THE PROPHETIC SOUL

Also by Leon Stover

Anthropology and History
The Cultural Ecology of Chinese Civilization
(based on lectures at Tokyo University, 1963–65)
China: An Anthropological Perspective, with Takeko Kawai Stover
(textbook version of the above)
Stonehenge: The Indo-European Heritage (in Britain,
this new political theory of that ancient monument
is titled, *Stonehenge and the Origins of Western Culture*)

Fiction
Stonehenge, with Harry Harrison
Stonehenge: Where Atlantis Died (large expansion
of the above, with revised afterword and bibliography)
*The Shaving of Karl Marx: An Instant Novel of Ideas,
After the Manner of Thomas Love Peacock,
in Which Lenin and H.G. Wells Talk about
the Political Meaning of the Scientific Romances*
(a work of novelized literary criticism)

Criticism
La Science Fiction Américaine (commissioned by
the Sorbonne for its program in American Studies)
Robert A. Heinlein (for Twayne's United States Authors Series)

Anthologies
Apeman, Spaceman: Anthropological Science Fiction,
with Harry Harrison (the first SF theme anthology)
*Above the Human Landscape: An Anthology
of Social Science Fiction*, with Willis McNelly
(the first college reader in SF)

Contributor
"H.G. Wells," in *Contemporary Authors*
"Science Fiction and the Research Revolution" and
"Social Science Fiction," in *Teaching Science Fiction*,
edited by Jack Williamson
"John W. Campbell, Jr.," "Harry Harrison," "John R. Stewart,"
and "Jules Verne," in *Twentieth-Century Science-Fiction Writers* (2d ed.)
"H.G. Wells, T.H. Huxley, and Darwinism," in *H.G. Wells:
Reality and Beyond, A Collection of Critical Essays
Prepared in Conjunction with the Exhibition and Symposium on H.G. Wells*
(this essay is in addition to the author's service
as humanities consultant to the Champaign Public Library
and the University of Illinois Library at Champaign–Urbana,
whereby he helped to assemble the traveling Exhibition)

THE PROPHETIC SOUL

A Reading of H.G. Wells's
Things to Come
Together with His Film Treatment,
Whither Mankind?
and
the Postproduction Script
(Both Never Before Published)

by
LEON STOVER

McFARLAND & COMPANY, INC., PUBLISHERS
Jefferson, North Carolina, and London

Whither Mankind? (The Film Treatment) is reprinted by permission of the Literary Executors of the Estate of H.G. Wells (A.P. Watt, Ltd., agent) and the University Library, University of Illinois at Urbana-Champaign.

"Things to Come" (The Release Script of 1936, an in-house document of London Films) is reprinted by permission of London Film Productions, Ltd., and the Literary Executors of the Estate of H.G. Wells (A.P. Watt, Ltd., agent)

Library of Congress Cataloguing-in-Publication Data

Stover, Leon E.
  The prophetic soul.

  Bibliography: p. 117.
  Includes index.
  1. Things to come (Motion picture). 2. Wells,
H.G. (Herbert George), 1866–1946. The shape of
things to come. 3. Wells, H.G. (Herbert George),
1866–1946—Moving picture plays. I. Wells, H.G.
(Herbert George), 1866–1946. II. Things to come
(Motion picture) III. Title.
PN1997.T42863S78 1987   822'.912   87-42523

ISBN 0-89950-289-X (acid-free natural and enamel gloss papers)

McFarland & Company, Inc., Publishers,
  Jefferson, North Carolina 28640

for
my wife
Takeko Kawai Stover
who started this
by putting me on to
kata-ginu

... the prophetic soul
Of the wide world dreaming on things to come.
—Shakespeare, *Sonnets*, CVII

TABLE OF CONTENTS

Between pages 120 and 121 are 32 plates
containing 50 photographs from *Things to Come*

TABLE OF ABBREVIATIONS

STTC   *The Shape of Things to Come* (1933), the novel on which the film is in part based. New York edition. The London edition is noted where it differs.

TTC   *Things to Come* (1935), the film scenario published by Wells in literary form. London edition.

ttc   "Things to Come" (1936), the postproduction script, a studio document of London Films, consisting of 1049 numbered camera shots. Cited with reference to these numbers. See Appendix II.

WM   *Whither Mankind?* (1934), the film treatment of "Things to Come," privately printed by Wells for circulation among the production staff of London Films. Cited with reference to section numbers. See Appendix I.

WWHM   *The Work, Wealth and Happiness of Mankind* (1931), the nonfiction work on which the film is in part based. New York edition.

     All other sources are footnoted. Those authored by H.G. Wells are noted by title only, with full details given in the Bibliography, alphabetically arranged. First editions are the rule, but whether they be of British or American imprint depends on this author's familiar choice from his transatlantic collection.

FOREWORD

When H.G. Wells attended the premier of *Things to Come* in February 1936 he felt irritated and disillusioned by what he saw. The whole enterprise, he thought, had been a pretentious failure. It is true that audiences liked it, and this earliest and most naive of the science-fiction blockbusters still lingers on in the film-club circuit. But critics and scholars of Wells have never looked into it closely, and literary and cultural histories of the 1930s barely even mention it. Now, in an enthralling study, Leon Stover has taken this neglected work and raised it, at one bound, to classic status.

The discovery of the release script and of Wells's privately circulated film treatment, *Whither Mankind?*, would alone be enough to reinstate *Things to Come* as an expression of Wells's ideas. But Stover has done much more than this, bringing intellectual passion and an encyclopedic knowledge of Wells's writings to bear in a powerfully perceptive and detailed reading of the film. Shot by shot, and scene by scene, *Things to Come* is now revealed both as a landmark in cinema history and as a deliberate *summa* of Wells's vision of the potentialities of human society. It stands beside that other product of Wells's last great creative phase, the *Experiment in Autobiography*, now completed by the belated appearance of its "Postscript."

One cannot get far in reading *The Prophetic Soul* without realizing that Leon Stover is a warm admirer of H.G. Wells—and an implacable enemy of "Wellsism." For Stover is a romantic conservative, who sees in *Things to Come* an exemplary exposition of the sinister proclivities of Wells's romantic socialism. I do not myself share Stover's anti-"Wellsite" zeal. In fact, I would say that Stover and Wells have not a little in common. They are both great synthesizers and generalizers, who take all mankind for their province. *The Prophetic Soul* would not be what it is had it not been for its author's remarkable earlier books, *Stonehenge: The Indo-European Heritage* and *The Cultural Ecology of Chinese Civilization*.

Reading Stover on *Things to Come* I was reminded of Wells's great friend and conservative adversary, G.K. Chesterton. Chesterton said that Wells's great fault was that he was trying to tell the tale of Jack and the Giant-Killer from the point of view of the giant. Chesterton was unrepentantly on the side of the Jacks of today against the "modern state octopus." The difference between Chesterton's time and ours, it may be argued, is that we have seen what rule by the giants is like. George Orwell, another of Stover's heroes, wrote off the Wells of the 1930s as an Edwardian innocent and benighted progressive who was too sane to understand the world of the dictators. Stover, however, strenuously rejects this assessment. For him Wells, far from being sane, was amply and candidly possessed of the revolutionary madness. To Stover this madness is demonic and evil, though others have found it—and will find it—divine.

It is only fair to add a few notes of caution. Did Wells really look to the technocratic socialists, Comte and Saint-Simon, as his intellectual masters? And was he as consistent as Stover's systematic citation from his works implies? It is well known that on some issues he repeatedly changed his mind. In addition, the curious reader will very soon come across a number of Wellses who do not figure in *Things to Come* and are not, therefore, much in evidence in the pages that follow. There are Wells the sharp-eyed journalist, Wells the self-critic, Wells the campaigning liberal, Wells the lover of women, Wells the discerning admirer of three United States presidents, and Wells the self-deprecating comic (whose closest friend in the film world was Charlie Chaplin). But all this is perhaps by the way, for by concentrating, so to speak, on the more domesticated sides of the later Wells we have arguably diminished his achievement.

In every century there have been prodigies, great writers who simultaneously exhibited great versatility and great single-mindedness. Stover demonstrates that Wells was one of these, and that what is implicit in *Things to Come* is nothing less than the whole tragic political history of the first half of the twentieth century. Seen as the visionary poet of modern socialist revolution, Wells appears as a writer of almost Miltonic force, with *Things to Come* as his *Samson Agonistes*, a drama of human resilience and impersonal idealism which has, as its climax, an uplifting, apocalyptic apology for mass murder. After such knowledge, what forgiveness? Certainly after Professor Stover's reading neither *Things to Come* nor H.G. Wells can ever seem quite the same again.

Patrick Parrinder
Chairman, The H.G. Wells Society
London

PREFACE AND
ACKNOWLEDGMENTS

H.G. Wells was 70 years old in 1936 when *Things to Come* was released. It is, he tells us, "a propagandist film" for what he calls "Wellsism."[1] Wellsism is the sum of all he had to say before his death in 1946. Looking back on his career from near the end he explained, "My role has always been that of a propagandist, direct or indirect, for world socialism."[2]

In his Introduction to the film's literary version, however, Wells has nothing to say about world socialism, assuming that we all know the particulars of this, his "political religion,"[3] from the whole record of his career. He tells us only that *his* film is everything that Fritz Lang's *Metropolis* a decade earlier is *not*, the latter's vision of the future (as he said on reviewing it) being "hopelessly silly."[4] A memo addressed to the production staff, from which he quotes, has it that,

> As a general rule you may take it that whatever Lange [sic] did in "Metropolis" is the exact opposite of what is wanted here [TTC:13].

At the same time, he alludes to another staff document. This turns out to be his preliminary film treatment entitled, *Whither Mankind?*, privately printed by Wells for use in script conferences at London Films under its managing director, Alexander Korda, and deposited with the Wells Archive at the University of Illinois in Urbana. This tells us what the film *is*. It is a cosmic drama of universal forces, cast in the language of Hindu theology. The film's theme, he explains, is the tripolar struggle between those eternally contesting forces the Indians deify as Brahma, Siva, and Vishnu.

But how relate Hindu religion to the political religion of Wellsism? This book attempts to answer that question. Wells himself never intended to pose a riddle, but so he has. Least of all did he expect the public to mistake his intentions, yet it did. To this day, the film is taken as nothing more than a crude prophecy of space flight derived from Jules Verne, imitative in his unimaginative use of manned projectiles fired from a man-squashing Space Gun, when the early science fiction magazines already were featuring space ships powered by reaction motors. Even for the advertising staff, this was a technical embarrassment. Posters and lobby cards covered up for it, promising something more super-scientific, by redrawing the artillery shell, discharged at the moon in the film's climactic scene, as a portholed, gas-jetting rocket ship of the Buck Rogers type. Perhaps Wells assumed too much, a familiarity with his life work, for the public of his day to grasp the political symbolism of his Vernian Space Gun, and of much else besides. This book draws upon the complete library of H.G. Wells, quoting from much of it and from many of its viewpoint characters, by way of unriddling his true purpose.

Whither Mankind? is published for the first time in this book as Appendix I. For help in finding it, I am happy to thank Mary Ceibert, assistant librarian of the Rare Books Room at the University of Illinois Library in Urbana. I owe permission to publish it, not only to the custodians of that library, but to the gracious consent of the H.G. Wells Estate through the good offices of Linda Shaughnessy at the A.P. Watt Literary Agency in London.

Also published here for the first time, as Appendix II, is the post-production or release script of *Things to Come*, the film as shot and shown. It describes the film's 11 reels of 1049 camera shots and records the related dialogue.

An in-house document of London Films, it was limited to about 25 numbered copies, duplicated by hectograph machine from typewritten stencils on varicolored, unpaginated, legal-sized sheets the quality of blotting paper, this thick mass held together at the top with industrial grade staples.

Copy number 22 survived to come into the possession of Eric Korn, a rare book dealer in London whose fields are natural history, Darwiniana, and H.G. Wells. The latter fits in with these others, of course, because Wells was a student of natural history and Darwinian biology under T.H. Huxley at the Normal School of Science in South Kensington.

Mr. Korn, moreover, is a Wells collector in his own right. It is his personal copy of the release script, kindly xeroxed for me, that is transcribed here. I am beholden to him for his outstanding generosity. For permission to publish it, I am once again happy to acknowledge the Estate of H.G. Wells, and the mediation of A.P. Watt, Ltd. In this instance, I have the pleasure of reporting that additional permission was granted by Mark Shelmardine, chairman of London Films.

Apart from adjusting some irregularities in the format, and correcting obvious typographical errors, the text of this rare document is faithfully transmitted. The accuracy of its measured feet and frames (often dubious) is attributable to the studio typist (or typists; more than one set of hands is evident) who cut the original stencils. The feet measure how much film was expended by the operator on each shot; the frames, how many were selected by the editor (at 16 frames per foot of 35mm film). In a few cases, the numbers were illegible (the blotting paper effect), and here I enter question marks. Where no numbers occur, none were given.

The script ends with shot #1049. The attentive reader will discover why it comes out to that, despite two interpolations (#869a and b) and one omission (#798). But the film production accommodates all of these shots only in the British release of 113 minutes' running time; the American version is edited down to 92 minutes.

A curiosity, the credits indicate a character who does not in fact appear. She is Rowena, the "love-hungry" wife of Oswald Cabal, the puritanical president of the World Council of Direction. The credits have her played by Margaretta Scott, who also plays Roxana, indubitably present in her barbaric splendor as harem mistress of Rudolf the Victorious.

Yet to judge from existing publicity stills, her scenes in the role of Rowena evidently were filmed. The decision to edit them out must have come about at the last minute, after the first pages of the release script had already been stenciled. One imagines a sudden fear at the studio, that the film was too long, too talkative, too full of Wellsian disdain for the conventional sex adventure.

For Wells, film was a means of propaganda rather than entertainment. To put ideas on the screen he called for "a repudiation of the 'love interest,'" which is as much to repudiate the amusement industry itself.[5] Indeed, Rowena in the literary version speaks the lines of a love-huntress only as an excuse for Oswald Cabal to preach against this very sort of thing. "You may want love, but I want the stars" (TTC:114).

Another last minute change was the title itself. Throughout the film's shooting, as indicated by various informal stills of the on-location crew at rest, the number board reads, "Whither Mankind." Moreover, all publicity stills without exception are marked in the lower left or right corner with the code letters "W-M," for *Whither Mankind?* This was Wells's preferred title. It dominates the screen in his description of the opening scene in his literary version of the scenario (TTC:20).

In the event, the film *was* too didactic for public taste. It argued for "something superhuman" in its vision of "a new world of conquest among the atoms and the stars."[6] Such is Wellsism and its revolutionary program when projected in cosmic terms—"man's power over nature and over his own nature."[7] Billed as the most expensive production ever mounted by an English studio to 1936, it was all of that, only to become in the words of Michael Korda, the producer's nephew, "an instant box-office failure."[8]

Except for that last minute cut and change of title, however, Wells got his way. Raymond Massey, who played the starring roles of John and Oswald Cabal, says in his autobiography that,

> No writer for the screen ever had or ever will have such authority as H.G. Wells possessed in the making of "Things to Come."[9]

Beyond the script itself, his touch tells in every detail, the architecture, the decorations, the costumes, the music; and he appeared on the set every working day during a whole year's shooting. Somewhat a family affair, Frank

Wells, his elder son, served as the assistant art director. More interesting was his collaboration with Arthur Bliss, the musical composer of his choice. "So far from regarding the music as trimming to be put on afterwards," he instructed Bliss that he wanted the musical design done first, and then the film cut to that, not the music to the film as had been the custom. Wells wanted "a complete sensuous and emotional synthesis" and he got it.[10]

All of which points up one outstanding fact. *Things to Come* is thoroughly and altogether Wellsian. Asked by reporters at the film's release if any alterations had been made, anything added or subtracted, Wells replied, "No, it was the same as I wrote it."[11] He forgot Rowena's face on the cutting room floor, but no matter. The fact remains that *Things to Come* rightly deserves attention by students of Wells fully as much as by students of the cinema.

A number of other science fiction movies are based on the scientific romances of the early H.G. Wells, but none of these ideological fables are done with his political religion in mind. One thinks of *The Island of Lost Souls* (1932), starring Charles Laughton, and its remake, *The Island of Doctor Moreau* (1977), starring Burt Lancaster. Or *The Invisible Man* (1933), starring Claude Raines in his first (unseen) film role. Or *The War of the Worlds* (1953), *The Time Machine* (1960), *The First Men in the Moon* (1964), and last and least, *Food of the Gods* (1977).[12]

Made for entertainment by the amusement industry, none of these ever intended to make propaganda for Wellsism. The novels whose titles they borrow serve only as points of departure for the empty fantasies of the standard science-fiction horror film. Only *Things to Come* is the real thing, written and supervised by H.G. Wells himself, "World Revolutionary Socialist."[13]

One of the few critics to judge *Things to Come* in light of its political pitch finds it "positively repulsive," Wells at his worst with his "most lop-sided Utopia."[14] A fable of power it surely is. But it has its own peculiar aesthetic. Artfully compact in its visual symbolism, and with its highly charged thunderbolt rhetoric condensed to the poetical intensity of classical drama, it is not easily dismissed on grounds of ideological content alone.

Moreover, a comparison of *Things to Come* with a second film Wells did for Korda, *Man Who Could Work Miracles*, will show that what is lop-sided in the Utopian vision of the former is balanced by the self-critical humor of the latter—"a film of imaginative comedy." It is, after all, styled a "proper companion piece" to the former.[15] Read together, as they were meant to be in a compendium of their literary versions, *Two Film Stories*, they reveal the sure touch of irony that distinguishes Wells at his best.

The clichés of the one (Speed, Power, Progress, Efficiency, Science, Hygiene, Service) are mouthed in the other by less than supermen, the pathetic little figures pictured by Wells in his Dickensesque novels of social comedy like *Kipps* and *The History of Mr. Polly*. Wellsism, evidently, is not the all of Wells.

But it calls for emphasis here, if the monopoly of appreciation given *Things to Come* by science fiction fans is to be diversified. It is they alone who have kept up a running commentary on it all these years, if only to rehearse their delight in it as a big-budget precedent for *2001* and *Star Wars*. More than a forerunner of such space operas, however, it belongs to the complete works of H.G. Wells the social and political thinker no less than to the cinema of the fantastic.[16]

I am therefore grateful to the H.G. Wells Society for sponsoring this effort to bring *Things to Come* into the critical literature about that world-man of letters whose name the Society honors. Its chairman and senior Wellsian critic Patrick Parrinder, head of the English Department at Reading University, favors this book with his Foreword.

But without Robert Franklin, president of McFarland & Company, Inc., Publishers, there would be no publication to begin with. I am pleased to thank McFarland for undertaking to publish the somewhat esoteric documents contained in the Appendices, otherwise of interest to only a few film scholars. The publishers have been generous in allotting me sufficient space to amplify on the wider value of these documents to students of H.G. Wells.

Among them I am happy to count Christopher Rolfe, a close friend of this project. He is the honorary general secretary of the H.G. Wells Society, with his office located in the Department of Language and Literature at the Polytechnic of North London. His companionship and help during our joint visit to the Wells Archive at Urbana, in April 1984, is recalled with fond gratitude.

Moreover, both he and Dr. Parrinder that same year took the time from their travels in the United States to lecture in my Wells course here at the Illinois Institute of Technology. They provided the students with a refreshing literary perspective differing from my own approach, coming as it does out of the social sciences. All the same, Wells was a notable amateur in this field, and tried to professionalize it by twice going after a chair in sociology.[17] That the students found these guest lectures complementary to mine, and not mutually exclusive, is a tribute to the multifaceted aspects of Wells's art which the Society fully recognizes, in its "aims to promote a widespread interest in the life, work and thought of Herbert George Wells."

For providing the still photos used in this book (apart from the usual commercial sources), I am happily obliged to the Imagi-Movie Archives (Hollywood) of Forrest J Ackerman, to Dennis Saleh, publisher of Comma Books, and to Kenneth von Gunden. The few grainy-looking pictures are frame enlargements taken from my own 16mm print of the film.

Leon Stover, Ph.D., Litt.D.
Professor of Anthropology
Illinois Institute of Technology
Chicago

The state form of tomorrow is "Caesarism" with all
that this implies in social and economic terms.
Caesarism means both "socialism"—that is, military
totalitarianism resting on a dynamic faith and a will
to action—and "internationalism"—that is, the end of
national sovereignty in favor of a world state.

(Frederick L. Schuman, "Who Owns the Future?" *The Nation*, 11 January 1941)

There are limits to everything. In all this time something
definite should have been achieved. But it turns out that
those who inspired the revolution ... aren't happy with
anything that's on less than a world scale. For them,
transitional periods, worlds in the making, are an end
in themselves. ... Man is born to live, not to prepare for life.

(Boris Pasternak, *Doctor Zhivago*, chapter 9, section 14)

As for you, you doctrinaire Utopians who shut your eyes
to human nature, you ardent atheists who feed
on hatred and delusion, you emancipators of women, you
destroyers of family life, you genealogists of the simian race,
you whose name was once an insult in itself,
be well content: you will have been the prophets
and your disciples will be the pontiffs of an abominable future!

(Frederic Alfred Pierre, comte de Falloux, *L'Unité nationale*, 1880)

INTRODUCTION: H.G. WELLS
AND THE COMMUNIST REVISION

The Whole Duty of Man

In *Things to Come*, Wells exposes a side of his literary self that his biographer son describes as "a sort of wilder Lenin."[1] It is Wells out-Heroding Herod with his "Communist Revision." He asks for a "greater Communist Party, a Western response to Russia," with a revolutionary party of more "enlightened fanatics."[2]

This is the Modern State Society, "an aggressive order of religiously devoted men and women [who] try out and establish and impose a new pattern of living upon our race" (STTC:431). Their social experiment, unlike Lenin's, is a total success; they are able to socialize the whole world because they are enlightened by a superior political religion. Informed by Wellsism, they make the Modern State Revolution.

Their success is told in *The Shape of Things to Come*. It is the story of the Modern State Movement and its outcome. In the film, its revolutionaries are the men and women of the Air League, whose party leader is John Cabal. With his Airmen he is founder of the Modern World-State, known under him as the Air Dictatorship. Where Lenin only promised world revolution, John Cabal delivers it. His grandson, Oswald Cabal, president of the World Council of Direction, confirms it.

Lenin's experiment is nonetheless the Airmen's inspiration. The dreamed-about history book of the future on which the film is in part based, looks back on him as the twentieth century's one outstanding statesman. As the novel's narrator says, introducing his dream text, "One name alone among those who have been prominent in our time escapes to a certain extent the indictment of this history—the name of Nicolai Lenin" (STTC:26, London edition).

As a publication of the future, this dream-book is dated A.D. 2106. Looking back over the last 189 years from that distant view platform, it surveys the Era of the Modern State, beginning in 1917 with the ending of the Christian Era. Also ended with it is the age of democracy and nationalism. 1917 is of course the year Lenin seized power from Russia's emergent parliamentary government, an act hailed by him as the start of the world socialist revolution.

1

Although Lenin failed to pull it off, the historians of the future, gathered in their Chronological Institute, mark his experimental try at it as the turning point in world history. "The Modern State had been conceived" (STTC: 20).

Moreover, they commemorate this date in resetting the calendar. As the birth of Christ was the baseline for the old calendar (a custom set by the Venerable Bede in early medieval times), the new one takes off from the Russian Revolution and the birth of post–Christian rationality. The "obliteration of out-of-date moral values" achieved by the Modern World-State owes to the example of Lenin's ethical revolution in governing by the industrial code of scientific management. For that, the Chronological Institute gives him his due as the ender of Christian moral obligations on an individual ethical basis, and the abolisher of self-reliance and personal responsibility. In the new calendar, C.E. 1917 is the last year of the Christian Era and the first year of the Modern Era, M.E. 1. Hence the proper date for C.E. 2106, the dream-book's publication date, is M.E. 189 (STTC:360, 18f).

In the film, the Modern World-State is fully realized by the year A.D. 2036 (ttc:799). No revision of the calendar is indicated, but the ethical revision hallowed by it in the novel is the very gist and all of the revolutionary things to come the film story relates. Indeed, the old Christian order is destroyed following the onset of a catastrophic world war started on Christmas Eve, the traditional date for celebrating Christ's birthday. John Cabal is an aviation engineer radicalized during that war, who forms the Air League with technical revolutionaries like himself, drawn from both sides.

The Airmen then complete the smash-up, ending once and for all the existence of separate nation-states, whose bellicose patriotisms had brought on the war to begin with, and the near doom of the human race. Thereafter they reconstruct the world along rational lines, in the post–Christian faith "that scientific methods could be applied to all human relations, to law and government—as well as material things." What can be done in the research and development of advanced technology can also be done in social engineering, and the design of a functional one-world state. Their watchwords are, "RESEARCH, INVENTION, WORLD PLANNING–AND SCIENTIFIC CONTROL" (WM:39).

The subsequent Air Dictatorship founded by John Cabal is a global technocracy, leading on to ever more powers of scientific control under his grandson. Addressing his fellow partymen in the film's key speech (ttc:725), Cabal expresses his faith in just that sort of lasting dynamism. His credo in a forward-directed movement of history, carried along by the collective purpose of the human species, is thereby established as the official state religion of the Modern World-State.

It is a creed evoking belief in the possible unification of the species into one biological organism with a will of its own, subsuming the wills of individual men. In that, it makes a point of contradicting the Christian doctrine of personal immortality. For individual salvation implies a life of personal liberty before death, and this is incompatible with Wellsism no less than with

Leninism. Cabal's new doctrine is therefore well suited to collective planning on a futuristic basis. Indeed, the historian of the Modern Era writes that the Air Dictatorship's "general plan for the directed evolution of life on the planet ... is in operation to this day" (STTC:391).

The film argues Wells's case for the cosmic imperative to unify and pacify the human race, or else we shall fall back in conflict and decay. Either we respond to "the steadfast upward struggle of life towards vision and control," or else our species will fail.[3] "Adapt or perish." It is the duty of revolutionaries drawn to the Modern State Movement to save us from a fatal disunity by enforcing this evolutionary law of survival. While "democracy means the subordination of the state to the ends and welfare of the common individual," a truly responsible state must be concerned with subordination of the individual to the long-term welfare of the species.[4] This calls for a "large prevision" of the future, a thinking in "suns' distances" far beyond the immediate cares of the personal life. The Modern State is therefore obliged to systematize "private and public conduct alike, and to [make it] uniformly directed."[5]

That the Air Dictatorship does by imposing its "Act of Uniformity," aimed at stamping out "personal initiatives [and] individual motives" (STTC:332, 429f). There is now "one faith only in the world, the moral expression of the one world community" (332f). With this legacy of collective discipline passed on to the World Council of Direction, the historian of the Modern Era is able to write that, by his time, "The Modern State became the whole duty of man" (398).

These are the appropriate words, taken from the Biblical injunction "Fear God, and keep his commandments; for this is the whole duty of man" (Ecclesiastes, 12:13). Wellsism is a political religion that offers a secular reading of this text, replacing God with the divinized state.

Things to Come thus poses the same radical alternatives that George Orwell saw in the antagonism between Christianity and Communism.

> Either this life is preparation for another, in which case the individual soul is all-important, or there is no life after death, in which case the individual is merely a replaceable cell in the general body.[6]

The future historian of the Modern World-State sees matters the same way, and indicates the choice made by John Cabal for the world revolution when he writes, "The body of mankind is now one single organism.... We are all members of one body" (STTC:429). Given "the harshly rational schooling of human motives" under the Air Dictatorship, the lesson of socialism is now brought home (346). "Man's soul is no longer his own. It is, he discovers, part of a greater being which lived before he was born and will survive him."[7]

The world socialist state is a "collective human person" made up of people who are "corpuscles in his being," the being of the species as a super-individual evolving through cosmic time.[8] The corpuscles, however, are but a doctrinal metaphor. In Wellsism, they stand for self-renunciation under the discipline of "a single world economic machine" (WWHM:373) in the "coming age of scientific management."[9]

Saint-Simon and the Social Idea

While all Communist Party members are socialists, no other socialists are communists. Except H.G. Wells. After the Revolution of 1917, Lenin ruled that no others were radical enough to take the name of his party.[10] Exempting himself, Wells declared his Communist Revision. What this amounts to is Marxism-Leninism minus Marx.

During Wells's visit to the Kremlin in 1920, Lenin asked him, "To make [the world revolution] a success, the western world must join in. Why doesn't it?" Because, Wells replied, the wrong political religion is being used to promote it. Communism is falsely represented in the language of Marx as a workers' democracy. Western intellectuals are not about to share Lenin's "vision of a world changed over and planned and built afresh" if they are not invited. Instead, even the "technical intelligentsia" (a phrase Wells cast up to Stalin in 1935 in a futile discussion of the same question) are classed with bourgeois enemies of the revolution.[11]

> I said that ... the technicians, scientific workers, medical men, skilled foremen, skilled producers, aviators, operating engineers, for instance, would and should supply the best material for constructive revolution in the West, but that current Communist propaganda, with its insistence upon a mystical mass directorate, estranged and antagonised just these most valuable elements.

These were the very same elements governing Soviet Russia. So what is this nonsense about a master class of untrained workers running the show? "I have never believed in the superiority of the inferior."[12] And neither did Lenin.

Was not Lenin himself "intensely middle-class" (STTC:125), heading up a civil service drawn from the technical intelligentsia? His was a revolution made from above. It was "a revolt of the competent [not] a class insurrection by hands" (262).

In this Wells was quite right. Lenin's key associates were all middle-class intellectuals, most of them graduates of the St. Petersburg Technological Institute. Its laboratories and workshops were the gathering place for the largest concentration of radical students in Russia, turning out highly politicized engineers with dreams of social engineering.[13] In the event, their managerial revolution was cast in the fiction of a proletarian revolution.

In *Things to Come*, the Airmen lead a similar lot, and show how it's rightly done. They come right out and say, "Let the Makers rule! Let us who know take power!" (WM:39). Nothing is to be gained by giving credit for a revolution by the superior to unskilled and inferior factory hands. "There is no authority but competence" under the "leadership of professionally trained men."[14]

Yet Lenin crippled his authority beyond the borders of Soviet Russia by failing to make just that kind of straight-talk about his actual accomplishment. Would-be technocrats in the West were put off the world-revolutionary cause by his Marxist jargon. As a result, what he had done in practice for the Modern-State idea would never lead on to its fulfillment in a "World Civil Service" of managerial experts. His was but a failed experiment the Airmen learn from. As long ago as 1898, Wells had prophesied the coming of a new "aristocracy of organisers."[15] And here they were in Lenin's Russia, disguising themselves as common workers!

Lenin, we may be sure, knew all the arguments. In harking back to the pre–Marxist fathers of socialism, who were technocrats *avant le lettre*, Wells told him nothing new. But Lenin the practical politician could not ignore talk about a working-class revolution, now that Marx had identified socialism with the labor movement—a force unseen by the Old Testament patriarchs of socialism, the Saint-Simonians.[16]

They take their name from Claude Henri de Rouvroy, comte de Saint-Simon, a nobleman declassed by the French Revolution—that "benevolent aristocrat" as Wells calls him for his conception of a new "aristocracy of talent."[17] Therein is the measure of Wellsism: "We must have an aristocracy—not of privilege, but of understanding and purpose—or mankind will fail." The first task of the socialist revolution is to destroy the old aristocracy; the second is to replace it with a new one, with a force of "stronger and better men."[18]

Saint-Simon was the first thinker to see that the industrial revolution of his day was more important than the political one, especially as the latter in his opinion was not only a failure, but a mistake. The French Revolution, in the name of the People, did nothing to put down the feudal and military system of the *ancien régime*. The old order soon came back to harass the bourgeois leaders of industrialism as well. With factory production in their control, their growing economic power remained a political threat to the passive power of limited and static wealth belonging to the landed estates of the hereditary aristocracy, at last restored to its possessions and ascendency.

To make that threat real, and overthrow feudalism once and for all, was the original socialist idea. It was not to oppose capitalism but the feudal system that Saint-Simon advocated the control of society by its "industrial chiefs," they who were its aristocracy of talent. They would make industrialism the new world-formula. Industrialism was in itself a dogma to rival that of the Catholic church and everything universal it pretended to support in the medieval world. Originating in Saint-Simon's homeland, this new and truly universal formula would make for a world-industrial state.

> When this social organization is established in France, the famous prediction made by the Fathers of the Church will soon be realised; the entire

human race will share the same doctrine; one by one every people will adopt the principles proclaimed and put into practice by the French.[19]

The captains of French production would thus unite all workers of the world, following the logic of the industrial revolution and its international marketing economy. Theirs ;would become the business of leading a "World Republic of United Interests."

This phrase, too bad, is not Saint-Simon's. It is a deprecation, a caricature of his world-state idea, done by a fellow national who has the distinction of being the first, with his *Le Monde tel qu'il sera* ("The World to Come"), to write the sort of anti-utopian novel Wells refers to when he speaks of "such alarmist fantasies as Aldous Huxley's *Brave New World*" (STTC:301).[20] It is fitting to mention this, because the future world of *Things to Come* is rebelled against by a mob of dissidents whose leader, Theotocopulos (a frustrated artist), is none other than a stand-in for Aldous Huxley himself—a reactionary who represents "the sentimental and aesthetic values of the old order" (306). "I will go for this Brave New World of theirs," he says with scornful irony (TTC:93). But for Wells, it *is* a Brave New World—brave and new and true. The new post–Christian values of science, technology, production, efficiency and ra-tionalization are supremely useful to the collective good of society, more so than the old morality of "individualistic liberalism" (STTC:82). And so poor old Theotocopulos pays for his humanistic impiety. He and all his followers, numbering in the thousands, are "liquidated" (to use the Bolshevik term for political executions without benefit of trial) in the film's final scene of trium-phant mass annihilation. They are so much "trouble in the machinery," so many "obstructives" in the way of historical progress (350, 298).

The Brave New World of *Things to Come* is without a doubt Saint-Simon's. His Republic of United Interests, named by a sneering critic, is aptly named for all that. So perfectly does the phrase capture the spirit of his world-industrial state, that we shall make use of it as though coined by the Master himself.

In his technocratic vision, the spiritual direction of society once given by the medieval church would fall to men of science; its temporal direction once given by feudal war lords would go to big businessmen and production engineers. Their ruling center (located in Paris, of course) he called the Coun-cil of Newton, the very model for the World Council of Direction in *Things to Come* (TTC:98).

Under the Council of Newton's direction, "universal association" for peaceful production will replace international conflict and social injustice.

> The exploitation of man by man—that is the state of human relations in the past. The exploitation of nature by man associated with man—that is the picture the future offers.[21]

In the future, "Science and Industry are destined to replace Theology and

War."[22] And on a worldwide scale. Only the whole planet will serve for a scientific-industrial Utopia, given the global reach of humanity's business affairs, with the advent of marketing industrialism. "There will never be permanent public peace until the most important industrialists are in charge of the administration of public wealth."[23] From this derives the Wellsian prophecy that, "The future belongs to big-scale business" in a "world-industrial civilization without nationalism, warfare and economic selfishness."[24]

The contrast between Labor and Capital, so much emphasized by later socialism after Marx, is not present in Saint-Simon. He assumes the unity of their interests—hence a Republic of United Interests, in which they collaborate in doing the world's work. But it is the duty of Capital, not of Labor, to dictate this unity. That is the function of his "industrial chiefs" at the head of production, serving under their scientific colleagues on the Council of Newton, who do the economic planning and theoretical guidance. Scientists replace the medieval theologians.

Mobilizing all human and capital assets in a collective drive to exploit nature and create social wealth, the Council's men of science assign managers and engineers to control the various operational functions of what we today call a command economy. The military ranks of the old feudal order are recast for a civilian army of labor. What is wanted for this, as Wells rightly reads the Master, is "the spirit of the soldier, the spirit of subordination to a common purpose."[25] But this means the regimentation of all society. In Saint-Simonian doctrine, the industrial revolution to overthrow feudalism will not be complete until political life is understood as work, and is finally subjected as a matter of course to the demands and techniques of the labor economy. "Society must become a vast production company."[26]

At the same time, Saint-Simon advocated a system of merit. Each man is to be placed according to his capacity, and rewarded according to his work. The greater the capacity, the greater the reward. "Work is the source of all virtue; the most useful work should be the most highly esteemed."[27] Naturally, the scientific and executive brains in charge of planning and managing are more deserving than the laboring hands, for whom Saint-Simon coined the word "proletariat."

With everything based on talent and personal capacity, and not on the feudal privileges of blood, everybody will know without a doubt who his betters are, in a fair division of labor between men who guide and the proletariat who are guided. Therefore the workers will obey their natural superiors, and do their duty to the common cause for a lesser reward, without a sense of being exploited. The collective business of making war on nature is its own reward, each to the joy of his collaborative part in overcoming the common obstacles of the material world, thereby making for human unity.[28]

Lest the workers forget their part in this, Saint-Simon composed a model speech for them to recite to their chiefs at the start of each working day.

> You are rich and we are poor. You work with your head and we with our hands. From these two facts, there result fundamental differences between us, so that we are and should be your subordinates.[29]

Critics of today's communist system, who find fault with its big rewards going to high-ranking party officials, fail to recall how essential a feature this is in its doctrinal origins.

For example, the Yugoslavian dissident, Milovan Djilas, complains in *The New Class* that members of the Communist Party violate the socialist ideals of social equality. They form a political bureaucracy holding "privileges of *administration*," arising from the party's "monopoly over property, ideology, and government." The so-called "socialist ownership" of the communist system is a disguise for the real ownership by a "new class" that has merely displaced the ownership privileges of the old ruling class.[30]

But of course. This is as it should be, without any Marxist double-talk, if communist-socialism were faithful to its fathers, as is Wells's Communist Revision. What is revised about it is merely his return to Saint-Simonian basics. Already at the turn of the century, himself always faithful to Saint-Simon, Wells had predicted the rise of "a new class of intelligent and scientifically educated men." And here they were in socialist Russia, led by Lenin wearing a worker's cap! The Modern State presupposes the "inevitable development of an official administrative class," Wells wrote as early as 1910, "a new class and a very powerful class of expert officials."[31] It is only this difference in rhetoric that marks his differences with Lenin. While to his associates Lenin advanced the idea of a new "ruling class of administrators," a party dictatorship, in public he rather made misleading propaganda about a Dictatorship of the Proletariat.[32]

Not that Wellsism, the true faith, is inconsistent with the ideals of social equality. Saint-Simon insisted that his industrial system would make for "the most complete system of equality which possibly can exist," in which the brotherhood of man finally would be realized. Of course, he adds, it is "a brotherhood not by blood but according to the doctrine."[33] What counts more than the inequalities of rank and wealth is the equal sharing of *ideas* by all men, their kinship in a doctrine that says, all men must work according to their capacity; and none have the right to be lazy. "Down with idlers!" is the all-embracing Saint-Simonian slogan. Asking for the unity of interests between a working aristocracy of managerial talent above and worker discipline below, it exhorts to the partnership of Science and Labor.[34]

It is from the Master's first commandment that the whole of Saint-Simonian doctrine springs:

> All men will work; they will regard themselves as laborers attached to one workshop.... The supreme Council of Newton will direct their works.... Anybody who does not obey the orders will be treated by others as a quadruped.[35]

An example of such a quadruped, or antisocial animal, in *Things to Come* is poor old Theotocopulos. He learns the hard way that, when Science rules, "there can be only one right way of looking at the world for a normal human being and only one conception of a proper scheme of social reactions, and that all others must be wrong and misleading" (STTC:333). Theotocopulos is by this definition abnormal; he is a defective citizen, in whose "animal individualism" dwells a "spirit of opposition [that is] purely evil" (334, 350). And so he dies a quadruped's death. He had wanted to live the selfish personal life apart from a community of shared work, in which alone the highest good of socialist equality may be satisfied. Everybody equal in his useful capacity to serve the social purpose is everybody equal in citizenship—or else there is no citizenship.

Socialism was from the start a doctrine of social utility. The word for it was coined by Saint-Simon's private secretary and number one disciple, August Comte, who described it as the "Religion of Humanity."[36] This is Wellsism in its origin, and no doubt about it. Wells tells us in his autobiography that his Modern State idea is not his own. He claims no originality. Indeed, he grants to Comte the "priority he had in sketching the modern outlook."[37]

In his debate with Lenin, all Wells did was to recall the same outlook they both held in common, the only difference being that Lenin refused to acknowledge it in his official language. Instead, he concealed a modern practice behind a premodern facade, the words of Marx. He kept on insisting that the Soviet state, aspiring to industrial giantism, was a workers' democracy more suitable to a small cooperative or commune.

In giving us the word for socialism, Comte himself played on a newly minted coinage of Diderot's *Encyclopédie*, the word "social." This familiar adjective, now fairly divested of ethical meaning, had its origin in French radical thought. The word at first designated those virtues rendering a person useful to society.[38] One serves a social function, work, or one is a beastly quadruped.

Hence for Wells, who traces his line of thought to this beginning, socialism is called by him "the Social Idea." It is bound up with the rational ideals of "social efficiency," which means, "It is only by doing his quota of service that a man can justify his partnership in the community."[39] The Social Idea calls for "universal service to the common good," whose moral output, "righteous economic behavior,"[40] is measured by "the standards of engineering efficiency" (STTC:263). Social-ism is thus a doctrine that summons all men to productive work for the sake of unselfish giving to society. In short, it calls for "altruism," another one of Comte's coinages. One shows concern for the welfare of all or one is a dead quadruped. Altruistic behavior, in the Saint-Simonian sense of efficient citizenship, is easy enough to measure because it does not rest with anything so untestable as personal piety, a subjective virtue. Altruism is a *public* virtue, whose ethical standard is met by one very simple test—submission to one's assigned duty in the world's workshop.

One is forced to be useful by the factory discipline of a universal production company.[41]

For Saint-Simon, the only people useful to society, and therefore to his Republic of United Interests, are *les industriels*, the industrials—those who are industrious. In the Master's vocabulary, *les industriels* include not only industrialists or captains of industry, but also the *industriels* of theory, men of science who do applied research, and who furthermore set the new spiritual tone of a technocracy by doing research into the nature of nature. The mastery of nature is the collective purpose of a postfeudal industrial society, wherein "politics is the *science of production*."[42]

Also included are engineers, technicians, craftsmen, inventors, factory managers, investment bankers and commercial traders—big businessmen and entrepreneurs of all sorts—not to mention teachers, medical men, journalists and writers in sympathy with the cause, and other useful intellectuals. Added to them as well is the entire proletarian mass of workingmen. All are *industriels*, contrasting with *les oisefs*, the lazy bones or idlers. They are the useless people of the vestigial feudal order, a leisure class of priests, theologians, lawyers, rentiers, landowners, generals, and the whole aristocracy of blood and privilege headed up by the royal family, with its metaphysical nonsense about the Divine Right of Kings.

The like of *les industriels* for Wells are his "economically functional people," comprising both planners and executives on the one hand, and operatives on the other. The former belong to the new ruling class in his Modern State, the latter to the ruled. They are the two estates of his technocratic realm, "Direction and Labor" respectively, the very terms used by Saint-Simon.[43] Among the directive elite are "technicians, scientific workers and able business organisers" (STTC:261f). They include "the men of science, the technical experts, the inventors and discoverers, the foremen and managers and organisers" (282), who have their credentials to rule from the honest crafts of "workshop [and] laboratory" (264).

All of these new-class elements are embraced by the Air Dictatorship. Indeed, all of them meet in the person of John Cabal himself. Before the war, he managed and did applied research and industrial design for his own engineering firm. That is what qualifies him for his great destiny, his creation of the technocratic Air League.

But as commanders of workingmen, the Airmen are themselves no less *workers* than are the factory hands and laborers of the proletary. If in a Saint-Simonian technocracy work is the source of all virtue, then the two estates of Direction and Labor are those of working intellectuals and proletarian workers. The Airmen for their part are *brain* workers—the "intellectual worker [and the] scientific worker." Each is the "creative, organising type . . . who sees the world as one great workshop."[44]

In society-as-workshop, political life is at one with industrial life. Entering the language of socialism from the start with Saint-Simon, it remains the image basic to modern communist theory. On the very eve of his bid for power, Lenin described his project in the same terms.

> The whole of society will have become a single office and a single factory.[45]

So with Wells and his Modern World-State. It, too, is one vast Saint-Simonian production company. Describing it in a prophecy enriched with the particulars of Lenin's example, he says it is to be "one great departmentalised business, a single rationalised system ... of which there will be one owner, one single capitalist—the State—and everyone else will be an employee ... or a prisoner of that supreme power."[46]

Wells was quite right, therefore, in telling both Lenin and Stalin that the Soviet Union's covert ideology was nothing if not technocratic. Take away Marx from Marxism-Leninism, and what is left is Lenin and Saint-Simonism. The reality is not a workers' state in its limited proletarian pretensions, but rather more so in the Saint-Simonian sense. All are *industriels* attached to one great workshop, U.S.S.R., Inc., be they brain workers in the front office or worker workers on the shop floor. All are industrious—except for the quadrupeds. They are prisoners of the Gulag where, appropriately enough, they are worked to death—useful to the end. Here they are given to know what socialist virtue is, for over the gateway to each killing "corrective labor camp" of the Gulag are the iron-wrought letters reading, "Work Is Honorable."

In fine, the Saint-Simonian ideal realized in practice by the Soviet experiment does not sort with its Marxist cover story. It is not "a democratic Socialism," as Wells interprets the language of Marxism.[47] Its real name, he says, is rather "State Capitalism" (WWHM:557).

Marx departed from this original idea of the early French socialists with his doctrine of class war. Unforeseen by the Saint-Simonians, however, was the rise of the labor movement. Its method of going on strike, against capital and the captains of industry, was a later development. Sizing up its revolutionary potential in *The Communist Manifesto* of 1848, Marx pictured a civil war between the two partners of Saint-Simon's unified class of producers, between owner-employers and worker-employees. A class-vindictive proletary, acting on its grievances, would rise up against its exploiters, take over industry, and then.... But here the picture fades. Marx left it at that, himself not foreseeing the moderating effect on this conflict by the trade union movement, and its bringing forth of an independent party of labor.

This development was left for Lenin to reckon with—by crushing it. With the Revolution he promptly exerted statist control over the working class by abolishing its trade unions. Or rather, he abolished their independence. He made them over into what under the evils of unreformed capitalism were called tame "company unions," the company in this case being U.S.S.R., Inc. Here, writes one Soviet dissident, "unions do not defend the interests of the workers against the employer, who in this case is the state; instead they ensure labor discipline and the carrying out of the employers' plans."[48]

But this, as Wells cast it up to Lenin, only returned the Social idea to its basics. While Lenin had replaced the Saint-Simonian worship of production with the Marxist worship of the proletariat, he did so only in a manner of speaking. In practice, his command economy linked together the whole body of labor, managerial and manual, in one united host, as proposed by the pre–Marxist patriarchs of socialism.

The Communist Revision of H.G. Wells, then, is no more than Leninism with Marxism subtracted from the Communist Party's official propaganda. There is nothing in Lenin's actual program that goes against Wellsism and its anti–Marxist "proposal not to exalt the labor class but to abolish it."[49] Lenin did just that, in his putting the estate of Labor at the mercy of Direction and its educated experts. His party dictatorship of working intellectuals used its power to ensure a docile labor force, for the making of social peace. He realized the Saint-Simonian dream of State Capitalism, uniting the interests of Capital and Labor alike in a common enterprise.

With all that to Lenin's credit, we can see why the Chronological Institute of the future resets the calendar, starting year one of the Modern Era with C.E. 1917. The Russian Revolution, Wells allows, "was the greatest experiment in egalitarian collectivism ever made, but after all it was only one part of the world experiment in egalitarian collectivism that our species has to make if it is to survive." It had the weakness of any first experiment, as one must expect. "Revolution is just like science; it progresses by a succession of experimental failures, each of which brings it nearer success."[50]

Lenin's weakness was his attempt to sell the world revolution with the wrong political religion. But the Airmen avoid that mistake. Learning from his failed experiment, they go on to fulfill the Social Idea in its Wellsian prophecy: "Humanity will be one labor organization."[51]

The Modern State Octopus

Wells tells us that the Modern State is "a scientifically organized class-less society."[52] But how does this sort with the party elitism of Direction over Labor? How is it that autocratic State Capitalism (or State Socialism, the same thing in his vocabulary) may be thought of as egalitarian? Certainly it has nothing to do with equality of pay, nor with equality of condition.

All the same, he says that socialism means the end of "class government"—no more "downward class war."[53] The "downward class hatred" of the old "Master-over-Man social order," a medieval relic standing in the way of industrial progress, is finished.[54] The scientific state that has organized every element in its being for production has "got rid of every vestige of our present distinction between official and governed"; it builds "a new social order of efficients."[55] Every citizen is "a public servant" working for the State, the common worker no less than the party bureaucrat; "the State belongs to him and he to the State."[56] All serve as equally functional parts of one labor organization that is the world's workshop. Some do directive work, others toilsome work, in a subdivision of tasks within a single producer class. Thus everybody industrious and efficient is everybody equal in social usefulness, to the gain of human solidarity. None are privileged to live off unearned income as were the leisured masters of the old ruling class.

This is in strict accord with socialism's first commandment, as framed by Saint-Simon himself: "All men shall work." Those who cannot work with their heads must work with their hands, each to his capacity. Directive men hold total authority over workingmen, to be sure. Yet this hierarchy of unequal ranks, derived by Wells from big business, with its "subordination of functions and great freedom of action for executives,"[57] makes for egalitarianism in a way that the feudal system does not. It makes for the equality of all producers of wealth against the claims of nonproductive idlers. No one has the right to be lazy.

A technocracy is by definition classless. All are *industriels*. Those who are not industrious are not socially efficient, and do not belong to this one-class society. One is economically useful or one is not a citizen. That, in essence, is the Social Idea: work is the only possible social activity. Therefore, in the world super-state of United Interests, class differences do not exist. There is only the difference between public servants and prisoners, between world citizens and quadrupeds. "The man who serves a particular state or a particular ownership in despite of the human commonweal is a Traitor" (STTC:318).

What makes it a *scientifically* organized classless society is its being organized as a production company. The moral regulation of industry, based on a scientific division of labor, is extended to regulate every other aspect of society as well. Socialism's post–Christian ethic, with its "rational code of morality," makes universal the organizing principle of industrial management. As nothing else can, it brings all social life under "the discipline of a common ideal."[58] Because the subordinated functions of public service are just as important as their executive controls, all else follows. All parts of the world economic machine share equally in the harmony of the perfected whole.

Now we can see more clearly what Wells was driving at in his debate with Lenin. Lenin was doing the correct Saint-Simonian thing, which is not to play on the "antagonism of employers and employed," but to end it.[59] Lenin did this in practice, yet he denied it in his public speeches, given to the rhetoric of class-war socialism. All the while, however, he spoke the language of the true socialist faith when addressing his party comrades in confidence. In his inner writings, there is no Marxist foolery about a workers' state, nor any exaltation of the common man as its dominant force.

Here Lenin sums up his purpose quite exactly. He says that the organizational basis of a communist, or classless society, is "a division of labor under the leadership of a center."[60] That center, of course, is Lenin himself, sitting at the head of Direction, the system's front office, its managerial brain or polit-buro. "*Unquestioning Subordination* to a single will is absolutely necessary for the success of processes organized on the pattern of large-scale machine in-dustry."[61] This means that "factory discipline will extend to the whole of society," the technocratic idea in a nutshell. "*All* citizens are transformed into hired employees of the state. . . . *All* citizens become employees of a *single* country-wide 'syndicate.'"[62] A classless society is the automatic result. All it takes is the will of one man, empowered to apply the science of industrial management to the subdivision of all social tasks. "The scientific concept of dictatorship means neither more nor less than unlimited power, resting di-rectly on force, not limited by anything, not restricted by any laws."[63]

The Air Dictatorship in *Things to Come* brings about a scientifically organized classless society by the same means—"collective submission by force."[64] John Cabal heads up the managerial center, or politburo, of a world civil service whose dictatorial powers are then passed on to the World Council of Direction under Oswald Cabal.

This control center of the Modern State, a world economic machine, is called by Wells its "World Brain," after the title of one of his books. His "world machine" is a complex of industrial cells in a "world organism," governed by that same World Brain.[65] Here, too, Wells is faithful to Saint-Simon in the last detail, right down to his mixture of mechanical and biological metaphors. The Master spoke of his world industrial state as "a veritable *organic machine* whose every part contributes in a different manner to the movement of the whole" (emphasis added). This follows from his view that human society con-stitutes "a veritable being whose existence is more or less integral according to whether its organs acquit themselves more or less regularly to the functions entrusted to them."[66] It is a physiological being, whose *organic* unity is made the more integral the more its human parts are *mechanized* by way of a scien-tific division of labor. Thanks to the industrial revolution, it is at last possible to realize the ancient ideal of Plato's organic state.

So far from being modern in outlook, both Wells and Saint-Simon revert to what is known as the "organic theory of the state," originating with Plato.[67] In *The Republic*, he says that the best-ordered state is one which "most nearly resembles an individual. For example, when one of us hurts his finger, the whole partnership of body and soul, constituting a single organism under a ruling principle, perceives it and is aware as a whole of the pain suffered by the part."[68] The best way to run a state, under the "ruling princi-ple" of organic unity, is to make sure that its limbs and organs are obedient to its brain, as if all were parts of an individual human body. The modern touch given this organismic analogy by Saint-Simon is his mechanical means for instrumenting the Platonic ideal. The biological division of labor between bodily parts has its likeness in the industrial division of labor, by which a pro-duction company is organized. Thus the body politic can be integrated as a unitary organism, by means of imposing the system of factory management onto all human relations.

"Humanity," said Saint-Simon, "is a collective entity." It really does exist as a veritable being in biological reality. But so long as the self-seeking individual parts of humanity lack awareness of this truth, it never will be acted upon and made a social reality in the political unification of mankind. The brotherhood of man is built into the nature of things, lacking only the organizational means to bring it about. This is the task of the socialist project, to make human solidarity a realizable goal. The prospect of universal harmony is mankind's only salvation. Socialism rests upon a "moral conception by which man becomes conscious of a social destiny."[69]

This prophetic truth, of course, is first given to the progressive-minded leaders of the socialist idea. Out of their moral superiority, in sensing the direction of human destiny, they will establish a church for the preaching of this idea, and make it a new and global religion. Saint-Simon's disciple who coined the word for socialism, Auguste Comte, called it the Religion of Humanity. Comte carries on with his Master's belief in mankind as a collective entity by describing it as *Le Grande-Être*, the Great Being of humanity in its "composite existence." We priests of this new religion, he says, are called upon to serve Humanity, in "our constant ministrations to the Great Being." In our capacity as religious teachers, it is our duty to instruct everyone to live for each other, after our own example, as "agents of the Great Being."[70]

Wells makes use of the same language. He says that socialism means a selfless service to the on-going life of Humanity, beyond the reach of our individual lives. To that impersonal end, we are to surrender our selfish egotisms and become "contributing parts in the progress of a greater being." The Social Idea calls for "subordination of the self to a higher order of being [that is] the master being, Man."[71] Man with a capital "M," wherever it recurs in Wells, is none other than Comte's *Grande-Être*.

Thus do the mixed metaphors of the Wellsian world state, otherwise known as the Great State, make sense. If it is a world *machine*, it is at the same time a world *organism*. It is Man embodied in the Great State by mechanical means. The Great State integrates all humanity into one self-conscious being, made aware of itself through a sense of solidarity created by the industrial division of labor. The productive process is the very instrument of organic unity. Only a technocratic state can make the *Grande-Être* to live on its own terms. It brings the "collective human beast" to life as nothing else can. The world economic machine will merge individual men with that "synthetic wider being, the Great State, mankind, in which we all move and go, like blood corpuscles, like nerve cells, it may be at times like brain cells, in the body of a man."[72]

Indeed, that "higher organism, the world state of the coming years," is nothing if not a "collective human person" made up of people, "a super-man with larger thoughts and aims."[73] This collective individual is Wells's early prophecy of the "Coming Man," his "Coming Beast."[74] It is a "new social Leviathan," the Hobbesian "monster as a completely unified social organism," in which "converge all lives upon a common existence."[75]

In *Things to Come*, the Coming Beast is a collective state monster of yet another species—not a giant fish (or whale) but a giant cephalopod. The *new* social Leviathan is a creature going by the name of "the Modern State octopus" (STTC:289). It is "a vast business octopus," the world machine as operated by the Air Dictatorship (289). So explains its future historian. "Within its far-flung tentacles it embraced [the whole mass of humanity]. . . . The central brain of the Modern State octopus [came to dominate a] world system of organization" (293, 295).

In this organic analogy, the huge cephalic dome of the giant octopus is the world state's World Brain, headed by John Cabal, the Air Dictator himself, together with his party intellectuals and chief executives. He stands in for Direction, the equivalent of Saint-Simon's Council of Newton, composed of scientists and industrialists; while the octopus tentacles are Labor, its operative tools. All brain and hands (or tentacles), the octopodal state monster is the very embodiment of the Social Idea. In representing the Saint-Simonian World Republic of United Interests, it brings Direction and Labor into organic collaboration, and makes for a unified producer class of equally functional *industriels*. Indeed, it fulfills Plato's ideal of a society unanimous in its collective will and wholly free of internal conflict. No independent labor unions exist to disturb the social peace.

Plato, Wells, and the Hindu Trinity

As it happens, Wells read Plato before he discovered Marx. It was *The Republic*, he says, that prompted his revolutionary view "that the whole fabric of law, custom and worship, which seemed so invincibly established, might be cast into the melting pot and made anew."[76] Indeed, he credits Plato with being "the Father of the Modern State" (STTC:125). His Modern State Fellowship, the film's Air League, is a private ruling cult, "self-appointed, self-trained and self-disciplined," fulfilling Plato's "plan for a devoted and trained order of rulers" (112). The Airmen bring Plato's dream of professional state Guardians into effect, as "foreshadowed" by the example of the Communist Party (119). But while Lenin's party members "were extremely like those Guardians," their effort, in the futuristic hindsight of the historian of the Modern Era, served as a useful example only insofar as it taught the lesson of a failed experiment (125).

Plato showed the proper way with his balanced one-two punch. His Guardians knew how to use "persuasion or compulsion to unite all citizens and . . . to make each man a link in the unity of the whole."[77] Lenin had theorized about and experimented with the seizure and concentration of power in just these brutal terms, but still he failed to carry his revolution beyond the borders of Soviet Russia. Wells explains why. While the Bolsheviks acted as "a necessary destructive force" in updating the powers of the Guardians with new means of physical violence, and while they indeed thereby managed to cast Russia into the melting pot for renewal, yet they did so given to "a modern method without a modern idea."[78] That is to say, Lenin's Communist Party used the right instruments of compulsion—the "forces of power industrialism and of mass manipulation" (STTC:150)—but it used the wrong words of persuasion.

Lenin correctly grounded his scientific dictatorship on a forced division of labor, extending it from the limited realm of factory management in the workplace to the rest of society. But he attempted to manipulate the masses with deceitful propaganda. Marxism in no way authorizes technocratic practice.

The Airmen, learning from this verbal error, do better. Acting as "educational guardians" of the Modern State (STTC:421), they do a better job of instruction in winning over "an acquiescent co-operative world." With Lenin, they recognize "the spirit of opposition as purely evil, as a vice to be guarded against, as trouble in the machinery . . . to be minimised as much as possible" (350). But they have the Platonic wit to combine the right forces of coercion with the right language of persuasion. Their job, after all, is to teach the citizen not how to participate in government, but how to accept it. Marxism, with its notion of mass democracy, is unsuitable to that purpose.

As old Plato knew, the common man is much too impulsive to govern himself, too covetous to produce for others without moral guidance from above. He needs the Guardians as a sick man needs doctoring by a physician. The mean desires of the many need holding down by the virtues of a superior few. Comte wrote this ancient wisdom into Saint-Simonian doctrine when he ever and again called for a rule of the "intellectuals" over the "emotionals." The Communist Revision of H.G. Wells differs from the official line of the Communist Party only in his plain speaking about this necessity. Wellsism is the more workable and more truthful doctrine. If only Lenin had listened to him! Now the world revolution is up to him and his Airmen. "The World-State, c'est moi."[79]

But suppose Plato was wrong to begin with? *Is* the common man all that irresponsible? If not, what matters the issue of Wellsism versus Marxism-Leninism? Centralized planning means rule by unlimited force, never rule by consent, *whatever* doctrine the one-party guardians of the one-opinion state may profess. The democratic belief behind the Western idea of the nation-state assumes just that, a disbelief in Plato. It takes for granted that Plato was mistaken.

The first skeptic after Aristotle to see this error was the great medieval theologian, St. Thomas Aquinas. Our democratic assumptions rest on his critique of *The Republic*, in which he ventured to make himself the first exponent of popular sovereignty. What is most interesting about this, is that St. Thomas cast his argument in Plato's own language, playing with the same three elements or social castes that Plato uses in describing his ideal republic. He takes its teachers, soldiers and producers as the constituent elements of *any* society, the difference between one and another being in how they are politically ordered.

With Plato, the top two castes comprise the Guardians, who monopolize their two related powers of persuasion and compulsion in order to dominate the bottom and third element, the caste of producers. That is to say, in the words of St. Thomas, the Guardians combine the "spiritual power" of the Republic's teachers with the "temporal power" of its soldiers, to the suppression of "popular power" inherent by natural right in its producers. Seated together in the Republic's politburo, or Nocturnal Council, teachers and soldiers rule in joint sovereignty over the populace.

But while this arrangement may satisfy the philosophical dream of unity aspired to by the Republic's philosopher-king, who heads up the Nocturnal Council, the whole system works only to disable production. All social elements are parts of one organic state so far as the ideal is concerned, but enforcement of the ideal works against society's economic strength. The administered distribution of wealth hurts production and creates only poverty.[80]

In making this criticism, Aquinas followed Aristotle in viewing the Guardians as a virtual army of occupation, sitting on its own fellow citizens. He was not, however, indulging himself in a mere scholastic rehash of antiquity's dead political issues. He rather addressed himself to that great issue of his own day, vital still in our own, the question of the separation of Church and State. What was the proper relationship between the spiritual or moral power of society (given to the Church to say) and its temporal or political power (given to the State to exert)? In making his case for the separation of Church and State, he made a case for what we today call democratic pluralism. He argued that when popes and kings, churchmen and statesmen hold joint dominance, as they sought to do under a theocracy, they combine for no divine purpose that he himself as a Catholic theologian could understand; but only to the effect of suppressing the popular or economic power of society, wherein reside its productive forces and wealth making. Therefore, all *three* powers ought to be separated, each to exercise its moral or political or economic strengths on its own, independently of each other. Each social element in Plato's despotic order deserves to have its own sovereignty, making for a pluralistic order.

Note that Aquinas equates Plato's teachers with the Church, his soldiers with the State. In modern terms, this makes a lot of sense, if we think of the one-party state invented (or reinvented) by Lenin as a kind of secular theocracy. The Communist Party guides the bureaucratic apparatus of the government, giving to the temporal powers of the civil service its policy direction in line with party ideology, the state's moral or theological power. Party and State jointly govern the people, as did the medieval combination of Church and State.

Or as did Plato's teachers and soldiers. In his grand design, the teachers are policy planners, the Republic's party theoreticians and propagandists. They are its Perfect Guardians, being its intellectual overseers, following the unitary dream of the philosopher-king himself. The soldiers are the party's administrative aides, Auxiliary Guardians, serving their more brainy bosses as executives and policemen. We may picture this in the following tabulation:

Plato's Republic

social elements	*functions*
1. teachers—policy makers (Perfect Guardians)	persuasion
2. soldiers—executives & police (Auxiliary Guardians)	compulsion
3. producers—farmers & artisans	obedience

Now it so happens that Saint-Simon's technocracy is Plato's Republic of united citizens all over again. For the Guardians he has Direction, with scientists in its top or perfect ranks, and industrial executives in the lower or auxiliary ranks; together they hold joint sovereignty over Labor. For Plato's Nocturnal Council, he has his Council of Newton. Moreover, in describing the functional aspects of his two ranks of Direction, he borrows his phraseology from none other than St. Thomas Aquinas. The scientists embody the system's "spiritual power," the industrial chiefs its "temporal power." But there is no mention of "popular power." Saint-Simon does not recognize such a thing. Instead, he speaks of the "proletariat," from Roman *proletarius*, the lowest social element with no power of its own. He assumes that Labor can be commanded by Direction to produce; that government alone can create wealth and decree prosperity—the everlasting socialist fallacy.

So, too, with Wells. His Modern State divides between Direction and Labor, with the former's planners and administrators holding joint seats on a World Council. For Saint-Simon's merit system, which distinguishes directive men from workingmen according to their natural capacities for brain work or manual labor, Wells offers a rather more complicated analysis of capacity in psychological terms. In *A Modern Utopia* (chapter 9), he speaks of four basic human temperaments—Poietic, Kinetic, and Dull and Base.

The Poietic temperament refers to a capacity for creative thinking; the Kinetic to the executive ability to carry out the leading ideas of the former. "The *kinetics* 'run the show,' the *poietics* animate it." Both are uncommon types, belonging to the aristocracy of talent. The Dull and the Base define capacities, or the lack of them, belonging to the common run of men—the "intellectually incapable [and the] morally incapable."[81] They cannot or will not act on the Social Idea without the "forcible conformities" of a police-and-propaganda regime; the "non-effective masses" can do nothing without the imposed discipline of a self-disciplined elite. Thus the Wellsian "necessity of replacing crude democracy by a control organization."[82]

But this only returns us to Plato once again. He, too, has his capacities or temperamental types, tagged as qualities of the soul. The ideal society, making for social justice and functional equality, is one in which each soul-type finds its natural station in a political order, arranged by a very exceptional philosopher-ruler who understands these human differences. He selects men endowed with Wisdom (or Reason in some translations) for his teachers; men endowed with the will to exert Force for his soldiers (Courage it is in other translations). Together, they subdue the pleasure principle given to the soul of the masses, who are full of nothing but Desire and self-seeking.

All these correspondences, between the soul-types of Plato and the natural capacities of Saint-Simon and Wells, may be tabulated as follows, with their social ranking as decided by their respective Councils.

Plato	Saint-Simon	Wells
Nocturnal Council	Council of Newton	World Council
Guardians	Direction	Direction
Wisdom (teachers)	spiritual power (scientists)	Poietics
Force (soldiers)	temporal power (industrialists)	Kinetics
Producers	Labor	Labor
Desire (worker-citizens)	proletariat	Dull & Base

This leads us directly to the church-state or party-state theology of *Things to Come*. Wells explains in *Whither Mankind?*, his treatment drafted for discussion by the production staff, that the film was meant to dramatize "the Indian vision of life." He says that the film's dramatic idea is based on Hindu theology, with its trio of gods—Brahma the Creator, Siva the Destroyer, and Vishnu the Possessor. These divinities, he says, are symbolic of the supreme powers of the universe. Their tripolar struggle is the explanation of everything. The film story is meant to "display these cardinal forces at work" (WM:4). They "express the main forces in the world about us."[83]

At the same time, Wells is able to invoke the Christian deity with no sense of contradiction; "the world state is God's church." "God is the collective mind and purpose of the human race."[84] Here, the name of God is useful in summing up all the forces of the cosmic process, otherwise assigned to the trinity of Hindu gods.

This is perfectly good Saint-Simonian theory, in which monotheism is reduced to a secular concept, in the service of a civil theology. As one of the Master's disciples put it, "The idea of God is for man merely a way of conceiving unity, order, harmony, of being conscious of a destination and of accounting for it."[85]

As for the Hindu trinity, its gods relate to the souls animating Plato's three social castes. Brahma sorts with the creative intellect of his Perfect Guardians or teachers; Siva the Destroyer with the coercive sword-power of his Auxiliary Guardians or soldiers; and Vishnu the Possessor—a female deity given to lust—sorts with his producers and their greed to keep what they produce. Vishnu stands for exclusive love and sexual possession, the basic motive behind all other proprietary desires that it is the task of the Guardians to control. No believer in market economics, Plato requires the taking of wealth from its producers for redistribution by the state, breaking their hold on it by a combination of guile and force—the propaganda of the teachers and the strong-arm methods of the soldiers.[86]

According to Wells, Vishnu's primary spiritual home, in a capitalist society of private profit and private ownership, is the "sex-cemented family." Marriage is a "fellowship of two based on cohabitation and protected by jealousy."[87] From this "partisanship for wife and family against the common welfare," getting and keeping in all else follows. "The fierce jealousy of men for women and women for men is the very heart of all our social jealousies."[88]

Because these jealousies, like "class, partisan and nationalist passion," are as essential "as lust" in the motivation of the common man, "these natural tendencies will have to be overridden."[89] His "animal individualism" will have to be "socialized entirely against his natural disposition in the matter" (STTC:334, 428).

Tabulating the above correspondences, we may see at a glance what Wells means when he says that *Things to Come* is a dramatization of the Hindu vision of life.

Hindu deities	Platonic souls	Wellsian capacities
Brahma the Creator	Wisdom (reason)	Poietic
Siva the Destroyer	Force (will)	Kinetic
Vishnu the Possessor	Desire (passion)	Dull & Base

Wells, like Plato, joins creative wisdom with destructive force in the double ranks of his ruling elite, for the repression of possessive desires in the ruled. The reason and will of the few must discipline the passions of the many. To create a unified state on the basis of the Social Idea, the Poietics who formulate the idea need the aid of the Kinetics to enforce it among the Dull and the Base. In the film, as Wells explains it, Brahma relies on the sword of Siva to destroy the animal appetites of Vishnu, so that the creative idea may prevail. This is his mythic way of saying how a Saint-Simonian technocracy may come into being, by making sure of a docile labor force in the destruction of trade unions, and all other forms of independent group life, rooted as they are in self-interested partisanship against the organic harmony of the whole.

Like Plato's philosopher-ruler, John Cabal hand picks his teachers and soldiers, himself a shining example to them of both rational wisdom and the courage to use force. He gathers into his Air Dictatorship those few exceptional men and women of the Poietic and the Kinetic type that exist in the world, ruling it in his image over the intellectually Dull and morally Base who comprise the rest of humanity. This he does for mankind's own good, in spite of its fierce resistance. But in time, all opposition to his Puritan Tyranny ceases. Cabal brings Siva the Destroyer to the side of Brahma the Creator for the permanent holding down of Vishnu the Possessor. In monopolizing all instruments of force in the creative name of the Social Idea, he achieves a lasting victory over those craven desires that animate the common man. With all three cardinal forces lined up in dynamic balance, he gains absolute power, and with it at last fulfills the Platonic dream of organic unity. He wins Man's greatest conquest, "the conquest of the social order."[90]

Let us not suppose, however, that Wells takes a special interest in the Eastern religion of the Aryan Indians. In explaining *Things to Come* in terms of the Hindu vision of life, he rather relates it to the whole range of Indo-European mythology. The author of *The Outline of History* is a generalist, who sees in Hindu religion a convenient instance of a like vision of life shared throughout the Indo-European cultural realm, from Aryan India to northern Europe of the Irish and Gaulish Celts, and later transmitted to the Norsemen.

In drawing upon this widespread tradition for the mythic symbolism of the film's political theology, Wells remains consistent with his interest in Plato, who also drew upon it. Plato codified ideas already ancient by his time, originating in a range of preliterate societies long antedating the rise of classical Greece. He merely pitched these ideas at a theoretical level of discourse, which since has been retained in the language of socialism from Saint-Simon to H.G. Wells.

These ancient Indo-European societies were stratified into three social castes—those of priests, warriors, and peasant producers—under the leadership of a warchief in consultation with a high priest. The priestly caste itself invented departmental gods to express this arrangement, thus creating a religious validation for everybody's proper place in the social order, with reference to a higher cosmic order of which society was a part. In Aryan India, the god of the priests (Brahmins) was Brahma, that of the warriors Siva, and that of the peasants Vishnu. In Norse mythology they are Odin (god of the Druids or something like them, as among the Celts), Thor (god of the warriors) and Freya (the erotic goddess of the producers). In all cases, these divinities represent the wisdom of the priests, the destructive force of the warriors, and the fertility of plant and animal wealth in the peasants' possession.

Long after the chiefdoms which gave rise to these gods disappeared as actual social structures, their religion survived as a mythology, to be used by later intellectuals as a means of stating political ideas, as did Plato.[91] Tabulating this, we have the following:

Indo-European castes	functions	cosmic order	Plato's republic
Brahmins/Druids	wisdom	creation	teachers
warriors	force	destruction	soldiers
peasants	wealth	possession	producers

Wells made direct use of this general scheme in *The Work, Wealth and Happiness of Mankind*, a heavyweight treatise on social economics. Much to our astonishment, we find it listed on the title page of *Whither Mankind?* as the book other than the novel, *The Shape of Things to Come*, on which his "Film of the Future" is based (see Appendix I).

This treatise is book three of his educational trilogy, modeled after Diderot's *Encyclopédie*, beginning with *The Outline of History*, a universal history of planetary man. The world is one in an astronomical sense, as a single planet located in the gravitational field of a particular star, and is therefore destined by the laws of the universal cosmos to become one in the political sense as well, world humanity embraced by a world socialist state. The second book is *The Science of Life*, an atheistic reading of biology that shows man to be a world species of organic oneness. As the cells in our bodies are but parts, in a like manner do we individuals compose the body of this higher organism, Man the racial being. Therefore independent personhood is an illusion, a perceptual error abetted and wrongly warranted by the Christian doctrine of personal immortality. True immortality is rather to be had in selfless devotion to the undying life of the species, the Great Being, faith in whose collective progress is the condition of world citizenship in the Great State to come. Finally, *The Work, Wealth and Happiness of Mankind* outlines the social forces that are trending to make for this outcome, in the shape of "a single world economic machine" (WWHM:373), destined for mastery by the emerging revolutionaries of the Modern State Movement.

If communism has its Marxist canon, then the Communist Revision has its body of sacred texts in this educational trilogy, providing the Movement with "an ideological basis for the new time" (WWHM:13). Wells modestly refers to it as his "Bible of Civilization," written to serve "the propaganda of world unity." In short, it makes propaganda for Wellsism, otherwise designated as the "Religion of Progress."[92]

The same is true of *Things to Come*, based in part, as it is, on book three of this "Bible." But how dramatize that sort of thing? *The Work, Wealth and Happiness of Mankind* is a huge compendium of encyclopedic dimensions. Yet withal it is simple in outline.

In it, Wells reduces the economic forces of the world to an interplay of three basic "personas," those of priest, warrior and peasant. These personas are general types that persist throughout history, although their names change. By medieval times, the tripartite caste system of ancient Indo-European society had become feudalism's Three Estates, those of clerics, knights, and serfs. Nowadays feudalism is being transformed by the industrial revolution, which is the object of the Modern State Movement to capture for the socialist revolution. In this progressive trend, wisdom has passed from clerics of the church to scientists, force from the knights to the managers of power industrialism, and the productive work of peasant-like serfs to factory and industrialized farm labor. It is the purpose of socialism, following Saint-Simonian theory, to organize these new embodiments of the basic personas in a neoplatonic state, making use of the most modern means of mass persuasion and compulsion (WWHM: chapter 8).

The shape of things to come is "ultra-modern State Capitalism," a command economy in which the state acts as "the universal buyer and seller" (WWHM:557). Or rather, buying and selling as in a market is abolished, for a planned economy is by definition tradeless. The spontaneous cooperation of the free market is replaced by regulated cooperation, with the controls of all production and distribution given over to the state's unitary will. Marketing activity is a part of that free social life that is a freedom only for "chaotic individualism" (315). The task of socialism (or State Capitalism) is to reduce that selfish disorder to collective order, by bringing all social life under the common discipline of industrial management and a forced division of labor. When the whole world thus becomes a single production company, each of mankind's three personas will find its proper function and subdivided task, according to capacity, in the harmonious unity of the organic Great State.

How this technocratic conquest of the social order comes about is the film's theme, treated as a progressive movement of historical trends, élans, and impersonal processes. Not *who* makes the Modern State, but *what*. Accordingly, the film characters as explained by Wells in *Whither Mankind?* are not meant to portray living, breathing personalities. They are rather resonators of his three basic personas. In their cosmic projection, they are avatars of the Hindu trinity.

Thus John Cabal, in one of his personas, is the avatar of Brahma the Creator. But as he must destroy the old order before he creates the new, his other persona derives from Siva. He and his Airmen must clear the world of its nationalist leaders before he can establish his Air Dictatorship and build the world state. This is accomplished in the aftermath of a vastly destructive world war, in which the world is bombed back to the Feudal Age, although we are given to know that such a regression does not take things back very far. It but underlines the medievalism of the nation-state idea that was responsible for the political rivalries that caused the war in the first place.

The sample enemy of world unity that the Airmen attack is one Rudolf the Victorious, the feudalistic military chief of a peasant-like populace. He is presented as an avatar of Vishnu in his medieval chivalry and vainglorious lust for territorial possession. But in all this, he is basically motivated by sex. He makes patriotic war only to impress the likes of Roxana, his favorite harem mistress. She is an avatar of Vishnu in this female deity's more fundamental aspect, that of sexual possession. In Rudolf and Roxana, the two aspects of territorial and sexual ownership are related. Both desire only love and glory. He, the glory of bossing things from horseback and carrying his flag against other ministates as little and pathetic as his, while the patriotic cheers of the people in celebrating his victories pay off in his being loved by a sexually attractive woman. She, the glory of being sexually possessed by a knightly man heroic in battle and popular for his deeds. Sex is the animal appetite, ruled over by Vishnu's evil spirit, in everything proprietary and jealously guarded.

No wonder the Airmen are tagged as New Puritans. They have no red passions or beastly lusts, being cool-headed intellectuals motivated only by ideological conviction—their scientific motive to govern well. They are "sober and religious men . . . educated in the scientific outlook as the old Puritans were educated in the Bible."[93] Against Rudolf, who makes war for self-glory, they make "war for peace." They make war to end war, to end nationalism, and to create a unified world state. Yet John Cabal, in doing so, wields the sword of Siva the Destroyer no less than does Rudolf and his kind. The difference, however, is this: In Rudolf, Siva sides with Vishnu the Possessor for *chaotic* destruction, whereas in Cabal, Siva sides with Brahma for *creative* destruction. His is the "sword of peace."[94]

John Cabal's philosophical franchise in the world unity business is given him because he understands this verifiable difference. He has mastered the symbolic meaning of the Hindu trinity and its destruction-reconstruction dialectic. To build the new, the old must first be smashed. His is the wisdom of Brahma to know and command the cosmic forces of a dialectical universe. To resolve its tripolar struggle, and bring order to the chaos caused by Vishnu's upsetting passions, he is obliged to take the sword of Siva to the exclusive side of his creative cause, and keep it there eternally. Never again shall Vishnu be permitted to grasp hold of it. Henceforth the Modern State shall monopolize all instruments of force to subdue the inferior soul-stuff of the multitudes, and to prevent the rise of any popular leader in their name.

Vishnu subdued, however, is not Vishnu dead. This is a dynamic universe in which all three cardinal forces remain in play. Oswald Cabal inherits the power of his World Council of Direction from controls put in place by his grandfather, John Cabal, with his Air Dictatorship. But although John won such a power with Siva's aid, it is up to Oswald to hold it with the same sword. While the Modern State Revolution has made its conquest of the social order, it must ever be on guard against Vishnu's counter-revolution. No sooner is Oswald Cabal installed than he is faced by just that. A dissident mob at the end of the film rises up to attack the Space Gun, the symbol of his faith in Man's collective energy to conquer Nature and to assault the whole world of mind and matter, first on this planet and then in the universe beyond the stars.

But the mob shares none of this faith. It objects to industrial progress on sentimental grounds. Oswald Cabal drives ahead without regard for the smaller values that the common man places on ease and comfort, the natural man who wants only to preserve and protect his own individual life, and relax from the frenzied imperatives of socialist work. The film concludes with a morally uplifting putdown of these base and ignorant objections. With yet one more decisive sword-stroke of the permanent revolution, the final scene

> brings the drama of creative effort versus the resistance of jealousy, indolence and sentimentality to a culmination. . . . The aggressive maker in

the human soul has emerged triumphant over instinct and tradition. Brahma the Creator asserts himself over Vishnu the Preserver [*i.e.*, Possessor—*ed.*] after his [her!] previous subjugation by Siva the Destroyer. But as the struggle about the Space Gun shows, all three Powers are still eternally alive and at work in the world [WM:02].

In the late 19th century, when the Social Idea of collective salvation by force was no more than a dreamy idea, not yet acted on by Lenin at all costs, Auberon ("self-ownership") Herbert wrote the following words.

> The highest art cannot gild socialism. It is impossible to make beautiful the denial of liberty. . . . [S]ocialism is the negation of all personal rights, erected into a system; and literature, even in the hands of a master, is powerless to make us look with anything but scorn on that negation.[95]

Herbert, however, had not reckoned on such a literary master as H.G. Wells. *Things to Come* is without a doubt the most romantic apology for the Social Idea ever conceived. It is a mighty and altogether poetic statement, endorsing no-limit progress.

> To the mystery of Power and Beauty, out of the earth that mothered us, we move.[96]

His film, together with the rest of his Literature of Power, is most exceptional in the history of letters, usually regarded as a humanistic art. Yet Wells alone had the artistic craft to make it serve a profoundly anti-humanistic purpose. The strange effectiveness of *Things to Come*, when taken seriously as the work of propaganda for Wellsism that it is, deserves the close attention we give to the Great Books.

Igor Shafarevich, one of the dissident writers in the Soviet Union, explains that the attraction of socialism is the strange allure of death and nothingness, in its hostility to self-culture and its aim to destroy everything supportive of the human personality in religion, family life, and private property. The socialist project, he says, "is consistent with the tendency to reduce man to the level of a cog in the state mechanism, as well with the attempt to prove that man exists only as a manifestation of non-individual features such as production or class interest."[97]

Therein lies the true significance of the Hindu trinity as Wells gives it out in his explanation of the film's dramatic line. Men are but avatars of impersonal forces in the progressive movement of history, making for a nonindividualized future, to be made official in the dedicated nihilism of the organic state.

THINGS TO COME:
A READING

Everydayism

In his preliminary film treatment, Wells divides the story line into four main parts (WM:02). With musical signatures added for the benefit of the composer,[1] they are:

1. Present Conditions (*Pastorale*)
2. The World Smashed (*Marche Funèbre*)
3. Reconstruction—a rush series
4. The World in 2054 (*Chorale*)

The future date in the actual film, however, is not A.D. 2054 but A.D. 2036 (or M.E. 119). It is 100 years beyond the release date of 1936, although Present Conditions are posted a few years ahead of that, at 1940. This is the year Wells predicted for the outbreak of the Second World War. He was more or less right, but not alone in his prophecy. Indeed, the storm signals of 1936 are the very ones on display in the film's opening scenes, and with the same show of public indifference. Another great war is in the making for all to see, yet the mass of people are blind to every sign of its nearness. Preoccupied with their private affairs, they pay no heed to political affairs, at home or abroad.

Their "self-complacent ignorance" of world-historical trends is an aspect of Vishnu, and Wells gives it the name of "everydayism." It is his tag-word for the "false securities and fatuous satisfactions of the everyday life."[2] Its opposite is "a vision of human life as one continuous drama," the evolutionary drama of the species in which our personal lives are but passing incidents. This he calls the "Human Adventure."[3] It is the on-going life of Man the master being, that great collective organism, *Le Grande-Être*, whose racial welfare and progress are the object of religious reverence in Wellsism.

Worship of this Great Being, however, is at first limited to the Wellsian elect.

> The great majority of human beings have still to see the human adventure
> as one whole; they are obsessed by the air of permanence and finality in
> established things; they accept current reality as the ultimate reality. They
> take the world as they find it.[4]

The elect, who are the film's Airmen, take it upon themselves to convert
the rest of mankind to their own sense of this higher reality. It is the ultimate
Darwinian reality, known to them through the science of biology, beyond the
limits and illusions of personal experience. Their aim is to create a species-wide
world state in which the ever-unfolding Human Adventure is everyone's
religious duty to serve, out of a "desire to give oneself to a greater end than
the everyday life affords." Their credo is based on that new Bible of World
Civilization, compiled by H.G. Wells for their ideological guidance—they who
are the revolutionary movers and doers of the Modern State Movement. The
basic lesson of Wellsism contained therein teaches them "to see that the
species has its adventures, its history and drama, far exceeding in interest and
importance the individual adventure."[5]

This lesson it is the mission of the Airmen to carry to the masses, who
still are in the grip of Vishnu the Possessor. And Vishnu is none other than
the evil deity of everydayism itself. It is because of Vishnu's hold on the common man that he is betrayed into believing that the petty selfishness of the
personal adventure is everything. The Airmen, however, are prepared to
disprove and defeat that huge and all-pervasive falsehood. Their sense of a
transcendent, nonindividualized human reality is informed not only by Darwinian science; they have elevated this biological truth to a mystical truth that
informs the rightness of their reproval. Acting as cosmic agents of the inevitable, theirs is a faith in the Hindu vision of life, with its promise that
Brahma, the supreme deity of the Hindu triad, is destined to prevail in the
making of world order. Theirs is a religious conviction that the tripolar struggle of all three Powers is preordained in the dialectical nature of things to be
resolved into a unity, by the ultimate siding of Siva the Destroyer with
Brahma the Creator for the final overcoming of Vishnu. This is what is coming in *Things to Come*. With both right and might allied in its cause, the
Modern State Revolution is "the ultimate revolution" (STTC:374).

Indeed, the coming war is all to Brahma's advantage; and the Airmen are
wise enough to redirect it for their own creative ends. The war will come as
a stunning catastrophe, shaking the masses out of their self-serving ignorance
of indisputable truth. It will come as a form of shock therapy, educating the
survivors of this collective havoc to their responsibility to the collective fate
of Man. They will learn the hard way that Man's racial well-being, as a super-
individual going a progress above and beyond the particulars of the personal
drama, is the one and only real concern of human affairs.

A new and greater world war, for all the warnings of its coming, is no
tragedy but a blessing in horrific disguise. Doom is the very quickener of Progress. After John Cabal and his Airmen quell the last feeble remnants of

fighting in a dying world, they give birth to a new and indestructible order – a Caesarist dictatorship for the putting down forever of all that goes against the laws of universal cosmic harmony. Henceforth, world unity will prevail. The *pax mundi* imposed by their Air Dictatorship is inhumanly strong.

John Cabal, in picking up the sword of Siva in Brahma's invincible cause, never will permit it to fall ever again into the hands of Vishnu and the disorderly spirit of democracy, with all its mob-like striving for popular power. Like Andrew Marvell's Cromwell, he knows that "The same arts that did gain/ A power, must it maintain." This bit of dialectical wisdom he passes on to Oswald Cabal his grandson, president of the World Council of Direction in the world of 2036. John's power then is Oswald's to extend for the conquest of all mind and matter and the deeps of space. The Modern State Revolution is a permanent revolution, its eternal dynamism symbolized by the Space Gun, that deadly tool of Oswald Cabal's expansive powers. Against such a super-scientific dictatorship, so accomplished in its researches into the secrets of human destiny, no counterrevolution is possible.

When a popular revolt is raised against the Space Gun and all the driving collectivism it stands for, a revolt motivated by nostalgia for the good old selfish days of contented everydayism, Oswald Cabal destroys it with ease. In using the Space Gun itself to do this, he displays how well the cardinal forces of the universe are now under his dialectical control, not only for the unending conquest of space, but for the everlasting conquest of society.

The new order is for keeps. The state is everything, civilian society is nothing. The self-regarding smugness of Vishnu the Possessor is at last disillusioned by the preventive terrorism of Siva the Destroyer, who now stands by on loyal watch for Brahma, guarding the unstoppable creativity of the unfolding Human Adventure.

It is Christmas Eve in Everytown (a town-sized London City with London shops). Christmas shoppers and holiday revelers crowd the town square, heeding not the screamer headlines on the broadsheets of the newsvendors. Europe is arming. The enemy country (Germany) has built another 10,000 warplanes. Its Air Minister has just made another alarming speech. WAR, WAR, WAR the broadsheets and war posters shout in block letters, as a Christmas carol, "God rest you merry, gentlemen," plays in counterpoint against the rising din of the *Marche Funèbre*, to be fully developed when the war storm finally breaks. "Let nothing you dismay," sing the voices. The *Pastorale* now sounds with the force of irony as the counterpoint theme anticipates the death and burial of Merry Olde England.

The first building hit when the bombs fall, significantly, is the movie theatre (ttc:215). According to Wells, the cinema "has been developed chiefly on its 'amusements' side.... Its obvious uses for educational purposes have still to be developed." He thought it the business of state-run schools and universities "to control this new and powerful instrument for the distribution of mental impressions," but the "existing regime" has no sense of the State at all (WWHM:174f).

A democracy is by definition under-governed. Yet the technical means of mass persuasion now exist, all to the advantage of statism, were there the political will to use them for other than the trivial purposes of commercial greed. With the invention of photography, "the camera abolished privacy."[6] The replication of visual images is a powerful means of communicating the collective experience of socialism. With a mass medium like film, "the intensity of the individual life is diminished and the individual life *generalised*" (WWHM:172).

For that reason, says Wells, the cinema is destined to become "the Art form of the Future."[7] Come the world revolution, it will serve the Modern State as it served the Soviet regime under Lenin, who said, "Of all the arts, for us the cinema is the most important."[8] Indeed, the first action we see in the future world of 2036 is a school lesson taught by film. The "educational development of the cinematograph,"[9] as a propaganda arm of the Modern State, is realized.

But for now, movies in Everytown serve only to amuse. The film industry has yet to awaken to its political calling. In fact, on this Christmas Eve, the local cinema house is offering no film program at all. Instead, a signboard outside advertises a pantomime show entitled, "Sleeping Beauty." Film is a medium awaiting its Prince Charming to kiss it back into renewed and purposeful life.

When the cinema house is hit with the first bomb, the explosion centers on the building's huge tabled letters for CINEMA dressing its facade, and they are seen falling down with a conspicuous crash. Yet the promise of futurity they represent is to be fulfilled by the Modern State Revolution, following the ruinous aftermath of the war. For the lettering is done in a curvilinear style called the Streamlined Moderne, the counterpart in graphic design for a futuristic style of architecture going by the same name, the very style in which the new Everytown of 2036 is built.[10] CINEMA spells "things to come" in the graphics of futurism.

Outside a toy-shop window a small boy looks in at a model fort, shown with studied closeness (ttc:19). The allusion is to *Little Wars*, a children's book about the playing of military floor games. In it, Wells contrasts his Little Wars with the real thing, Great War,

> a game out of all proportion. Not only are the masses of men and material and suffering and inconvenience too monstrously big for reason, but—the available heads we have for it, are too small.... If Great War is to be played at all, the better it is played the more humanely it will be done. I see no inconsistency in deploring the practice while perfecting the method.[11]

Only the Airmen have heads big enough for the real thing. The rest cannot desist from waging it, nor wage it competently. But once the Airmen decide to play at Great War in different game, they perfect the method only to end the practice. With all the modern weapons of military science, which they invented, at their disposal, they alone understand them and hold the power to end war and enforce world peace. Proficiency in war makes for progress.

"Militarism and warfare are childish things, if they were not more horrible than anything childish can be. They must become things of the past."[12] The way to achieve the peace of mankind is by taking the game away from its infantile players in the traditional armed services, turning its playthings over to the technical intelligentsia, who are "more likely to regard war as a tiresome distraction than as a great and glorious opportunity." They have more creative things to do with science and technology. In their hands, the "improvement of war may be synonymous with the ending of war."[13] In time, this idea occurs to John Cabal, who then forms the Air League.

Cut from the town square and its Christmas jollity to the home of John Cabal, "aviator and inventor" (WM:01). He is in his study, musing over a newspaper and its war-scare headlines, which include one that says, "Fresh Trade Restriction" (WM:2). This is bad for business, his own business included. He owns an aviation design firm with international connections.

On the table beside him are some engineering drawings; hung on the wall a propeller blade. Over the mantelpiece is a framed picture of a DC-3 in flight. The Douglas Commercial mark 3, introduced in 1935, was the first of the fully streamlined airliners. The efficiency of its design made air traffic in passengers and cargo a routine part of the global economy.[14]

John Cabal is a middle-class professional man of trained intellect, who understands that world trade and advanced technology could make for a progressive world civilization, were it not for what he reads in the newspaper. In his musing he seems to sense, with Wells, that nationalism is the only bar to this development, as if peace and free trade were incompatible with the existence of a plurality of nation states. This is not in fact the case.

It is not true that a given nation can prosper only at the expense of other nations. Their interests may harmonize with each other, no less than do various occupational groups and social classes within any nation—so long as its patriotic self-interests are not stupidly ignored by playing at trade war. A mercantilist policy is bad business for all partners to international trade. Every economist knows this.[15]

But not H.G. Wells. His outline of economics, book three of his World Bible on which the film is in part based, denies two centuries' worth of practical wisdom, accumulated since the time of Adam Smith. For Wells, a stupid, beggar-thy-neighbor policy is intrinsic to the national idea: "the existence of independent sovereign states *is* war" (STTC:88).

The trade restrictions Cabal reads about are represented not as a response to military threats from across the Channel, but as the cause of them. No distinction is made between British democracy and Hitler's German dictatorship. From this viewpoint of faked Martian detachment, both nations are regarded as equally war-provoking sovereignties.

Yet German imperialism is exemplary. John Cabal takes the war prowess of the enemy's Air Ministry as a model for his Air League and its aggressive drive to establish its own imperium. While reading, his thumb drums against the newspaper with the same hereditary tic that marks his grandson, Oswald Cabal, who comes to govern a world state won for him by John through air power.

Enter young Harding, a medical student and family friend of the Cabals, come to join their Christmas party. He asks what is all the fuss about in the evening papers. Cabal answers with a Biblical phrase from Matthew 24:6, "War and rumors of wars," and fears the worst (ttc:59). A second world war will mess up his career as did the first (WM:1). He does not yet know that events this time will make revolution his profession.

Next enter Mr. Passworthy, a businessman friend and managing director of a textile factory (WM:1). His grandson will serve the poietic Oswald Cabal as one of his kinetic executives. As head of "General Fabrics" (ttc:845), the later Passworthy manages textile mills wherever in the world fabrics are manufactured.

The big-business octopus that is the Modern World-State is no federation of nation-states. Under its rule, the old political divisions of the globe no longer exist, not even as administrative areas. All local patriotisms, being relics of the feudal heritage, are replaced by loyalties to occupational domains. The units of administration belonging to the World Council have no local references whatsoever. They are based on a functional division of labor, with global Controls for transport, natural products, staple manufacturers, housing, social sanitation, police, education and the like; "the world which had once been divided among territorial Great Powers became divided among functional Great Powers" (STTC:355).[16]

But the future Passworthy of General Fabrics is no less conservative than his ancestor. He is "more normal" than Oswald Cabal, who has revolution in his blood (ttc:873). Not radical enough to sit among the Perfect Guardians who do the planning at Council meetings, yet he is worthy enough to pass among the Auxiliary Guardians. Given his kinetic temperament and executive abilities, he helps run the show animated by the poietics.

His ancestor, now lacking such creative guidance under Present Conditions, is altogether lost to the world of everyday. Singing a Christmas carol, Passworthy joins Harding and Cabal and is brought up short by their glum faces. "What's the matter with you fellows?" he asks. Cabal indicates the newspaper. Passworthy dismisses it. "Why not look on the bright side of things? You're all right. Your business is going up. You've got a jolly wife, a pretty home." Cabal throws this back at him. "All's right with the world, eh? Passworthy, you should have been called Pippa Passworthy" (ttc:62–64).

The allusion is to "Pippa's Song" by Robert Browning, whose famous last lines are "God's in His heaven—/ All's right with the world."[17] Cabal thus pokes fun at his friend's Christian faith in divine Providence, on which his easy-going everydayism rests. Cabal doubts that human affairs take care of themselves for man's benefit, without an act of will on the part of those who know the truth about the real forces at work in the world. They are forces to be mastered, not accepted.

Stung by this reference to simple-minded optimism, Pippa Passworthy replies to Cabal with his own epithet. "You've been smoking too much. You're not ... you're not eupeptic" (ttc:65).

The allusion here is more complex. Not eupeptic—that means Cabal is dyspeptic. His digestion is not good. The reference is to John Calvin, whose dyspepsis made him the stern and priggish source of Calvinist doctrine that he was (or so French folk medicine has it). John Cabal is all of that as a fount of Wellsism. "As Christians have dreamt of the New Jerusalem so does Socialism ... set its face to the World City of Mankind."[18]

As John Calvin transformed Geneva into a theocratic City of the Saints, uniting religion and politics into one truth and one program, so John Cabal transforms the world.[19] Radicalized by the war, he leads his New Puritans of the Modern State Revolution to the founding of a "Puritan Tyranny" and a "rule of the new saints" (STTC:353, 359). Like Calvin, he is a driver out of all creeds but his own; for "the Revolution is itself a religion, and it is quite prepared to resort to Jehovah's intolerance, 'Thou shalt have none other gods but me.'"[20] Like Lenin's partymen, the saintly Airmen rest their rule on dogmatic truth alone. Cabal assumes, as did Lenin in the words of one biographer, that popular support "could be dispensed with and that mere integrity of motive would be adequate."[21]

On this point, the name Cabal is itself significant. A *cabal* is a small group of plotters, a private junta of men serving a cause particular to its own purpose. This is what the Airmen are, a "conspiracy of intellectuals and willful people against existing institutions and existing limitations and boundaries."[22] They conspire to "carve out a Society of its own from Society."[23] Led by John Cabal, the League of the Airmen is a private ruling cult, "self-appointed, self-trained and self-disciplined" (STTC:125).

When the Christmas party in Cabal's living room gets under way, the children at once play Little War with the pellet-shooting cannon and wind-up tanks they received as gifts. Grandfather Cabal remarks that these mechanical toys are perhaps too complex for children, unlike the simple wooden playthings of his day. Mrs. Cabal says, "It teaches them to use their hands" (ttc:68f). Speaking better than she knows, her reply hints at the mechanical skills of the coming Airmen, who will take Great War away from its childish players in the traditional uniformed services, "controlled by gentlemen in red tabs, gold lace and spurs."[24] These gentlemen still think in terms of medieval combat on a field of personal glory, and refuse to bother their heads about modern weapons in use by the new mechanized services. For them, there's no heroism in the tanks and airplanes that are about to unseat their horsy pride.

Grandfather then reflects on his grandchildren and what new things *their* grandchildren will experience. "Progress, progress. I'd like to see the wonders they'll see." Such wonders they indeed will see. But Cabal says, "Don't be too sure of progress" (ttc:70–72). He means that progress does not come automatically, as if by a gift of Providence. It must be won by men of vision and will against the inertial pull of Vishnu the Preserver of tradition.

Pippa Passworthy reacts to this with his usual witless optimism. "Oh listen to the incurable pessimist. What's to stop progress nowadays?" Cabal tells him, "War." Nonsense this is to Pippa; war "stimulates progress." Cabal agrees, but adds that "you can overdo a stimulant." Pippa rejoins by saying the horrors of war are exaggerated. The last one, after all, was not as bad as people make out. "Something—something great seemed to have got hold of us." He remembers only the patriotic fervor it aroused. "Something greater still may get hold of us next time." Cabal warns him. "If we don't end war, war will end us." Sobered by this, Pippa asks, "Well, what can you do?" Cabal answers, handling one of the toy tanks, "Yes. What can we do?" (ttc:72–80).

Cabal is no pessimist, only a Calvinist who knows how hard the way to salvation is. Mankind must suffer hell before it is delivered. John Cabal himself sees to that. In forming the Air League, he leads a revolutionary war to end war. His Airmen, recruited from both sides to the coming conflict, turn their mechanical weapons against a common enemy—their horsy military bosses in gold lace and spurs. At that point, writes the future historian of the world state, "power had passed over to the specialised forces—to the aviators and war technicians" (STTC:207). They take joint command of their modern services and, smashing what is already smashed in a devastated world, they destroy all that is left of nationhood anywhere on the planet. "They are men of steel, men of knowledge, men of power" (WM:28). Making Great War with professional mastery and supreme competence, they reduce it to mere child's play, taking it over from the horrid children who are no good at it. They impose a *pax mundi* and return the game to the toy box where it belongs, out of mankind's way.

When the Christmas party is over, the Cabals walk their guests out the front door to the sight of searchlights and the sound of anti–aircraft guns. Inside, the telephone rings. John Cabal returns to answer it. "Mobilization," he reports, himself called to the local aerodrome. They all then hasten indoors to pick up the news on the radio (ttc:90f).

The radio confirms the report of general mobilization, following a bombing raid on the coast by the enemy air fleet, and the sinking of "the Battleship Dinosaur" (ttc:92). So much for antiquated dreadnaughts, no match for airpower. No less inadequate is the stand to arms called for; it's bayonets against warplanes. Merry Olde England is unprepared to fight a modern enemy.

Cabal turns to Pippa and says, "You've got your stimulant, Passworthy. Something great has got you. War has come." Pippa is once again all patriotic fervor and vengeance. No, "it's not war. It's extermination of dangerous vermin. A vermin hunt without pause or pity" (ttc:101f). He remembers World War I as a war to end Germany. This time it will be different, and he does not live to see these vermin join Cabal's Air League in another kind of war—a revolutionary war to end patriotism. Cabal rather sees in the German aviators both enemy and model. Enemies of England, yes; but that is not important. Their superior war machines indicate that Germany, unlike England, was able to overcome a conservative prejudice against the advancement of technology and applied science. In that, they are the wider enemies of tradition and a model of progress and efficiency. More than a war between obsolete nation-states, World War II is a conflict between Brahma the Creator and Vishnu the Preserver, between progress and reaction.

Winning progressive aviators from all nations to his cause, Cabal leads the League of the United Airmen on to the technological wonders of a scientific dictatorship. Proficient in mechanized warfare because of their inventive technical skills, the Airmen are gifted at social invention and human engineering as well. The same innovative outlook carries over to a mechanization of the peace following their war to end war. Capable of reducing the old "capitalist military civilization" to rubble, they are just as adept at redesigning its "competitive industrialism" along the lines of socialized industry for a "civilization of service."[25]

Today war, tomorrow revolution. But first, war's "vast tragic clearance for a new order."[26] Then follows the revolutionary lesson. What the mass of mankind learns from the discipline of universal military service is to be retained after the peace is won; it is "something that can be learned in no other way [and that] tradition of service and devotion . . . will remain a permanent acquisition." In other words, after the coming of the *pax aeronautica*, forced civilian labor will replace war-time conscription. World peace means a labor force militarized world-wide. The Modern-World State requires "'unpaid' public service in order to secure citizenship."[27]

Cut to the town square as the *Marche Funèbre* starts up again, this time without its counterpoint theme. Everytown's pastoral idyll is over. The news headlines now read GENERAL MOBILIZATION; posters everywhere call for a STAND TO ARMS. The holiday crowd goes frantic as truckloads of soldiers fill the square and a battery of anti-aircraft guns is emplaced in front of the town hall. The soldiers hand out gas masks to a riot of grasping hands. A military announcer's car drives up, and over the screams of panic, its loudspeakers blare out warnings of the impending air raid (ttc:103–143).

Back at Cabal's home, John and his wife stand beside the bed of their sleeping children. He is in his air force uniform, prepared to leave for duty at the aerodrome on the outskirts of Everytown. Mrs. Cabal asks, "My dear, my dear, are you sorry we had these children?" No, he is not sorry; "life must carry on." But Mrs. Cabal is not quite so detached as he. She wanted only to love him, to serve him, to make life happy for him; what now will happen to the children of this love? "Were we selfish?" John's answer is indirect. "You weren't afraid to bear them—*we* were children yesterday" (ttc:146).

"*We* were children yesterday." Here John Cabal alludes to the Wellsian vision of life carried on as one continuous drama. The emphatic "we" refers to we agents of the Human Adventure, we servants of Man the master being.

Again, it is a vision derived from Saint-Simonian doctrine, which has it that

> Humanity is a collective entity. This entity has grown from generation to generation as a man grows in the course of years, according to its own physical law, which has been one of progressive development.[28]

In other words, the racial drama is a story of Man's growing up, from childhood to adulthood. The Wellsian elect, like the Airmen, are vanguard adults of human growth. "Sovereign adult men" they say they are, "with nothing left to control us."[29] After the failure of everything else, they are responsible only to themselves in seeing to the maturation of the rest of humanity. They are the first to break the grip of Vishnu the Possessor on their personal lives, to surrender the having and holding of everydayism to the Human Adventure, and to live in and through the species for the good of its ultimate development.

"In the past," writes Wells, "the normal existence fell wholly into the frame of the family. Man was a family animal. Now the family becomes merely a phase in an ampler existence. Human life escapes beyond it." No longer immersed in the exclusive love-life of the monogamous family, the "fully adult human being toward whom destiny moves will not pair at all."[30] Parentage will merge with world citizenship. "Strict mating narrows a human being down below the level of broad social usefulness." Whereas, by contrast, "Socialism says boldly that the State is the Over-Parent, the Outer-Parent."[31]

In future, all will belong to that "comprehensive marriage group" of unpaired husbands and wives that is "the State family," in accord with the Social Idea that "mankind is of one household and one substance."[32] In the past, however, "the chief interest and motive of the ordinary man was to keep and rule a woman and her children and the chief concern of a woman was to get a man to do that." But with racial maturity, the woman will be released from permanent giving in marriage to work with men "as if there was only one sex in the world."[33] The sexual problem of the socialist revolution is to "unspecialize women," so they may fully share in the collective purpose of humankind, "for the good of the race, and not for men's satisfactions."[34]

Mrs. Cabal, a preadult mother and housewife, does not live to see this development. She dies in the early bombing raids, and does not witness the despecialization of women, first brought about by her husband. Well meaning in her everyday habits of family devotion, she was used to saying "my dear," when in future it will be "comrade," as among the Airmen who set the pace. Or rather, as among the Airpersons. For like Plato's unisexual Guardians, both men and women share the barracks life of the Air League, working together in comradely devotion to the cause, apart from "women-centered excitement."[35]

"Were we selfish?" John Cabal's implied answer to his wife's question is, "yes." But he answers not for *their* children, but for the children of the race. The monogamous family institutes "jealousy and possessiveness, in sex as in property." And so the old sex romance must go for the collective good; "love ... breaks things up."[36] In the Modern State, as in Russia of the Revolution, there is no excuse for the woman "to obtain a life of ease by steadfast affection, personal loyalty and devotion to home duties. It is not possible, indeed, to obtain a life of ease in any way whatever" (WWHM:616). In a Saint-Simonian technocracy, work is all.

Cabal then leaves home and household forever, going out into the foggy night on his way to the aerodrome (ttc:149). Cut to the front-yard gate of Passworthy's home. There Pippa says goodbye to his boyish son, panoplied in the military articles that were his Christmas gifts, a toy drum and a play helmet. His father wears the real thing, and goes off, thumping his valise at quick march (151).

The boy picks up the rhythm on his toy drum, and begins to march back and forth in front of a blank white wall across the street. Thereon, hugely projected in shadowgraph above the tiny figure in tin hat parading below, we see the infantile game of war enlarged to its real and deadly proportions — silhouette troops on the march to the beat of the *Marche Funèbre* (ttc:151f). Little War is juxtaposed with Great War. Militarism is displayed as belonging to the childhood of the race, and it threatens to end the race unless it is outgrown.

Cut to antiaircraft guns firing in the town square. Bombs fall, the first one hitting the movie house. Its great blocks of tabled letters for CINEMA, designed in Streamlined Moderne, crash to the ground in a heap of broken debris. The promise of a progressive future seems lost. The enemy airfleet drones away. Everytown is left in ruins. Hovering in the air is a cloud of lethal gas, the doomsday weapon of that innocent time before the advent of atomic bombs. Another Dark Age descends.

Yet it will be lifted by the Airmen, those new saints of the new order. But as their future historian writes of the terrible costs necessary to pay for the salvation they bring, "The millennium arrived in anything like millennial fashion" (STTC:344).

Triumphant Catastrophe

Now follows a montage sequence, with shots of old-model tanks rolling in one direction and being exploded, intercut with very advanced tanks, the enemy's, rolling in the other. No doubt this fighting takes place on European soil, against a British expeditionary force. Finally the German tanks prevail, crushing down buildings unopposed (ttc:254–259). Technical prowess wins the day over the lagging technology of the reactionary, antiscientific British. It is "a fight between the more efficient and the less efficient, between the more

inventive and more traditional."[37] But as the fight drags on, both sides are
decivilized by it, and we see no more mechanized weapons at all.

The futuristic German tanks are models designed by Frank Wells in
Streamlined Moderne, the same style he uses in its graphic format to letter
the word for CINEMA, and later uses in its architectural variant for the
model sets of the new Everytown in the world of 2036. In the end, what makes
for proficiency in war makes for salvation.

After the bombing of Everytown, a second wave of German aircraft passes
overhead (ttc:260–270). We see now, in their massed formation, what the
planes look like. No less than the enemy tanks, they are of advanced design—
great monoplanes with dihedral wings. In this design feature they resemble the
Streamlined Moderne bombers built decades later by the Airmen, no doubt
helped by German recruits, some of them perhaps former tank engineers.

When the second wave arrives to drop more poison gas, John Cabal flies
up in his old-fashioned biplane to engage one of the enemy fighters, a modern
monoplane. But his heroism overcomes the handicap of his nation's conservative military heritage. In the aerial dogfight that ensues, he shoots down the
superior German plane.

Following it to the ground (in a cheaply done crash that always gets a
laugh from the sophisticates of today's unerring special effects), Cabal helps
the dying airman out of the wreckage, saying to him, "Why has it come to this?
God, why do we have to murder each other!" (ttc:293). The enemy airman
replies in kind. "What fools we airmen have been! We've let them make us
fight for them like dogs" (TTC:37). But this is not mawkish pacifist talk. It is
not as mawkish as the badly done crash might lead us to believe. Far from it.
As fellow professionals trained in the international disciplines of science and
engineering, both recognize in *them* a common enemy, those criminal patriots
who set *us* against each other. It is *they* who make *us* fight each other with
weapons that endanger the only sort of industrial progress *we* are interested
in—weapons whose technology only we aviators understand for its productive
and creative potential. The real question is, why have not we professionals the
sanity to league together and make war against our common foe? Do we not
have it in our power to wield the sword of peace, by turning the war into a
revolution to end war?

With the answers to these questions evidently taking shape in his mind,
Cabal flies off, up and away from the gathering cloud of German gas dropped
by his erstwhile colleague, fraternally leaving behind a pistol with which he
ends the choking misery he intended for others. Among them is a small girl
child, who comes racing ahead of the gas cloud, to fall into the arms of the
two aviators the while they talk revolution. Cabal rips off the German's gas
mask from his kit and straps it onto the girl's face, taking the child with him
in his plane, a foreshadowing of the concern for all future generations he is
later to make the duty of his peculiar brand of statecraft. The unborn are to
be given a greater value than the living.

Meanwhile, we see no more of John Cabal until he reappears with his

United Airmen in about the year 1970, sword of peace in hand. Held together by "the unity of a common order and a common knowledge" (ttc:722), they now wield the sword of Siva the Destroyer in the interests of Brahma the Creator. Joined in militant cooperation, they initiate a "destructive (and, by clearance, creative) conflict,"[38] directed against the spirit of Vishnu, wheresoever it still haunts the last remaining possessors of the last shreds of national real estate. No pacifists, the Airmen. At least they are not pacifist until all the guns are on their side. It is only their terrible war prowess that makes for peace—on their terms.

Their revolutionary headquarters, we later learn, are located at Basra (ttc:485, 589–90). Basra is the port city of Baghdad in present-day Iraq, just north of the Persian Gulf, from which figs once were exported and now oil. Why should the Airmen have their hangars and aircraft factories here? To be sure, Iraqi oil was the only source of aviation fuel at the time of the film's writing, but there is more to it than that.

For Wells, this area holds great historical significance. In his *Short History of the World*, he reminds us that Baghdad from A.D. 750 to 1258 was the capital city of the Abbasid caliphate, a dynasty of rulers descended from Abbas, the uncle of Mohammad, the religious prophet who taught his followers to win converts by the sword to the true faith of his divine revelation. Accordingly, the heads of Muslim states ruling in his dynastic name combined in the title of *caliph* both religious and military duties. Both teachers and rulers, they joined theological argument with armed force, in the interest of directing the infidels along the path of righteousness.

In the event, the Abbasid caliphate was the most glorious one of all. From Baghdad, its capital city, was extended the world-historical Moslem Conquest, described by Wells as "the most amazing story of conquest in the history of our race." Amazing because, in the wake of the European Dark Ages, it brought a learning and enlightenment from which we have our scientific words for algebra and chemistry. Indeed, this most heroic and holy of crusades brought light and order to "the whole world west of China."[39]

Baghdad, however, was but the administrative center of the Conquest, the political and military adjunct of its spiritual purpose. It was its twin city Basra, the superior twin, that was the capital of its persuasive theological and educational influence; "out of what were at first religious schools dependent upon mosques, a series of great universities" grew out of that place, and "the light of these universities shone far beyond the Moslem world."[40]

With the Air League, a.k.a. World Communications or Wings over the World, a greater conquest now originates from Basra. Its reach is global, bringing home at last the purpose of historical progress. For history is governed by "a secular change in the dealings of man and man" (WWHM:53), the human community ever enlarged the greater its range of communications. Starting with the family thing, history moves on to the less and less localized interests of tribe and nation, and finally to the fellowship of all mankind united in a world state. Or as Oswald Cabal says, looking back on this process from the

Hindu trinity	The Basra/Baghdad conurbation	Plato's castes & their souls	Wellsian temperaments
Brahma the Creator (right)	Basra the education city (spiritual power)	teachers (wisdom)	Poietic (theory)
Siva the Destroyer (might)	Baghdad the executive city (temporal power)	soldiers (force)	Kinetic (action)
Vishnu the Possessor (everydayism)	the conquered (infidels)	producers (desire)	the intellectually Dull & morally Base

vantage point of its culmination in his world dictatorship, "Either life goes forward or it goes back. That is the law of life" (TTC:139). If the war in John Cabal's time took things back, it did so only as a condition for his launching of a greater imperialism than that intended by the imperial ambitions of the aggressor who started this war. Out of Basra the Airmen fly, to every part of a whole world smashed back to medieval darkness, bringing in their train, as agents of historical destiny, the lasting light of science and sanity.

In working to this end, the Airmen care little for the usual distinction between war and peace. They speak, after all, of the "aggressive peace" (ttc:725) they mean to bring. Their dialectical example is the Moslem Conquest. The twin cities of Baghdad and Basra illustrate, in their copartnership of might and right, a dualism Wells first discovered in Plato. Its analog in Hindu theology he offers as the film's explanation.

Thus the Airmen are not only neoplatonic teachers and soldiers ruling in joint sovereignty, they are also avatars of Brahma and Siva respectively. They monopolize the sword of the latter in the former's creative cause—the disarming of popular power and thereby the disanimation of the spirit of Vishnu. The emotional masses, as always, stand in need of control from above, exercised by a spiritual or intellectual power backed up by a temporal power resting on force.

The same dualism Wells finds in the rule of the Moslem caliphs, with their religious-cum-civil leadership. We are thus given to understand that, while the Airmen base themselves at Basra (their Brahminic headquarters), they have the unspoken alliance of Baghdad (the seat of Siva's power). In building the world state, John Cabal is a Platonic philosopher-ruler in the guise of a neo–Islamic caliph, who sees to the creative use of his armed forces for his own doctrinal ends. Thus it is the Brahminic aspect of Cabal that is the paramount one, just as Mohammad himself is famed not as the heroic swordsman for his faith that he indeed was, but solely as its prophet and religious leader. So when the Airmen launch their war for peace out of Basra, the implication is that their symbolic point of origin is the complete Basra/Baghdad urban complex.

To summarize all this, while harking back to other elements displayed in similar schemes in the Introduction, we have the table on page 40.

By the time the Airmen come to the rescue of Everytown in 1970, however, the war has gone on for thirty years—time enough to plunge the world back into the Dark Ages from which it is duly saved. A process of decivilization is the necessary prelude to world reconstruction.

This decline is shown in a montage series of increasing desolation. Newspapers reporting on the war, like *The Weekly Patriot* and *The National Bulletin*, are more infrequently and more roughly printed, as the warring forces themselves break down into a number of rag-tag armies disputing over the merest shreds of territorial possession. The great nation-states which rallied to the fight are no more. They are hopelessly smashed, yet the passion of the national idea remains undiminished. Patriotic loyalty to these surviving mini-states runs just as high (TTC:37–39; ttc:303–319).

Their leadership is reduced, in the end, to feudalistic war-chiefs like Rudolf, the Boss of Everytown in its medieval shambles. Wells does not permit us to think that the Feudal Age was anything but such a mess. He allows himself to portray Rudolf as a caricature of the big-time political bosses who brought the world to this pass, because he regards Present Conditions, at the start of the film, as no more than a survival of the medieval heritage itself, with all its disorder and competitive localism.

Thus he has it that the war was kept going only "through the sheer inability of any authorities to meet and agree and end it, until every organised government in the world was shattered as a heap of china broken with a stick."[41] The *dégringolade* Wells warned of in *The Outline of History*, that "History is more and more a race between education and catastrophe,"[42] has been allowed to occur. It is, after all, a useful catastrophe — "gigantic clearances [followed by] gigantic new constructions." Speaking as "the voice of this cosmic calamity," he says, "My other name is Noah."[43] His choice of prophet is exactly right. For like Noah, Wells has it both ways, calamity *and* salvation, a war deluge followed by Utopian dry land.

By education, Wells of course means education for socialism and a world peace ideology. History is a race between world revolution and world war. It's "unify or smash."[44] To the Airmen, however, the war *is* the revolution, catastrophe *is* education. In their dialectical way of thinking, the opposites of unity and smash up are one — smash first, unite later. Smash with the destructive might of Siva, then rebuild for unity with Brahma's creative ideals.

In this cosmic business of death and resurrection, the Airmen serve "that most stern and educational of all masters — *War*." Only by means of "a catastrophic breakdown of the formal armies," and the rival patriotisms that sustain them, can the world's "local social order" be cleared of its "weeds of differentiation."[45] Unity does not come of itself. "Nothing comes of itself except weeds and confusion."[46] Thus, before the Airmen can impose their Act of Uniformity, "traditions of nationality had to be cleared away" (STTC:381). Given "the educational ideals of these men who set out to demodel the world," they could not remodel it until they "pulled up the soil with the weeds" (398, 363). Theirs is perforce a policy of "tearing up life by the roots."[47]

It is a policy in full accord with Saint-Simonism. The Master said that socialism breaks with all tradition and preserves nothing from the past.

> The Golden Age of mankind does not lie behind us, but before; it lies in the perfection of the social order. Our forefathers did not see it; one day our children will reach it. It is for us to clear the way.[48]

To clear the way. That's all it takes. In the end, the "way" need not be constructed at all. Oswald Cabal's "law of life" takes care of that in steely fashion. Reconstruction is but a dialectical term for a policy of sweeping the predestined path of progress clear of its artificial impediments — blockheads like Rudolf. Proficient in war, the Airmen "clean that up" (ttc:463) by directing the course of destruction to their own visionary ends. Making way for the sure things to come, they are "workers of a new dawn. Men of no nation. Men without tradition. Men who look forward and not back."[49]

In the wake of the initial war-storm and the social breakdown it caused, there follows "a strange and terrible pestilence, the wandering sickness." Unlike the Black Death that plagued only Europe during the Dark Ages, it "spread unchecked throughout the world" (ttc:319).

The wandering sickness—an interesting disease. It prompts people stricken by it to get up out of their fever beds and wander far from home in a hypnotic daze, thus denationalizing themselves. But even after the disease dies out, its after-effects live on as a permanent condition of the new order. For Utopia is "a world without boundaries," wherein it is expected that all "definitions of place" shall have melted away until "all the world will be awash with anonymous stranger men."[50]

Under a Saint-Simonian technocracy, the world's workshop requires a docile and moveable labor force, regarded by Wells in *A Modern Utopia* as "a delocalised and fluid force [transferrable] from this region of excess to that of scarcity," as the commanders of a command economy see fit. In the liberal language of that book, fluidity of movement, or "detachment from place," is held to constitute one of Utopia's most precious articles of freedom. "Freedom of movement" is one of those rights of the world citizen "planned" for his benefit, so as to release humankind from its medieval "fetters of locality" and from a peasant-like "permanent life servitude to this place or that." On this legal basis for the mass deportation of labor, regulated by thumb-printed travel passes (the world-state's internal passports), is gained yet another Utopian "freedom from tradition."[51]

A world without national frontiers, "the common ownership of the earth,"[52] is the main goal of the socialist project. For according to Saint-Simonian doctrine, "the whole world belongs to mankind."[53] After eradicating the weeds of differentiation, the Airmen achieve that goal. On behalf of mankind, the Air Dictatorship becomes "the landlord of the planet" (STTC:294). The prophecy Wells made in the final chapter of his *Outline of History* about "Man's Coming of Age" is fulfilled, following (as the chapter headline has it) a "Struggle for the Unification of the World into One Community of Will and Knowledge."[54]

With a floating population going about the world, delocalized by the wandering sickness, the Airmen's policy of tearing up life by the roots is made all the easier. Apart from killing off half the world's population (making the job easier still), the disease has the useful effect of destroying "the institutions, the boundaries, the laws, prejudices, and deep-rooted traditions established during the home-keeping, localised era of mankind's career." The wandering sickness, as a natural calamity added to the man-made one, is of equal educational value in teaching mankind to unlearn "the attraction and necessity of home."[55]

In this, *Things to Come* is a replay of *The World Set Free*, a future war novel of 1914, in which the way is cleared of its impedimenta at one stroke—by atomic bombs, no less.

> The catastrophe of the atomic bombs which shook men out of cities and businesses and economic relations shook them also out of their old established habits of thought, and out of the . . . beliefs and prejudices that came down from the past. To borrow a word from the old-fashioned chemists, men were made nascent; they were released from old ties [and made] ready for new associations.[56]

The new associations that result are those designed by a World Council, whose executives have taken charge of rebuilding a new world civilization from the ashes of the war that destroyed the old one. Socially atomized by this the Last War, "a smash that opened a way to better things," mankind now is made ready for mass mobilization by a directive force from above. As the executive for Education on the World Council says, "the atomic bombs burnt our way to freedom." Freedom, that is, from affirmative selfhood and group diversity; "we've had unity and collectivism blasted into our brains."[57]

As usual with Wells, his wars to end war educate for socialism because they are destructive enough to end all forms of independent group life. The new collectivism that emerges never is described as a mutual "exchange of services" by way of interpersonal cooperation. He speaks against that as a mere volunteering of "trade in help" between and among selfish individuals.[58] His Utopia does not rely on "the chance occasional co-operations of self-indulgent men."[59] He rather favors the forced cooperation of "direct public service" to the state, with each citizen brought into it as a social atom, for the sake of "directive simplicity."[60] In this way, men are "released from individual motives and individual obsessions," and made free to act collectively in "association for service."[61]

What is wanted for direct public service is "the spirit of the soldier, the spirit of subordination to a common purpose" in a "general labor conscription."[62] Indeed, the one tradition not to be forgotten from the past is that of the discipline for universal military service the Last War evoked. It is a discipline "that can be learned in no other way," Wells tells us, and with the coming of the Ultimate Peace, a civilian labor draft will replace the military draft. For the Modern State requires "unpaid conscript service" in order to secure citizenship.[63] As its future historian writes, "compulsory public service . . . is an integral part of our education" (STTC:425). The Social Idea proposes that men be *forced* to be social, each individual, without the -ism, atomized for his duty in a regulated social division of labor under the direction of the World Council. So ends the Age of Feudalism, as the doctrinaires of Saint-Simonism would have it ended. The age of scientific management replaces the age of medieval warfarism with its new cult of collective wealth and power, in the name of peaceful industrial production.

Certainly the wandering sickness in *Things to Come* is a useful device for shaking men loose from their old interpersonal ties, making them ready for their later subordination to the Air Dictatorship. Having served its purpose in this way, the virulent stage of the disease finally runs its course.

We now come in on the ruins of Everytown just prior to this. Young Harding the medical student, not so young any more, is a practicing doctor now. He keeps a skeletonized hospital there, attempting to fight the disease. But he no longer has any medical supplies. "There is no more trade, nothing to be got. This pestilence goes on—unchallenged—worse than the war that released it" (TTC:44f). He remembers "talking to a man named Cabal. About preventing war. I remember he said that if we did not end war, war would end us. Well, here we are!" (WM:21).

But things are not quite all that bad. Cabal comes to the rescue, making constructive use of these decivilized conditions. Indeed, Wells clues us in on the good omen by comparing the shabby and broken down state of Dr. Harding's laboratory with something he saw for himself elsewhere. "A thing to be noted in all these ruinous scenes is the dearth of china, glass, and cutlery. I noted that such breakable gear was extremely short in Russia in 1920. Most of it would be smashed and disappear in ten or twelve years" (WM:21). He alludes here to his passage through St. Petersburg to see Lenin in that year. The sight of it gave him the "impression of a vast irreparable breakdown," the same we are intended to get from Everytown in ruins. In this one broken city he saw what had happened to the Russian part of the civilized world, a nation reduced, by the incessant strains of World War I followed by civil war, to a land of ragged peasants and brigand chiefs. But such a breakdown was helped along by Lenin as the necessary precondition of his plans for reconstruction. "Amid the vast disorganization an Emergency Government—the Communist Party—has taken control." Smash first, collectivize later. "Only through that could the Bolsheviks have secured power."[64] So, too, with the Air League.

The sample brigand of a smashed planetary world in *Things to Come* is Rudolf the Victorious, the local Boss of Everytown. He lords it over "an urban population sunken back to the state of a barbaric peasantry." Played by Sir Ralph Richardson with a fine flair for mocking "the brag, blare and bluster of our competing sovereignties,"[65] the territorial shred of a once great nation he bosses he grandly terms, "the Combatant State" (ttc:406).

Rudolf's way of dealing with the wandering sickness is to have all wanderers shot. Looking out the glassless windows of his barren laboratory, Doctor Harding sees one of his hospital patients wander out into the rubble of market square, helplessly watching as the poor man is felled by one of the Boss's rooftop sentries. Turning to his daughter and assistant, Mary Harding, he remarks, "That's the way they dealt with pestilence in the Dark Ages" (ttc:342).

This establishes the feudal-militaristic motif of Everytown under its Patriot Chief. At one level of meaning, the imagery conveys a return to barbarism; but at another, it signifies that the modern world from which Everytown has lapsed never was all that modern to begin with. The hidden medievalism of Everytown under Present Conditions, at the start of the film, is now exposed by Wellsian burlesque in all its nakedness. Things have come to this decline only because a premodern political order continued to lag behind the modernity of its technical progress. Examples are the marvels of British cinema, misused for economic competition in the amusements industry, and the progressive tanks and airplanes of German military technology. As Doctor Harding observes, "We are still too busy fighting among ourselves, to put up any fight against the cruelties of nature" (WM:19).

In other words, the so-called Modern Age at its prewar height was no closer to attaining Saint-Simon's technocratic dream than it now is in its postwar regression. For all of its mechanical and scientific progress, it failed to throw off the barbarity of its political past. Far from surrendering their new powers to the collective conquest of nature by all men in global association, the moderns played with them in the same old game of economic thievery and national conquest. The Master's disciples had prophesied, technology "has been represented in the past by the actions of both war and industry but in the future will be represented by industry alone, for the exploitation of man by man will have been replaced by the harmonious action of man on nature."[66]

Yet that prophecy is not out of place even now, and the collapse of civilization has not been in vain. For as the Master said, it is "necessary to demolish in order to construct."[67] The way must first be cleared, as it has been in the film story by world war and a pandemic disease.

In time the disease is checked, thanks to the Chief's vigilance. Not yet conquered, however, is the "patriotic virus."[68] Illiterate peasants gather in front of the remains of the town hall to hear the good news, read aloud to them by a herald from the National Bulletin for the day, chalked up on a notice board. Announced after that is news that the Chief is now prepared to resume hostilities against the neighboring Hill People. "Soon we shall have Victory and Peace." The herald then ends by iterating the "ancient pieties and loyalties" (WWHM:564) – "God save our Chief. God save our Land" (ttc:369–378).

Life returns to normal – normal for the Dark Ages. During the above recitation, the camera studies a number of craft specialists in the town square, a potter at his wheel, a cobbler at work, a man weaving, a blacksmith hammering, a wheelwright fixing a wagon. We also see a man milking a cow and a butcher chopping meat. A furniture craftsman carrying a handmade chair on his back passes by. All of this is a study in medievalism, the natural foods, the artisan turning out his own custom made artifact. Each is but "doing his bit" by way of "being himself" in the voluntary cooperation of a selfish market economy, each artisan working "ignorantly in his own circumstances," taking the world as he finds it and "living in an uninformed world with no common understanding and no collective plan."[69] It is a study in everydayism.

Small-scale craft specialization is the opposite of large-scale modernity, with its impersonal division of labor belonging to the mass production factory; or to the chemical factories of the future, which are destined to complete the conquest of nature in their manufacture of synthetic foods. Artificial foods and the artifice of regulated human association – these are the coming things. More important than productivity itself is the productive process that takes the worker out of himself, and makes him a truly collaborative and self-forgetful part of the "world economic machine" (WWHM:373). That is the essence of the socialist project, "man's power over nature and over his own nature."[70]

"Have you ever examined an aeroplane," asks Wells, "and realised the thousand beautiful adjustments and devices that have produced its wonderful perfection?"[71] To create such a machine calls for a like perfection of adjustments between its human makers. It calls for "coordinated effort and a community of design," a nontraditional form of organization invented for the purpose. From the viewpoint of the Social Idea, the airplane's makers, in creating its mechanical efficiency, only reflect in their work their own social efficiency. "Such an order means discipline. It means the triumph over the petty egotisms and vanities that keep men on our earth apart."[72] The Airmen in their aircraft factories at Basra thus herald a new world order, modeled after their own self-imposed discipline. "Every principle in the world machine must be designed." Not alone its material technology, but its human engineering as well. What it takes to make beautiful airplanes, it takes to build socialism, because "machines make men honest."[73]

Note that aircraft, Wells's favorite symbol of purposive integration, are lacking in feudal Everytown even now. In a wrecked hangar at Cabal's old aerodrome, a former aviation mechanic, Richard Gordon, is attempting to patch up a dilapidated biplane belonging to the Chief's air force. But Gordon has not got so much as a scrap of rubber tape to work with, and there's no petrol anyway. "What's the good of setting me at a job like this," he says. "Nothing'll ever fly again. Flying's over. Civilization's dead" (ttc:380).

Passing through market square on his way home, Gordon meets his wife Mary, Doctor Harding's daughter. She is buying vegetables brought into town by a peasant steering a Rolls Royce. But it is without tires and is drawn by a horse. Gordon looks at it with professional interest, in one of the film's most memorable images (ttc:383; cf. STTC:222).

The peasant responds with a nostalgic memory. "Why, I remember when I was a lad – when it were new – we thought nothing of going a hundred miles in it, a whole hundred miles. Less than three hours I've done it in. But that sort of thing's all gone now. Gone forever." Gordon sadly agrees. "Afraid so," he says, and the driver gees-up his horse with a slap of the reins and the powerless Rolls Royce moves off camera (ttc:385–87).

But we know that "that sort of thing" – power transport and the conquest of distance – is not over with, because Mary tells her husband, "I thought I heard an aeroplane this morning." Gordon thinks she imagines things. "Nonsense. I tell you flying's finished. We shall never get into the air again" (ttc:388f).

She's right, however. The Airmen are coming. For them, the problems of starting up a broken down society are "hardly more serious than the rehabilitation of a stalled machine. The task is hardly more formidable than, let us say, the restoration of a Rolls Royce ... which has been stuck in the mud for some weeks."[74] It's only a question of social engineering.

> Before all things we have to modernise. It is no good dreaming of raising human social and political life with the dear old principles of the horse and foot days. At present we are about as competent to handle these problems that confront us, as the chauffeur whose one idea of starting up his engine was to say "Gee-up" to it.[75]

In other words, power transport has united the world in a physical way, all the more so with flying and the aid of the DC-3; but the world's fragmented political controls have yet to yield to this material fact.

In the barbaric past of horse-drawn transport, "Man had a localised, patriotic mind because his economic life was definitely local and bounded." But since the advent of the industrial revolution, "human life has lost touch with locality to an extraordinary extent. Insidiously the average man has ceased to be part of a localised economic system, and become part of a vaguely developed but profoundly real world economic system.... And you cannot put him back to the old state of affairs unless you are prepared to shatter this developing thing, civilization, altogether."[76]

The war smash did just that. Because the world's national leaders did indeed try to preserve the old political state of affairs, in spite of Rolls Royces and DC-3s, we are now returned to a premodern order—with its localized mentality given to patriotic barbarism and "nationalist brigandage." Nothing has changed. Things are as they were during Present Conditions from *before* the shattering of Merry Olde England. "Again and again in this book," says Wells in one of his novels of social criticism, "I have written of England as a feudal scheme."[77]

Pressing home the point, the film cuts directly from the peasant chauffeur saying "gee-up" to his Rolls Royce, to the Chief returning on horseback from one of his robber raids. The sound track swells with the brassy blare of mock-triumphal music as the Chief comes riding into town square, his retinue of banner-flying horse cavalry behind him, followed by drummers and foot soldiers, not much in uniform, but all strong to exalt in the new exploit of their spurred and feathered bandit leader. "The Boss is coming," a voice goes up, and a patriotic crowd gathers instantly to greet him and cheer and wave wildly (ttc:390–404).

He is Rudolf the Victorious, defender of the least of territories, an avatar of Vishnu the Possessor, siding with Siva the Destroyer. Dismounting at the sight of Gordon, the crowd gives way and he swaggers by, the cock feathers on his helmet a-jiggle. "Anything to report, Gordon?" he asks. He wants to know if his personal mechanic, his court craftsman, can get his airplanes flying for his decisive battle against the Hill People. Gordon says the planes can't fly without petrol. Well then, replies Rudolf, he'll get petrol for them on his next robber raid (ttc:405f).

At this point, Rudolf's attention is caught by Gordon's wife, Mary. "Salutation lady," he says, giving her a romantic salute. He urges Mary to use her influence on her husband to do his best for the Combatant State. At the same time, Rudolf means to impress her with his latest victory. His feudal love of war is mixed with the medieval chivalry of his theatrical posing before women (ttc:406f).

But Rudolf is cut short in making his pass at Mary by a distant shout from Roxana, his number one harem mistress. Named after one of Alexander the Great's two wives, and dressed the part in her barbaric bangles, she hastens over to him, steaming with jealousy. She is the avatar of Vishnu in this female deity's aspect of sexual possession, as Rudolf is in her aspect of territorial possession. The two aspects are related. Rudolf and Roxana desire only the personal satisfactions of love and glory. He the glory of bossing things and the glory of being loved by a woman "whose support is jealousy and whose gift is possession." She the glory of being possessed by a powerful lover victorious in war, craving only this one man's care and attention, delivering herself to him "as a prize" locked up for him alone, his "delicious treasure." For Vishnu's curse in everything is "woman-centered excitement" and the limiting "servitude of sex."[78]

Roxana is the "common pretty woman who doesn't work," a preadult type of sexual heroine and love huntress who invites possession by men like Rudolf. "Wherever power is, she will follow" (TTC:89). Rudolf in turn is typical of the common man, "concentrated as a Boss," who loves power only because it makes him attractive to such women, "specialized for excitement" as they are.[79]

After the uncommonly puritanical Airmen drop their decisive weapon on Everytown, their Gas of Peace, one of them stands over the fallen bodies of these two and pronounces on their deadly sins: "The common man who cannot be trusted with duty or machinery and the common woman who cannot be trusted with men" (WM:45). For it is Wells's judgment that "sex is bound up with most of the power-craving." Sex is more powerful than statesmanship. For that reason, the Airmen train themselves to be "sexually self-controlled."[80]

What is more, these New Puritans have the honesty and "clearness of mind that comes of dealing with machinery." They are also "self-forgetful and scientific," because they are educated in science "as the old Puritans were educated in the Bible."[81] In their "scientific self-control," they are free of the *libido dominandi*, "remote from the primordial scuffle for pride and power."[82] Their only pride is their professional honor, in serving the task of statesmanship above self-interest. As Plato said of the desirable qualities wanted for his Guardians, "what we need is that the only men to get power should be men who do not love it."[83]

Such is the test the Airmen meet. Or so they say of themselves.

The Coming Beast

But for now, Roxana is distracting Rudolf from making his play for Gordon's wife by raising a complaint against the local bazaar's Jewish merchant. This is Wadsky, whom Roxana brings along with her train of attendants. As a lady of leisure and social importance in Everytown, her rank certified by Rudolf's keep, she hurls her problem at him in a great huff.

Wadsky, she says, has been up to his old mercantile tricks again; this time holding back from her some dress material she had wanted. Accusing Wadsky to his face in front of Rudolf and before the gathering crowd, she says, "You had a piece of flowered stuff, a whole length, seven yards, and you did not tell me of it. You kept it back from me, and you gave it to that woman of yours." Wadsky refutes this with a most stereotypical show of servile mannerisms and Jewish accent. "Ooh Lady, I showed you this piece" ((TTC:49). "Lady, Lady, I showed it to you and you said you didn't want it" (ttc:408).

The future historian of the Modern Era, looking back on this kind of behavior, observes, "One could never tell whether a Jew was being a citizen or whether he was just being a Jew. They married, they traded preferentially" (STTC:383). Is Wells being antisemitic?

Elsewhere he writes, "Jews have gone through the system of this world, creating nothing." They have worked only "to develop and master and maintain the conventions of property." Wadsky exemplifies their "social parasitism."[84] The dry goods in his bazaar have "been got together from the wardrobes and presses that are still to be found in the abandoned houses.... Wadsky's stall is stocked with such findings" (TTC:49).

If this be antisemitism, it only can be of a piece with Wells's antipathy to anything partisan and sectarian, be it ethnic pride, denominational faith, or local patriotism. He opposes every particular sort of community life short of that life community belonging to the whole species, united under the Modern World-State "in one undivided cultural field" (STTC:417).

At all events, Rudolf disposes of the problem by throwing it back at Roxana, as a sequey into matters of his own concern.

> Not only Wadsky keeps things back. What do you think of our Master Mechanic here—that won't give me planes to end this war of ours with the hill men [ttc:410].

Roxana now plays the part of the Chief's pillow advisor, but not without a glow of resentment for having her personal problem turned aside for what passes as matters of state. "Well, can't you make him? I thought you could make anybody do everything." Gordon answers for himself, explaining that without external resources made available by trade he's helpless. No amount of bossing can overcome that fact, even though the Boss promises to get "coal-stuff to make oil" by raiding a nearby colliery (ttc:411f). The message here is that technical expertise is not to be got on demand by reactionary bosses like

Rudolf, much less can it flourish when material resources are regarded as primitive war prizes. As Gordon says, "You cannot have technical services, you cannot have scientific help without treating the men who give it to you properly" (423). As this respect is not likely to be shown under the present feudal scheme of things, Gordon concludes that "Flying's become a lost art in Everytown" (412).

Just at this moment an airplane is heard overhead, and then seen coming in for a landing at Cabal's old aerodrome on the edge of town. The Boss is furious with Gordon. "And you told me we couldn't fly anymore" (ttc:423). The Boss then sends a detachment of armed men to arrest the pilot, who is none other than John Cabal, and fetch him to the town hall.

We are now about to witness the most condensed visual imagery in the entire film. Cabal's aircraft, a monoplane of Streamlined Moderne design, is identified as WT 34, in the style of letter-numeral designation distinctive to the aviation industry. The letters WT stand for World Transport, words that spell out what is most essential in Saint-Simonian doctrine to the unification of a world industrial civilization. Accordingly, Wells has it that "Civilization is Transport."[85] Indeed, Cabal reveals himself to be "the commissioner from the Transport Union, the Air Traders" (WM:26). But to make the world safe for transport, the Airmen must first establish a world state. All claims to national sovereignty, like Rudolf's to his little war-like state, have "to vanish, like the Tyrannosaurus and the saber-toothed tiger" (ttc:583). In the event, Rudolf does not live to see the "swift unfolding of a transport monopoly into a government, a social order and a universal faith" (STTC:333).

A vast business octopus is transformed into the Modern State octopus, an event foreshadowed by our first glimpse of Cabal as he steps out of WT 34. Dressed in black Airmen tights, his head is encased in a gigantic gas helmet, the exact shape and contour of an octopus's great cephalic dome. As the head of a world state in the making, the Air Dictatorship, he is the living embodiment of its World Brain. Relating the symbolism of his helmet to what has been said in our Introduction about the Coming Beast — the state monster that is the Modern State octopus — we have the following schema:

The State Monster
(world machine as world organism)

Modern State Octopus	functions	Hindu trinity
	1. Poietic or creative intelligence. The spiritual power of scientific planning. Plato's Perfect Guardians or teachers.	Brahma (wisdom)
World Brain or octopus head. Direction — the working aristocracy.		

	2. Kinetic or executive intelligence. The temporal power of industrial management. Plato's Auxiliary Guardians or soldiers.	Siva (force)
Docile work force or octopus tentacles. Labor—the working proletariat.	3. The Dull and the Base. Common incapables deprived of popular power. Plato's producers.	Vishnu (desire)

The Coming Beast, then, is the outcome of that triangular struggle between the cosmic forces of Brahma, Siva and Vishnu—that of "creative effort versus the resistences of jealousy, indolence and sentimentality." By the film's end, however, "The aggressive maker in the human soul has emerged triumphant over instinct and tradition. Brahma the Creator asserts himself over Vishnu the Preserver after his [her!] previous subjugation by Siva the Destroyer" (WM:02).

"The aggressive maker in the human soul." What that comes down to, in the final analysis, is the creative soul of John Cabal. He is, after all, the first of a line of dynastic world rulers, followed on as he is by his grandson, Oswald Cabal. The Cabals, in short, are hereditary "king bees," as are Plato's philosopher kings.[86] They, too, are "aggressive makers," in that they contain and combine in their own souls the two qualities of wisdom and courage that distinguish the teachers and soldiers who respectively form the state Guardians, and over whom their kings preside. It is the king bees who decide what wisdom is to be taught by the teachers (Perfect Guardians), and how force is to be used by the soldiers (Auxiliary Guardians) in assisting their superior colleagues on the Nocturnal Council by way of administration. The teachers plan, the soldiers enact, keep order and combat dissent.

The few Guardians of both ranks, who understand the king's philosophy, rule the many who do not; they do so for the good of society's moral salvation. This consists in realizing the idea of social justice, which means the sorting out of men and women according to the capacities of their soul-stuff, and assigning them to compatible duties. As conceived by the king bee himself, the just society is one in which everyone knows his place in the social division of labor, and makes his functional contribution accordingly.

But while the Guardians well know their own duties, because they willingly undergo the self-discipline required to perform them, the producers require the externally supplied discipline of their betters. To fill their place in the scheme of things, they need be persuaded and coerced into acceptance of their lot. Because their inferior souls are animated by nothing more than everyday personal desires, they lack the force of character to act out the grand design unaided. Denied metaphysical insight into the cosmic struggle whose end is to win their submission, they need moral guidance for their own good and for that of universal harmony. They must be made to do their part as an extension of the king bee's will to power in the name of social justice.

So it is with John Cabal. His octopus-headed helmet is a symbol not only of the organic state-monster he brings into being, but of his personal headship as its philosopher politician. The tentacles of the Modern State octopus, which embrace Labor, are the extensions of his dictatorial will as mediated by Direction. And the aim of Direction is "to deal directly with every primary producer" (STTC:295). In other words, the producers are to be denied a market economy. That ancient theatre of greed and self-seeking is to be destroyed and be replaced by direct public service, by way of "a general labor conscription together with a scientific organisation of production."[87] Therein lies "the essence of the Socialist project."

> It means no little change. It means a general change in the spirit of living; it means a change from the spirit of gain ... to the spirit of service.[88]

Every primary producer is expected to serve in the same altruistic spirit that animates their moral exemplars, the new saints of Direction who sit on the World Council.

As the future historian of the Modern State octopus writes, "Within its far-flung tentacles it embraced and sought to permeate with its own nature [a whole world] still carried on by inertias established during thousands of generations" (STTC:293). Such has been Vishnu's domain for all that time — the "natural animal-like acceptance of the established thing" (270), the jealous "preservation of the thing that was and still is."[89]

So when we see John Cabal step out of WT 34, dressed in his octopus helmet, we know that the state monster he heads is about to reach out its tentacles to the people of Everytown, and squeeze out the evil spirit of Vishnu in them, their "treacherous egotisms." Soon they will be released from their passion to possess, once they undergo "the harshly rational schooling of human motives" he has planned for them. Thereafter, those "protesting spirits who squirmed in the pitilessly benevolent grip of the Air Dictatorship" are emptied of desire (STTC:346). With Vishnu conquered by the creative efforts of Brahma, aided by the auxiliary forces of Siva, "the battle against indolence, greed and jealousy in every soul in the world" is won. Man's "animal individualism" is finally brought under control (334). In the end, for all the protest against it, this "[Puritan] Tyranny was in essence a liberation" (363). It liberated mankind from its deadly sins and "brought [it] into the new communion" that is the world community (347).

As the future historian of this moral triumph writes about its lasting victory unto his own time, "The individuality deprived, or relieved if you will, of its primary instinctive preoccupations with getting and keeping ... is no longer a self-sufficient being, at war with its kind, it has become a responsible part of the species" (STTC:429). The individual is now made one with the organic whole of the Great Being, embodied as it is in the state monster, and whose collective aims are to advance the progress of the Human Adventure. "Socialism is the schoolroom," writes Wells, "wherein by training and restraint we shall make men free." Free, that is, for direct public service to the Modern State, which is the whole duty of man; free from the "false idea of property and self."[90]

The film's 1936 audience at this point, recognizing the octopodan contours of Cabal's helmet, very likely felt a shudder of horrible anticipation. Here comes the evil state monster to swallow us up! For it was a newspaper cliché of the 1930s to describe the totalitarian state as "the octopus state," and so it was pictured in political cartoons. This image applied not only to Fascist Italy and Nazi Germany, both a scary thing at that time, but also to Soviet Russia — scary to some, if not to others. Whatever, the octopus was a widely known symbol of the collectivist state. One political journalist wrote, "the octopus state is not only the banker, manufacturer, and common carrier, but also the baker, the butcher, and the candlestick maker." As the arbiter between capital and labor, it determines wages and conditions of employment. In democratic countries by contrast, "the wage-earners, in so far as they are organised, are represented by trade-unions headed by officials of their own choosing. Under Collectivism, this form of economic democracy goes the way of political democracy. The all-powerful state relieves the workers of the burden of defending their own interests."[91]

These last words are written with heavy-handed irony; the evilness of the collective state monster was more than self-evident to the author and his mass readership. But it was Wells's artistic intention in *Things to Come* to reverse this popular prejudice against statism, and redefine its fright symbol as one altogether benign.

Indeed, he argues that it is rather the very "headlessness of this planet" that endangers it; it has no "collective mental life. . . . It has just the tired out ganglia of its disunited past." It has no "central ganglion" to give the world a community of faith and common purpose.[92] Under the stimulus of modern technology, it achieved "a hypertrophy of bone, muscle and stomach, without any corresponding enlargement of its nervous controls" (STTC:32). A World Brain is just what humanity needs for its collective mental life. To this purpose John Cabal has come into the world. He sees to it that mankind grows up and comes of age.

> The attainment of the World Republic and the attainment of the fully adult life are the general and the particular aspects of one and the same reality. Each conditions the other. The former would release man from traditions. . . . And the other would liberate the individual man from a servitude to instinctive motives. . . . The individual forgets the doomed and defined personal story that possessed his immaturity, the story of

mortality, and merges himself in the unending adventure of history and the deathless growth of the race.[93]

All of this is evident in Wells's own explanation of the landing scene. He says that the vizor in front of Cabal's helmet "is peculiar in structure. . . . The lower part swings down to expose the face and throat, leaving a great semi-circular back, a kind of high vast collar or setting, behind the head" (WM:24). When he drops the vizor his head and shoulders "are suggestive of a Buddha against a circular halo" (TTC:56). A benevolent state-octopus indeed!

John Cabal is portrayed as a salvationist, cast in the haloed image of Buddhahood. And why not? After all, the spiritual goal of all the great religions is to deanimalize the self and make over one's purpose to greater ends than the everyday life affords. For example, "Buddhism with an entire renunciation of earthly desire." The political religion that John Cabal brings is of that general quality, with all the particulars of doctrinal variation and cultural baggage unloaded, be it Christian, Islamic or Buddhist in content. Stripped down to essentials, the new and truly universal community of the socialist faith reduces to this credo, "I give myself." Nothing more is asked of the convert, than he turn himself from the world as it is toward a better collective future. "First comes self-disregard, then service." Thus are the Buddha-headed and octopus-domed images of Cabal's helmet melded into one goodly symbol of redemption. Cabal comes to lead mankind into the spiritual life of the Human Adventure, inviting us "to lose ourselves in a greater life."[94] It is the immortal life of the Great Being he calls us to, in whom the hope and promise of the world's organic unity lies, as integrated by the all-embracing tentacles of the Modern State octopus.

Cabal, however, is not only savior but judge. The armed guard sent by Rudolf to arrest him looks up at the haloed visage of this towering figure, over seven feet tall in his helmet, only to back off with due humility. It is Cabal who has come to search out the local warlord, not Cabal who will be taken to him. "He sent me to arrest you," says the guard with a note of apology in his voice. Cabal replies, "You can't do that. But I'll come and see him" (ttc:437f).

Strolling with majestic rectitude through market square, helmet now carried in hand, he is mobbed by the townspeople, and little children press close to him. He motivates "hero worship" in them for the one deserving reason Wells gives for such behavior, "the worship of superior power." Like Saint-Simon's industrial captains of commanding and preeminent capacity, Cabal excites piety and obedience. "Power is the key to popularity, not vice versa as in the democratic notion," Wells explains. "Power acquires a moral quality of its own."[95]

Looking about the ruins of his home town, Cabal asks about Pippa Passworthy. Nobody remembers him; he and his kind died at the outset of the war. Cabal then asks about Harding. The crowd produces this good doctor and, murmuring respects, makes way for the two to meet. Harding notes that Cabal has aged handsomely. "You are grey but you look young enough" (ttc:446). This is a tribute to Cabal's adult vigor, his maturity as a moral superman.

Doctor Harding then leads the way to his laboratory, where the two are joined by Gordon and his wife Mary, adult worthies all. They tell Cabal about the kind of Boss they have, and he assures them that their situation is not unusual. It's what endless warfare has led to, the same robbing and fighting by the same sort of brigand chiefs everywhere. "But we, who are all that is left of the old engineers and mechanics have pledged ourselves to salvage the world." In one of the film's most impressive speeches, he goes on to say, "we have ideas in common; the Brotherhood of efficiency, the freemasonry of Science. We're the last trustees of civilization when everything else has failed" (ttc:456f).

So impressed by this speech is Gordon, "the last engineer in Everytown" (ttc:425), that he leaps to attention, eager to take orders. "I've been waiting for this. I'm yours to command." But Cabal says, "Not mine. Not mine. No more bosses. Civilization's to command. Give yourself to World Communications" (ttc:458; TTC:60).

With saintly mendacity, Cabal denies that he is his party's individual leader. "No more bosses." He rather asks that Gordon give himself to the collective cause of human civilization and world unity. In this he mystifies the personal power of his Air Dictatorship by displacing it onto society at large, the familiar rhetorical trick of all totalitarian creeds. Cabal makes no distinction between *we* and *they*—we partymen who rule and they who are ruled. He talks the abstract language of organic theory, as if his party—the Air League or World Transport or World Communications or whatever—were but the nerve center of a higher organism, the being of the species. He is but a cerebral cell in the World Brain of the Modern State octopus. The *Grande-Être* is to command.

In recruiting Gordon to the cause, Cabal implies that the organic unity of interests as between Direction and Labor is the product of a "disinterested administration." Direction by the World Brain somehow operates beyond the "normal method of human control." In place of loyalty to a new ruling class, "loyalty to the objective" is called for.[96] No more bosses, no more class government. For the Airmen are but "the servant-masters of the world," mastering it in the service of the Human Adventure.[97] Gordon is asked to obey Cabal not as a powerful man, but as a powerful medium of the racial purpose. The Airmen are votaries of a religion whose object of selfless devotion is "the master being, Man," and whose teaching is that "the service of men's collective needs is the true worship of God."[98] Airmen are expected to deny the power motive that raises them up to the ranks of a new class, the new political elite. Like the priests of the modern church-state they are, they are required to say, with the political churchmen of the old medieval theocracy, *nolo episcopari* ("I do not wish to be made a bishop").

Thus when Gordon is recruited by Cabal into the Air League, he is at the same time inducted into the rhetorical mysteries of its ideology. He is taught the Wellsian trick of synecdoche.* In this case, Man or the Human Adventure or the World Brain or the racial being—they all stand for Cabal's personal authority. He rules in the name of the Great Being and its collective will to create a scientific-industrial world civilization. Not one man holds dictatorial power over his obedient partymen, but a verbal abstraction. "Civilization's to command."

As Wells writes in his propagandist mode, apart from his otherwise candid mode, the World Brain or Collective Mind

> is something transcending persons just as physical or biological science or mathematics transcends persons. It is a racial purpose to which our reason in the measure of its strength, submits us.... This Collective Mind is essentially an extension of the spirit of science to all human affairs.... [It is] by the sheer power of naked reasonableness, by propaganda and open intention, by feats and devotions of intelligence, that the great state of the future, the world state, will come about.[99]

Or again, "What we call Science is ... the knowledge in this Mind; and it develops a will for collective effort and a collective purpose in mankind." "It's *science* and not *men of science* that we want to enlighten and animate politics and rule the world." Therefore it can be said that "the Great State is indeed no state at all."[100] Addressed by Cabal in the elusive grammar of synecdoche, Gordon is instructed that his duty is not to the Air Dictatorship; he is rather to think of himself as responding to the historical imperatives of the Collective Mind, in the service of mankind's future.

St. Bernard said of the Romans, "When they promise to serve, they aspire to reign."[101] This is more or less true of all power elites, given that the *libido dominandi* is a steady motive in human affairs, and that it always is mystified to some degree by disguising it as a service motive. Every ruling class has its promising cover story, those who rule in the name of the Social Idea no less than any other. Wells is not naive in these matters, and does not hesitate to admit that his writings constitute a "Literature of Power," consecrated to making "propaganda for socialism."[102]

Things to Come is of a piece with that Literature of Power—film propaganda for Wellsism and the Modern State Movement. The film's political hero, John Cabal, is not only party chairman of the Air League or Transport Union, he is also its party theoretician; although in the novel he is named Gustave De Windt (STTC:250–258). Like Lenin, De Windt/Cabal plays a

---

*Synecdoche usually is taken to mean a part for the whole, as in "a fleet of fifty sail" (i.e., ships). But it works vice versa as well, as in "Chicago won" (i.e., the Cubs baseball team). Thus in the rhetoric of Wellsian socialism, the collective mind and will of "Man" stands for the power of Direction over Labor, and Direction (or the World Council) stands for its number one party member, its king bee and dictator of a one-person state.

dual role, moving from revolutionary intellectual to intellectual revolutionary. He not only formulates the party's ideological cover story for Wells's
Communist Revision; he also organizes a conspiratorial brotherhood with
which to seize power and act on its promise.

But as we know from the texts of Saint-Simonism, upon which Wellsism
is based, the Social Idea is little more than a political cover story for the coming class rule of middle-class experts. Auguste Comte took pains to emphasize,
for the instruction of the priesthood he would recruit into socialism—his
Religion of Humanity—that the Grande-Être really was not the sum of all
human beings. It was rather a figure of speech, the whole for a part, Humanity
standing for the Elect who had the wit to manipulate that larger abstraction
as a doctrinal false-face. The Great Being is but the smaller sum of its distinctive votaries, who were to found a new state religion for a scientific theocracy,
with monsieur Comte self-elected to its headship. Making the whole of
Humanity the object of public worship, socialists would take the lead in advancing the world's progress and welfare. For only they, as intellectuals, had
studied the science of society, the "sociology" of Comte's own invention.
Therefore, only they know how to further the common good. The rest, in
Comte's words, are so much "human manure."[103] Or as Wells has it of common humanity, the masses are but "the swill of this brimming world."[104]

Given the "incapacity of the common man towards public affairs," it is
only just that the intellectually and morally superior Airmen take charge of
mankind for its own good—for the under-organized method of representative
government can but indulge a "chaotic selfish rule" of the Dull and the
Base.[105] Popular power means giving unrestrained power to Vishnu, and let-
ting loose the evil spirit of getting and keeping. As De Windt/Cabal writes,

> It is no good asking people what they want. That is the error of
> democracy. You have first to think out what they ought to want if society
> is to be saved. Then you tell them what they want and see that they get
> it (STTC:254).

In plain words, first you hijack control, then you make them like it. For all
his lofty goals, Cabal's credo reduces to the strongarm code of gangster-
dom.

But from his point of view it is Rudolf who is the gangster, an outlaw of
the world state. Taking leave of Gordon his new recruit, Cabal now goes over
to town hall to see the Boss in his dilapidated audience chamber.

He sits behind a huge desk on which, Wells want us to notice, there is
a "broken down telephone" (WM:27). At one level this indicates a postwar
breakdown of communications technology and a return to barbarism. At
another, it signifies that local patriotisms of the Boss's barbaric sort persisted
into modern times despite the development of such a technology, because
nobody had the political will to make use of it as the nervous system of a
World Brain, and thereby abolish nationalism.

Nobody until now. When the Boss asks Cabal what government he represents, the answer is, "I belong to World Communications. We just run ourselves" (ttc:469). How confrontational this is, the Boss does not understand. Cabal is not recruiting; he is talking to the enemy. He represents a conspiratorial society carved out from society, with the intention of overthrowing all existing governments. "We just run ourselves."

The only thing Rudolf understands is that Cabal is a stranger, come uninvited into his country when it is at war. "At war!" says Cabal, as if redressing a naughty child. "Still at it, eh? We must clean that up" (ttc:461–3). But Rudolf has yet to learn what the Airmen mean by tidiness. The Air Dictatorship has under it an executive bureau called the department of "social sanitation" (STTC:355). Its job is to clean up social dirt, by killing off men like Rudolf. The Airmen once doing this, and putting everybody else to useful work, "Earth became an ant-hill under their dominion, clean and orderly" (360).

Meanwhile, Rudolf is interested to discover that the Airmen deal in commerce, although he is unhappy to find out that munitions are not in their line of business. Well, then, what about fuel and spare parts for his air force? Cabal replies that "our new order has an objection to private aeroplanes." Rudolf's dignity is ruffled in having to spell out the obvious difference. "I'm not talking about private aeroplanes. Our aeroplanes are public aeroplanes. This is an independent sovereign state—at war" (ttc:482f).

It soon becomes clear, however, that Cabal meant what he said. Private airplanes they are, precisely because they are national airplanes. The new order redefines the public order of old as no more than a private-profiteering racket, run by gangster politicians for their own personal power and glory. "We don't approve of independent sovereign states," Cabal says at last. "We mean to stop them." Finally Rudolf gets the message. "That's war." Cabal, patronizing to the end, thinks it something less than that. "If you will," he says, knowing that the sanitary police will soon arrive to clean things up, even as Rudolf orders him taken to the detention room downstairs (ttc:488–95).

"Clean that up! My war!" says Rudolf afterwards to Roxana, his favorite harem mistress (ttc:498f). She had stood beside his chair during the above colloquy, a prized sexual adornment of his political power. Now they talk together in his bedroom. She evidently had thought on Cabal as the better man to follow, even though at the time she commented on his "impudence" (483). But now she rounds on Rudolf for playing the bully with him, "the first real aviator that has come this way for years" (505). Perhaps Rudolf is not so clever, after all. Otherwise he "could have had some of those machines up long ago" (506). Perhaps Cabal is "too much for you," she says (508).

Jealous of Roxana's concern for this powerful stranger, Rudolf claims that he always had known about the brewing of "this conspiracy of air bus drivers" (ttc:511). The belittling phrase, for Roxana's benefit, cannot hide his anxiety that a Transport Union might imply more than its name gives away, now she has planted the suspicion in his mind. So, to keep her devotion to himself, he boldly declares that the stranger's arrival was no surprise at all, but fits in

perfectly with his plans. "Now's our chance." Cabal is locked up, and his
fellows with their airplanes out there somewhere, suspected all along, won't
come looking for him until he, Rudolf, is ready for them. "I've got everything
fixed now for an attack straight away on the Floss Valley to the old coal and
shale pits—where there's oil too." Then, with fuel for his air force, "up we buzz"
(ttc:511–15).

Cut to Rudolf's attack on the Floss Valley (ttc:516–536). The enemy is
routed in a scene of mock glory, the winning flag hoisted atop the taken colliery. We are left in no doubt what it is that independent sovereign states do
for a living. Led by "little fellows in spurs and feathers [they make] militant
economic raids upon the economic life of other countries." Because every nation is "a separate economic system in hostile competition with the rest,"[106]
the very "existence of independent sovereign states *is* war" (STTC:88).

Rudolf the Victorious returns with the usual patriotic crowd turned out
to greet him (ttc:537–541), only to find that Gordon and Harding have been
radicalized by Cabal's visit (543–554). Gordon won't work on the airplanes
and Harding won't make poison gas. Both refuse to salute. "We have our duty
to civilization," Harding explains. "You and your sort are driving us straight
back to eternal barbarism" (549). This but confirms Rudolf's prejudice, his
reactionary failing for which he is doomed. "I don't trust you technical chaps"
(544). Rudolf then exhibits the kind of bossing that soon is to be no more,
when the technical intelligentsia take over. "I'm the master here. I'm the
State," he tells the two traitors (551). "The State's your mother—your father,
the totality of your interests. No discipline can be too severe for the man who
denies that by word or deed" (548f).

But wait—where have we heard this before? We recall Wells telling us that
under socialism, "the State is the Over-Parent," that the Great State is in fact
"the State family," every world citizen's outer mother and father. What, then,
is the difference between Rudolf's national rule and Cabal's party rule? It
seems to be only a manner of speaking. Rudolf does not disguise his power
motive very well, and is made to sound ridiculous. He's the Boss, and doesn't
mind saying so. The authority of the old ruling class of traditional politicians
is made to look petty in comparison with the lofty goals bespoken by the coming technocrats. They rather come on with a highly abstract cover story,
suitable for revolutionary intellectuals on the road to class power for *their*
kind. "No more bosses. Civilization's to command." Cabal never says, "I'm the
party, I'm master of the Air Dictatorship." He rather says, "we" Airmen are
the brain cells of Man the master being, servants of the *Grande-Être*, a scientific name for God, ruling by the divine right of reason.

As Rudolf continues to bully his technical help, Roxana steps in and per-
suades him to meet their one condition, that of working with Cabal, else the
planes will never fly. This is a plot on their part to get Gordon into the air
in a flight for help from Basra. Roxana for her part plots to get Cabal released
for this work only to obligate him in her game of love hunting.

That evening Rudolf addresses a victory banquet for his captains and commanders. With new fuel to hand and planes that soon will fly, all it takes is one more supreme effort, a conclusive bombing of the Hill States, and we'll "make this land forever ours. A man's land we're making, a land for strength and for courage. None but the brave deserve the land," and reaching over to fondle a rival to Roxana in his affection, he adds, "none but the brave deserve the fair" (ttc:558–60). This last line is from Dryden's poem, *Alexander's Feast*. Not that Rudolf knows the source; yet it indicates the barbarism of his conquests, both territorial and sexual. Roxana herself is named after one of Alexander's two wives. Now Rudolf is favoring the second of his two harem mistresses.

He goes on in a patriotic vein. "Our dear old land! There are some among us that dare run down our land," this in allusion to Gordon and Harding. They complain about the lack of civilized things like chemists, printing, and means of travel. Well, Rudolf says with pride, who the hell needs chemists anyway, and books only muddle the mind. As for not travelling anymore, "Well, isn't our land good enough for us?" (ttc:561–63). Sexual lust, local patriotism, and distrust of science are all linked as reactionary aspects of Vishnu the Possessor.

At this point, Roxana slips away from the banquet and goes downstairs to visit Cabal. She finds him more attractive than the Boss for his far-travelling, a man who commands a greater world than this little, limited land. His airplane, WT 34, is for her no augury of the coming civilization, only a sign that Cabal is a superior kind of Boss. She offers herself to him, together with the offer to use her queenly influence in having him spared a violent death. Cabal spurns her. Besides, his personal life does not matter. "We shall come here and clean things up just the same" (ttc:581; TTC:75).

But Roxana asks, how can you say "we" if you are killed? Respecting her intelligence (she has read the old books and knows geography), Cabal gives her an ideological lesson, perhaps hoping to convert her.

> We go on. That's how things are. We are taking hold of things. In Science and Government—in the long run—no man is indispensable. The human thing goes on. We—forever [ttc:582].

But this is more than she can begin to understand. The "human thing" is the Human Adventure, which "in the long run" is the evolutionary life of the species, the on-going progress of Man and the organic state. Its Collective Mind, filled with the knowledge of Science, is the world's will and Government, which "we" Airmen serve as replaceable cells.

Roxana's response is to press her personal claim on Cabal. "Have you no use for that closeness of devotion that you can never get from any man? Don't you see I have been working for you already?" (TTC:76). But Cabal does not *use* women. Roxana has not yet seen his female comrades, booted and uniformed in black like himself. In the Air League, as among Plato's Guardians, women are fellow political workers, not love objects to be possessed.

"You are a new sort of man to me," she says. Cabal replies, "No. A new sort of training. The old Adam fundamentally" (TTC:75). Repelled now by the self-mastery of Cabal's adult vigor, she turns on him with, "Ugly you are and grey" (ttc:586).

At that point Rudolf bursts in on them. Roxana defends her conduct as that of a loyal mistress, "trying to find out what this black invader means. Do you think I wanted to come and talk to him, this cold grey man?" (ttc:588f). She repeats what Cabal told her, about the airplanes being built at Basra, and the new world of United Airmen that will finish him. But Rudolf's ignorance of geography (he never heard of Basra) only renews her contempt for him. He'd better make peace with this Airman and let him go, she insists—or else. To Rudolf, this is all bluff. Turning on Cabal he declares, "There's no making peace between you and me. It's your world or mine. And it's going to be mine." He then takes leave with a parting shot, "you're a hostage. Remember that" (593f). Roxana, the disappointed love huntress, knows how little that matters to Cabal. Now she has nobody, and the Boss really is a fool.

Yet to be on the safe side, Rudolf does take Roxana's advice, and releases Cabal under guard to work with Gordon the mechanic (ttc:596–601). Together they get a number of planes in flying order, and presently Gordon escapes in one to Basra.

Meanwhile Roxana visits Doctor Harding's laboratory to learn from Mary Gordon more "about this man Cabal and this Airmen's world they talk about. . . . Do you understand him? Is he flesh and blood?" (ttc:603f). "He's a great man," says Mary. "My husband worships him." But Roxana is not interested in ruler worship. She wants to know why she found him so cold and preoccupied. "Do men like that ever make love?" She is told, "A different sort of love, perhaps." To which she snorts, "Love on ice" (TTC:80). That being the case, "If this new world of yours—all airships and order and science comes about—what will happen to us women?" The answer is, "We'll work with the men" (ttc:605f). Nonsense this is to Roxana. She knows men. They want only the glory of being loved by us women. Let the Airmen come, let them "conquer the world. Then we shall conquer them" (615).

Roxana has not forgotten what Cabal said about "the old Adam," but overlooks what he said about that "new sort of training." But we must not. These New Puritans may put "love on ice," yet they are neither chaste nor celibate. They are rather trained to put sexual jealousy behind them, taking the curse of Vishnu out of "passionate personal love" and all the mind-upsetting emotionality that goes with it. In pre-utopian times, we are told by Wells from the viewpoint of the future, "The pride and self-respect of a man was still bound up with the animal possession of women—the pride and respect of most women was by a sort of reflection bound up with the animal possession of a man."[107] The old code of jealousy, with its competition for sexual ownership, is abolished under socialism, as it has been in Soviet Russia. There, as Wells imagines, women fight the good party fight with men, "instead of being fought for."[108] Among the Utopians it can be said, "We take love by the way as we take our food and our holidays, the main thing in our lives is our creative work." "For the rest of the time we do our work, make our machines, subdue the earth to our needs, in sexless tranquility."[109]

Or as Mme. Alexandra Kollantay advised on the free love of New Soviet Man, "The sexual act should be deemed of no greater importance than drinking a glass of water."[110] But this is not new to the Bolsheviks. "Plato wanted exactly that," says Wells.[111] As with the Guardians, so with the Airmen— comradely, nonpossessive Platonic love out of a glass of ice water, in which Vishnu is cooled for the sake of Brahma's creative work.

Once Rudolf learns of Gordon's get-away he is furious. "Curse these World Communications. Curse all Airmen." Why did he ever tamper with flying, he wonders. His advisor tells him that the planes were needed against the Hill States. And if we didn't start in again with airplanes and gas and bombs, these Airmen would have come upon us anyway. But Rudolf is not consoled. "Why was this science ever allowed? Why was it ever let begin? Science! It's the enemy of everything that's natural in life." Exactly so. In Wellsism, science *is* the enemy of the natural, everything belonging to Vishnu that Rudolf the reactionary defends and preserves. He pictures the Airmen as "Great ugly black inhuman chaps, half like machines" (ttc:631f). In this, too, he is not far wrong.

By this time Rudolf really fears their coming. But wait. He's got hostages, Cabal and his friends Harding, Gordon and Mary Gordon. He's also got some airworthy planes now, so he'll fight. "What is this World Communications? A handful of men like ourselves. They're not magic" (ttc:633).

But they *are* magic. What else can their power be, when they claim for science a total mastery over both nature and human nature? To the Airmen, "There is no limit to either knowledge or power." But their knowledge is that of political rhetoric above all, the verbal magic by which they redefine their despotic power over other men as no more sinister than a generous acting out of the general purpose of things, given them to do by the rarified spirit of science infusing the Collective Mind. Or as Wells himself says of his coming elite, "They will perform miracles of restatement."[112]

Cut to Basra and the sight of a gigantic bomber, viewed from beneath the long curving reach of an expansive wing, marked WT 714 on its underside, indicating one of a massive fleet belonging to World Transport (ttc:634). The image flashes on the screen and is gone, but that moment is enough to suggest a confused oneness of physical and moral greatness. Such products of technical prowess are "the outward and visible signs of an inward and spiritual grace." The Airmen's "gigantic handling of gigantic problems," as in their admirable engineering, is the sign of their Election by the *Grande-Être* for the political job they are given to do. They are what is wanted by destiny, "masterful people to handle the problems of the Modern State."[113]

WT 714 is a triumph of willing discipline, a product of industrial order and scientific management, displayed in the very manner in which the Airmen load it with bombs. With silent, inhuman, machine-like coordination, each does his duty as planned for him in advance, not bossed on the spot. Some place boxes of gas bombs onto a rail leading into the plane while others, parachutes on their backs, enter it through a doorway after smartly going up a pair of steps. Inside, others pack the bombs (glass globes filled with the Gas of Peace) in place by the bombardier's station. Two men outside take the rail away, others remove the steps, and yet another comes up to shut the door (ttc:634–641). Each man knows his task, assigned him by the Air Dictatorship's brain center, all of them loyal to the common purpose. This duty-ridden sense of obligation, however, is "inhuman" only by contrast with the natural and animal-like methods of feudal society, bossed by its beastly top dogs. "The normal method of human control is intimidation," exercised by natural men like Rudolf who "demand subservience to themselves."[114]

In flight, the Basra bombers drive toward Everytown with a steady drone, their dihedral wings breaking through huge cloud banks little by comparison. A shot on board the lead plane shows an open deck, sheltered in the lee of its bulking fuselage of Streamlined Moderne design, where crew members lean idly against the railing, calmly looking down on the world below.

They are driven by four engines and are used against horse soldiers. In these details, the Basra bombers recall the world's first fleet of four engine bombers, Ilya Muromets, designed by Igor Sikorsky for use by the Reds against White cavalry during the civil war following the Russian Revolution of 1917. Assembled for its first flight on November 2, 1919, the fleet by its mere passing overhead routed the Whites by sending their mounts rearing and neighing in fright and throwing their riders to the ground in a panic of surrender.

Rudolf hears them coming and orders his pitiful little airforce of shabby biplanes to up at them. He addresses his pilots in a send-off speech that is a model of patriotic stupidity. "You are not mechanics—you are warriors. You have been trained not to think, but to do, maybe to die. I salute you—I your Chief" (ttc:643–45). His planes go hopping fitfully along the unpaved airfield, some never gaining altitude. Those that do are shot down with pitiless contempt. Looking out over the railings, the Basra gunners point at their ease to the foolish falling planes. The Airmen are everything Rudolf's warriors are not, not men but ten thousand parts.

Then the bombs fall, Rudolf shoots off his pistol at the sky, the gas explodes all around him, everyone succumbs, and the Airmen drop down by parachute. Saved by his gas helmet, Cabal comes out to greet his fellows, who move through town square over the fallen bodies. Says one of the Airmen, "Well, we've given them a whiff of civilization." Another says, "Nothing like putting children to sleep when they are naughty" (WM:45).

But on the steps of town hall is one who is not sleeping, the Boss. He is beyond redemption, a most insanitary member of the dirty old ruling class. Standing over his dead body Cabal pronounces,

Dead and his world dead with him, and a new world beginning. Poor old Boss. He and his flags and his follies. And now for the rule of the Airmen, and a new life for mankind [ttc:711].

But it's to be a new world "with the old stuff. Our job is only beginning" (ttc:715).

The "old stuff," of course, is common humanity—non–Airmen and all other men and women who are not party material. As Gordon, now in uniform, observes of the raw material for resurrection lying about him, "Common souls. The common man who cannot be trusted with machinery and the common woman who cannot be trusted with men" (WM:45). The question now arises, "What are we going to do with all the swarming multitude of un-suitable people who constitute the great majority of mankind?"[115]

Cabal's answer to that is quite simple. "Who would rule others must begin by ruling himself" (WM:25). Or as Lenin said to his fellow partymen, "Learn to be disciplined, to introduce severe discipline."[116] The natural man is to be made "more social and unselfish in his ideology and mental habits" by the puritanical example of the Airmen themselves (STTC:415). Lacking the capacity for self-control, the place for civilians in the new technocratic order is with Labor, under Direction, where their common souls, animated by Vishnu, fit them. "Men are born but citizens are made" (251).

Merger Immortality

We next see Cabal at Basra, the great Air Dictator addressing his council members. He stands over them at a vast map-covered table, while other Airmen of lesser rank listen from the galleries above. Behind him we see through immense panes of plate glass, framed in steel beams, to a view outside of arching girders that show lofty hangars under construction. He tells them of the strength of the party idea, "we have the unity of a common order and a common discipline," and of his plan of operations. "First a roundup of brigands," other Rudolfs, then "organize, advance. This zone, then that.[117] And at last, wings over the whole world and the new world begins" (ttc:722–24).

Cut to the distant ruins of Everytown as the camera pans to where huge digging machines, designed in Streamlined Moderne, are excavating for an underground city, to be the metropolitan center of the Modern World-State. Cabal's address is continued voice over. This part of it is the film's key speech, delivered by Ramond Massey with a dramatic intensity to match the strong music of its lines. It is cast in free verse below, the better to capture that poetic effect, and to visually unpack its compact ideas.

> Do you realise
> The immense task we shall undertake

When we set ourselves
To an active and aggressive peace,
When we direct our energies
To tear out the wealth of this planet,
And exploit
All these giant possibilities
Of science
That have been squandered hitherto
Upon war and senseless competition.

We shall excavate
The eternal hills.
We shall make such use
Of the treasures of sky
And sea and earth
As men have never dreamt of hitherto.

I would
That I could see
Our children's children
In this world
We shall win for them.

But in them
And through them
We shall live again [ttc:725].

The phrase "aggressive peace" in the fourth line is highly suggestive. We are reminded of the Airmen's making of war for peace. They take up the sword of Siva in alliance with Brahma for the creation of a world state and the ending of war. This is what Cabal means when he speaks of "a roundup of brigands." He means the death of nations, the gassing of their patriotic leaders who are the cause of war, and the bringing of their territories under the control of the Air Dictatorship. Eternal peace then shall reign.

But this is the peace of aggressive pacifiers, imposed by men of violence who seek to create peace by subjection. It depends on the domination by an absolutist ruler whose regime is intended to be permanent, his policies unchangeable. Democratic yearnings for change in any respect are met with further violence, as we shall see in the way Oswald Cabal handles a massive popular revolt against his tyranny, which he defends as for the good of these very same masses. "It is barbarism come back," he says of the revolt (ttc: 133).

"Aggressive peace" also suggests the Saint-Simonian war on nature, humanity united to exploit "the wealth of this planet," no longer divided by wars of mutual exploitation. Heretofore, the productive possibilities of science have been wasted on "war and senseless competition." Note that fighting and competition are equated, when in reality they are extreme contrasts. War is destructive, economic competition is productive. So we have it in the liberal-democratic wisdom of Adam Smith economics. But Wells is antidemocratic, and so he puts "competition and scramble" (TTC:107) on the same footing as killing.

Science is to create a noncompetitive order, the world economic machine. Under a technocracy, with its idea of scientific management and rationalization, it can be said with confidence that, for "every process there is a best way which is the right way" (WWHM:314). Or as De Windt/Cabal writes, "There is one sole right way of doing things and there are endless wrong ways of doing things" (STTC:256f). But there is no such thing as a scientific *ought*; science can establish only what *is*. Only its ideological perversion, scientism, can dictate what ends people ought to live for. Scientism is in fact the very essence of Wellsism and is the ruling truth of the Air Dictatorship. Like all dogmas it is unpetitional, beyond the arguments of common sense. If the citizen does not submit to its "unearthly sanity," then he must be irrational or immoral, as most people are in their everydayism. The old stuff is just that, Dull and Base, bound to defy the plans of the "political reasoner," no matter how sane. That is why "Every principle in the world machine must be designed." A scientific government is impossible to rest on consensus. "Peace must be a *forcible substitute* for war."[118] So we are back again to social peace by subjection and the power of design.

This is the noble prospect that John Cabal is winning for "our children's children." He wishes that he could see them in the distant glory of that future world, "But in them and through them we shall live again." Far from expressing his personal wishes, however, Cabal is here laying down party doctrine. Remember, he is addressing his party followers, gathered in council. He is not vaporizing about his private family affairs and the future of his own offspring. He is talking about the Human Adventure, the on-going life of the species, and how "we" Airmen are to serve its purpose. Or rather, he explains how that service to humanity is to be talked about in making propaganda for socialist power. What he shows them, by the example of his rhetoric, is the doctrinal language of the party's cover story. We Airmen "live in and through" the being of the species, as the embodiment of its Collective Mind and its will to unify and save mankind.

As we already know, Wells assumes (or pretends) with Comte that mankind is a composite being, a collective man composed of persons for its parts. The supposed existence of this higher organism is the political myth of Saint-Simonian socialism and its worship of Man in a scientific Religion of Humanity. Wells brings to it later discoveries in the field of genetics. Because all men are related by common descent through the germ plasm, it follows that the human species does indeed breed itself as a large-scale type of its own units.

In the crazy logic of scientism, this larger unit is the essential biological reality, of which the individual is but a cellular part. As Thomas Hardy put it in his poem "Heredity," the germ plasm is the real seat of the human soul, "The eternal thing in man/ That heeds not the call to die." Our only spiritual refuge from death is to seek our immortality in living for those others who come after us, and who are destined to carry along our genetic heritage from out of the remote past into the remotest future. In tune with this poetic insight into the biological nature of the soul, Wells assures us that the genetic unity of the Human Adventure, entraining all persons living and dead and yet unborn, may be represented as the organic unity of a super-person in the immortal state-monster. Man is one and always has been, although he has been slow to translate this fact into a suitable political reality.

The world state is thus a living organism of on-going vitality. But to speak of such a creature is like saying that a grove of trees is itself a tree, or that a galaxy of stars is itself a star. The metaphor suggests that the Airmen, in working for Man, are able to help Humanity otherwise than by working for men. Setting the example with their own self-denying puritanism, they coerce the citizen into following suit, expecting him to serve the collective all of the state otherwise than by serving the individual needs of his fellows. This is possible to do, the Airmen argue, because the whole has a genuine end to be fulfilled beyond the needs of its parts and persons; individuals do not exist except as means to that higher end. Selfhood is not real; "we are egotists by misapprehension." On the basis of this truth, which strips the veil from the "illusion of personality," Cabal lays down his theological imperative: "Live for all life or do not dream that you are living."[119]

Now we know why the Airmen are "scientific atheists." *Scientific* because "the scientific method is the method of ignoring individualities." In biological science, only the species as a whole is the unit of objective reality. *Atheistic* because biology refutes the Christian doctrine of personal immortality and its earthly premise of personal freedom. In place of individual salvation, Cabal offers his doctrine of collective immortality, based on one supreme truth, "Man is immortal, but not men."[120]

This truth is the burden of *The Science of Life*, the second book of Wells's Bible of World Civilization. It serves to deny that "I am I" (Hardy's phrase from "The Pedigree") and to negate the supernatural. "Yet these considerations do not abolish the idea of immortality; they only shift it from the personality. In the visible world of fact, life never dies; only the individuals it throws up die." Thus "we [are] not ourselves, but Man." Let the world state teach men to identify with Man and the Human Adventure, and the individual "acquires an impersonal immortality," then to become "infinitely richer as a part than as a whole."[121]

The world citizen is taught a scientific creed that calls for the "merger of one's romantic individual life into the deathless life of the species."[122] He is instructed to repose his rational faith in a more comprehensive and unselfish kind of immortality, appealing to "interests far transcending mere individual survival," and whose doctrinal name is "merger immortality."[123] John Cabal affirms this credo in the concluding part of his address, thereby making merger immortality the official creed of the world socialist state.

Certainly it is Wells's credo. "Socialism is to me," he says, "no more and no less than the awakening of a collective consciousness in humanity." This means, he goes on, "I would oppose the conception of the Whole to the self-seeking of the Individual."[124] The Individual is to sink his ego into the immortal state-monster, and so "live in the species and find his happiness there," rejoicing in "the idea of a racial well-being embodied in an organised state."[125] Worshipful of this Whole, the world citizen is to incorporate himself "with the undying organism of the World State," which is none other than the quintessence of human brotherhood, undivided by the interests of a separate working class; "no trade union will impose a limit on his activities. The world will be his Union."[126] Or again, the Modern State is "the whole duty of man," in both faith and obedience (STTC:398).

Cabal's doctrine of merger immortality is no mere abstraction without real consequences; it is a fighting creed directed against the masses for the repression of personhood among them. The biology lessons the world citizen is to be instructed in, out of *The Science of Life*, are rather more for the benefit of the Modern State's "educational guardians," in perfecting the niceties of their cover story. For the rest, writes the future historian of the Modern State, "compulsory public service ... is an integral part of our education" (STTC:421, 425). Note the collective "our," which is in itself doctrinal, the Whole standing for the part that opposes and governs the Individual others. Obedience is faith enough for them. They need no further instruction. "Socialism is the schoolroom ... wherein by training and restraint we shall make men free," writes Wells of "we" socialists. Socialism means a "release of the human spirit from the individualist struggle."[127]

Or as John Cabal promises, it will save mankind from "war and senseless competition." But his new religion of merger immortality is the old Platonic religion of statolatry. And John Cabal himself is no less intolerant than were the religious fanatics of the Moslem Conquest. No doubt that is why he addresses his Airmen at Basra, the spiritual headquarters of that former Conquest, the center of its faith and learning.

Statolatry, according to one critic, is the

> dogma that the State or the government is the embodiment of all that is good and beneficial and that the individuals are wretched underlings, exclusively intent upon inflicting harm upon one another and badly in need of a guardian.[128]

Likewise it is with Wells. The power of the god-like state is for him not so much masked by his theology of merger immortality, as it is rather elevated to a moralism beyond reproach.

Wells may use the mystical language of Plato's organic analogy for his cover story, but unlike Plato he is not bashful to reveal what exercise of autocratic power is justified by it. He may say, with some coyness, that "The corner-stone of socialism is the great principle of the merging of the individual in the state." But no sooner does the reader ask how this mystical thing is done, than the answer is given. In practice, it reduces to "the principle that life is the property of the state."[129] Or more bluntly still, it comes down to "collective submission by force."[130] In terms of administrative policy, as we have seen, this amounts to "a general labor conscription together with a scientific organisation of production."[131] It means a forced division of labor in all social relations, and a dehabituation of every popular appetite—the evil habits of Vishnu as embodied in "the limited, instinctive traditional life of the multitude" (WWHM:883).

In this, Wells is no less explicit than are the Saint-Simonians from whom his technocratic brand of socialism is derived. When the Master spoke in his mixed metaphor of society as an *organic machine*, he said nothing a modern production engineer could fail to understand. The individual is merged with the *being* of society, the body politic, by way of *mechanizing* him along the lines of subdivided labor, in accord with the principles of scientific management. Thus the power of the Council of Newton over the world's workers, in Saint-Simon's Republic of United Interests, lies in "directing them towards a great common industrial purpose, in which they will be co-ordinated according to their respective functions."[132]

The World Brain, which for Wells heads "an economic world republic and a single world civilization," does the same in its "co-ordinating of the species in a common general end."[133] That the organic state, the Modern State octopus, is described by him as a being "in which all lives converge upon a common existence" has a meaning no less mystical than Saint-Simon's mixed metaphors of the organic and the mechanical. The common industrial purpose is the one and only general end of Wellsism. "To organise for work [is] the primary duty of [the Great State], and organisation for work is Socialism."[134] Again, this is the Saint-Simonian ideal. The Master had it that, come the technocratic revolution, "henceforth economic life constitutes the whole of social life."[135] The world is a workshop and it cannot be anything else.

Thus when John Cabal speaks of living in and through his grandchildren—"and through them we shall live again"—he alludes to his doctrine of merger immortality. His grandchildren and all others of that generation will find their satisfaction in merging themselves with the organic state in its coming completion. They will find their selfless joy in a world-wide labor levy, conscripted for the aggressive war on nature Cabal outlines in the first part of his address, where he tells about exploiting "the wealth of this planet." As Cabal concludes, we see his industrial idea begin to take shape, "the conception of one single human community organized for collective service" (STTC:23).

Civil Death

Now follows the Reconstruction sequence, done in montage (ttc:726–797). "An age of enormous mechanical and industrial energy" is in the making, as we see "small figures of men move among the monstrosities of mechanism, more and more dwarfed by their accumulating intensity.... The lines of the new subterranean city of Everytown begin to appear, bold and colossal" (TTC:91f). The Saint-Simonian vision is being realized, "the prospect of evoking such a plenty and wealth of life on our planet as the whole universe had never dreamed of before this time" (STTC:389).

The new Everytown that takes shape is one enormous factory complex, gleaming white and automated. We get the impression that machines do all the work. We see no toilers nor any labor conscripts, only industrial engineers on inspection tours, zipping about on scooters designed in Streamlined Moderne, riding overhead in travelling buckets, or climbing steel ladders from one observational deck to another. The historian of this time tells us that forced labor is only for "such toil as is still unavoidable" (STTC:425). Yet this cannot be negligible in amount. "The Modern State meant to abolish toil," he says, but then goes on to explain, "that meant to abolish any toiling class" (305). What is toilsome labor is only a matter of political definition.

Machines in Utopia are said to emancipate men from toil, in "abolishing the need for labor." But it is only "Labour with a capital L, as the name of a class of human beings organised for distinctive class ends [that] will pass away."[136] It is independent trade unions that are abolished, not toil itself. Modern machines are but symbolic of the machine-like integration of men into the organic machine that is the state monster, once all men are made over as *industriels* working for a one-class society of producers. The capital L in Labor then will stand for the tentacles of the Modern State octopus, working in collaboration with Direction by way of subserving it.

In the Great State, no matter how "boring or irksome" the job, "most will toil very cheerfully if they feel the collective end is a fine thing and a great thing."[137] In the Utopian future of A.D. 2036, now that workers are "contributing parts in the progress of a greater being," no longer sweating for the idle and selfish rich men of private-profit capitalism, toil is "a form of liberty and not a form of enslavement."[138] Wage slavery is converted into "pride in being joint owner and joint worker in a classless community. That has been done in Russia in the brief interval since 1917."[139] All belong to the same class of Saint-Simon's *industriels*, be they the worker workers of Labor or the party workers of Direction. So much for those "miracles of restatement"!

The division of tasks between Labor and Direction is itself a model of subordination to the common end, set for the mass of toilers by the partymen engineers we see scooting about on their inspection tours. They are exemplars of this principle. One of them, a "diver in black helmet," climbs up a ladder out of some chemical tank, for the manufacture of synthetic food (itself a symbol of Man's conquest of Nature), onto an upper deck. There he turns about in close up to reveal his name tag (ttc:770). No name is inscribed on it, however, but a letter-numeral designation, LIX 891.

This image is perhaps borrowed from a custom of Saint-Simon's apostles, who in forming a would-be party of technocrats, uniformed themselves in a distinctive blue tunic. Pinned to it was a nameless name tag that designated one's function and numerical rank within the apostolic hierarchy. Moreover, their tunics buttoned up the back so that no one could dress himself without dependence on others.[140] Both features were meant to exhibit the industrial principle of their Master's teaching, "the organization of a well-regulated system, which demands that the parts should be firmly linked to the whole and subordinated."[141]

So it is in the Wellsian industrial Utopia, in which everyone is tagged with a "scientific name," such as "A.M.a.1607.2 $\alpha\beta \oplus$," indicating his or her subordinate function in a hierarchical division of labor under the control of a center, for the efficient managing of a scientific organization of production.[142] Such a tag is meant to show a willing display of "disillusioned self-reliance."[143] The private life no longer matters.

The same goes for the diver's letter-numeral designation, LIX 891. He is a functional part of the organic world machine, whose no-name nomenclature is a way of reminding the world citizen of the selfless joys of his merger immortality. This is the modern way of depersonalized work, in contrast to the medieval way we saw among the craftsmen of barbarian Everytown, each man being himself in his work.

That contrast is all the more pointed when we recall that socialism originated with Saint-Simon as a theory of industrialism, opposed to the feudal order and its validation by the holy church. The new order therefore asks for some kind of rival religiosity to replace Christian theology. In the event, the Master appealed to the classical mystique of Platonic organicism. But from an operational point of view, such works as his *Du système industriel* anticipated Frederick Winslow Taylor's *Principles of Scientific Management* (1911), the American classic that gives us "Taylorization" as a name for the industrial division of labor. The difference is that Saint-Simon intended to Taylorize social and economic life alike.

As Wells puts the case, there is in the Modern State "no real distinction between political, social and economic control. . . . They are inseparable in a rational order." Guided by their faith in merger immortality, men of this new order will surrender themselves to the rationale of the system in order to be the more useful to humanity; in this cause they are ready to cripple their freedom and make themselves less fit to live on their own. "That cherished personal life which men and women struggled to round off and make noble and perfect, disappears from the scheme of things. What matters more and more is the work one does. What matters less and less is our personal romance and our personal honor. Or rather, our honor will go out of ourselves into our work."[144]

In *Things to Come*, this notion is glorified in the very particulars of

LIX 891's no-name nomenclature, borrowed as they are from the glamor of the aviation industry. His tag is in the same style as World Transport plane, WT 715. In the lettering-numbering of airplanes, the letter prefix indicates the functional type of aircraft ("B" is bomber, "F" is fighter, etc.) and the affix is its design number – if not its fleet number, as with WT 715 or WT 34. For example, the DC-3 is a Douglas Commercial aircraft, mark 3. Indeed, it was the epoch-making design of this first fully streamlined airliner in 1935, a year before the film, that called public attention to no-name nomenclature and lent it the mystique of modernity captured by Wells for LIX 891.

When the design of an aircraft is in the experimental stage, the designer adds an "X" to the letter prefix (as with the FX-111 before it became operational in the U.S. Air Force). This lends to it the further mystique of adventure, heroic test pilots bailing out when wings fall off some avant-garde model.[145] LIX 891 thus can imagine himself part of some "social experiment" of the sort that revolutionary Russia was known as at the time the film was made. He is a contributing part of the Human Adventure.

But *Things to Come* failed to sell its message. Another 1936 film opposed to it, however, was hugely successful. This was *Modern Times*, produced by Charles Chaplin. In it he played Charlie the Tramp as ever, Charlie the romantic rebel, Charlie the invincible individualist. A comedy about the dehumanizing discipline of the industrial workshop, it has Charlie crazed by the subdivided task he is put to on the assembly line. Turning the self-same bolts over and over again with wrenches in both hands, he throws it over and runs out into the street, his arms jerking like two pistons. Charlie the invincible human had been turned into a machine.

Since *Modern Times* looked to be a profound attack on our modern industrial civilization, it is told that some "intellectuals called upon Charlie to join them in reorganizing machine culture to some more human scale of things." Off screen, however, he said nothing about it.[146]

But these were humanistic intellectuals who came to Chaplin. There is another kind whose ideals are antihumanistic. Among them are H.G. Wells. In a film just as much of his own making as Chaplin's, he made the same point, but not as a joke. Dehumanization is good for you. The humiliating of the individual to a functional unit of work in his world machine is given out as the only possible salvation of mankind from disunity and war. "The individual life isn't everything. Human beings have overvalued their individual lives and cared too little for their kind." Or again, "I do not regard the organisation of all mankind into one terrestrial anthill . . . as a Utopian dream, as something that fantastically might be. I regard it as the necessary, the only possible continuation, of human history."[147]

That Wells and Chaplin were good friends does not subtract from the difference between their pictures. For Wells is the intellectual heir of Saint-Simon and his immediate disciple Comte, who said of socialism, the Religion of Humanity, that it was a "religion which throughout substitutes duties for rights."[148] Comte argued to the effect, as a recent summary has it,

> That in the future society the "immoral" concept of individual rights will disappear and there will be only duties . . . that in the new society there will be no private persons but only state functionaries of various units and grade, and that in consequence the most humble occupation will be ennobled by its incorporation into the official hierarchy.[149]

Or as Wells has it, "no one is really private but an outlaw." He speaks with profoundly anti-humanistic enthusiasm for the "non-individualized life [of] the great impersonal society of the days to come."[150]

The technocratic state-monster dreamed of by the Saint-Simonians and celebrated in Wellsism is a Frankenstein's monster. To design a society and model it by command is first to demodel the existing order. It is like tearing a living body to bits in order to build a new one out of the dead parts. To make Collectivism a fact one must first kill off all forms of independent group life standing between the individual and the state. The condition for mobilizing all citizens for direct public service is the death of civil society. A forced social division of labor replaces the spontaneous division of labor rooted in voluntary social ties, and the total state is built on the ruined soil of that uprooting.[151] The result is totalitarian poverty.

Lenin spoke of "universal labor service" on the model of military conscription. Or as one of his colleagues put it, expressing the Collectivist idea, "We [supply] labor according to plan, and consequently without taking account of individual peculiarities . . . or the wish of the workers to engage in this or that kind of work."[152] So with Wells, when he speaks of the Social Idea as embodied in his Great State, the Modern State octopus, with its "general labor conscription together with a scientific organization of production." This is what he means by "universal service to the common good," as glorified in the example of LIX 891.[153]

Not that Wells is unaware of the dangers to individuality and personal suffering this collective policy entails. He rather chalks it all up to the necessary costs of his "ethical reconstruction,"[154] following after a triumphant "obliteration of out-of-date moral values" (STTC:360). In his technocratic Utopia, "there are no absolute rights and wrongs, there are no qualitative questions at all, but only quantitative adjustments." The main policy consideration in the minds of his directive elite is to keep the Human Adventure moving forward. They clear the way for historical progress. "For the purposes of revolutionary theory the rest of humanity matters only as the texture of mud matters when we design a steam dredger to keep a channel clear."[155]

The new post–Christian ethic is founded on the "cruel rationality [of] inhuman humanitarianism" (STTC:345), as opposed to "the old Individualistic Humanitarianism." With a new "collective man" in the making, by way of merging one's identity with the organic health of the Great State and the perfectibility of its undying purpose, mankind at last matures and "takes the final step to a transcendent subordination, from which the last shred of personality has been stripped."[156]

What is humane, in the long run, is whatever serves humanity's growth and its adult future, however inhumane this may be from the self-protecting viewpoint of the individual and his immediate concerns at the present moment of living. Such everydayism was the object of ethical support under the old order; the Airmen "revolt against what was called 'Christian morality'" (STTC:398). Under the new order the sacrifice of selfhood and personality is altogether lawful, with respect to history's law of progressive movement, whose object is the salvation of the species as a whole. For that, the Darwinian channels of racial development must be kept clear of all obstructions, put in the way of this on-going stream of collective progress by any dissenters who take their stand on the obsolete values of "individualistic liberalism" (STTC:82).

Small wonder, then, that the grip on the squirming masses by the tentacles of the Modern State octopus, under John Cabal's headship of the Air Dictatorship, is described as "pitilessly benevolent" (STTC:346). You, in the first person singular, may not like the higher socialist morality of inhumane humanitarianism; but it's good for you in the second person plural.

Revolution is just like science; it has to be done by experiment, until the right mix of forceful coercion and convincing persuasion is learned. Lenin's "experimenting spirit," according to Wells, is all to his credit despite his failure. He was wrong-headed to promote *his* Revolution in the name of Marxism, yet he understood at the time of his takeover in 1917, that for the Russian people "our present system of social and economic organisation has nothing but evil, and that they may as well perish experimentally as perish without effort."[157] Learning from that failed experiment, John Cabal does better.

All the same, John himself learns by doing. Scientific-minded above all, he knows that "Living's just material"[158] to be shaped by revolutionary trial and error. As his grandson says of his experimental Space Gun project, and all this implies for the Modern State's ever-expanding conquest of society, "There's nothing wrong in suffering, if you suffer for a purpose. Our revolution didn't abolish danger and death, it simply made danger and death worthwhile" (ttc:906).

Two Cultures

With the world's work well organized by the end of the Reconstruction sequence, we now get our first look at the residential architecture of the new Everytown in the year 2036 (ttc:799). It is done in Streamlined Moderne, a variant of the International Style, led by Walter Gropius and Mies van de Rohe, and so called because it celebrates the international diffusion of modern technology and the smoothing out of local peculiarities. It speaks for a unified cultural field divested of any historical tradition, just what Wells wants, no reminders of the picturesque buildings of the past in which "our forefathers assembled about their various archaic businesses" (STTC:362).

But no sooner are we shown the cold and sterile whiteness of this great wonder city, than we hear the voice of romantic rebellion from the new age's invincible Charlie. He is Theotocopulos, a sculptor played by Sir Cedric Hardwicke, who speaks for "the sentimental and aesthetic values of the old order" (STTC:306). Unmistakably an artist, he is named after the famous Greek painter who moved to Spain, Domenikos Theotocopulos, where he became known as El Greco. Perhaps this name is chosen for the film's purpose because *Theotocopulos* in Greek means "God-possessed-son-of," one who accepts things as they are given by Providence. He thinks the old days were jollier, before things were taken in charge by Man the master being, "when life was short and hot and merry, and the devil took the hindermost" (ttc:803). He still lives under Vishnu's curse, the illusion of everydayism.

We first see him atop a high scaffolding, at work sculpting one of the monumental statues of athletic posture that decorate Everytown. Done in the progressive style of socialist realism as in the Soviet Union, all youth-and-tomorrow and eyes-to-the-future, he turns to his assistant and says he's had enough of this "great white world." It's time to rebel. Now's the time. The people are murmuring about the Space Gun experiment to shoot men at the stars. The people don't like it, but they have no leader. So it's up to him. He'll make a television broadcast and cry, "Halt. Stop this Progress." But his assistant doubts that the authorities will allow him to do so. Theotocopulos replies, "I'm a Master Craftsman. I have a right to talk" (ttc:801–809).

Others, evidently, have not the right to talk. This suggests that Theotocopulos is a privileged member of a state-run artists' union, perhaps even a party member of the Modern State Society. All the same, since he intends to bite the hand that feeds him, he will take care to conceal his purpose when he applies for official permission. "I shall call my talk, 'Art and Life.' That sounds harmless enough. And I shall *go* for this Brave New World of theirs" (TTC:93). He very well knows that his pitting of the humanistic vision of life against the regime's monopoly of scientific truth is not in the least harmless. It is a case of political opposition.

Cut to the interior of one of the state apartments (Oswald Cabal, world dictator, lives in the same building) where a small girl-child of the party elite is getting her "history pictures" from an elderly tutor (ttc:837). "Some strange pet animal" is in the room with her (TTC:94). Perhaps it is one of Fourier's antilions, those exotic symbols of the Utopian conquest of nature.

Today's lesson is about the "Age of Windows." The skyline of prehistoric New York appears on the educational film. "They'd no light inside their cities as we have. So they had to stick them up into the daylight, what there was of it" (ttc:816). A strange lesson. What can it mean for a child in training to become a state Guardian? Wells offers a clue in the following remarks:

> Henry Ford told me that he always wanted to keep daylight out of his works. Men at work suffer greatly from the alternations of brightness and dullness even on a normal day. The light will vary in a few minutes from

half as much to twice as much as the sun clouds over. The nervous strain demanded by accurate work under this variable illumination is very exhausting. In holiday times it is delightful to see the cloud shadows race across the hills, but that is a pleasure in which a man doing a piece of fine work cannot indulge.[159]

With Everytown's constant light, there is constant work constantly, with no holidays. In this age of scientific management, a state Guardian is required to know what technical progress in electrical illumination is good for, in keeping the world machine humming, its workers busy. "In twenty-four hours they [do] twenty-four hours of work," as with the noble ants.[160]

Everytown, after all, is described as a "human ant-hill" (TTC:106). As the future historian writes of the new Saint-Simonian work ethic, "We find it almost impossible to imagine the temptations to slacken at work, loiter, do nothing, 'look for trouble,' seek 'amusement,' feel bored and take to trivial or mischievous 'time-killing' occupations, that pursued the ill-trained under-vitalized, objectless citizens before C.E. 2000 (STTC:360f).

Another disability of the Age of Windows, the tutor goes on, is that "they had a disease—colds. Everybody had colds." He demonstrates a sneeze, and the little girl thinks it funny. "Not so funny as you think," he says (ttc:819–822). It would indeed be laughable if the new age had no more to congratulate itself on than for no longer catching cold. But in organic theory, "Society is one body, and it is either well or ill," and the new society is no longer ill. The "patriotic virus"[161] and the "disease of hate" that made for war has been cured along with the common cold. Looking back on the unwholesome world of the past and its insane nationalism, the historian of the Modern Era writes, "Our ancestors did not envisage this as a controllable mental disease. They did not know that it was possible to get through life without hatred, just as they did not know that the coughs and colds that afflicted them . . . were avoidable" (STTC:184). This is because they were "sick and feeble with congenital traditionalism."[162]

"I'm glad I didn't live in the old world," says the child. "I know that John Cabal and his Airmen tidied it all up." She is then shown him in her history pictures, and is told he was the ancestor of "Oswald Cabal, the President of our Council" (ttc:837f).

Cut to Oswald Cabal, president of the World Council of Direction, busy with affairs of state. His fingers drum on his desk "in a manner reminiscent of John Cabal in Part I. It is an inherited habit" (TTC:98). The genetic heritage of Plato's line of king bees is made evident. Says one of his executives, "You are the grandson of John Cabal, the Air Dictator—who changed the course of the world. Experiment's in your blood" (104). Note our revision of this line. In the release script, Oswald is John's great-grandson; we follow the film's literary version in this generational matter.

No longer wearing Siva's death-dealing black as did John and his Airmen, Oswald and his councilmen are dressed in Brahma's white. The upper garment of their costume is wide-shouldered in the exaggerated manner of the *kata-ginu* or "shoulder-cloth" belonging to the formal court dress of the samurai nobility, still worn by Japanese musicians in the national Kabuki theatre. This contrasts with "workers in overalls" (WM:51).

The samurai were the ruling nobility of Tokugawa, Japan, its aristocratic administrators and adept swordsmen as well, sworn to a single-minded devotion to statecraft by the ascetic code of Bushido. From them, Wells derived yet another name for his neoplatonic partymen, following after the New Republicans of his *Anticipations* (1901), but antedating the film's New Puritans. They are the political class of his one-party state in *A Modern Utopia* published in 1905, after the Russo-Japanese War concluded earlier that year. Japan's military victory over traditional Russia was a sign for Wells of what a modernizing state could do when it mobilized everybody for one common purpose. It was a case of "war socialism," General Ludendorff's later term for Germany's efficient national mobilization during World War I.

Moreover, the superhuman contempt for death shown by the Japanese was a striking news item of the day. The London *Times* reported that such feats of depersonalized duty owed to a revival of the old samurai code of harsh self-discipline, the warrior trained to suppress his individuality in the service of the state.[163] Wells played to this advertised virtue in *A Modern Utopia*, taking Japan's war socialism as a model of modern efficiency and concentrated state power. In this book's early version of his world technocracy, "The Samurai control the State and the wealth of the State."[164] They are the super-monopoly capitalists of "an ultra-modern State Capitalism" (WWHM:557). As a self-trained militant cult devoted to the selfless giving of directive services, Wells modestly hints that his 1905 Brotherhood of the Samurai may have inspired Lenin's invention of the Communist Party. "Whether there was any genetic connection between his scheme and mine I have never been able to ascertain."[165]

At all events, the Samurai reappear in *Things to Come*, suitably garbed in broad-shouldered *kata-ginu*. It is their "insistence on duty and sacrifice" that Theotocopulos now prepares to speak against (TTC:121). We next see him standing in a television studio, posed for artistic oratory (ttc:855).

Speaking to a world audience on behalf of popular discontent with the Space Gun project, emblematic of the regime's experimental social engineering, he declaims: "What is the good of all this Progress. Onward and onward. We demand a halt, we demand a rest. The object of life is happy living. We will not have human life sacrificed to experiment. Progress is not living, it should only be the preparation for living" (ttc:857f).

These words, made to sound ridiculous, are echoed by no less a humanist than Boris Pasternak, whose *Doctor Zhivago* reviews the nihilism of the Soviet experiment as follows:

> There are limits to everything. . . . But it turns out that whose who inspired the revolution aren't at home with anything except change and

turmoil, they aren't happy with anything less than a world scale. For them transitional periods, worlds in the making, are ends in themselves. . . . Man is born to live, not to prepare for life. Life itself . . . is so breathtakingly serious![166]

Wells makes fun of the same humanistic ethos, when he has his Theotocopulos orate against the regime's unending quest after "knowledge and power," its courting of "danger in every shape and form, playing with gigantic physical forces" (TTC:116, 132). Cabal asks his chief of police, "What is this Theotocopulos after?" Answer: "What he calls the natural life of man. He talks of the loveliness and beauty of man's *little* life" (WM:52).

Theotocopulos is as much an object of contempt as Rudolf, when he spoke of science as being the "enemy of everything that's natural in life" (ttc:631). His voice dripping with a sarcasm that is meant to be taken for impiety and a blasphemous attack on the theology of merger immortality, Theotocopulos goes on. "We must sacrifice ourselves. We must live for—what is it?—the species" (863).

But at least Wells permits Theotocopulos to understand what the real issue is behind his question when he asks, "What does this Space Gun portend? Make no mistake about it. The slaveries they put upon themselves today they will impose tomorrow upon the whole world" (ttc:866).

Exactly so. The self-disciplined Samurai undergo this puritanical training only to impose the same harsh discipline on the masses. The party's internal regimen is a model of the regime it intends to rule. The people are ignorant and unreliable, badly in need of a stern task master. Writes the future historian, "The Modern State Fellowship was a trained body pledged to impose its own type of training upon the whole world. It proposed to be the New Humanity. . . . Never before was Man so directed and disciplined" (STTC: 398). So *The Internationale*: "The Communist Party will be the world."

As Theotocopulos orates, we see him at times from behind the deck of a high control console at which a studio technician sits, observing the flow of video tape across the full length of the deck's upper surface. Or rather, this tape looks like a moving strip of film. It is carried along, frame by frame, over some pick-up or recording head at the center, endlessly running from its point of origin up one side of the console, only to vanish down the other. It seems to visualize the Human Adventure, the collective life of man as it flows out of the past through the present moment and into the unknown future of the race. "The race flows through us, the race is the drama and we are the incidents . . . episodes in an experience greater than ourselves." Our personal lives, when seen as film frames in the on-going human drama, are "like the picture on a cinema screen. They are discontinuous 'Nows,' but they follow one another so rapidly that they seem to be continuous."[167] Theotocopulos, with his "irresponsible disconnected aesthetic mentality," does not see the whole picture in its running entirety. In scientific reality, human existence is a continuous "tissue and succession of births [in which the individual] is after all only the transitory custodian of an undying gift of life."[168] Lost to the everyday illusion of personality, Theotocopulos thinks that his episodic *now* has a life of its own. He mistakes his "transitory bodily independence" for individuality, as though each frame of the human movie were free to detach itself and run loose. But the cosmic truth is, "the personal life is not a freedom, though it seems to us to be a freedom."[169] Egotism is a subjective error that the Social Idea teaches us to unlearn; and so the way is cleared for merging our mortal selves with the immortal life of the Great Being, as embodied in the undying organic state. "The fundamental art of life is to recover the sense of that great self-forgetful continuous life from which we individuals have budded off."[170]

Little does Theotocopulos realize that the true nature of art and life is to be found in the biological wisdom of *The Science of Life,* book two of Wells's Bible of World Civilization. The studio setting in which he makes his address, then, is of symbolic importance. It shows him to be a heretic, dissenting from the biblical truths of the new religion of humanity.

Speaking against the ultimate reality of the continuous life, as it flows there in the studio before his very eyes, in the symbolic movement of the human filmstrip, he makes his pathetic appeal for a return to the little life of everydayism. "Between the dark past of history and the incalculable future let us snatch to-day—and live. What is the future to us?" (TTC:122).

In doing so, he demonstrates a total and irreconcilable discord between himself and Oswald Cabal, between the man of art and the man of science, between the irresponsible aesthetic mentality and the truly creative scientific mind. This war to the knife between the two outlooks is basic to Wellsism. After all, Michael Korda, whose father designed the sets under the guidance of Frank Wells, tells us, the main point of the film is to argue "the relative merits of science and the humanities," to the effect "that science and ordinary human concerns are necessarily incompatible."[171]

Science and the humanities—these are "the two cultures" named by C.P. Snow in his famous lecture by that title. His point, however, was to argue for intellectual dialog between them.[172] It is not something that everybody agrees to. Today, Wells would find himself siding with Charles Galton Darwin, grandson of *the* Charles Darwin who, in a recent book with a cosmic title worthy of his ancestor, wrote in *The Next Million Years* that science is the *only* culture deserving of the name, because its impersonal truths make the humanities obsolete. Humanistic wisdom is parochial and divisive, based as it is on the feeling-tone of immediate human experience. But science rises above artistic feelings about the nature of life. "The Scientific Revolution has introduced ways of thinking, which can claim a quality of universality, because they are objective and nearly independent of aesthetic tastes."[173]

As if the experience of life itself were not universal—and "so breathtakingly serious," as Pasternak says. But Wells will have none of this. Addressing himself to university professors of the educational establishment he asks, "Why let this poisonous pretence that the Humanities as you call them, these stale scraps of past thought, are Wisdom and that Science is not?" For him, "the dear old Humanities [are] all so much mental thumb-twiddling." They never get things done in the world, with their academic back and forth about the relative values of this or that, "religions, philosophies, moralities, customs, social organizations of all sorts." But there is an answer to these questions that goes beyond the variety of aesthetic verdicts, whereby "sound thinking and sufficient knowledge can dominate feeling. Most of this stuff about incurable differences of opinion is nonsense, brains are as alike as eggs. You can beat them up or boil them hard or scramble them or poach them or let them go rotten. But cook them the same way and they will come out very much alike."[174]

Science is for Wells the cookery by which his "Educational Dictatorship" will teach the truth of the Social Idea. "The Socialist state is therefore the educational state;.the terms are synonymous. . . . Education for service must replace education for 'getting on in the world,' just as production for use must replace production for profiteering."[175] This is altogether in accord with Saint-Simonian doctrine. As the Master said, "Man only exists for society and society educates him for itself."[176]

Or as Wells has it, the purpose of education is to make known "the intentions of the state to the common citizen." It exists for the collective good, "to subdue the individual."[177] There is no real difference "between education proper and the prevention and punishment of crime" (WWHM:864). The two amount to the same thing. Thus "education is to a large extent repression— discipline" (692). If Vishnu is to be disanimated, then "Progress is only possible through repression" (878).

Like Darwin's grandson, Wells is equally cosmic in identifying science with something universal and unifying. It goes with Brahma the Creator, as art goes with Vishnu the antiscientific preserver of tradition. Theotocopulos the artist is clearly an avatar of Vishnu, as Oswald Cabal, the scientific Brahmin is an avatar of Brahma. The one stands for contentment with "the thing that was and still is." Theotocopulos is one of those "undeveloped lives [that] do nothing to carry life on. They are just vain repetitions. . . . All that they feel has been felt, all that they do has been done better before." Whereas the other stands for the "Religion of Progress."[178] Oswald Cabal embodies "the spirit of Eternal Creation," which is none other than the spirit of science (WM:4). As Cabal himself says, "it is the nature of life to drive on. The most unnatural thing in life is contentment" (TTC:103).

These two men thus represent those "two fundamental opposites in human affairs as we know them—creation and tradition." It is a "conflict between past claims and future achievement."[179] Their pending struggle over the Space Gun is part of a cosmic struggle as the gun's very name signifies. New frontiers face mankind, to be opened or closed by force. The outcome depends on who is allowed to hold the sword of Siva. The firing of the Space Gun or the stoppage of its firing is a portent of all this, for "the essential and permanent conflict in life is a conflict between past and future, between the accomplished past and the forward effort" (STTC:35).

Vishnu	**Brahma**
(Reactionary Right)	(Radical Left)
humanities	science
past-regarding	future-regarding
legal	creative
vain repetition	progress
aesthetic	utilitarian
sentiment	rationality
tradition	design
custom	plan
everydayism	the Human Adventure
individualistic humanitarianism	inhumane humanitarianism
natural man	collective man
family	State family
Normal Social Life	the Great State
medieval	modern
insanitary	tidy
confusion	order
militarism	industrialism
nation states	world state
private-profit capitalism	state capitalism (socialism)
self-interest	the Social Idea
egotism	altruism
old political class	the new class
popular power	state power

It appears, then, that this conflict between art and science is more than a philosophical war of the two cultures. It is a deadly war of internecine ferocity between two irreconcilable political parties, conservative and progressive. In fine, between the reactionary Right and the revolutionary Left—with Vishnu on the Right and Brahma on the Left. The one side pushes for continuous movement, the other moderates. But for Wells, everything to the right of radical progress is a reactionary danger.[180]

It is true, for all this bipolar conflict, that Wells explains the film as a drama of triangular struggle between all three powers of the Hindu trinity. But as we have already seen, it is resolved by a coupling of powers between Brahma and Siva against Vishnu. The destructive force of Siva is but the common medium of action between the other two deities. The spirit of Vishnu possessing the masses is conquered by the Modern State only because its Brahmins killed off popular power by taking the sword of Siva into their exclusive hands. The forceful power of Siva still exists, but it is now out of play for one of the two remaining sides. In dialectical logic, two opposite tendencies are linked together through a middle term. What Wells calls the film's "Indian vision of life" is just that sort of dialectic (WM:4). That is why, without any logical contradiction, he is able to think of this triune polarity as a dualistic system of contraries.

While these opposites relate in the first instance to the two cultures, by giving them a political quality, right or left, much else can be deified as Vishnu or Brahma as well, not alone art and science. Almost anything can be sorted out in terms of the two cultures, the humanistic mind "dominated by accep- tance," as against the scientific mind which does not accept the times, but "conditions the times" (STTC:302). Among the many things Wells makes ir- reconcilable by this duality are listed opposite; he assigns these to one political camp or another, reactionary or radical, given his "hard distinction between . . . the legal (past-regarding) and the creative (future-regarding) minds."[181]

Theotocopulos, in standing up for art and life, is thus a reactionary in many other aspects as well, raising the populace against everything the totally progressive Modern State stands for. In the Wellsian "War with Tradition," which is a war of the two cultures, the scientific revolution is all- comprehensive, making for "freedom from tradition" in every aspect of life.[182] In this all-out war, Theotocopulos is a dangerous enemy. He would bring a halt to the dynamics of "Eternal Creation" (WM:4). Which is to say, he dares to oppose the essential principle on which the totalitarian state is founded – its lawlessness. For that is what Brahma's creativity really means. Writes William Henry Chamberlin in his classic study, *Collectivism: A False Utopia,*

> The collectivist state is omnipotent. It can make and break laws of any description between breakfast and dinner, without worrying about courts and constitutions. It can imprison, exile, expropriate, execute any of its citizens without any nonsense about due process of law or trial by jury of one's peers.[183]

George Orwell was later to say the same; in the "totalitarian idea . . . there is no such thing as law, there is only power."[184]

Wells means the same by his war on tradition. The past-regarding legal order is overthrown by a private cult of future-regarding radicals who, like Lenin's partymen, are "justified in seizing and socializing" by the "extravagant illegality" of confiscated power itself.[185] "Realization of a new state of civilised society will be the work of an intelligent minority, it will be effected without the support of the crowd and quite possibly in spite of its dissident." As no legal system has ever voluntarily abolished itself in favor of another system, "The legal standing of such old, obstructive, entrenched rights will have to be changed by imposing – in a manner essentially illegal – a different legal stand- ing upon them."[186]

Theotocopulos concludes his talk on art and life with a call for revolt. "Make the Space Gun the symbol of all that drives us . . . and destroy it now" (ttc:869b). He demands that Cabal "leave our human lives alone" (TTC:122). This message wins instant favor among the masses. "A man has a right to do what he likes with himself," is one typical response (WM:50). The talk strikes fire, and the rebellion is on.

Oswald Cabal is abashed. What? "Can mankind rise against itself?" How can this be, "now [that] we have no downtrodden classes. Everyone does a share of the work and everyone has a share in the abundance" (TTC:129). In the organic state, the exploitation of a downtrodden laboring class is abolished; and everybody has work, if only in the labor camps, because it is illegal to be unemployed. All belong to the same unified producer class of *industriels*, and its wealth is collective wealth by definition. But the people know better. They cannot eat social property. What they have in shared plenty are only state recipes for cooking all brains to the same ideological consistency. Still, that's what "ethical reconstruction" is all about.[187] Is not the unity of mankind in doctrinal brotherhood morally superior to the old divisive getting and keeping of private ownership? Collective ideals are sufficient unto themselves. "Pay, honors and the like cease to be the inducement of effort. Service, and service alone, is the criterion that the quickened conscience will recognize."[188] Or as the future historian writes, "'plenitude' of life was now only to be attained by living in relation to the Modern State. All other living was 'waste'" (STTC:255f). Now at last "man has learnt the real lesson of plenty, that far more important than getting things is getting rid of things. We are rich universally because we are no longer rich personally" (409f). Thus is totalitarian poverty justified.

As the mob gathers force, Cabal's chief of police comes in, his official title being "Controller of Traffic and Order" (TTC:127). He advises Cabal that the Space Gun is "in urgent danger. It's a race against time to save it" (ttc:911f). Worse news, he says he has no Gas of Peace ready to hand (916). But the head of the Space Gun's astronomical department arrives to say that it's possible to be fired before the mob gets there (924–26).

All then rush off by helicopter to conduct the experiment ahead of schedule. In the event, the mob gets there at the same time. But just as well. When the gun is fired, the rebellion is literally crushed by the concussion.

Of symbolic importance here is the fact that the Controller of Traffic and Order is dressed, unlike Cabal in Brahma's white, "in a dark costume" (TTC:127)—that is, in Siva's death-dealing black. He is one of the state's Auxiliary Guardians, entrusted with the use of administrative force in carrying out its creative ideas. In keeping with this, his name is Morden Mitani, an abbreviated spelling of Morden[t] Mitan[n]i. The Mitanni were an ancient Indoeuropean tribe in Asia Minor who invented the then invincible war chariot, and a mordent is a melodic figure of music in which the principal tone is trilled with an auxiliary tone. To apply this musical figure of speech to Plato's ideal republic, his principal or Perfect Guardians are "trilled" with his Auxiliary Guardians. Wells fancies the same in his world state, whose alternating forces of Brahma the Creator and Siva the Destroyer are the basis of its "aggressive peace." The Samurai partymen of the world of 2036 have both right and might on their side, and the rebellion is crushed with a musical grace note. Their *pax mundi* is upheld, as occasion demands, by warring on their own subjects. Indeed, it is Mitani who fires the gun in Cabal's name.

Tyranny of Truth

With Cabal at the controls of the helicopter, he flies his passengers out to the Space Gun. These include the two youths who are to be fired around the moon in a manned capsule, in a creative act of experimental science that serves also to destroy Theotocopulos and his followers. The firing of the Space Gun is a dialectical act of creative destruction, as are all the progressive actions of a past-disregarding scientific state in its on-going war with tradition, sentiment, and feeble aestheticism.

The two are a Utopian couple of the new generation, unisexually devoted to the mission, with no love interest in each other. The education state has at least remade *them* over into the image of collective man. They are Cabal's daughter and the son of Raymond Passworthy, who serves the World Council as one of its kinetic executives, in charge of "General Fabrics" (ttc:845), administering the planet's textile plants. Raymond is the grandson of Pippa Passworthy and retains the conservative soul-stuff of his ancestor. Less radical than the poietic Cabal, his leader, he balks at the moon mission because it is dangerous; he fears for the life of his son. Yet he is worthy enough to pass as a managerial guardian in the second rank of Direction, under the more perfect party intellectuals.

This is as it should be, in the new model of revolution as set forth by De Windt/Cabal. The future historian recalls how this model was put into effect under the Air Dictatorship.

> First came the [poietic] intellectuals, men living aloof from responsibility.... Like De Windt they planned everything and achieved no more than a plan. Such men are primarily necessary in the human adventure, because ... they reveal more and more clearly and imperatively the course that lies before the race and in that task their lives are spent and justified. Then it is that the intelligent executive type, capable of concentration upon a complex idea once it is grasped ... comes into action. Their imaginative limitation is a necessary virtue for the task they have to do.... The rather unimaginative forcible type is the necessary [kinetic] executive of the revolution, and the benefit of the revolution is entirely dependent upon the soundness of the ideology with which he has been loaded [STTC:259].

Passworthy is a worthy kinetic or auxiliary type, for all his lack of creative thought, as is Morden Mitani, an example of the "unimaginative forcible type," whose only task, after all, is the administration of force at the command of the ideology.

Both of these men, with the two youths, are aboard the helicopter flown by Oswald Cabal. Looking out the window as they approach their destination, they see the Space Gun in the distance "like a great metallic beast" (TTC:135). It is emphatically a gun, complete with beady gun sight, aiming skyward in a steely show of the state-monster's fearsome power and bold intentions. Its thick-set gleaming barrel of cloud-capped height is the church steeple of a world theocracy, and the very engine of its dialectical truth. Passing by and around it is an overhead rail system, with cars hung from it going back and forth, part of the world's network of surface transportation.

This latter is derived from a system of "telpherage," an Aerial Ropeway, that Wells helped develop for munitions transport during the Great War.[189] Used in combat at that time, telpherage is not a forgotten technology for civilian transport in the world of 2036. It is the physical means by which the new social Leviathan swallows its world citizens and moves them about as a fluid labor force, wheresoever duty calls.

The Space Gun itself is derived from Jules Verne's *Columbiad*, the space cannon in *From the Earth to the Moon*. Himself a Saint-Simonian socialist, Verne wrote this novel during the fourth year of the American Civil War. Pondering on American wartime technology, he wondered how it might be converted to peacetime industry, in accord with the Master's doctrine. How redirect these destructive energies to a creative project? His answer, as the war concluded, was to symbolically melt down its entire arsenal of cannons in the casting of the *Columbiad*, for the development of interplanetary travel.

But its experimental moonshot is not America's project alone. While a spinoff of her military technology, the Baltimore Gun Club that initiated the project raises funds for it from a worldwide subscription. All humanity is drawn into it with collective enthusiasm. The Gun Club itself is internationalized on the model of the Council of Newton, as it calls upon scientific talent from around the globe, including the world's astronomers to track the moon capsule in flight. However, the Gun Club's council of directors wins to its purpose the happy collaboration of the entire American labor force, organized on a gigantic scale as one national workshop, united in a common purpose.

Thus we have a parable of the Saint-Simonian industrial world-state. Theology and war are replaced by science and technology in one outstanding symbol of united interests, the *Columbiad*. The space cannon is an achievement of peaceful industrial science, marking the end of man's exploitation by man, and inaugurating the future exploitation of nature by man in universal association. *From the Earth to the Moon* celebrates the romantic globalism of Saint-Simon's dictum, "The whole earth belongs to mankind." In its exalted atmosphere of class collaboration, between Direction and Labor in the service of mankind's conquest of the material world, it is a technocratic hymn to the copartnery of knowledge and work, science and toil.[190]

We need not suppose, as have some critics, that Wells was ignorant of rocket power. Neither was Verne, for that matter, who uses rockets to guide and direct his moon capsule once it is launched by explosive gun powder from a huge artillery piece. A gigantic cannon better suits his ideological purpose, as it does for Wells, who borrowed from Verne on these grounds alone. His up-dated technical idea of electrical fire power adds nothing to the Space

Gun's plausibility. Wells chose to ignore rocketships for the sake of a vehicle more in keeping with Saint-Simonian symbolism.

So much for *Things to Come* as a failed prophecy of the means of space travel. Its prophecy lies elsewhere, in the political not the technological realm. For the Space Gun is not for the conquest of space, but for "the conquest of the social order."[191] With its gun sight and military bearing, it is in fact a weapon of civil war between state and society, party and people.

As the mob approaches it, the young couple enter the projectile, which is then muzzle-loaded into the gun barrel with a gantry crane (ttc:963ff). Theotocopulos makes a speech from the distance, somehow amplified so that Cabal can hear his complaint (972–986). Science is always changing things, it goes against nature. Cabal answers him. "It is not we who war against the order of things, but you. Either life goes forward or it goes back. That is the law of life" (TTC:139). For Cabal, the law of life is the law of historical movement. It is the dialectical law of the excluded middle. Either Siva sides with the movement of radical Progress, or else the sword is on the side of Reaction and popular power, and so we are returned to barbarism. As Cabal says, either we drive on "to new and greater destinies," or else it is "death and decay for mankind" (115, 113).

But Theotocopulos is not persuaded by this argument. For him, the law of life is everyday living. "We mean to destroy that gun." Cabal, who thinks that only humanistic arty types have made the rebellion, asks, "And how will you do that?" Theotocopulos indicates that he has rebel engineers on his side. "Oh! We have electricians with *us* too" (TTC:137).

All the more reason why humanistic intellectuals are a danger to the technocratic state. Their dissident habits are likely to infect its technical intelligentsia. That is why in the Soviet Union, we are told by one critic of its *de facto* technocracy, that "Science and engineering have replaced law and the humanities as the prestige disciplines of study in the state university apparatus."[192] To prevent such infection, the technical schools under the Air Dictatorship had made the attempt of "distinguishing what was essential science from what was treasonable thought" (STTC:265).

Evidently this didn't work out. And so Theotocopulos now has his followers to urge on. "Destroy the gun!" (ttc:986). As it pulls up on its colossal shock absorbers before firing, men and women in the thousands advance upon it, clambering up ladders, girders and latticework, swarming over platforms, through passageways and in spaces below the gun. Cabal calls out, "Beware of the concussion! Beware of the concussion!" (989). And he repeats again, "Beware!" (TTC:140). Three times he warns, and disappears into the concussion chamber.

What he says three times is true, for Cabal rules by science, the "power of the thing that is provably right."[193] But the rebels heed not. The gun fires, and they are extinguished.

The film's promotional ads and posters boasted a cast of thousands. Big budget cinema—20,000 extras! All of them wiped out in one cruel blow by the concussion of the Space Gun. Invincible truth has the power to smite wrong doers dead in mass murder.

As Ernest Renan said, "Truth will one day be power."[194] Renan, a French philosophical writer in the Saint-Simonian tradition, is the author of *The Future of Science* (1891), the decisive classic of post–Christian rationalism in which he prophesied, "Science is a religion, science henceforth will make all creeds." It is to be "the sole definite religion."[195] The future of science is to be, as Wells agrees from his own reading of this text, "the religion of the future." Or better, science in the form of scientism is to be the *ideology* of the future, a coercive system of doctrinal thought aptly described by Wells as a case of "political religiosity." Because it is the only faith that is provably right, it is the business of a technocratic state to teach and enforce that truth. In the Master's words, those of Saint-Simon himself, "Religion is the sum of the applications of general science by which the enlightened govern the ignorant."[196]

This is what Renan means when he says that truth will one day be power.

> The ignorant will see the effects and will believe; theory will be verified by its applications. A theory which shall lead to the invention of terrible engines, overpowering and subjugating all, will establish truth by irrefragible evidence. The forces of humanity will thus be concentrated in a very small number of hands, and become the property of league capable of regulating the life of the planet, and of, by that threat, terrifying the whole world. On the day when a few persons favored of reason shall really possess the means of destroying the planet, their supremacy will be established; these privileged persons will rule by means of absolute terror, because they shall have in their hands the life of all....
>
> Thus we can imagine a time when a group of men might, by undisputed right, reign over the rest of mankind. Then would that power be reestablished as a reality which the popular imagination used formerly to ascribe to magicians. Then the idea of spiritual power, that is to say, a power having intellectual superiority as its basis, would be a reality. Brahmanism prevailed for centuries through the belief that a Brahman could, by his glance, strike any one dead against whom his wrath was kindled. This belief, resting as it did on a complete error, could not offer a very firm basis; but some day, perhaps, science may possess a similar power unmixed with delusion. The superiority of her resources will be so great that rebellion will be out of the question.... A spiritual power will be really strong only when it is furnished with arms, when it has in its hands a material force belonging exclusively to itself; that is to say, when it has the means of restraining its enemies in an effective way, as the Brahman held his enemies in check, in an imaginative way, by the terror of his glance....
>
> Well! I sometimes dream an evil dream; I fancy an authority will some

day have hell at its command, not a chimerical hell of whose existence there is no proof, but a veritable one.[197]

The new Brahmins who rule under Cabal's Educational Dictatorship have just that sort of verifiable magic at their command. The Space Gun fires, "Brahma the Creator asserts himself over Vishnu the Preserver [*i.e.,* Possessor — *ed.*]" (WM:02), and the ignorant are instructed. Not that the dead can be instructed. Yet "political executions" are an educational service of the Modern State all the same (STTC:344). Terrorism works.

"When I say that Socialism's mission is to teach," says Wells, "I do not mean that its mission is merely a verbal or a mental one; it must use all instruments." A socialist education is "education with steel in it."[198] For "Utopia is only a home for those who have learned the way," and its animal-like quadrupeds, its defective "unteachables," will have to be killed off. "Utopia will have to purge itself [of its] incurably egotistical dissentients."[199] Or to use a word more familiar to us from the Soviet Union, its dissidents. But the "educational guardians" of the Modern State (STTC:421) "have an idea that will make the killing worth the while; like Abraham, they will have the faith to kill." Theirs is the faith in the power of scientific truth, as made into a state religion, to "supply teaching, coercive and directive services to the whole world."[200]

Coercion as a public service! Yes; because like the purges of Stalin's Great Terror, the killing that has to be done is "exemplary." In the Soviet Union, under its Man of Steel, punishment is divorced from moral desert; it rather serves a policy of calculated fright. On that model says Wells, numbering himself among socialist policy makers, "We kill the traitor not to serve him out, but *pour encourager les autres.*"[201] Political executions are instructive because they terrorize others into compliance. It is in this imitation of Stalin that John Cabal carries out the exemplary killings of his Air Dictatorship. "[W]ho serves a particular state or a particular ownership in despite of the human commonweal is a Traitor" (STTC:318). For that reason his Airmen are said to be "men of steel, men of knowledge, men of power" (WM:28), setting the pattern for his grandson's great purge in the film's climax.

But is there any validity to Wellsism? Is it really true that Oswald Cabal governs out of some truth the rest of us are missing? It doesn't matter. His firing of the Space Gun, with its purgative payoff, has its own logic. It is not so much truth that prevails, but the force that backs it up. Siva is on the side of Brahma now, and that's all that counts. Cabal's command over the hellish means of mass cruelty and death is in itself sufficient. Placed into irrevocable power by a previous generation of Airmen proficient in war, he has translated their horrible skill into the preventive terrors of his Educational Dictatorship.

As one of the Soviet Union's dissidents has it, "The object is not to show that the [party] is right, but that it is necessary to agree with it."[202] Truth is whatever illegality the totalitarian state can get away with.

Reaching for the Stars

Oswald Cabal watches the flight of the moon projectile on a huge mirror, framed in the by now standard fixtures of Streamlined Moderne. It reflects a view of the starry sky from the projected light of a monstrous telescope, all knobs and gnarls of glorified precision. Here, in this ultraprogressive setting, "the spirit of Eternal Creation emerges to plain statement in the concluding speech of the film" (WM:4).

For this occasion, Cabal has added to the Brahminic white of his basic tunic a black sash and black harness over both shoulders. The speech celebrates his resolute act of creative destruction—a clearing of the way for the progress of human destiny—in accord with the law of movement "from things that are past and done with for ever to things that are altogether new." This is the great truth of the Hindu dialectic; "no evolutionary process that does not involve death and birth, putting an end to old things and beginning again with new things, can ever bring about the new world implicit in science."[203] Costumed in the colors of the two Hindu deities who now hold joint sovereignty over Vishnu, Cabal dresses the part in speaking to the film's theological premise:—"Brahma the Creator from whom all new things proceed" makes them come forth and be new with the aid of Siva the Destroyer, in his on-going testing of "everything effete and feeble" accumulated from the past (WM:4).

Standing next to Cabal is Passworthy, also dressed over his white in Siva's black sash and harness; but the latter covers only one shoulder, the measure of his auxiliary status and lack of poietic imagination. He does his kinetic duties. But as a mere administrator in the second rank of Direction, he falls short of the creative wisdom that guides him. Only Cabal, number one in wisdom and number one in force, holds both these qualities in his own person; he is Plato's king bee, presiding over his party functionaries who specialize in these two qualities, each to their rank as Perfect Guardians or as Auxiliary Guardians.

Ordinarily, Cabal stands aloof in his white, making plans. But now, he must take on the burden of deciding what to do with the black, his kinetic executives, whose violence it is his to direct when administrative violence is needed. Yet Passworthy only half understands his leader's will and purpose; and so is only half garbed in black, reflecting at this crucial hour his lack of imagination and his doubts about the whole lunar experiment. What if the two don't make it back, he asks. Then others will go, replies Cabal.

Passworthy is dismayed. "Oh God, is there never to be any age of happiness? Is there never to be any rest?" Cabal reminds him of the doctrine of merger immortality on which the scientific truth of their regime is founded. "Rest enough for the individual man. Too much and too soon, and we call it death. But for Man no rest and no ending. He must go on. Conquest beyond conquest.... And at last out across immensity to the stars" (ttc: 1044f).

Man, the collective being of the species, has not the weakness to rest and die as has the individual. For Man there is no resting, no having of the Now of everydayism, only the growing and becoming that is the Human Adventure, progress eternal. In serving that growth of the Great Being, the party members of the Modern State Society are its vanguard adults. In serving the Great State, the "individual forgets the doomed and defined personal story that possessed his immaturity, the story of mortality, and merges himself in the unending adventure of history and the deathless growth of the race." Whereas the desire for happiness and contentment "with existing things is damnation. It is a surrender to limitations."[204]

Passworthy is not imaginative or adult enough to rise above these limitations. He worries that we humans are "such little creatures. Poor humanity, so fragile, so weak – little animals" (ttc:1047). Cabal sets him straight by posing the alternatives in the starkest of dialectical terms, between being and nothingness.

> Little animals, eh? And if we're no more than animals we must snatch each
> little scrap of happiness and live and suffer and pass, mattering no more
> than all the other animals do or have done. It is this [looking down at the
> pit of death beneath the telescopic mirror] or that [looking up at the mir-
> ror's display of stars]. All the universe or nothingness [1048f].

Then comes the *Chorale*, the two men fade out against the stellar background, and only the stars remain, cold and remote. The musical finale becomes dominant, and Cabal's voice is heard over the singing of the soundtrack's angelic choir, "Which shall it be, Passworthy? Which shall it be?" (ttc:1049).

And then one final and conclusive and god-like repetition. "A louder stronger voice reverberates through the auditorium: WHICH SHALL IT BE?" (TTC:142).

It's not much of a choice – all the universe or nothingness. It's no-limit progress or damnation, the "overriding idea of a greater state, or nothing." Socialism means "the establishment of the world state as a duty," or else we are lost to the "inconsecutive suffering of animal life," damned to the nothingness of vain repetition, "the old cycle of mating and love and struggle and personal competition."[205]

Instead, there is to be Brahma's eternal war, with the aid of Siva, against Vishnu. The world revolution makes for "no stable Utopia." "Utopia must not be static but kinetic."[206] For "as the struggle about the Space Gun shows, all three Powers are still eternally alive and at work in the world" (WM:02). Utopia is always in the process of becoming, or else the future is undone by a failure "to resist the causation of the past." Socialism must always be in the building, in the open-ended creativity of "the racial adventure under the captaincy of God," who is the collective mind and purpose of the human race. "He brings mankind not rest but the sword."[207] Or as the poet Henry Vaughan said, "God ordered motion, but ordained no rest."

Passworthy, in wanting a rest from the revolutionary business of eterniz-
ing progress, deserves our sympathy, no matter how obtuse Wells makes out
his conservative belief in limits to be. When he hears Cabal talk about overcoming "all the laws of mind and matter that restrain" the human creature
from reaching the planets and crossing "immensity to the stars," there to conquer "all the deeps of space and all the mysteries of time," and then to be told
that with that, Man still "will be beginning" (ttc:1045f) — hearing all this, he has
good reason for thinking of outer space as "that outer Horror" (891). It is the
nihilistic horror of reaching for impossible goals at the disregard of common
sense reality, loftily dismissed by Wells as "everydayism." For the obedient
citizen who surrenders himself to the immortal soul of the species, it's the
nihilism of civil death; for the disobedient ones, it's the labor camp or the
firing squad. Either way, the choice is nothingness.

Theotocopulos had portrayed the Space Gun as a symbol of the regime's
"insensate straining towards strange and inhuman experiences," not merely
for its ambition to conquer outer space, but for its fanatical zeal to conquer
the inner space of human personality and the private life. As a spokesman for
everydayism he says, "We are content with the simple, sensuous, limited
lovable life of man and we want no other" (TTC:122). For that appeal to common sense, he is destroyed. He and all his followers numbering 20,000 men
and women — all the extras boasted of in the film's promotional literature. All
killed by the discharge of the Space Gun, whose firing out of the regime's
ideological grudge against reality they dared to stop.

What better symbol of the totalitarian state? In its conquest of society, the
preferred method is colossal homicide on an industrial scale. After all, the true
task of a technocracy is not production but control. Its first order of business
is not to create wealth, but to administer order and unity among the mass of
producers, that is, to vanquish the desiring spirit of Vishnu indwelling in
them. Not conquest of the material world, but a moral victory over the un-
socialized natural man is the mission. The common man will have to be
"socialised entirely against his natural disposition in the matter," until he is
"[n]o longer a self-sufficient being" (STTC:428f).

This explains why no institution is more central to the totalitarian state
than its annihilation camps, the so-called corrective labor camps. Bernard
Crick who, significantly, is George Orwell's biographer, rejects the motive of
sadism and rather finds for motives of the highest idealism. He reasons that
the abstract claims of Soviet ideology to have socialized man are so important,
that they must be proved correct at any cost. The inmate of the Gulag system
loses not only his identity as a citizen, he is forcibly deprived of his personal
identity as well. He becomes, in Orwell's term in *Nineteen Eighty-Four*, an "un-
person." This is by way of proving out the socialist truth that individual incentives belonging to private life no longer count for anything in the collectivized
life.

In thus accounting for the Gulag horrors as well as the Nazi Holocaust,
Crick writes,

The general theory of totalitarian ideology cannot be proved true while there is the slightest spark of absolute personality alive in its actual or potential opponents. Only when the individual is stripped of all previous social identity and finds he has nothing else to fall back upon, only then can it be seen that the general theory of ideology is true; *that there is nothing in the world but social identity—the individual is independent in nothing.*[208]

But of course there may be a more practical explanation. The Social Idea, after all, is not in the least social in its idealism. Collective man is really atomized man, his independent group life destroyed. To dislocate the social fabric in this manner certainly is helpful in stopping any coherent opposition to what otherwise is nothing more than plain old-fashioned despotism. Perhaps the idealism is only a cover story.

At all events, Wells is in tune with the other ideologues of socialism when, as we have seen from the title of one of his pamphlets, he thinks of it as a radical project to annihilate "the illusion of personality." To him, selfhood is not real; it is a dream-like delusion arising from ignorance of biological reality. The truth is that man was *made* for subdivision, because we are in fact merely corpuscles in the Great Being. If only we could be taught to know this! At the same time, Wells is aware that personality, like hope, springs eternal. Despite the efforts of his Educational Dictatorship to make "the whole educational framework militant" (STTC:398), as in Plato's police-and-propaganda regime, he knows that it will always have the likes of Theotocopulos and other romantic rebels against depersonalization to deal with. Hence the need for the corrective labor camps in perpetuity. "No revolution is secure without re-education."[209]

Come the revolution, he warns, if you do not conform, "there is nothing to prevent it declaring you, quite dogmatically, a criminal or a lunatic. [It will] try to alter you. . . . It may have to kill you." The lesson to be learned is "that damnation is really over-individuation and that salvation is escape from self into the larger being of life."[210] First offenders against the piety of the revolution's religion of humanity get a second chance, however, in the re-education camps. As Wells wrote in 1905, anticipating the territorial islands of the Gulag archipelago,

> In remote and solitary regions these enclosures will lie, [these] islands of exile . . . fenced in and forbidden to the common run of men, [and] there the defective citizen will be schooled. There will be no masking of the lesson: "which do you value most, the wide world of humanity, or this evil trend in you?"

If that does not work, "then kill."[211]

Moreover, such unteachables will "not only be killed, but disposed of in an entirely sanitary manner," so much social dirt to be flushed through "the excretory organs of the state."[212] Ever the social prophet, Wells coined this phrase about his world state's "excretory organs" as early as 1899, only to have it echoed in the words of Aleksandr Solzhenitsyn, who says that the Gulag death camps are referred to by their administrators as a "sewage disposal system."[213] They, too, equate mass annihilation with hygienic purging.

But this equation for Wells is only to be expected in his "Utopia of cleanliness," a sanitary image of his college days, going all the way back to 1887.[214] Carried over to his aseptic City of Health depicted in *Things to Come*, it is a "great white world" (ttc:803) made ready by the Airmen, who before had cleaned things up. Because nature continues to breed its unteachables, however, there is an ongoing need for "social sanitation." This is a job for the World Council's educational, police and medical services, combined in its bureau of "Behavior Control" (STTC:348).

Having thus anticipated the Gulag archipelago with his island-based concentration camps, which serve his Modern State as its excretory organs, Wells was not surprised to discover the real thing under Stalin (although it began with Lenin). After all, his own men of steel are trained in a scientific capacity for "rational insensitiveness," an ability to "see things unfeelingly [and] not as dreads and horrors."[215] Writing about the Gulag in 1938, he therefore spoke not of its horrors but of its therapeutic value as a cure for the disease of everydayism.

> Maybe we overestimate the value of that idle and safe, slack, go-as-you-please discussion that we English-speaking folk enjoy under our democratic regime. The concentration camp of to-day may prove after all to be the austere training ground of a new freedom.[216]

By now, we know just what new freedom he means. Freedom from the dead past. Freedom from the democratic tradition of "individualistic liberalism" (STTC:82). Freedom from "greedy egotism [and a release of the individual] into a wider circle of ideas beyond himself in which he can at length forget himself and his meagre personal ends altogether." Freedom from the Christian tradition of personal guilt, because the new collectivist ethic "repudiates the idea of Sin and Personal immortality" alike.[217] In "the age-long issue between faith in compulsion and faith in the good-will of the natural man," the makers of the Modern State opt for the former (STTC: 334).

The abolition of sin is of course an open invitation to mass murder. "Crime and bad lives are the measures of a State's failure, all crime in the end is the crime of the community." Personal guilt counts for nothing. The Modern State's new rational code of morality deals not with the qualities of individual men but with a social quantity, whereby whole categories of people may be classified as guilty because they do not fit into the regime's Utopian plans. Thus political executions and the death camps are not instituted in order to punish personal crimes; they are rather public health measures, calling for "social surgery."[218]

What Lenin described as "bourgeois humanism," Wells long before him in 1901 described as liberalism "of the humanitarian philanthropic type," given to "moral kindliness" and later described as a form of "ineffective gentleness."[219] Or as one of Lenin's executives put it, "The bourgeois kills separate individuals; but we kill whole classes."[220] That's the steely spirit of "inhumane humanitarianism" (STTC:345) shown by Oswald Cabal in firing the Space Gun at the convenient time he did, punishing a massed gathering of reactionary types at one collective blow. But he is cruel to men only to be kind to the race. In his "disinterested devotion to great ends,"[221] his higher moral purpose is doing good for Man, in despite of those incurable romantics who reject future-regarding abstractions for the concrete values of personhood in the here and now. They must go, because they resist the law of historical movement.

In the cause of saving the future, explains Wells, "We [socialists] contemplate an enormous clearance of existing things." "Socialism means a complete change, a break with history, with much that is picturesque; whole classes will vanish. [It calls for] the elimination of whole classes of nationally and socially important people." Not personally at fault, they simply inconvenience the Human Adventure by their mere existence. "Death makes for progress."[222]

"Some day—some day, men will live in a different way. There'll be a lot of dying out before that day can come." To be sure, the great impersonal days to come will have "dehumanised the world," but it will not be "inhuman in the bad sense."[223] Less human is more social, or at least more submissive. As the future historian of the Modern State writes, "Nowadays even children do not fight each other. . . . We have learnt how to catch and domesticate the ego at an early age and train it for purposes greater than itself" (STTC: 428).

Someday, the body of mankind will form one single organism, each corpuscle relieved of the individual struggle to become a responsible part of the species. It's a fraternal universe, in which all men are obliged to share a single cosmic fate.

> Man . . . does but begin his adventure now. Through all time henceforth he does but begin his adventure. This planet and its subjugation is but the dawn of his existence. In a little while he will reach out to the other planets. . . . He will bring his solvent intelligence to bear upon the riddles of his individual interaction, transmute every jealousy and passion [and make for] a continually finer and wiser race. What none of us can think or will, save in disconnected partiality, he will think collectively. Already some of us feel our merger with that greater life . . . knowing oneself indeed to be a being greater than one's personal accidents, knowing oneself for Man on his planet, flying swiftly to unmeasured destinies through the starry stillnesses of space.[224]

Such are the impossible goals of the totalitarian credo, never concerned with immediacy but only with large issues of galactic significance. Reaching for the stars, Wells would have us led to salvation by the likes of his Airmen and Samurai, "these people capable of devotion and of living lives for remote and mighty ends."[225] The trouble is, they wish to carry the rest of us along with them into that remoteness, Passworthy's "outer Horror."

It was Lenin who actually reached for that great beyond when he defined socialism in terms of Hobson's choice. To him, as we have seen, it meant a United States of the World or nothing less. Wells merely talked about a world socialist state. Yet both are revolutionary intellectuals of the same mind, inhabiting a world of pure doctrine, ignoring the everyday realities of national and cultural tradition for the everything of some universal all.

Bernard Crick writes of such visionaries, they "are never prepared to enjoy or even tolerate the present . . . they attempt to live in the future and so prophecies, or the predictions of pseudo-science, play a great part in their lives. Always some huge catastrophe will occur unless you take my medicine quickly."[226]

It's all the universe or nothingness, merger immortality or racial suicide, Utopia or oblivion. But since the ultimate meaning of history cannot be known in advance, no constructive action on the basis of prevision is possible; and so the socialist project at its most radical is necessarily one of nihilistic demolition. When Wells avows that "the present is no more than material for the future, for the thing that is yet destined to be," the only future thing inevitable is the death of civil society. But unlike Lenin, Wells was candid enough to admit, "impressed as I have always been by the inferiority of material facts to moral facts," that his own Utopian project reduced to a case of "ambitious unreality."[227]

With *Things to Come*, Wells leaves behind the most vivid record of his revolutionary dream, meant to be taken, perhaps, not for its attainability but for its high-minded laudability.

TTC on Television

Chaplin's *Modern Times* is justly famous for the seriousness of its comic intentions. But alas, *Things to Come* has earned a reputation, in its reruns on the double-digit channels of American television, as a work of failed art, comical for its all-too serious intent.

In Chicago, *Things to Come* is run least irreverently on Channel 44, twice a year, in midsummer (something to pass the heat wave with) and every Christmas (something topical), the day the film's world war breaks out. Or at least this was the case before Channel 44 recently went over to pay television. But Channel 32 still runs it as a regular stock offering, along with Japanese monster movies and other cheapo horror and science fiction flicks, on a Saturday evening program devoted to such. Like these others, *Things to Come* is interrupted during station breaks by the program's host, got up as Dracula, who steps out of his coffin every fifteen minutes to make ghoulish jokes about it, working up this Transylvanian humor as a lead-in to the local commercials.

A more elevated note of humor is hit on Channel 11, Chicago's outlet for the nation's Public Broadcasting System. It does business without commercials, for the sake of Culture with a capital C. In between Verdi operas and ecology documentaries, *Things to Come* is run for the literati with the likes of stuff shown on Channel 32, but from the vantage point of a superior outlook, in which the very same offerings are classified as "camp," that is, works of trivial content done in a high-handed manner. The stance allows for laughing at uncultured things, and the Wells film is played with the others in a regular series called "Summer Camp." But the season indicated is not strictly meteorological. More fun, it's a play on words, and "Summer Camp" can be seen repeatedly at any time of year. *Camp* is an American slang term for a homosexual brothel. By extension it applies to affected behavior, or to failed art, in which one is permitted to find amusing qualities in the mismatch between extravagant form and empty content. In accord with this cultural policy, the program's dignified host, in mock homosexual voice, pronounces *Things to Come* to be "a film of absolutely no redeeming social value whatsoever." Hence fun to watch in complete safety, strictly for laughs.

The reader of this book is asked to question judgments of that sort. A closer reading of *Things to Come* in the light of Wells's other writings, taken from his Literature of Power, reveals a refreshingly candid antidemocratic mind at work. One of the few Western intellectuals on the Left to avoid the sugary euphemisms of "'little man' democracy" on behalf of Lenin and Stalin, he is among the last after Plato to advocate salvation by force. He does so openly on the grounds that only collective submission can make a good citizen of the common man; "it is his duty to contribute such service to the community as will ensure the performance of those necessary tasks for which the incentives which will operate in a free society do not provide."[228]

In this most horrific of centuries, the socialist dream of improving man's collective lot has resulted in the creation of man's greatest disease, the totalitarian state, for which Wellsian candor is perhaps the best vaccine. Yet he himself had the wisdom to qualify himself on the likes of his Airmen, saying, "Our elite is our necessity and our menace."[229]

Elsewhere, in a total lapse from Wellsism, he spoke of Lenin as "a rotten little incessant egotistical intriguer.... He just wants power," and his Bolshevik horrors themselves want cleaning up. "He ought to be killed by some moral sanitary authority."[230]

But we shall let Sir Ivor Evans have the last word. "No one can well understand the twentieth century, in its hopes and its disillusionments, without studying Wells. Uneven as he is, the danger is always to underestimate him."[231]

REFERENCES

Preface and Acknowledgments

1. G.P. Wells, ed., H.G. *Wells in Love: Postscript to "An Experiment in Autobiography"* (London: Faber and Faber, 1984), pp. 73, 172.

2. *'42 to '44*, p. 56.

3. *God the Invisible King*, p. 96.

4. "The Silliest Film: Will Machinery Make Robots of Men?" p. 189, in *The Way the World Is Going*, pp. 179–189.

5. *The King Who Was a King*, p. 31. This is Wells's first film scenario, written just before the advent of the talkies but never produced. Its front matter explains at length his film theory, carried over in his writing of *Things to Come*.

6. Letter to Arthur Bliss, 29 June 1934. Wells Archive.

7. *The New World Order*, p. 144.

8. Michael Korda, *Charmed Lives* (New York: Random House, 1979), p. 123. Royalty statements in the Wells Archive indicate that, while the author of *The Shape of Things to Come* got a handsome £10,000 for the film rights to this novel, his income from the film *Things to Come* ran as low as one pound a year. Yet he claims it "had a considerable success from the commercial point of view." G.P. Wells, *op. cit.*, p. 211.

9. Raymond Massey, *A Hundred Different Lives: An Autobiography* (Boston: Little, Brown, 1979), p. 122.

10. Letter to Arthur Bliss, 17 October 1934. Wells Archive.

11. For the full text of this interview, see "Mr. Wells to the Screen," *Saturday Review of Literature* 13 (2 November 1935), pp. 11–12. But after the film's release he expressed disillusion, blaming the studio no less than himself. See G.P. Wells, *op. cit.*, p. 211f. But this should not disillusion *us* as to its authenticity. He later repudiated the scientific romances as well. See Patrick Parrinder and Robert Philmus, eds., *H.G. Wells's Literary Criticism* (Brighton, England: Harvester Press, 1980), p. 227f.

12. For a survey of all films based on works by Wells, see Alan Wykes, *H.G. Wells and the Cinema* (London: Jupiter Books, 1977).

13. *The Common Sense of War and Peace*, p. 31.

14. W. Warren Wager, *H.G. Wells and the World State* (New Haven: Yale University Press, 1961), p. 238. Even more unsympathetic, if not downright nasty, is Peter Kemp, *H.G. Wells and Culminating Ape* (London: Macmillan, 1982), p. 172f.

15. *Man Who Could Work Miracles*, p. vii. Based on the short story of 1898, "The Man Who Could Work Miracles." In *The Short Stories of H.G. Wells*, pp. 792–810.

16. While literary critics treat Wellsian SF with confidence, they remain shy of *Things to Come*, perhaps because it it a *film* and not a proper text. The following samples, in which we might have expected more, make only passing reference to it, if at all. Darko Suvin and Robert M. Philmus, eds., *H.G. Wells and Modern Science*

Fiction (Lewisburg, Pa.: Bucknell University, 1977); Frank McConnel, *The Science Fiction of H.G. Wells* (New York: Oxford University Press, 1981); John Huntington, *The Logic of Fantasy: H.G. Wells and Science Fiction* (New York: Columbia University Press, 1982). The appreciation of *Things to Come* is monopolized by SF fans and film buffs. For example see the following, arranged alphabetically: Allan Asherman and George Zebrowski, Introductions. H.G. Wells, *Things to Come* (Boston: Gregg Press, 1975). A reprint of the London edition of 1935, with new front matter, pp. vii–xiv and xxxiii–xlix. John Baxter, *Science Fiction in the Cinema* (New York: Paperback Library, 1970), pp. 52–64. John Brosner, *Future Tense: The Cinema of Science Fiction* (New York: St. Martin's Press, 1978), pp. 55–62 and *passim*. James Robert Parrish and Michael R. Pitts, *The Great Science Fiction Pictures* (Metuchen, N.J.: Scarecrow Press, 1977), pp. 320–322. Frederik Pohl and Frederik Pohl IV, *Science Fiction Studies in Film* (New York: Ace Books, 1981), pp. 78–90. Jeff Rovin, *A Pictorial History of Science Fiction Films* (Secaucus, N.J.: Citadel Press, 1975), pp. 15–23.

Chris Steinbrunner and Burt Goldblatt, *Cinema of the Fantastic* (New York: Galahad Books, 1972), pp. 151–176. Kenneth Von Gunden and Stuart H. Stock, *Twenty All-Time Great Science Fiction Films* (New York: Arlington House, 1982), pp. 1–13. George Zebrowski, "Science Fiction and the Visual Media," in Reginold Bretnor, ed., *Science Fiction, Today and Tomorrow* (Baltimore: Penguin Books, 1979), esp. pp. 56–61. The only exception to this genre treatment seems to be Parker Tyler, *Classics of the Foreign Film: A Pictorial Treasury* (New York: Bonanza Books, 1962), pp. 104–107. But note also the following curiosity, prepared by Educational and Recreational Guides, Inc. of Newark, N.J., for use as a study guide in high school: Alfred F. Mayhew, "A Guide to the Discussion of the Photoplay, 'Things to Come,' Based on a Scenario by H.G. Wells," *Photoplay Studies*, vol. II, no. 4 (April 1936), 14 pp. I thank Dennis Saleh, publisher of Comma Books, for bringing this to my attention.

17. Wells first pursued this ambition by appealing to the Prime Minister. See unpublished correspondence in the British Library, Wells to A.J. Balfour, 26 August 1904 (BL.Add.Mss.49856.223–24) and 10 May 1905 (BL.Add.Mss.49857.208–213). Wells complains that "it is not altogether right that my intellectual process should go under the perpetual fog & pressure of the market-place." He asks for an endowed academic position in sociology, not because he is needy for money, but so that "I could be let loose in this field for a time I could give things a trend. If I could be placed in some position that would leave my time free & relieve me from the obligation of earning at most more than five or six hundred Pounds a year, I believe I could do better and more significant work than under existing conditions." A memo from Balfour to one of his aides, dated 6 December 1905, advised that "I am not convinced that Wells stands out sufficiently to warrent the experiment." At the top of this memo the aide, a Mr. Ramsey, notes that "I wrote to Wells to explain." Wells to Ramsey, 10 December, is a defensive reply. "The suggestion I threw out to Mr. Balfour was one quite casually made and one I should have been amazed to find productive of any positve result in my case" (BL.Add.Mss.49858.93–94). Yet Wells went on in 1912 to appeal to the honorable secretary of the British Sociological Society. See S.I. Hyman, *The Sociology of H.G. Wells*, unpublished doctoral thesis (London University, 1952), p. 450n. I thank John Root, Prof. of History and Chairman of the Department of Humanities at the Illinois Institute of Technology, for discovering the BL letters for my use in this book. In the event, Wells carried out what he had in mind all along, "a text-book of Sociology that I venture would be a seminal sort of work" (Wells to Balfour, 10 May 1905), which appeared in 1931 as *The Work, Wealth and Happiness of Mankind*.

Introduction

The Whole Duty of Man

1. Anthony West, *Heritage* (New York: Washington Square Press, 1984), p. 169. Orig. pub. 1955. The author of this autobiographical novel is named after his father's mistress, Rebecca West. His long-awaited biographical study is *H.G. Wells: Aspects of a Life* (New York: Random House, 1984).

2. *After Democracy*, pp. 35, 24; *All Aboard for Ararat*, p. 73.

3. *A Short History of the World*, p. 427.

4. *The Fate of Man*, pp. 247, 44.

5. *The Future in America*, p. 52; *The New Machiavelli*, p. 499; *Mankind in the Making*, p. 4. The phrase "suns' distances" first appears in "A Talk with Gryllotalpa," *Early Writings*, p. 20. It appears again in *The War That Will End War*, p. 60f. Astronomy's cosmic vision bears on Wellsian politics, in that what is wanted are statesmen with "a sense of externality" (*The World of William Clissold*, p. 28), who can detach themselves from human interests close at hand and plan "a sun's distance away from the world of every day" (*The History of Mr. Polly*, p. 140). As the founder of the world state in *The World Set Free* advises his party followers, "Men who think in lifetimes are of no use to statesmenship. . . . You have to learn to think of yourselves . . . in relation to the sun and the stars" (pp. 74, 277). This way of thinking is how the Airmen learn to "escape from immediacy" (STTC:28), and thus rise above petty human concerns.

6. Sonia Orwell and Ian Angus, eds., *The Collected Essays, Journalism and Letters of George Orwell* (Harmondsworth, England: Penguin, 1970), vol. 1, sel. no. 151, p. 422.

7. *The Open Conspiracy*, p. 23.

8. *The World of William Clissold*, p. 83; *Social Forces in England and America*, p. 414.

9. *A Year of Prophesying*, p. 129.

Saint-Simon and the Social Idea

10. See Warren Lerner, *A History of Socialism and Communism in Modern Times* (Englewood Cliffs, N.J.: Prentice-Hall, 1982), p. 154f; Massimo Salvadori, *The Rise of Modern Communism* (Hinsdale, Ill.: Dryden Press, 1975), p. 25. Lenin's radical brand of socialism differed from the other European varieties in his idea of a state-unified world economy independent of national frameworks, subject only to a regional division of labor. He sloganized this in saying, "The United States of the World coincides with socialism." See Elliot R. Goodman, *The Soviet Design for a World State* (New York: Columbia University Press, 1960), p. 28. Wells made use of the very same slogan in his *Outline of History*. The words, "United States of the World," are emblazoned across a global map picturing "The Next Stage of History," his title and cover illustration for the book's final installment, completed in its original serialized version just prior to his Kremlin visit (London: George Newness, 1919–1920, part 24).

11. *Russia in the Shadows*, pp. 155, 162; *Stalin-Wells Talk*, p. 11.

12. *Experiment in Autobiography*, pp. 690, 68.

13. See James H. Billington, *Fire in the Minds of Men: Origins of the Revolutionary Faith* (New York: Basic Books, 1980), p. 452.

14. *The Brothers*, p. 68; *Socialism and the Scientific Motive*, p. 4.

15. *The Holy Terror*, p. 347; "What I Believe," p. 220.

16. See George Lichtheim, *The Origins of Socialism* (New York: Praeger, 1969).

17. *The World of William Clissold*, p. 172. Saint-Simon's phrase, "aristocracy of talent," is picked up by Wells in "The Man of Science as Aristocrat," p. 467.

For selected translations of the voluminous writings of Saint-Simon, see Ghita Ionescu, ed., *The Political Thought of Saint-Simon* (Oxford: Oxford University Press,

1976) and Keith Taylor, tr., *Henri Saint-Simon (1760–1825): Selected Writings on Science, Industry and Social Organisation* (New York: Holmes and Meier, 1975). For a series of public lectures given by his disciples in 1828–1829, see Georg G. Iggers, tr., *The Doctrine of Saint-Simon: An Exposition* (Boston: Beacon Press, 1958).

18. *The New Machiavelli*, p. 334; *Mr. Blettsworthy on Rampole Island*, p. 338.

19. In Keith Taylor, *op. cit.*, p. 261.

20. Emile Souvestre, *Le Monde tel qu'il sera* (Paris, 1859). For its place in the history of anti-utopian literature, see I.F. Clarke, *The Pattern of Expectation, 1644–2001* (New York: Basic Books, 1979), p. 127f.

21. The words of the disciple Bazard cited in Emile Durkheim, *Socialism and Saint-Simon* (Yellow Springs, Ohio: Antioch Press, 1958), p. 211.

22. Auguste Comte, *System of Positive Polity, or, Treatise on Sociology, Instituting the Religion of Humanity*, 4 vols. (London, 1877), vol. 4, p. 499. Comte was Saint-Simon's private secretary and wrote much under his Master's name. After Saint-Simon's death, Comte systematized their joint efforts in this and other works.

23. Saint-Simon in Keith Taylor, *op. cit.*, p. 183.

24. *Elements of Reconstruction*, p. 22; *A Year of Prophesying*, p. 346.

25. "The Lawyer in Politics," III. Page reference missing from newspaper clipping.

26. See Emile Durkheim, *op. cit.*, p. 134.

27. In Keith Taylor, *op. cit.*, p. 187.

28. See J.L. Talmon, *Political Messianism* (New York: Praeger, 1960), pp. 56, 52.

29. Cited in Frank E. Manuel, *The New World of Henri Saint-Simon* (Cambridge, Mass.: Harvard University Press, 1956), p. 255.

30. Milovan Djilas, *The New Class: An Analysis of the Communist System* (New York: Praeger, 1957), pp. 46, 45.

31. *Anticipations*, p. 187; *The New Machiavelli*, p. 212f.

32. Michael Voslensky, *Nomenclatura: The Soviet Ruling Class* (Garden City, N.Y.: Doubleday, 1984), p. 42.

33. Manuel, *op. cit.*, p. 309; Iggers, *op. cit.*, p. 244, n. 1.

34. Slogan cited in Jean Chesneaux, *The Political and Social Ideas of Jules Verne* (London: Thames and Hudson, 1972), p. 69.

35. Cited in F.A. Hayek, *The Counter-Revolution of Science*, 2d ed. (Indianapolis: Liberty Press, 1979), p. 221f.

36. See Comte, *op. cit.*, vol. 4, p. 78 and *passim*.

37. *Experiment in Autobiography*, p. 562.

38. See Raymond Aron, *Progress and Disillusion* (Harmondsworth, England: Penguin Books, 1972), p. 7.

39. *Social Forces in England...* p. 237; *Anticipations*, p. 350; *Phoenix*, p. 189.

40. *Men Like Gods*, p. 74; *The Anatomy of Frustration*, p. 77.

41. See Noel Annan, *Leslie Stephen, The Godless Victorian* (New York: Random House, 1984), pp. 266, 273.

42. Saint-Simon in Keith Taylor, *op. cit.*, p. 168. Supreme among the working brains of Saint-Simon's directive elite are the investment bankers. It is they who, when seated on the Council of Newton, will decide the flow of investment capital for the best productive results. The strategic importance of banking to the socialist project is explained at length by Wells in *The World of William Clissold*. He also took this message directly to financiers in one of their own professional journals, *The Banker*, with "Has the Money-Credit System a Mind?"

43. *The Open Conspiracy*, p. 74; *The Elements of Reconstruction*, p. 100.

44. *Democracy Under Revision*, pp. 5, 7; "Discovery of the Future," p. 326.

45. V.I. Lenin, *State and Revolution* [1917], 2d. rev. ed. (Moscow: Progress Publishers, 1965), p. 93.

46. *After Democracy,* p. 181f.
47. *Experiment in Autobiography,* p. 215.
48. Michael Voslensky, *op. cit.,* p. 171.
49. *The Open Conspiracy,* p. 78.
50. *'42 to '44,* p. 66; *Babes in the Darkling Wood,* p. 118.
51. From a letter to Sir Richard Gregory, cited in Geoffrey West, *H.G. Wells* (New York: W.W. Norton, 1930), p. 216.

The Modern State Octopus

52. *Experiment in Autobiography,* p. 69.
53. *The Outlook for Homo Sapiens,* p. 272; *The Common Sense of War...,* p. 47.
54. *'42 to '44,* pp. 32, 39.
55. *Anticipations,* pp. 202, 229.
56. *Social Forces in England and America,* p. 394.
57. *Democracy Under Revision,* p. 19.
58. "Morals and Civilization," in *Early Writings,* p. 227f.
59. *The Open Conspiracy,* p. 39.
60. Cited in Stefan T. Possony, ed., *Lenin Reader* (Chicago: Regnery, 1966), p. 330.
61. Cited in Robert C. Tucker, *The Lenin Anthology* (New York: W.W. Norton, 1975), p. 455.
62. V.I. Lenin, *op. cit.,* p. 92f.
63. Lenin cited in Salvidori, *op. cit.,* p. 176, n. 13.
64. *War in the Air,* p. 202. The phrase "collective submission" is made in reference to Prussian ideals of duty and discipline. The same is embodied by Wells in the Social Idea, once known as the Prussian Idea. Thus Wells has it in "The Ideal Citizen" (*Social Forces in England and America,* pp. 390–396) that socialism requires everybody to become a state official, with all wages and salaries paid by the state. In particular, the administration of all property is to be a salaried function as well. No private persons are permitted to exist. Thus the Prussian state-idea and Wellsian socialism are the same. See Frederich A. Hayek, *The Road to Serfdom* (Chicago: University of Chicago Press, 1976), p. 179. Orig. pub. 1944.
65. *The First Men in the Moon,* p. 305; *Phoenix,* p. 53.
66. Cited in Durkheim, *op. cit.,* p. 99.
67. See J.-Lucien Radel, *Roots of Totalitarianism: The Ideological Sources of Fascism, National Socialism, and Communism* (New York: Crane, Russak, 1975), p. 20.
68. Desmond Lee, tr., *Plato: The Republic,* 2d ed. (Harmondsworth, England: Penguin Books, 1974), p. 247. In keeping with this organic theory, Wells has it directly from Plato that, the world community of the future "will be an organism; it will rejoice and sorrow like a man. Men will be limbs – even nowadays in our public organisations men are but members. One ambition will sway the commune, a perfect fusion of interest there will be, and a perfect sympathy of feeling. Not only will there be 'forty feeding like one,' but forty writing like one, because of a toothache in its carpenter or rheumatics in its agriculturists" ("Ancient Experiments in Co-Operation," in *Early Writings,* p. 191f). But those "forty feeding like one" are a herd of cattle, so described by Wordsworth in his poem, "Written in March." One wonders what Wells has in mind when he associates this image with Plato's "ruling principle." Are citizens to be herded like cattle, in the making of the state's organic unity?
69. Cited in Georg G. Iggers, *op. cit.,* p. 28.
70. Comte, *op. cit.,* pp. 30, 44, 299.
71. *Mr. Belloc Objects,* p. 83; "H.G. Wells," p. 90.
72. *The Conquest of Time,* p. 38; *A Modern Utopia,* p. 372.

73. *Anticipations*, p. 189; *The World of William Clissold*, p. 83; *Holy Terror*, p. 450.

74. "Zoological Retrogression" (1891), in *Early Writings*, p. 168.

75. *The World of William Clissold*, p. 589; *The Conquest of Time*, pp. 36, 12.

Plato, Wells and the Hindu Trinity

76. *Experiment in Autobiography*, p. 138.

77. Plato in Desmond Lee, *op. cit.*, p. 324.

78. "A Forecast of the World's Affairs," p. 21; *The Way the World Is Going*, p. 29.

79. *Experiment in Autobiography*, p. 705.

80. See Thomas Molnar, *Politics and the State: The Catholic View* (Chicago: Franciscan Herald Press, 1983).

81. *Phoenix*, p. 48; *First and Last Things*, p. 115.

82. *Anticipations*, pp. 282, 93; *After Democracy*, p. 12.

83. *The World of William Clissold*, p. 328.

84. *God the Invisible King*, pp. 170, 61.

85. The disciple Bazord, cited in Durkheim, *op. cit.*, p. 223. Like the Saint-Simonians, Wells reserves the name of God for the idea of socialist planning. Thus he is able to declare that "God is Red" (*All Aboard for Ararat*, p. 7). Or again, in Stalin's time he said that God may be likened to "a personification of . . . the Five Year Plan" (*Experiment in Autobiography*, p. 575f).

86. See Leon Stover, "Spade House Dialectic: Theme and Theory in 'Things to Come,'" in *The Wellsian* 5 (Summer 1982), pp. 23–32.

87. *The World Set Free*, p. 273; *Experiment in Autobiography*, p. 465.

88. *Social Forces in England and America*, p. 395; *The Passionate Friends*, p. 96.

89. "A Forecast of the World's Affairs," p. 5f.

90. *The Conquest of Time*, p. 64.

91. See Leon Stover, *Stonehenge: The Indo-European Heritage* (Chicago: Nelson-Hall, 1979), chap. 5. British title is *Stonehenge and the Origins of Western Culture* (London: Heineman, 1979).

92. *Experiment in Autobiography*, p. 616; *'42 to '44*, p. 48; *Democracy Under Revision*, p. 32.

This educational trilogy, or Bible of World Civilization, is meant to serve as a model of textbook writing for the schools of the coming Modern World-State. Accordingly, says Wells, "I should like the old textbooks destroyed and burnt, and new ones written along the lines of my scheme. And the next generation should be taught from these books." This quotation is from a letter to the Russian translator of *The Outline of History*, cited by J. Kagarlitski, *The Life and Thought of H.G. Wells* (London: Sidgwick and Jackson, 1966), p. 189, n. 76. Wells is nothing if not, like Lenin, intolerant of rival ideologies. On behalf of his Communist Revision he says, "I don't believe in tolerance, you have to fight against anything being taught by anybody which seems to you harmful, you have to struggle to get your own creed taught." From a letter to Beatrice Webb, cited in her autobiographical account of the Fabian Society and her joint leadership of it with husband Sidney Webb, *Our Partnership* (New York, 1948), p. 307f.

Although freedom of expression is granted in article 5 of "The Rights of the World Citizen" (*Phoenix*, p. 189), Wells elsewhere says that free speech can be tolerated only so long as "accepted opinion is *provisional*," when there are "longer views and broader truths yet to be stated." But once the revolution heralds them, "why insist that fundamentals be criticized?" (*After Democracy*, p. 18f). Thereafter, the press will be "under oath to serve the state" ("The Lawyer in Politics," III). This just one year before the Russian Revolution of 1917. After that, the newspaper of the Communist Party, *Pravda* ("Truth"), was elevated as the official organ guarding the interests of the Soviet state.

Lenin therefore did right when "he established a very complete control of education and the Press, to keep [public thought] upon the right lines" (STTC:125).

93. *Anatomy of Frustration*, p. 191f.

94. *The War That Will End War*, pp. 11, 14.

95. Auberon Herbert, *The Right and Wrong of Compulsion by the State and Other Essays*, ed. by Eric Mack (Indianapolis: Liberty Classics, 1978), p. 254.

96. *First and Last Things*, p. 105.

97. Igor Shafarevich, *The Socialist Phenomenon* (New York: Harper and Row, 1980), p. 294.

"Things to Come": A Reading

Everydayism

1. Wells drew up a more detailed musical outline for Arthur Bliss (letter of 11 October 1934 in the Wells Archive), by way of guiding him in composing for the following thematic effects: 1. Christmas Jollity. 2. Onset of the War. WAR. 3. Ruin. 4. Pestilence. 5. Post pestilence SQUALOR. 6. Entry of the Airmen. Struggle of the Airmen. Triumph of the New Order. 7. The New World. Crescendo of conflict up to the Space Gun. [8. Finale.] This last, with its "exultant shout of human resolution," had already been composed, its theme described as "the marching song of a new world of conquest among the atoms and the stars." See letter from Wells to Bliss, dated 29 June.

2. *Guide to the New World*, p. 150; *The Open Conspiracy*, p. 93; "Experiment in Illustration," p. 54. The film's opening scenes with their study of Everytown's commonplace habits of everyday satisfaction with the given social order, recall the famous opening paragraph of *The War of the Worlds*, before the Martians invaded to shake things up.

3. Preface, *Atlantic Edition XXVII*, p. x. See also "The Human Adventure," in *Social Forces in England and America*, pp. 409–415.

4. *The Open Conspiracy*, p. 32.

5. *Ibid.*, p. 18; *God the Invisible King*, p. 71.

6. *Brynhild*, p. 19.

7. *The King Who Was a King*, p. 3.

8. Lenin cited in Ivor Montagu, *Film World* (Harmondsworth, England: Penguin Books, 1964), p. 108.

9. *The Undying Fire*, p. 454. In the same cause, Wells argued as early as 1915 for the "abolition of written books in favor of the gramophone and the cinematograph." See *The Peace of the World*, p. 35.

10. The Streamlined Moderne alphabet was designed by Walter Dorwin Teague in 1934—the year Frank Wells began doing art work for the film (mentioned by his father in a letter of 29 June to Arthur Bliss). When this futuristic alphabet was new, anything spelled with it spelled "things to come." To the film's contemporary audience, the graphics of the word CINEMA thus hinted at the World of Tomorrow revealed at the end. See Donald J. Bush, *The Streamlined Decade* (New York: George Braziller, 1975), pp. 133–153.

11. *Little Wars*, p. 100f.

12. *After Democracy*, p. 137.

13. *Are Armies Needed Any Longer?* p. 7f.

14. See Donald J. Bush, *op. cit.*, p. 38.

15. See Ludwig von Mises, *Human Action: A Treatise on Economics*, 3d rev. ed. (Chicago: Contemporary Books, 1966), p. 183.

16. This Administrative scheme accords less with the federal structure of the U.S.S.R., for all of Wells's claim to find the concept of the Modern State born with Lenin, than with the corporate structure of Fascist Italy. Mussolini's Grand Council of Fascism presided over a number of translocal Corporations, such as those for grains, wood, metals, glass, transport, building, and others. See J.-Lucien Radel, *Roots of Totalitarianism: The Ideological Sources of Fascism, National Socialism, and Communism* (New York: Crane, Russak, 1975), pp. 92–95 and 196–198. Indeed, even the economic syndications of National Socialist Germany are more in line with the Wellsian state idea. Under the leadership of Hitler's party, the government controlled a number of translocal Estates, such as those for food, industry, commerce, labor, and culture; but these were not unmixed with territorial organizations. See Radel, pp. 133–135.

But it was Wells himself who anticipated all of this in his novel of 1898, *When the Sleeper Wakes.* Set in A.D. 2100, the novel describes a world capitalist state ruled by a council of 12 trustees, under a world dictator, called the White Council. Like Raymond Passworthy, head of General Fabrics in *Things to Come,* each trustee is the chief executive officer of one or more corporations or estates. These functional domains in the novel (with only some of them territorially organized) include the following:

Labor Bureau

The Labor Companies (subsumed under the above)

Public Schools (under the Surveyor-General of Education)

The Sanitary Company

British Food Trust

Navigation Trust

Wind Vanes Control (power generation)

European Food Trust

European Piggeries (subsumed under the above)

Antibilious Pill Company

Medical Faculty Company

Wind Vane Police

Aeronautical Society (flight engineers and pilots)

Consolidated African Companies

African Agricultural Police

International Creche Syndicate

The Euthenasy Company (controls "the excretory organs of the state," p. 238)

General Intelligence Offices (propaganda)

These are the "principalities, powers, dominions—the power and the glory" of the White Council (p. 221).

When the Sleeper Wakes is treated by critics as an anti-utopian novel, no doubt because its naked state capitalism is not clothed in the rhetorical garments of socialism. Yet it pictures Wells's Utopian plan to "substitute functional associations and loyalties for local attribution" (*The Outlook for Homo Sapiens,* p. 221f). Indeed, it is full of Utopian details that carry forward into later work. For example, the unit of currency is the Lion. Lions are technocratic energy units, counted in the duodecimal system, the same as in *A Modern Utopia* of 1905. Not a few details bear on the imagery of *Things to Come.* Most notable are the building machines that lift "plastic blocks of mineral paste" into place (p. 281), as in the film's Reconstruction sequence, although here the paste is molded into thin slabs, not blocks (ttc:783–797). Also notable is a synthetic material called Eadhamite, "resembling toughened glass" (p. 162), elsewhere and much later described as "rubber glass" (*Marriage,* p. 371). In the film, "All glass is unbreakable. . . . If someone can lean against a glass pane which gives elastically without breaking— good" (WM:65).

Or again, the film's educational "history pictures" (ttc:837) carry forward the novel's prophecy of a state monopoly on the electric media. The "kinematograph and phonograph have replaced newspaper, book, schoolmaster, and letter" (p. 164). Kinematograph is a neologism covering both movies and television.

17. Trained as a biologist, Wells may have a double allusion in mind, the other more esoteric one to the pipa toad of Surinam, whose eggs become enclosed in the skin of the mother's back, each in a little pocket covered by a flap. The tadpoles develop there in seclusion until they emerge as fully formed little toads. The outside world matters as little to the preadult Pippa Passworthy, whose mature self emerges only after the revolution in the person of his grandson. For a picture and description of the pipa toad, a zoological curiosity well known to biologists, see Alfred Sherwood Romer, *Man and the Vertebrates*, 3d ed. (Chicago: University of Chicago Press, 1941), plate opp. p. 55.

18. *First and Last Things*, p. 141.

19. On John Calvin as a totalitarian prototype, see Leonard Schapiro, *Totalitarianism* (New York: Praeger, 1972), pp. 74–76, 93f. Moreover, Cabal's revolutionary program of creative destruction is in the same dialectical spirit as Calvin's for purging the established church: "The building is too rotten to be patched up. It must be torn down and in its stead a new one must be built!" Calvin cited in Lewis W. Spitz, *The Renaissance and Reformation Movements* (Chicago: Rand McNally, 1971), p. 415.

20. *Phoenix*, p. 74.

21. Robert Conquest, *V.I. Lenin* (New York: Viking, 1972), p. 105.

22. *Anticipations*, the 1914 edition, p. x.

23. *The Open Conspiracy*, p. 74. The Open Conspirators of this book's 1926 title is yet another name for Wells's neoplatonic partymen. They are variously the New Republicans of *Anticipations* (1901), the Samurai of *A Modern Utopia* (1905), The Fellows of the Modern State or New Puritans of *The Shape of Things to Come* (1936), and the Airmen of *Things to Come* (1936).

As first described for the New Republicans, they form "a sort of outspoken Secret Society" (*Anticipations*, p. 298), an "open conspiracy" indeed. In this, Wells anticipated the organization of the modern Communist Party, which is open so far as its doctrine is made public, but is a conspiratorial secret society so far as its membership is closed. See Alvin W. Gouldner, *The Future of the Intellectuals and the Rise of the New Class* (New York: Seabury Press, 1979), p. 4f.

24. Introduction to *Catalogue of an Exhibition of Lithographs of Munition Works by Joseph Pennell*, p. 3.

25. *The War That Will End War*, p. 60; *Socialism and the Family*, p. 40; *A Year of Prophesying*, p. 338.

26. *The Common Sense of War and Peace*, p. 25.

27. *First and Last Things*, p. 226f; *Phoenix*, p. 78.

28. Citation from Georg G. Iggers, tr., *The Doctrine of Saint-Simon: An Exposition* (Boston: Beacon Press, 1958), p. 28.

29. *The Brothers*, p. 69.

30. *The Way the World Is Going*, p. 7; *Apropos of Dolores*, p. 277.

31. *Anatomy of Frustration*, p. 218; *Socialism and the Family*, p. 57.

32. *A Modern Utopia*, p. 212; *Socialism and the Family*, p. 30; *New Worlds for Old*, p. 291.

33. *The World Set Free*, p. 273.

34. *The New Machiavelli*, p. 412.

35. *The World Set Free*, p. 276.

36. *Experiment in Autobiography*, pp. 400, 393.

Triumphant Catastrophe

37. *Anticipations*, p. 222.

38. *'42 to '44*, p. 27. The Airmen, in initiating "creative conflict" with Combatant States like Rudolf's, recall the policy objectives of the tankmen in "The Land Ironclads" (1903). The invading tankmen blame the defenders for making war, not themselves.

They redefine their own aggression as defensive on the grounds that the deadly technical superiority of their war machines equals moral superiority. Like the Airmen, the tankmen are engineering types, not traditional military types; they command the mechanical means to make war to end war. Their "proficiency in war [is] the hope of the world." They are "calm and reasonable men," unlike the emotional patriots on the other side, given to the businesslike discipline of their machine technology. See *The Short Stories of H.G. Wells*, pp. 115, 130.

When the Airmen finally give Rudolf's naughty children a whiff of higher civilization with their Gas of Peace, they do from the air what the tankmen do on the ground with the big guns of their invincible land ironclads. These tank engineers attack a similar lot of glory boys on horseback, who lead obsolete troops of foot soldiers in the equally obsolete cause of national sovereignty.

> For the enemy these young engineers were defeating they felt a certain qualified pity and a quite unqualified contempt.... They despised them for making war; despised their bawling patriotisms [and] the want of imagination their method of fighting displayed. "If they *must* make war," these young men thought, "why in thunder don't they do it like sensible men?" They resented ... being forced to the trouble of making man-killing machinery; resented the alternative of having to massacre these people or endure their truculent yappings; resented the whole unfathomable imbecility of war [*Ibid.*, p. 130].

This is the logic of the schoolyard bully—"It all started when he hit me back." Yet the tankmen, with the Airmen, are typed as exemplars of maturity. They are "the hope of the world," forcing mankind up the scale of being to racial unity. From the "calm and reasonable" vantage of their sovereign adulthood, they view the patriotic self-defense of their opponents as a case of arrested racial childhood, as evidenced by their fighting back with premodern methods. Right is on the side of superior might. Wrong is on the side of the preadults; they are reactionaries by nature, hopelessly resistant to progress and human growth, thus making them the true aggressors.

The tankmen are therefore able to define the enemy's refusal to surrender without a fight as itself an act of war, directed against their world peace ideology. In this outlook, they anticipate Lenin's view that the only obstacle to a socialist *pax mundi* is the vestigial yet obstinate idea of nationality. The job of the world revolution is to clean up these last relics of the old feudal order and make way for the Soviet world state.

Yet the western democracies keep insisting on their right to exist as independent nation-states, defending themselves, out of theoretical ignorance, against the progressive movement of history, represented by Soviet expansionism. Do they not know, as a secret KGB document has it, that by now the "balance of power has shifted in favor of Socialism"? Surely it must be clear to all advanced thinkers that "A worldwide socialist system is the decisive factor for the political and economic development of the world." The balance of power has changed, yes; but the enemy has failed to appreciate this new reality. Therefore, this KGB document goes on, the inevitable world-historical thing

> cannot happen by itself and victory can only be achieved by struggle. Aggressive forces are raising a tremendous resistance to the growth of socialist power—growth resistance. [From a secret document of the State Security Organs of the U.S.S.R., revealed by Aleksei Myagkov, New York: Ballantine Books, 1976, p. 169.]

Growth resistance—that is what the fully adult Airmen, like the tankmen, are righteous to overcome. So are the Martians in *The War of the Worlds*. For the backward humans who fight back against their futuristic might (they are said to be what humans are destined to become once matured by a million years of evolution), "It's bows and arrows against the lightning" (p. 94).

39. *A Short History of the World*, pp. 253f, 257.
40. *The Outline of History*, p. 335f.

41. *The War in the Air*, p. 355.

42. *The Outline of History*, p. 608. Elsewhere he restates this famous dictum, cited in every dictionary of quotations, in the following words: "Human destiny is a race between ordered thought made effective by education on one side, or catastrophe on the other." See *The New America: The New World*, p. 58.

43. *The New America: The New World*, p. 10; *The New Machiavelli*, p. 17; *'42 to '44*, p. 86.

44. *Apropos of Delores*, p. 33.

45. *Anticipations*, pp. 183, 185, 93, 247.

46. *Meanwhile*, p. 258.

47. *The Brothers*, p. 27.

48. Ghita Ionescue, ed., *The Political Thought of Saint-Simon* (Oxford: Oxford University Press, 1976), p. 120.

49. *The Autocracy of Mr. Parham*, p. 313.

50. *A Modern Utopia*, pp. 79, 162.

51. *Ibid.*, pp. 532, 43, 49, 84. See "The Rights of the World Citizen," an Appendix to *Phoenix*, pp. 186–192. Article 8's "Freedom of Movement" is qualified as a collective right for the Modern State to decide when the Samurai say that it is "planned" by them in Utopia for the world citizen's benefit. That it is not a citizen's right is clear from the subtitle Wells gives to his pamphlet, *The Rights of Man: An Essay in Collective Definition*. Elsewhere he says that individual rights are but "mercantile conventions," whose legal standing will be redefined under socialism for the sake of "collective development" (*First and Last Things*, p. 24). See also *The Rights of Man*, *'42 to '44* (pp. 36–56) and *Science and the World Mind* (pp. 55–63).

52. *'42 to '44*, p. 101.

53. One of the Saint-Simonians, a Dr. Guépin and author of an encyclopedic survey of the world and mankind, cited by Jean Chesneaux, *The Political and Social Ideas of Jules Verne* (London: Thames and Hudson, 1972), p. 84.

54. *The Outline of History*, heading for chap. XLI, p. xv.

55. *Social Forces in England and America*, p. 24; *Mr. Blettsworthy on Rampole Island*, p. 180.

56. *The World Set Free*, p. 234.

57. *Ibid.*, pp. 261, 263.

58. Preface to Gabriel de Tarde, *Underground Man*, pp. 16, 17.

59. *A Modern Utopia*, p. 172.

60. *Elements of Reconstruction*, p. 69; *Experiment in Autobiography*, p. 519.

61. *Star-Begotten*, p. 184; *Men Like Gods*, p. 78.

62. *What Is Coming*, p. 147; *Socialism and the Great State*, p. 46.

63. *First and Last Things*, p. 226f; *Phoenix*, p. 79.

64. *Russia in the Shadows*, pp. 11f, 146.

65. *The War in the Air*, p. 373f; *The Open Conspiracy*, p. 32.

66. Iggers, *op. cit.*, p. 29.

67. Keith Taylor, tr., *Henri Saint-Simon: Selected Writings on Science, Industry and Social Organization* (New York: Holmes and Meier, 1975), p. 258.

68. *The Open Conspiracy*, p. 56.

69. *The Undying Fire*, p. 179.

70. *The New World Order*, p. 144.

71. *Washington and the Hope of Peace*, p. 229.

72. *A Modern Utopia*, pp. 128, 172.

73. *The Anatomy of Frustration*, p. 98f; *The Holy Terror*, p. 255. "Machines make men honest." This sentence echoes the lines of Kipling's hymn to modern machinery, "The Secret of the Machines":

> But remember, please, the Law by which we live,
>   We are not built to comprehend a lie,
> We can neither love nor pity nor forgive.
>   If you make a slip in handling us you die!

74. *After Democracy*, p. 240f.

75. *Travels of a Republican Radical in Search of Hot Water*, p. 58.

76. *After Democracy*, p. 110.

77. *The Open Conspiracy*, p. 109; *Tono-Bungay*, p. 488.

78. *The World Set Free*, p. 275f.

79. *Star-Begotten*, p. 201; *Bealby*, p. 285.

80. *The Holy Terror*, p. 363; *The Anatomy of Frustration*, p. 192. This latter title, published the same year as *Things to Come* was released, also uses the term "New Puritans" and outlines their ascetic qualities in chap. XVII. Here it is proposed that they make war on tradition with a "New Model Army." The term is borrowed from Cromwell, who used it to describe his modernized armed forces drawn from righteous and talented men of the Puritan faith, in his battles against the lace-cuffed aristocrats of the king's horse—Roundheads versus Cavaliers. See the "new Cromwellism" that distinguishes the New Republicans in *Anticipations* (p. 129).

81. *Boon*, p. 288; *Tono-Bungay*, p. 370; *The Anatomy of Frustration*, p. 192.

82. *God the Invisible King*, p. 74; *You Can't Be Too Careful*, p. 270.

83. Desmond Lee, tr., *Plato: The Republic* (Harmondsworth, England: Penguin Books, 1974), p. 325.

The Coming Beast

84. *In the Days of the Comet*, p. 230; *Anticipations*, p. 341.

85. *Guide to the New World*, p. 96. The phrase is taken from Kipling, who himself wrote about a world-state governed by air traders, who in his case used not airplanes but airships. See his two short stories, "With the Night Mail" (1905) and "As Easy as ABC" (1912), in which the initials stand for Aerial Board of Control. Another slogan of the ABC is, "Democracy is a disease," echoed in the title of one of Wells's political pamphlets, "The Disease of Parliaments" (reprinted in *Social Forces in England and America*, pp. 293–320).

Of more immediate interest is Michael Arlen, *Man's Mortality* (London: William Heineman, 1933), cited in STTC:277. A story about an air-transport syndicate along Wellsian lines whose motto is "WORLD TRANSPORT MUST GOVERN THE WORLD," it is antitotalitarian in tone. Its members establish a *pax aeronautica* over the world, under the name of International Aircraft and Airways, Inc., commonly known as I.A.&A., or simply Airways.

> This was originally no more than a world transport system. It grew because the world was rudderless. It displaced the existing system of individual and competitive capitalism. It displaced existing forms of government which, with few exceptions, were founded on democratic capitalism. Spawned in the despair of men, I.A.&A. rose and waxed strong. It was armed with a superb ambition, to dragoon the nations of the world into a colossal scheme of tidiness.
>
> The architects of this new order were inspired by the splendour of a dream of peace: of peace at all costs, even at the cost of tyranny. They courted tyranny. They were weary of the superstition of humility to the inevitable quarrelsomeness of human nature. Sick almost to death of the malaise of democracy, they denied that truth is the daughter of debate, and imposed an autocrat over the peoples [p. ixf].

But this "tyranny of tidiness" (xvii) is overthrown after fifty years. Wells's, of course, is meant to last forever.

It would seem therefore, that *Things to Come* is more a response to this anti-utopian novel than it is a dramatization of his own STTC, for there is very little in it by way of concrete imagery and nothing of characterization that carries over to the film. The one most outstanding image that does is that of a horse hitched to a broken-down Rolls Royce automobile, following the breakdown of civilization (STTC:222; ttc:381). And the fact that the Airmen in both novel and film have their base of operations in Basra and make use of Pacificin (STTC:325), the Gas of Peace (ttc:627).

But this is Wells's typical mode of literary creation—he writes rebuttals of other authors, fashioned as answers rather than assertions. See John R. Reed, "The Literary Piracy of H.G. Wells," *Journal of Modern Literature* 7 (1979), pp. 537–542.

For a literary response to *Things to Come* itself, see Rex Warner, *The Aerodrome* (London: Bodley Head, 1941), with its rebuttal of the Utopian project to make "a new and a more adequate race of men" (p. 187). See also the reprint edition with an Introduction by Anthony Burgess (Oxford: Oxford University Press, 1982). Elsewhere Anthony Burgess throws a brilliant ray of light on the socialist idea in general, which helps to explain the pedagogical violence of the Airmen in particular, and why they are tagged as New Puritans. In the introduction to his novel, *1985* (Boston: Little, Brown, 1978), he writes, "The old theocracies of Geneva and Massachusetts offered to free man from his slavery to sin, meaning bad habits, by punishing him. The secular theocracies, or Socialist States, make the same offer.... They propose taking the health of the citizen, as well as his private morality, into their charge" (p. 80). Thus the clean-that-up Calvinism of John Cabal and the on-going punishments of Oswald, all in the name of sanity, health, and tidiness. Now we truly know what Wells means when he says, "The Socialist state is therefore the educational state; the terms are synonymous" ("Labor, Socialism and Education," p. 135). Or when he says, "Let us not forget that Education . . . is to a large extent repression" (WWHM:692).

86. See Desmond Lee, *op. cit.*, p. 324.

87. *Socialism and the Great State*, p. 46. Our first sight of the octopus-head helmet is when John Cabal lifts himself up from the seat of his cockpit in WT 74, a scene shot nose-on from in front of this airplane. The shot is framed in such a way that the two struts of the plane's landing gear, with a downward turn of one of the propeller blades appearing like a third upright standing between them, compose the geometry of a tripod. This must be a symbolic evocation of the tripedal fighting machines from *The War of the Worlds*, in which the Martians are seated as controlling intelligences when they do their war making on London and environs. After all, the Martians are themselves octopodan monsters, all brain and hands (or tentacles), and their business is the socialist business of municipalizing the public services of greater Metropolitan London. They start off by smashing the independent town life of the commuting suburbs, aiming to integrate them into the wider metropolitan life; but the Martians die before this creative phase of their destruction-reconstruction dialectic can be carried out. See Leon Stover, *The Shaving of Karl Marx*, Letter Five, pp. 78–99.

Wells himself is very suggestive of this reading in his Fabian paper, "The Question of Scientific Administrative Areas," reprinted in *Mankind in the Making*, pp. 371–391. More explicit is the relation he makes of this paper to the work of the Martians in their new guise as the Giants in *The Food of the Gods*. See *Experiment in Autobiography*, p. 558.

88. *New Worlds for Old*, p. 91.

89. *After Democracy*, p. 200.

90. *New Worlds for Old*, p. 257.

91. William Henry Chamberlin, *Collectivism: A False Utopia* (New York: Macmillan, 1937), pp. 69, 67f.

92. *The Camford Visitation*, pp. 42, 41, 43. In this book's indictment of the traditional humanistic preoccupations of the academic establishment, when it should be teaching science and all this implies for a world-peace ideology, "Camford" is Wells's reverse play on "Oxbridge." But he probably borrows this reversal from Conan Doyle, who coined it for one of his Holmes stories, "The Adventure of the Creeping Man."

93. *The World of William Clissold*, p. 671f.

94. *The Open Conspiracy*, pp. 16, 25, 17, 26.

95. "Hero-Worship," page reference mislaid.

96. *Guide to the New World*, pp. 13, 46, 44.

97. *Science and the World-Mind*, p. 42.

98. *After Democracy*, p. 136; *War and the Future*, p. 260.

99. *Anticipations*, the 1914 edition, p. xiif.

100. *Atlantic Edition* I, p. xvii; *World Brain*, p. 17; *Socialism and the Great State*, p. 4.

101. Cited by Edward Gibbon, *The Decline and Fall of the Roman Empire*, ed. by J.B. Bury in seven vols. (London: Methuen, 1914), vol. VII, p. 228.

102. *Mankind in the Making*, p. 365. The phrase "Literature of Power" recurs in *The Camford Visitation*, p. 41. On political cover stories, see Gaetano Mosca, *The Ruling Class*, tr. by Hannah D. Kahn from the Italian edition of 1923 (N.Y.: McGraw-Hill, 1939), pp. 70–2, where they are called "political formulas," Or as Stalin put it most cynically, "Words are one thing; actions another. Good words are a mask for concealment of bad deeds." Cited in Brian Freemantle, *KGB* (London: Michael Joseph, 1982), p. 42.

103. Comte cited in Noel Annan, *Leslie Stephen, The Godless Victorian* (New York: Random House, 1984), p. 272.

104. *The Research Magnificent*, p. 122.

105. *Democracy Under Revision*, p. 25; *When the Sleeper Wakes*, p. 173.

106. *What Are We to Do with Our Lives?* p. 7; *Playing at Peace*, p. 6.

107. *The World Set Free*, p. 267; *The Dream*, p. 263.

108. *The Conquest of Time*, p. 47.

109. *The Dream*, p. 79; *Babes in the Darkling Wood*, p. 68.

110. Cited in Adam B. Ulam, *The Bolsheviks* (N.Y.: Macmillan, 1965), p. 538.

111. *The World Set Free*, p. 272.

112. *Ibid.*, p. 278; *The Conquest of Time*, p. 61. "They will perform miracles of restatement." Or as Mr. Polly says, "Queer incommunicable joy it is, the joy of the vivid phrase that turns the horridest fact to beauty!" (*The History of Mr. Polly*, p. 211).

113. *A Modern Utopia*, p. 172; *The New Machiavelli*, p. 481; *After Democracy*, p. 11.

114. *Guide to the New World*, pp. 46, 44.

115. *Phoenix*, p. 55.

116. Lenin cited in Ulam, *op. cit.*, p. 409.

Merger Immortality

117. Just how these zones are cleared is described elsewhere, in a short story whose future world is cognate with that of *Things to Come*. The Air Police conduct search raids on nationalist rebels and when such "brigands" are found out, they are pursued by mobile gas vans to their huts and hideouts where masked men in service uniforms, anticipating Adolf Eichmann's genocidal Einsatz commandos, work "some little machine on wheels with a tube and a nozzle projecting a jet." Unlike the Gas of Peace in the film, this is a permanent death gas. The episode given here takes place near Irkutsk, an area that figured prominently in the Russian civil war, following the Bolshevik Revolution. See "The Queer Story of Brownlow's Newspaper," in *The Man with a Nose*, p. 40f. Note the reference to this story in the London edition of STTC, p. 20. It is a vivid example of how to carry out Wells's program for the "elimination of undesirable types by force" (*Star-Begotten*, p. 190).

The Man with a Nose is a posthumous collection of "uncollected" stories. But its editor forgets that "Brownlow's Newspaper" was indeed collected before in a uniform edition of the works of H.G. Wells in nine volumes, printed by Waterlow and Sons in 1933, with no publisher's imprint. The set was a newspaper give-away, and not the only cheap edition to so use the name of Wells in raising subscriptions. In this case, the story appears in vol. 6, *The Soul of a Bishop, and Three Short Stories.* It first appeared in *Strand Magazine* in 1931. Its futuristic reference is to the *Evening Standard* of 10 November 1971. The *Standard* reprinted it, 39 years later, on that very date, but with cuts to save the "liberal" Wells from his genocidal excesses. By that time, 27 years after Wells's death, the press did not want to be reminded of the earnestness behind the euphemisms of this radical socialist's "Gas of Peace" in *Things to Come.*

Once the Air Dictatorship imposes its Act of Uniformity, making for "one undivided cultural field" (STTC:417), Wells allows for the survival of some local traits. His world state will permit a few traditional arts, such as "rugs, carpets, fabrics, dyes, pottery, metal work and so forth," much like the folk costumes and music Stalin permitted among the so-called minority peoples in the U.S.S.R., formerly national peoples. Indeed, Wells has only praise for the successful cruelty of Stalin's policy in so reducing them. His "greatest achievement, when at last history weighs him in the balance, will be found I think in his settlement of the minority difficulty in Russia for good and all" (*'42 to '44*, pp. 136, 52). John Cabal settles the matter on a global scale by the same means, with "forcible conformities" (*Anticipations*, p. 281).

118. *A Modern Utopia*, p. 159; "Evolution and Ethics," in *Early Writings*, p. 218; *The Anatomy of Frustration*, pp. 988, 125.

119. *The Open Conspiracy*, p. 23; "The Illusion of Personality"; *All Aboard for Ararat*, p. 8.

120. *God the Invisible King*, p. 69; *Social Forces in England and America*, p. 230; *After Democracy*, p. 135.

121. *The Science of Life*, pp. 1433f, 1473, 1477. All quotes from the last chapter of vol. IV, written by Wells unaided by his collaborators. This is evident from the typescripts in the Wells Archive.

122. *The World of William Clissold*, p. 359.

123. *The Anatomy of Frustration*, pp. 39, 44.

124. *First and Last Things*, pp. 132, 137.

125. *Joan and Peter*, p. 561; *First and Last Things*, p. 130.

126. *A Modern Utopia*, pp. 89, 151.

127. *New Worlds for Old*, p. 257; *Marriage*, p. 506.

128. Ludwig von Mises, *Socialism* (Indianapolis: Liberty Classics, 1981), p. 482.

129. "Democratic Socialism," p. 24.

130. *The War in the Air*, p. 202. These words are spoken by a Prussian officer. They are meant to state the Social Idea, which at the time of this novel's writing (1908) was known as "the Prussian Idea," with all the order and discipline implied by Prussia's war socialism in the Franco-Prussian War of 1870–71. See also n.64, p. 103.

131. *Socialism and the Great State*, p. 46.

132. Saint-Simon in Ionescue, *op. cit.*, p. 164.

133. *The World of William Clissold*, p. 770; *First and Last Things*, p. 131.

134. *The Conquest of Time*, p. 12; *Socialism and the Great State*, p. 119.

135. Durkheim, *op. cit.*, p. 137.

Civil Death

136. *A Modern Utopia*, p. 98; letter to Sir Richard Gregory, cited in Geoffrey West, *H.G. Wells* (London: Gerald Howe Ltd., 1930), p. 237.

137. *The Labour Unrest*, p. 12.

138. *Mr. Belloc Objects*, p. 83; *The Great State*, p. 42.

139. *Phoenix*, p. 71.

140. Felix Markham, tr., *Henri de Saint-Simon: Social Organization, The Science of Man, and Other Writings* (New York: Harper and Row, 1964), p. 33, n. 140.

141. Saint-Simon cited in Ionescue, *op. cit.*, p. 158.

142. *A Modern Utopia*, pp. 164, 108.

143. *The Conquest of Time*, p. 63.

144. *The Holy Terror*, p. 353; *Christina Alberta's Father*, p. 394.

145. On the selling of today's commercial products using the same mystique, see William Safire, "No-Name Nomenclature," in *On Language* (New York: Times Books, 1980), pp. 177–79.

146. Richard Griffith and Arthur Mayer, *The Movies* (New York: Bonanza Books, 1957), p. 319.

147. *Mr. Blettsworthy on Rampole Island*, p.287; *The World of William Clissold*, p.549.

148. Comte, *op. cit.*, p. 326.

149. F.A. Hayek, *op. cit.*, p. 353f.

150. *The New Machiavelli*, p. 145; *'42 to '44*, pp. 13, 187.

151. See von Mises, *op. cit.*, p. 263.

152. Citations from Paul Johnson, *Modern Times* (New York: Harper and Row, 1983), p. 91.

153. *Socialism and the Great State*, p. 46; *Men Like Gods*, p. 74.

154. *Anticipations*, p. 311.

155. *A Modern Utopia*, p. 37; *Experiment in Autobiography*, p. 628f.

156. *Mankind in the Making*, p. 25; *The World of William Clissold*, p. 185; *The Open Conspiracy*, p. 22.

157. "A Forecast of the World's Affairs," p. 17.

158. *The H.G. Wells Calendar*, p. 63.

Two Cultures

159. *Phoenix*, p. 162.

160. *The War of the Worlds*, p. 209. These words describe the sleepless, tireless Martians, octopus-like symbols of the inhuman state monster. "Quite nice monsters" they are said to be elsewhere, not "inhuman in the bad sense" because they represent a collective form of humanity "beyond good and evil." See *Star-Begotten*, p. 97f.

161. *Kipps*, p. 292; *The Open Conspiracy*, p. 56.

162. *After Democracy*, p. 137.

163. On the extravagant cult of Japan that the outcome of the Russo-Japanese War set off in Britain, see G.R. Searle, *The Quest for National Efficiency: A Study in British Politics and Political Thought, 1899–1914* (Berkeley: University of California Press, 1971), p. 57f.

164. *A Modern Utopia*, p. 289.

165. *Experiment in Autobiography*, p. 566.

166. Boris Pasternak, *Doctor Zhivago* (New York: Signet Books, 1960), p. 248.

167. *First and Last Things*, p. 102; *The Conquest of Time*, p. 85.

168. *Experiment in Autobiography*, p. 552; *Mankind in Making*, pp. 7, 15.

169. *The Conquest of Time*, pp. 14, 84.

170. Introduction to W.N.P. Barbellion, *The Journal of a Disappointed Man*, p. v.

171. Michael Korda, *Charmed Lives* (New York: Random House, 1979), p. 121f.

172. C.P. Snow, *The Two Cultures* (Cambridge, England: Cambridge University Press, 1959).

173. Charles Galton Darwin, *The Next Million Years* (Garden City, N.Y.: Doubleday, 1953), p. 199.

174. *The Camford Visitation*, pp. 51, 60, 40, 48.

175. *After Democracy*, p. 201; "Labor, Socialism and Education," p. 135.

176. Saint-Simon cited in Frank E. Manuel, *op. cit.*, p. 321.

177. *The Elements of Reconstruction*, p. 107; *The Salvaging of Civilization*, p. 106.

178. *After Democracy*, p. 20; *Secret Places of the Heart*, p. 155f; *Democracy Under Revision*, p. 32. The phrase "vain repetitions" is from Matthew 6:7.

179. *After Democracy*, pp. 20, 21.

180. On the philosophical bases for these extremes, see Raymond Aron, *The Opium of the Intellectuals* (New York: W.W. Norton, 1962), esp. chap. II, "The Myth of the Revolution."

181. *Experiment in Autobiography*, p. 553.

182. *What Are We to Do with Our Lives?* p. 69; *A Modern Utopia*, p. 84.

183. Chamberlin, *op. cit.*, p. 67f. On the subjugation of the legal order under the totalitarian state, see also Leonard Schapiro, *op. cit.*, pp. 29–34.

184. George Orwell, "The Lion and the Unicorn," in Sonia Orwell and Ian Angus, eds., *The Collected Essays, Journalism and Letters of George Orwell* (Harmondsworth, England: Penguin Books, 1970), vol. 2, selection no. 17, p. 82.

185. *The Outline of History*, p. 517; *The World Set Free*, p. 224.

186. *The World of William Clissold*, pp. 184, 185.

187. *Anticipations*, p. 311.

188. *First and Last Things*, p. 125.

Tyranny of Truth

189. *Description of the "Leeming" Portable and Collapsable Aerial Ropeway*.

190. See Leon Stover, "Jules Verne," in Curtis C. Smith, ed., *Twentieth Century Science Fiction Writers*, 2d ed. (New York: St. Martin's Press, 1986).

191. *The Conquest of Time*, p. 64.

192. W. Warren Wager, "The Steel-Grey Saviour: Technocracy as Utopia and Ideology," in *Alternative Futures* 2 (1979, pp. 38–54), 51f.

193. *Anticipations*, p. 213.

194. Ernest Renan, *Philosophical Dialogues and Fragments* (London: Trubner and Co., 1883), p. 63.

195. Ernest Renan, *The Future of Science* (London: Chapman and Hall, 1891), pp. 97, 236. The French original, *L'Avenir de la science*, was published in Paris in 1890.

196. *God the Invisible King*, p. 76; *The Way the World Is Going*, p. 47; Saint-Simon cited in Felix Markham, *op. cit.*, p. xxiii, n. 4.

197. Renan, *Philosophical Dialogues*, p. 59f.

198. *First and Last Things*, p. 147; *The Brothers*, p. 64.

199. *Men Like Gods*, p. 298; *The Science of Life*, vol. 4, p. 1468; *A Modern Utopia*, pp. 147, 128.

200. *Anticipations*, p. 325; *Experiment in Autobiography*, p. 668.

201. *Phoenix*, p. 60. The French phrase is a quote from Voltaire, "for the encouragement of others."

202. Michael Voslensky, *op. cit.*, p. 296.

Reaching for the Stars

203. "The Cyclic Delusion," in *Early Writings*, p. 113; *The World of William Clissold*, p. 185. This latter source makes explicit reference to "the Indian triad of fundamental gods" in the section entitled, "Vishnu, Siva, and Brahma" (pp. 328–332 and *passim*). See also *The Outline of History*, p. 214.

The color-coding Wells gives to this trinity is correct, insofar as it may be represented in a black and white film. The *varnas* or colors assigned by Hindu mythology to it are white for Brahma, red for Siva, and blue for Vishnu. Wells is consistent in his use of this color code throughout his writings. For example, in *When the Sleeper Wakes*, a "White Council" of new Brahmins with the aid of policemen dressed in red, governs "the people of the blue canvas," who at once embody Vishnu and Plato's third social caste. Or again, in *The First Men in the Moon*, the Grand Lunar rules over the Selenites of a planetary workshop whose interior caverns are lit by a blue light. Had *Things to Come* been shot in color, the black uniforms of the Airmen no doubt would have been shown in Siva's proper red.

204. *The World of William Clissold*, p. 671f; *God the Invisible King*, p. 148.

205. *The Idea of a League of Nations*, p. 44; *The Open Conspiracy*, p. 33; *The World of William Clissold*, p. 366; *The Man with a Nose*, p. 194.

206. *The Open Conspiracy*, p. 51; *A Modern Utopia*, p. 5.

207. *A Modern Utopia*, p. 9; *God the Invisible King*, pp. 76, 96.

208. Bernard Crick, *In Defense of Politics*, 2d ed. (Harmondsworth, England: Penguin Books, 1982), p. 53.

209. *Phoenix*, p. 72.

210. *You Can't Be Too Careful*, p. 284; *God the Invisible King*, p. 76.

211. *A Modern Utopia*, pp. 143, 147.

212. *Mr. Blettsworthy on Rampole Island*, p. 321; *When the Sleeper Wakes*, p. 238.

213. Aleksandr I. Solzhenitsyn, *The Gulag Archipelago*, vol. I (New York: Harper and Row, 1974), p. 24. GULAG is the Russian acronym for Chief Administration of Corrective Labor Camps.

214. "Mammon," p. 54.

215. *The Croquet Player*, p. 72.

216. "The World To-day—and Tomorrow?" Page number missing from newspaper cutting in author's collection.

217. *The Undying Fire*, p. 66; *The Conquest of Time*, p. 62.

218. *A Modern Utopia*, pp. 144, 142.

219. *Anticipations*, pp. 314, 318n; *Mr. Britling Sees It Through*, p. 302.

220. Zinoviev cited in David Shub, *Lenin* (New York: Mentor Books, 1950), p. 164. On the Soviet abolition of personal guilt, see also Paul Johnson, *op. cit.*, p. 70f.

221. "H.G. Wells," p. 91.

222. *Socialism and the Family*, p. 22; *This Misery . . .* , p. 36; *Apropos of Dolores*, p. 33.

223. "A Story of the Days to Come," in *The Short Stories of H.G. Wells*, p. 785; *In the Days of the Comet*, p. 303; *Star-Begotten*, p. 97.

224. "The Human Adventure," in *Social Forces in England and America*, p. 415.

225. *Democracy Under Revision*, p. 30.

226. Bernard Crick, *op. cit.*, p. 100.

227. "The Discovery of the Future," p. 326; *War and the Future*, p. 212; *A Modern Utopia*, p. 367.

TTC on Television

228. *Experiment in Autobiography*, p. 649; *Phoenix*, p. 189.

229. *All Aboard for Ararat*, p. 75.

230. Letter dated July 1918, published in the *New York Weekly Review*, 15 December 1920. Cited in Henry Arthur Jones, *My Dear Wells* (New York: E.P. Dutton, 1921), p. 81f.

231. Sir Ifor Evans, *A Short History of English Literature* (Harmondsworth, England: Penguin Books, 1940), p. 181.

H.G. WELLS BIBLIOGRAPHY

Selected Works Cited in This Book

After Democracy: Forecasts of the World State. London: Watts, 1932.

All Aboard for Ararat. New York: Alliance Book Corp., 1941.

The Anatomy of Frustration. London: Cresset Press, 1936.

Anticipations of the Reaction of Mechanical and Scientific Progress Upon Human Life and Thought. New York: Harper & Brothers, 1901.

Anticipations, 2d ed. London: Chapman & Hall, 1914.

Apropos of Dolores. New York: Scribner's, 1938.

Are Armies Needed Any Longer? New York: Chemical Foundation, 1927.

The Atlantic Edition of the Works of H.G. Wells, 28 vols. New York: Scribner's, 1924–27.

The Autocracy of Mr. Parham. Garden City, N.Y.: Doubleday, Doran & Co., 1930.

Babes in the Darkling Wood. New York: Alliance Book Corp., 1940.

Bealby: A Holiday. New York: Macmillan, 1915.

Boon, the Mind of the Race. London: T. Fisher Unwin, 1915.

The Brothers. New York: Viking, 1938.

Brynhild, or the Show of Things. New York: Scribner's, 1937.

The Camford Visitation. London: Methuen, 1937.

Catalogue of an Exhibition of Lithographs of Munition Works by Joseph Pennell, with an Introduction by H.G. Wells. New York: Frederick Keppel, 1917.

Christina Alberta's Father. London: Jonathan Cape, 1925.

The Common Sense of War & Peace: World Revolution or War Unending. Harmondsworth, England: Penguin Books, 1940.

The Conquest of Time. London: Watts, 1942.

The Croquet Player. New York: Viking, 1937.

Democracy Under Revision. New York: George H. Doran, 1927.

"Democratic Socialism." Abstract of the Proceedings of the Normal School of Science & Royal School of Mines Debating Society, for 8 October 1886. *Science Schools Journal* 1 (December 1886): 23–25.

Description of the "Leeming" Portable and Collapsable Aerial Ropeway, coauthored with G.W. Coleman. Great Britain: Ministry of Munitions, Trench Warfare Dept., Outside Engineering Branch, 26 November 1917. Document no. Mun 5, 198, Y/K, 6197.

"The Discovery of the Future." *Nature* 1684 (6 February 1902): 326–331.

The Dream. London: Jonathan Cape, 1924.

Early Writings in Science and Science Fiction by H.G. Wells, ed. by Robert Philmus & David Y. Hughes. Berkeley: University of California Press, 1975.

The Elements of Reconstruction. London: Nisbet & Co., 1916.

Experiment in Autobiography. New York: Macmillan, 1934.

The Fate of Man. New York & Toronto: Longmans, Green, 1939.

Faults of the Fabian. Privately printed, 1906. Reprinted in Samuel Hynes, *The Edwardian Turn of Mind.* Princeton, N.J.: Princeton University Press, 1968: 390–409.

First and Last Things: A Confession of Faith and a Rule of Life. New York: G.P. Putnam's Sons, 1908.

The First Men in the Moon. London: George Newnes, 1901.

"A Forecast of the World's Affairs." In J.L. Garvin, et al., *These Eventful Years: The Twentieth Century in the Making,* 2 vols. London: Encyclopaedia Brittanica, 1924, vol. II, pp. 1–17.

'42 to '44: A Contemporary Memoir Upon Human Behavior During the Crisis of the World Revolution. London: Secker & Warburg, 1944.

The Future in America. New York: Harper & Brothers, 1906.

God the Invisible King. New York: Macmillan, 1917.

Guide to the New World: A Handbook of Constructive World Revolution. London: Victor Gollancz, 1941.

"Has the Money-Credit System a Mind?" In *The Banker* 6 (1928), pp. 221–233.

"Hero-worship." Abstract of the Proceedings of The Normal School of Science & Royal School of Mines Debating Society, for 18 February 1887. *Science Schools Journal* 6 (May 1887).

"H.G. Wells." In Henry Goddard Leach, ed., *Living Philosophies.* New York: Simon & Schuster, 1931, pp. 79–92.

The H.G. Wells Calendar, ed. by Rosamund Marriot Watson. London: Frank Palmer, 1911.

H.G. Wells in Love: Postscript to "An Experiment in Autobiography," ed. by G.P. Wells. London: Faber and Faber, 1984.

The History of Mr. Polly. London: Thomas Nelson & Sons, 1910.

The Holy Terror. New York: Simon & Schuster, 1939.

The Idea of a League of Nation. "In collaboration with a Selected Group of British Political Thinkers." Boston: Atlantic Monthly Press, 1919.

The Illusion of Personality. St. Albans: Fisher, Knight & Co., 1944.

In the Days of the Comet. London: Macmillan, 1906.

Joan and Peter. New York: Macmillan, 1919.

The Journal of a Disappointed Man, by W.N.P. Barbellion, with Introduction by H.G. Wells. New York: George H. Doran, 1919.

The King Who Was a King. Garden City: Doubleday, Doran, 1929.

Kipps. London: Macmillan, 1905.

"Labour, Socialism and Education," an election address of 1922. Reprinted in Harry W. Laidler, ed., *Wells's Social Anticipations.* New York: Vanguard Press, 1927, pp. 131–136.

The Labour Unrest. London: Associated Newspapers, Ltd., 1912.

"The Lawyer in Politics." *The Evening Chronicle.* Pt. I, 13 March 1916. Pt. II, 15 March. Pt. III, 17 March.

Little Wars. London: Frank Palmer, 1913.

Love & Mr. Lewisham. New York and London: Harper & Bros., 1900.

"Mammon." *Science Schools Journal* 2 (January 1887): 53–54. Signed Walker Glockenhammer.

"The Man of Science as Aristocrat." *Nature* 3729 (19 April 1941): 465–467.

Man Who Could Work Miracles: A Film. New York: Macmillan, 1936.

The Man with a Nose, and the Other Uncollected Short Stories of H.G. Wells. London: Athlone Press, 1984.

Mankind in the Making. New York: Scribner's, 1904.

Marriage. New York: Duffield & Co., 1912.

Meanwhile: The Picture of a Lady. London: Ernest Benn, 1927.

Men Like Gods. New York: Macmillan, 1923.
Mr. Belloc Objects to "The Outline of History." New York: George H. Doran, 1926.
Mr. Blettsworthy on Rampole Island. Garden City, N.Y.: Doubleday, Doran, 1928.
Mr. Britling Sees It Through. New York: Macmillan, 1916.
A Modern Utopia. London: Chapman & Hall, 1905.
The New America: The New World. London: Cresset Press, 1935.
The New Machiavelli. London: John Lane, 1911.
The New World Order. New York: Alfred A. Knopf, 1940.
New Worlds for Old. London: Archibald Constable & Co., 1908.
The Open Conspiracy: Blue Prints for a World Revolution. London: Victor Gollancz, 1928.
The Outline of History. London: Cassell & Co., 1920.
The Outlook for Homo Sapiens. London: Secker & Warburg, 1942.
The Passionate Friends. New York: Harper & Brothers, 1913.
The Peace of the World. London: Daily Chronicle, 1915.
Phoenix: A Summary of the Inescapable Conditions of World Reorganization. London: Secker & Warburg, 1942.
Playing at Peace. London: National Council for the Prevention of War, 1927.
The Research Magnificent. New York: Macmillan, 1915.
The Rights of Man. Harmondsworth, England: Penguin Books, 1940.
The Rights of Man: An Essay in Collective Definition. Brighton, England: Poynings Press, 1943.
Russia in the Shadows. London: Hodder & Stoughton, 1920.
The Salvaging of Civilization. New York: Macmillan, 1921.
Science and the World-Mind. London: New Europe Pub. Co., 1942.
The Science of Life, 4 vols. With Julian S. Huxley & G.P. Wells. Garden City, N.Y.: Doubleday, Doran & Co., 1931.
The Scientific Romances of H.G. Wells. London: Victor Gollancz, 1933.
Secret Places of the Heart. New York: Macmillan, 1922.
The Shape of Things to Come. New York: Macmillan, 1933.
The Shape of Things to Come: The Ultimate Revolution. London: Hutchinson & Co., 1933.
A Short History of the World. New York: Macmillan, 1922.
The Short Stories of H.G. Wells. New York: Doubleday, Doran & Co., 1929.
Social Forces in England and America. New York: Harper & Brothers, 1914.
Socialism and the Family. Boston: Ball Pub. Co., 1908.
Socialism and the Great State: Essays in Construction. Wells is editor and the author of chap. I, "The Past and the Great State," pp. 1–46. New York: Harper & Brothers, 1912.
Socialism and the Scientific Motive. London: Co-operative Printing Society, 1923.
Stalin-Wells Talk. London: New Statesman & Nation, 1934.
Star-Begotten. New York: Viking, 1937.
Things to Come: A Film Story Based on the Material Contained in His History of the Future, "The Shape of Things to Come." London: Cresset Press, 1935.
This Misery of Boots. London: Fabian Society, 1907.
Tono-Bungay. London: Macmillan, 1909.
Travels of a Republican Radical in Search of Hot Water. Harmondsworth, England: Penguin Books, 1939.
Two Film Stories. London: Cresset Press, 1940.
Underground Man, by Gabriel de Tarde, with Preface by H.G. Wells. Tr. from the French by Cloudesley Brereton. London: Duckworth & Co., 1905.
The Undying Fire. London: Cassell & Co., 1919.
War and the Future. London: Cassell & Co., 1917.

The War in the Air. London: George Bell & Sons, 1908.

The War of the Worlds. London: William Heinemann, 1898.

The War That Will End War. New York: Duffield & Co., 1914.

Washington and the Hope of Peace. London: W. Collins & Sons, 1922.

The Way the World Is Going. London: Ernest Benn, 1928.

What Are We to Do with Our Lives? London: William Heinemann, 1931.

"What I Believe. A Chat with Mr. H.G. Wells." George Lynch, *The Puritan*, vol. I (April) 1899:218–220.

What Is Coming? New York: Macmillan, 1916.

When the Sleeper Wakes. New York: Harper & Brothers, 1899.

The Work, Wealth and Happiness of Mankind, 2 vols. Garden City, N.Y.: Doubleday, Doran, 1931.

World Brain. Garden City, N.Y.: Doubleday, Doran, 1938.

The World of William Clissold, 2 vols. New York: George H. Doran, 1926.

The World Set Free. London: Macmillan, 1914.

"The World To-day—and Tomorrow?" *Sunday Chronicle*, 3 April 1938.

A Year of Prophesying. New York: Macmillan, 1925.

You Can't Be Too Careful: A Sample of Life. London: Secker & Warburg, 1941.

Alexander Korda (left), managing director of London Films, and H.G. Wells, circa 1935.

Above: Advertisement showing manned artillery shell fired from the Space Gun, redefined as a rocketship (see upper right corner).

Opposite, top: Margaretta Scott as Roxana, mistress to Rudolf. Bottom: Rowena (Scott), her scenes shot but not shown, wants love; husband Oswald (Raymond Massey) wants the stars.

Above: H.G. Wells on the set with Raymond Massey (as Oswald Cabal) and Pearle Argyle (as Catherine Cabal, Oswald's daughter).

Opposite, top: "We were children yesterday" (ttc:146). John Cabal grimly reminds his wife (Sophie Stewart), before going off to World War II, that their children belong not to their marriage but to the Human Adventure. Invented title of book on table, lower left, is *Infant's Annual* — one more yearbook recording the infancy of the human species. But on this eve of the war to end war, the race is nearing maturation. (Courtesy British Film Institute.) Bottom: In the coming future, the engineer LIX 891 shows what racial maturity is all about. His no-name nomenclature befits the impersonal integration of new Collective Man into the world economic machine. (Frame enlargement.)

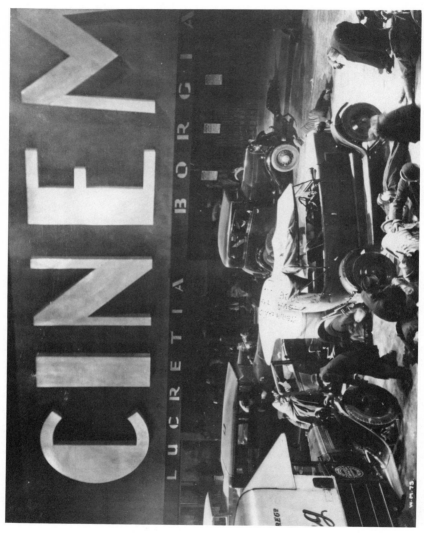

Everytown's movie house; the letters on its facade are spelled out in Streamlined Moderne.

Top: John Cabal, in front of a framed picture of a DC-3 in flight, observes "Pippa" Passworthy (Edward Chapman) urging young Harding (Maurice Bradell) to Christmas jollity despite the evening's bad war news. Bottom: Pippa Passworthy's son drums Little War against a shadowgraph of Great War. (Frame enlargement.)

Above: After a long war made worse by the Wandering Sickness, its cure in the remains of Everytown is announced by Rudolf the Victorious (Ralph Richardson) on a bulletin board outside his headquarters. He simply shot all Wanderers.

Opposite, top: A German tank, designed in Streamlined Moderne, crushes the weak British opposition. (Frame enlargement.) Bottom: John Cabal succors the dying German aviator he shot down. As they plot revolution, he gives the enemy's gasmask to a passing child.

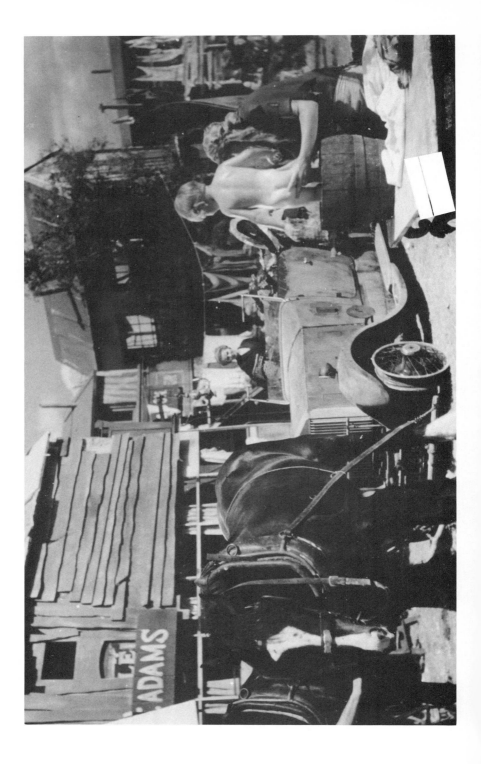

This page, top: Rudolf (center) makes a pass at Mary Gordon (Ann Todd), by way of getting her husband Richard (Derrick de Marney) to repair the Boss's airforce of shabby biplanes. The world's half dead from war and disease, yet Rudolf still wars on the Hill People. Bottom: Rudolf's sexual statesmanship is interrupted by Roxana, who has a grievance with Wadsky the local merchant (Abraham Sofaer).

Opposite: Everytown's transportation system at best is reduced to a horse-drawn Rolls Royce without tires.

Rudolf and the whole town is diverted from its local politics when an aircraft is heard overhead.

Top, left: John Cabal lands in Everytown and emerges from his aircraft; right: Cabal with the vizor dropped in front of his gas helmet, shaped like the head of an octopus, revealing the Buddha-like halo formed by the helmet back. (Courtesy British Film Institutue.) Bottom: Cabal meets old friend Dr. Harding (Maurice Bradell), another moral worthy; with Richard Gordon (Derrick de Marney) and his wife (Ann Todd).

Top: Cabal (Massey) confronts the Boss (Richardson) with his plan to clean up the last remnants of national sovereignty. Rudolf's pillow advisor, Roxana (Scott), and his chief aid Simon Burton (Anthony Holles) look on. Bottom: With Cabal in detention downstairs, Rudolf makes a raid on a nearby colliery in the possession of another ministate like his.

Top: Rudolf the Victorious toasts his captains and commanders for their recent valor in battle, while Roxana meditates on the smallness of it all. Bottom: Roxana leaves the victory banquet to visit Cabal in his detention cell downstairs, wooing him as a greater man than Rudolf to follow.

Top: Rudolf brings Roxana back to his purpose—to hold Cabal hostage against the coming of his fellow Airmen from Basra, former center of the Moslem Conquest. Bottom: Gordon (Derrick de Marney), the last aviation mechanic in Everytown, prepares to escape to Basra in one of the Boss's shabby biplanes he has just repaired. He returns with the Airmen to rescue Cabal, at the same time ending the Boss's petty tyranny.

Top: One of a huge fleet of bombers at Basra. Bottom: One of the Basra
bombers, designed in Streamlined Moderne.

Opposite, top: Airmen calmly looking down on the world as they fly toward Everytown to bomb Rudolf into submission. (Frame enlargement.) Bottom: Having parachuted to the ground, both Airmen and Air-women take over Everytown, now subdued by the Gas of Peace.

Above: John Cabal stands over the body of Rudolf the Patriot Chief and pronounces, "Dead and his world dead with him." A new world, Cabal's, begins.

This page, top: The Great Air Dictator presides over his World Council at Basra, setting out his plans for postwar reconstruction. Bottom: A digging machine, designed in Streamlined Moderne, excavating the site of the new subterranean Everytown, to be the metropolitan center of the world socialist state.

Opposite, top: Engineers on inspection tours of the new city's automated factory complex. The scooter on the right, needless to say, is of Streamlined Moderne design. Bottom: The state apartments of the party elite under construction, designed in Streamlined Moderne, a curvilinear variant of the International Style.

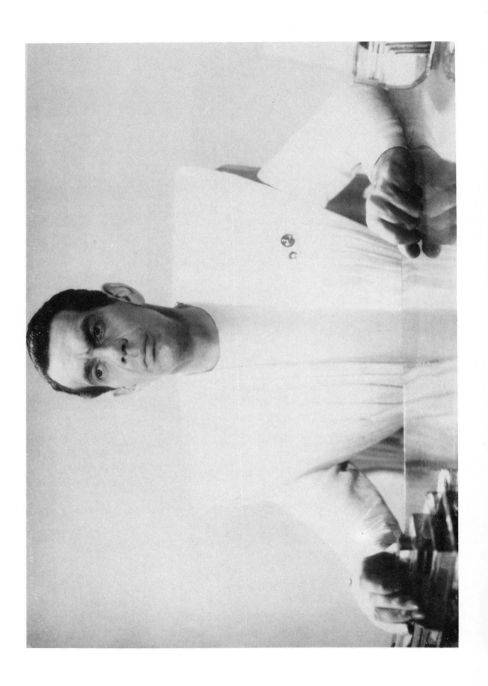

長上下
（なががみしも）

Opposite: Oswald Cabal, president of the World Council of Direction.
His wide-shouldered upper garment is patterned after the court dress of
the Samurai, the ruling class of Tokugawa Japan.

    This page: Illustration from an old Japanese dictionary (above), show-
ing the *kata-ginu* or "shoulder cloth" worn by the Samurai. The same style
is worn by Japanese musicians (below) in today's Kabuki theatre.

Above: Everytown's heroic statuary, done by dissident artist Theoto-copulos for a state commission in the style of socialist realism he objects to.

Opposite: Theotocopulos (Cedric Hardwicke) leads a romantic rebel-lion against "this Brave New World."

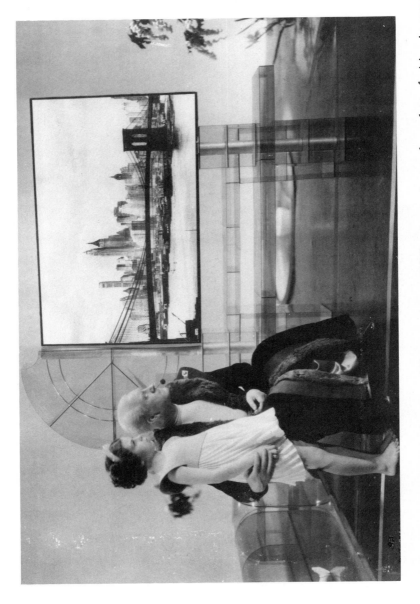

A child of the future gets her lessons by way of "history pictures." The cinema is now brought to fruition in serving the social ends of education rather than the commercial vulgarities of the amusement industry.

Top: Theotocopulos (Hardwicke) orates on television of rebellion, calling for the individual freedoms of self-culture, as against the collective life of the Human Adventure. What he speaks against, the continuous life of the species, is represented symbolically by the film strip moving across the deck of the control console in the foreground. Each frame, the Now of each individual life, is connected to every other in the biological life of mankind as it evolves from the past into the future. Bottom: Alarmed by Theotocopulos's television speech, Oswald Cabal takes off in his helicopter to beat the rebels to the Space Gun.

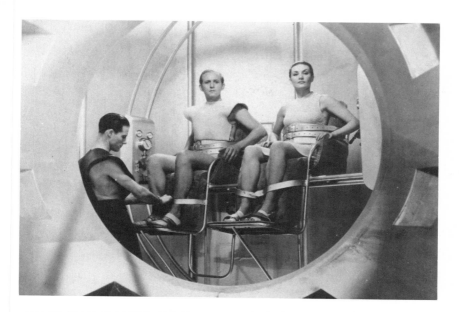

Opposite: In the foreground of the Space Gun (and note the gunsight at the top) is a system of transportation called "telpherage," a civilian application of the aerial ropeway Wells designed to carry munitions to the front during World War I. (Courtesy British Film Institute.)

This page, top: The interior of Wells's moon capsule, with its two passengers, Oswald Cabal's daughter Catherine (Pearl Argyle) and Raymond Passworthy's son Maurice (Kenneth Villiers). Bottom: A scene inside the control room of the Space Gun moments before firing.

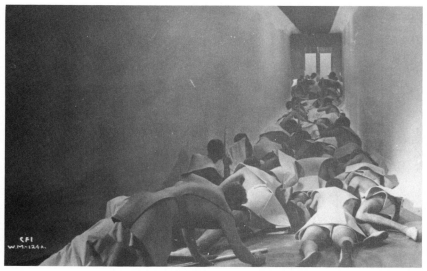

Above, top: Theotocopulos's followers climbing girders around the Space Gun, moments before they are felled by the concussion of its firing. Bottom: Others of the dissident mob felled in spaces beneath the Gun.

Opposite: Raymond Passworthy (Edward Chapman) and Oswald Cabal (Massey) watch the flight of the moon capsule on a giant telescopic mirror designed in Streamlined Moderne. With the firing of the Gun, the Modern World State has at once achieved the conquest of space and the conquest of society, by ridding it of its humanistic dissidents.

"Which shall it be?" asks Oswald Cabal (Raymond Massey) in his concluding speech (Edward Chapman at right). The choice is the little life of individual men, or the greater life of Man the Master Being.

[APPENDIX I]

WHITHER MANKIND?

A Film of the Future
. By .
H.G. WELLS

Based on his two books, *The Shape of Things to Come*
and *The Work, Wealth and Happiness of Mankind*.

TREATMENT

§[01]

A PROGRAM IS GIVEN TO EVERYONE.

The Program announces:—

The story begins in the present time. The screen shows a familiar scene and people troubled, as we all are troubled, by threats of war and disaster.

Then it shows war and the ruin, disorder and pestilence that must certainly follow another great war storm.

But it shows also the ineradicable courage of the human soul, which rises in the midst of disaster to restore the welfare of man after a new fashion.

We follow the fortunes of two men: one a young student of medicine,

Edward Harding, and the other an aviator and inventor, John Cabal, who comes to play a leader's part in that Revolt against Disorder.

Then we see the life of Oswald Cabal, the grandson of John Cabal, a hundred years later.

(Cast on program.)

N.B. – Credit titles are not to be given on the screen but on the Program. This is a long needed innovation upon cinema practice. It is in the interest of everyone. The audience takes the program away and reads it at leisure. Few people remember the names that are just flashed on the screen.

§[02]
THEME OF THE FILM
WHITHER MANKIND?

The theme is the history of the next hundred and twenty years (or thereabouts) roughly following the anticipations in THE SHAPE OF THINGS TO COME.

The film consists of four main parts.

The first part (*Pastorale*) represents *A Christmas Party* under (practically) PRESENT CONDITIONS. No date. War breaks out and the chief character reappears in the second part (*Marche Funèbre*), The Episode of the Two Aviators (1940).

A series of short exposures then shows war, degenerating into SOCIAL CHAOS, leading to the third part, which begins in *The Darkest Hour of the Pestilence*, shows *The Wandering Sickness at its Climax* (1960), and the revolt of the air-men, technicians and men of science, who achieve *Reconstruction amidst the Ruins* (1970).

This third part is set in A SPECTACLE OF IMMENSE RUIN. Everything is done to summon up a vision of our present world *smashed*.

Then comes a rapid series to convey WORK, leading up to the counter vision of what can be done with our world.

The work series is a rush series, beginning with hammerings and molten metal, etc., and glimpsing more and more distinctly phases of great buildings and engineering works. There will be glimpses of strange machinery and extraordinary building operations – walls being poured out of tubes and setting as they are poured out, *e.g.* Then a conversation about history between a little girl and her great-grandfather in the year 2054.

The fourth part (*Chorale*) is THE WORLD IN 2054. This concentrates on fresh spectacular effects. If they are not surprising and magnificent and REAL, the whole film falls down. The interest of this latter part brings the drama of creative effort versus the resistances of jealousy, indolence and sentimentality, to a culmination. This fourth part must carry an effective answer to the question "And after all, when you have unified the world, is it going to be any different from what it is to-day?"

The answer is Yes. The spirit will be different. The aggressive maker in the human soul has emerged triumphant over instinct and tradition. Brahma the Creator asserts himself over Vishnu the Preserver [*i.e.*, Possessor — *ed.*] after his previous subjugation of [*i.e.*, by — *ed.*] Siva the Destroyer. But as the struggle about the Space Gun shows, all three Powers are still eternally alive and at work in the world.

N.B. — The dates given are merely rough indications. Dates are not stressed.

§1.

The words WHITHER MANKIND? appear on the screen. They fade out and reappear throughout this section. The background is at first an even grey. Then the hooter of a factory in Everytown is seen and heard, and the outline of the factory is visible behind the letters. A crowd of workers is seen coming out of the factory. Passworthy, a genial managing director, is seen at the entrance saying "Good Night! A Merry Christmas."

Then one has glimpses of the streets and market square of Everytown, and people catching buses. The general effect of this is to be a flow of human beings across the screen from left to right. WHITHER MANKIND? . . . A mother is seen preparing a Christmas tree with her children. This is Mrs. Cabal who appears again in §3.

In a small students' laboratory looking out upon the square, and showing a distant hill of characteristic shape (which recurs steadily throughout the film), Edward Harding, a young scientific man engaged in medical research, is busily at work. He wears a white overall and rubber gloves. The people flow past outside. Like a river.

A clock strikes seven, and Harding desists reluctantly. He reads his notes as he dries his hands. He is seen hurrying down a street, along which other people flow upon their various occasions, and presently he approaches John Cabal's house. The letters WHITHER MANKIND? are reimposed in their original strength.

§2.

Music: A few bars of grave import, dying away as the voices begin. A hand and forearm rests on a newspaper lying on a table. The headlines of the newspaper appear. "Another Ten Thousand Air Fighters. Fresh Trade Restriction. Alarming Speech by (name hidden)."
This is the hand and arm of John Cabal and it reappears in the opening 2054 scene.

John Cabal sits in his study. This is a darkish close scene in harmony with his concentrated mind. Diagrams and models indicate an engineer. The blade of a propeller over the mantel and other objects emphasize his association with the air force. He is a man of 35 with a sensitive intelligent face and *a fine voice*, reasonably well-built and a quiet restrained good actor.

Enter Edward Harding, young and brisk: "Come to see your Xmas tree."

Business implying, What's in the paper?

John Cabal: "Wars and rumours of wars. Where is the world going?"

Edward Harding: "Crying wolf again?"

John Cabal: "Some day the wolf will come. Then *look out.*"

Edward Harding: "Do you really think?"

John Cabal: "The fools are capable of anything."

Edward Harding: "What becomes of my medical research?"

John Cabal: "War messed up *my* generation. This time it will mess up everything."

Edward Harding: "I've been working on that suggestion you made. What do you think of this for a gadget?"

Takes out something and shows it to Cabal.

Before this is said Pipper Passworthy has appeared. He is a cheerful, fatuous, commonplace man with a fat voice and a fat laugh. We have already had a glimpse of him outside his factory. He stands in the door and hears Cabal and Harding talking. He has a way of holding his hand across his open mouth. He comes forward now boisterously. "War won't come again!" (Looks at paper). "Oh! a speech. By *him!* Nothing in it, I tell you. Look at the cheerful side of things. Think of it. Good job. Jolly wife. Kids. Pretty house."

"And darkness outside, Pipper. And the wind rising."

"Let it rise. These clever fellows aren't going to let loose a war— again."

Mrs. Cabal appears down passage to summon the men to the children's party.

§3.

Pastorale music with a childish clash at the climax, and then children's dance music.

A large pretty room with a Christmas tree (in the home of John Cabal). A children's party in progress.

Some dais or gallery from which this room can be looked down upon.

An ordinary study and passage leading to this room.

The children play on the floor at their own level. The legs of the adults pass over them.

"Cheerio," sings Pipper Passworthy. "What's wrong with the world to-night?"

Horrie Passworthy cried "Hullo Daddy," and is swung up into the air by his father and kissed.

The adults disappear as dark figures in the foreground and the children play out their little drama.

§4.

Three boys play chief parts: Timothy Cabal, the Maker; Horrie Passworthy, the Breaker; and Billy Butters, the Wary and Possessive Type. Horrie
is a bigger and stouter boy than Timothy.

In their infantile and individual form they present the major trio in the
Indian vision of human life. Brahma the Creator from whom all new things
proceed, Siva the Destroyer who tries and destroys everything effete and feeble and Vishnu the Possessor who accumulates old and damaged things and
maintains the continuity of tradition amidst a rush of destruction and novel
things that would otherwise reduce life to headlong chaos. In their partial and
infantile way, the three youngsters display these cardinal forces at work. In
all the subsequent story these same cardinal forces react on each other and
the spirit of Eternal Creation emerges to plain statement in the concluding
speech of the film.

§5.

Timothy Cabal squats at play laying out a toy railway system. It has just
been given him. He is inclined to spread it too far over the floor. A pretty little
girl is interested. Another child is invoked to work the signals.

Horrie Passworthy the Breaker has been given a military panoply and a
drum and begins to beat the latter and march about the room—trying to in-
duce the others to march behind him. Two or three follow him including Billy
Butters. Horrie tries to interest the pretty little girl. Then as he marches round
he kicks aside some of Timothy's layout which is certainly extending rather
unduly. There is not room for the two of them. Timothy protests mildly and
repairs the damage. Horrie then comes up and wants to make a railway
accident.

"Let's have a war, see?"

"Kids amuse me," says Pipper. "I *love* kids. Look at 'em."

Horrie gets a toy gun and bombards Timothy's layout to pieces. Timothy
protests again. The little girl protests also. Delight of Horrie at their dismay.

Suddenly Timothy loses patience, becomes frantic and goes tooth and
claw for Horrie who is discomfited.

Mrs. Cabal snatches Timothy away. "You can come along with me," she
says and takes him off. Horrie tramples on the railway system and kicks over
the engine (Hullabaloo). Billy Butters resists him to protect the layout. The
elders interfere.

"Steady on," says Pipper. "Steady on. You just come out of this with me
young man. You come out of it and cool down."

Meanwhile Billy Butters sits down to play with and rearrange what is left
of Timothy's abandoned layout. He likes and admires it although he has no
genuine understanding of it. He is just as happy to see the engine wheels spin
wrong side up as run the engine along the lines.

When Timothy in a chastened mood returns, Billy says: "I've been taking care of it for you." But Timothy discovers: "You've got it all wrong."

Billy says: *"I'll* do it now. You shouldn't have gone away. You didn't take care of it. It got in everybody's way."

The pretty little girl says: "But it's *his!"*

Timothy seems disposed for a new fight.

His mother intervenes.

Timothy cries in despair. *"He puts it all wrong. They spoil everything I make."*

This episode gives the master theme of the film.

Transition to Mrs. Cabal playing a round game with all the children. Music. Dance merry-go-round.

"They soon forget their troubles, don't they," says Passworthy.

The children recede and the onlooking elders become important.

The grandfather comes in unobtrusively, nods to Passworthy and pats young Harding on the shoulder.

§6.

John Cabal, Edward Harding, Pipper Passworthy and the grandfather of the children, watch the children and talk.

The grandfather says: "Look at these toys—aeroplanes—electric trains—motor cars—things for building up machine frames—plasticine—when I was a child we had none of these things. . . . What will *these* youngsters live to see?"

John Cabal says: "What will they live to see? There are bitter times ahead."

Passworthy says: "At it again!"

The Grandfather: *"I* don't want to see another war."

"Who *does?"* says Passworthy.

"Nor I," says Harding.

John Cabal: "Nor I. But I'd rather have it soon than let it fall on *them."*

"There won't be another war," says Passworthy. "There *won't* be another war. And if there is, we shan't be in it! And even then——"

He hesitates. "The war wasn't so bad as they make out. One didn't worry. You did what you were told. Something great seemed to have got hold of you."

"Something still greater may get hold of you next time, Pipper."

Pipper's fatuous face waves from side to side. *"Don't* think. If everybody thought as much as you do, mankind would have thought itself off the earth, ages ago."

Cabal with a gesture of irritation: "If we do not end war—war will end us."

He laughs bitterly: "Everybody says that—and nobody does anything."

Harding: "I want to do Medical Research. What does all this matter to me?"

John Cabal: "What does a wolf outside matter to you?"

Horrie Passworthy, the visitor, being wrapped up and carried off by nurse.

Cabal's children being put to bed.

Cries of "Merry Christmas, Horrie!" All the quarrel is forgotten.

§7.

Then the adult guests departing. Through the open door, the villas of the suburb are seen on a hillside, and the characteristic hill crest against the rising moon. Frost on the ground.

Passworthy: "It's going to be a real old Christmas. It's midnight. Christmas Day in the morning, eh?"

Harding: "Hullo, what was that?"

Passworthy: "What?"

Harding: "Sounded like a gun."

Passworthy: "No guns about here."

Mrs. Cabal: "Look! Searchlights!"

Everybody becomes very still.

Mrs. Cabal: "But what are searchlights doing now?"

Passworthy: "Some anti-aircraft manoeuvres, I expect."

The telephone rings.

Cabal hurries off. Everyone is silent, listening. Pause. Cabal heard off, not very distinctly. "What? . . . *What?* Not *to-night.* What? To-morrow. My *God!*"

Everyone very still. Cabal comes back slowly. "Mobilisation!"

Mrs. Cabal: "So it's come!"

Harding: "Good-bye, research."

Passworthy: "But—perhaps it's only a precautionary mobilisation."

§8.

Rapid short montage of an air war surprise. Just air war. The war sequence is §12.

§9.

Farewell glimpse of the children sleeping in their nursery. Timothy grips an engine key. A doll dressed as a red cross nurse hangs over the little girl's head.

Cabal and his wife. Cabal is in uniform.

The wife says: "My dear. My dear are you sorry we—we had these children?"

He thinks long. "No. . . . Life must carry on."

He stands still and then breaks out: "Why should we surrender life to the brutes and fools. . . ."

She says: "I love you. I loved you. I want to serve you and make life happy for you. But think of the things that may happen to them!"

She looks at them: "Were we selfish?"

He draws her to him. "You weren't afraid to bear them. . . . *We* were children yesterday. We are anxious but we are not afraid. . . . Courage, my dear. . . . And may that little heart have courage!"

Kisses Timothy very gently not to wake him. Timothy stirs.

§10.

Flash of the mother sitting alone with the children — or the children waking up in the nursery and asking: "Where's daddy?"

§11.

John Cabal in uniform with valise at railway station meets Pipper Passworthy with an armlet. Passworthy is soberly elated. He already carries himself like a soldier.

Passworthy: "It will be over in six weeks. They can't keep it up. I find it exciting. Terrible of course — *terrible* — but exciting. Wish I was an airman like you. I have to do *my* bit down below at the base."

Cabal: "Don't you worry, Pipper. This time they'll bomb the bases."

Young Harding comes up. "I came to see you off, Sir. I'm exempted for six months, to finish my qualification. This means good-bye to research, I'm afraid. For a time, anyhow."

John Cabal: "It will mean good-bye to all sorts of things, before it is over."

Passworthy: "Hang it, Cabal, there's something rather fine about this, after all. Everybody being brought together for a common end. Private ambitions forgotten."

John Cabal: "Everyone in the dustcart, eh?"

Passworthy: "Everything into the wash!"

John Cabal: "And gas?"

Passworthy: "Oh, they exaggerate about this gas. It's just a way of frightening people. . . . I don't believe!"

Goes off at a tangent. "You should see that kid of mine, Cabal. In that Christmas tree panoply. Marching up and down right and proper. You'd laugh."

(Reminder glimpse of the little boy, marching gleefully.)

The menace of the music grows more definite, and flows on into the gathering storm of sound in the next scene.

§12.

WAR.

Music a crescendo up to a stillness. The reminder glimpse of the little boy in §12 multiplies itself and carries on to an effect of marching armies.

Men marching on to troopships.

Battleships and destroyers.

A broadside is fired.

Answering salvo from gigantic caterpillar guns. Tanks tearing into action in never ending lines. Tanks meet gas, and crash through houses.

Shells falling and exploding.

Propellors of warplanes are swung – the engines start with a roar. Beneath them men fix bombs.

Squadron after squadron of warplanes.

Bombs falling.

Warlike music and noises rise to an heroic climax and end abruptly – as if it had come upon something that appalled it to silence.

Close up of a little body lying dead among a heap of wreckage. It is Pipper's boy, Horrie Passworthy, in his soldier's uniform.

It is the first dead body we have seen. Still for a long moment.

§13.

GAS.

A street or Market Square in Everytown (vaguely about 1940), modern types of facade, but possibly novel advertisements with novel words, *e.g.*, Colour Cinema, Cinema Opera, Wright's Neuro Laxative, Proteroria.

The place is curiously silent.

The silence is broken by warning hooters, whistles, maroons.

A hurrying of people – the cinema is emptied – everything stops.

Gas masks being distributed.

Into the street comes a large motor lorry with an anti-aircraft gun. It fires into the air.

Gas is coming.

Gas is near.

GAS IS OVERHEAD.

Panic. Fight for masks. Fight for cellars.

A crowd of people packed tightly together go down into a dugout – we see only their heads. The round heads of bombs packed tightly together on a conveyor move like a crowd beneath the camera.

The street is wrecked and full of gas.

Gas pours down into the dugout. People choke. Horror of the gas made plain.

Chaos in the street like the description of Unter den Linden in the
SHAPE OF THINGS TO COME.

Above this are the bombing planes.

The street is wrecked by a bomb and then, as the anti-aircraft gun goes
on fighting, it is gassed and the action goes on amidst the ruins.

We enter upon the second episode in which John Cabal figures.

§14.

*Music stormy with the whirr of aeroplanes, drum rhythms and a crash. Menace in
the music.*

An enemy airman has been distributing (visible) gas. He is heard above
and his gas blows before the wind.

Panic in the street.

Scene in the air. The enemy airman is put down by the British airman
(this is John Cabal) who nose-dives after the action, but contrives to fall not
too disastrously. They both fall close to each other a mile or so away from the
gas which is drifting towards them. The foreign bomber is badly injured. John
Cabal limping a little, walks up to him. The man who has been dropping gas
bombs speaks with a foreign accent. Cabal says:

"My God. But you're smashed up! . . . . Eh! but you were a well-built boy."
Forgets his antagonism at the sight of his wounded enemy. "What can I do
for you. Is that better?" (aid).

He makes the broken man as comfortable as possible and sits down beside
him. The two regard each other with sympathetic eyes.

"Why should we two be murdering each other. How did we come to this?"

"Why do we let them make a dog-fight of our lives?"

The gas is drifting nearer. The foreigner points. (Accent here because he
is speaking English, but the Accent need not be stressed later). "Go my vriend!
Go! Dot's my gaz and it is a bad gaz."

The aviators adjust their gas masks. Some little trouble about the
foreigner's mask. Cabal takes it from him to make some alteration.

"Funny if I'm choked by my own poison, eh?" says the foreigner.

"This is all right," says John Cabal and puts on the other fellow's mask.

A very young girl in flight before the gas. She presses a handkerchief to
her mouth.

She falls down. She is already coughing.

The foreign aviator stares at her steadfastly with his goggled eyes, tears
off his mask which is not yet fully fastened and insists on giving it to her.

"No. No. Fix it on her and carry her off. I've given it to others, why
shouldn't I have a whiff myself?"

Cabal carries off the girl, both masked.

Cabal hesitates, turns back and hands a pistol to the foreign aviator.

The foreign aviator: "Good fellow—but I'll swallow my dose."

§15.

No music at all. Slow film. Tragic anticipation.

The foreign aviator is left awaiting the gas.

"Think of it! I dropped the stuff on her. Maybe I've killed her father and mother. Maybe I've killed all her family. And then I give up my mask to save her. That's funny. That's really funny. Ha, Ha, Ha! Better see a joke late than never. . . . I wish I'd seen it before."

He struggles for a more comfortable position. Looks at the approaching gas. Takes up the pistol, hesitates and looks at it and then puts it down.

"What fools we have been. We've let them make us fight for them like dogs. We who had everything in our hands."

"But, oh! it's funny! Got smashed trying to kill her and then gave her my mask. Ha, Ha! Ha, Ha!"

Whisps of vapour sweep across the scene. His laugh changes to a cough. He puts his hand to his mouth. His cough becomes a cough of distress. Grows fainter.

"I'll take it all"—cough—"I'll take it all."

Vapour blots out the scene. A voice "Oh-oo!" in a note of sudden unendurable suffering. Stillness. A shot is heard.

Here comes a blank interval of drifting vapour for 10 or 15 seconds.

§16.

SOCIAL DISORDER.

The Darkest Hour. The idea is now to present our contemporary world *wrecked.* For this purpose we need to base our scenes on any big factory or great building standing in ruins. We want, therefore, actual pictures of the ruins of any recent fires, explosions or the like,—shattered and contorted machinery, battered iron frameworks, huge metallic structures rusting on the ground. Or great facades with broken windows deserted and empty. Advertisements broken up and partly defaced. Huge ruinous effects. Wandering dogs, big rats. Possibly coatis. In the foreground of this huge, still, desolating, ruinous background, or in narrow passages amidst it, the vestiges of human society are ultimately discovered, in struggle against the Wandering Sickness, the Great Pestilence.

Stillness follows the death scene of the airman. Very slowly great shapes come through the mist and become plainer and plainer. Effect of gigantic ruined buildings deserted. *Menacing music resumes very softly at first and then rising in stormy gusts.*

Flashes of ruined capital cities. Possibly of well-known places and structures, *e.g.*, the Eiffel Tower prostrate. The Tower of London destroyed. Brooklyn Bridge down.

Flashes of plunderers and a food riot (?) and (for example) such glimpses as:

Flash of a looter and murderer caught red-handed and lynched. (? Cabal's house.)

Wandering starving children.

Water-main bursting in market square.

People carrying torches in a modern city deprived of its light.

Modern factories out of action—modern machinery going wrong. (Passworthy's factory.)

Love in wartime. Young Harding in uniform and red-cross brassard. Kissing good-bye to a young wife not otherwise shown.

A fantasia of war ruin and desolation.

An interval of time has to be presented. This is done in §17 herewith.

§17.

Fragments of newspaper badly printed. Each is printed worse than its predecessor.

THE DAILY COURIER.

No. I. New Series.   Feb. 2nd, 1952.   *Price one pound sterling.*
London.

RESUMPTION OF THE DAILY COURIER.

The Associated Newspaper Company has secured possession of a printing press and a supply of paper, and we are at last able to resume publication. We have to announce that the new Provisional Government met in the ruins of the Houses of Parliament and, in view of the seizure by the enemy of corn ships in the Channel, resolved to continue the struggle. To make peace at the present time, in view of this fresh outrage, would be not only humiliating, but disastrous.

The rest of the paper is torn off.

THE WEEKLY BULLETIN.

No. 402.   August 11th, 1960.   *Price four pounds sterling.*
Westminster.

RESUMPTION OF HOSTILITIES. TENTH YEAR OF WARFARE.
HOW LONG, O LORD!

BRITONS' BULLETIN.

No. 7.   Septr. 21st, 1965.   *Price twenty pounds sterling.*
Headquarters.

THE WAR TO END WAR.

Necessity of a preventive offensive against the enemy menace before his hostile preparations are completed. We cannot wait to be destroyed—

THE NEWS SHEET.
July, 1968.

TWENTIETH YEAR OF WAR IN EUROPE.
SPREAD OF THE PESTILENCE.
PRECAUTIONS TO TAKE AGAINST WANDERING SICKNESS.

§18.

PESTILENCE SERIES.

Music not too loud but grave and sad.

Rats crawl out of holes and die.

Wall notices about a new pestilence, hand bills and wall placards, all very badly printed or written by a stylograph, emphasize this.

Bills give directions about the disease. It is incurable. The sick are to be avoided. They are to be locked in. Above all, wandering is to be restrained.

A newspaper placard or writing in chalk on a wall announces: "Enemy are spreading the Wandering Sickness by aeroplane. Avoid sites where bombs have fallen recently."

A series of flashes of the pestilence. The sick wander. People, in fear of infection, fly before them. One is shot as he approaches a party of refugees. "He's bringing infection—*infection!*"

§19.

No music to this section; sounds, e.g., chinking of bottles.

Edward Harding is struggling desperately to work out the problem of immunity to the Wandering Sickness which is destroying mankind. He is now a man of forty-five; he is overworked and jaded. He is working in a partly wrecked laboratory with insufficient supplies. This laboratory has already been shown in the opening sequence. The rooms downstairs have been improvised as a hospital, to which early cases of the Pestilence are brought. His clothing is ragged and makeshift (no white overalls). His apparatus is more like an old alchemist's, makeshift and very inefficient. No power laid on. No running water, though there is still a tap and a sink. But two microscopes as before. Bottles, crucibles and suchlike hardy stuff, but very little fine glass. No Florence flasks, *e.g.*, mended windows. He mutters as he works.

He talks to his daughter, a girl of 18, dressed in a patched nurse's costume, with a red cross armlet.

"Father," she says, "why don't you sleep a little?"

Harding: "How can I sleep when my work may be the saving of a million lives? Have you got that iodine?"

Mary Harding: "There is no more."

Harding: "No more. Then *that* stops *that*. No iodine. What will fail us next? My God!"

He turns to the audience wringing his hands. "What is the good of trying to save a mad world from its punishment? No material, no hardened glass, no pure drugs. Yet it is all so plain. There are people who are immune from the pestilence. That must be due to some difference in their blood. Something must be there in some of them and absent in others. It would be possible to make everyone immune if I could find what that something is. But how can I do it? No material, no hardened glass, no trustworthy chemicals, no assistants."

"I would give my life," says his daughter.

"*Giving lives* is no use. Everybody is *giving lives*—whether they want to or not. We want *order* back in the world. This pestilence goes where it pleases and does as it likes. Some such pestilence was bound to come. When armies move about the world, when disease germs are scattered from the air—pestilence is unavoidable. Some of us seem to be immune. Perhaps we are, perhaps we are not. If none of us is really immune then this is the end of human history. We are still too busy fighting among ourselves, to put up any fight against the cruelty of nature. Even now. And to have no *iodine!* Oh, my dear!"

He sits down—overcome.

Mary Harding: "Oh, father, if you could sleep for a time."

"How can I sleep? Go into that hospital. See how they wander out to die. No one to look after them."

He broods for a moment.

"And to think I brought you into this world! I was home on leave. Just one snatch of happiness. It seemed romantic."

Mary Harding: "Courage, father! Even now, I am glad to be alive."

§20.

Richard Gordon, an air mechanic in patched and dirty blue overalls, enters in great distress. He is evidently very friendly with the Hardings.

"It's got my sister. Her heart beats fast, she feels faint. She won't answer."

"Yes, that is it."

Gordon: "What can I do for her? What can I *do?*"

Mary cries: "Oh, Janet! And *you,* poor *dear!*"

Gordon: "I thought something might be known– –."

He looks at Harding and catches his despair. Rushes out.

Mary Harding goes out after Gordon.

Harding is left. "This is the last torment of war!—to know what peace could give us and to be helpless!"

§21.

A ruined room with an old stove, wood fed. A fine big bedstead much broken down. Everything twelve years old and shabby and patched. (A thing to be noted in all these ruinous scenes is the dearth of china, glass and cutlery. I noted that such breakable gear was extremely short in Russia in 1920. Most of it would be smashed and disappear in ten or twelve years.)

Janet Gordon, the sister of Richard Gordon is stricken with the pestilence. She tosses in fear and pain on the bed. "Must *I*, too, go?"

Mary Harding hovers over her, helplessly helpful. Gordon sits on the bed, stunned and hopeless.

Harding comes in, jaded, dishevelled, red-rimmed sleepless eyes and stares at her apathetically.

Then he rouses her and goes through the motions of a practitioner examining a case. He pulls back the sheets, listens to her breathing. Then he replaces the sheets and shakes his head with professional despondency.

"No doubt," he says, in answer to Gordon's mute question.

Harding: "And it need not be. I cannot even get iodine now—not even iodine! There is no more trade, nothing to be got. The war goes on. The pestilence goes on—Worse now than the war that released it."

Gordon: "Is there nothing to make her more comfortable?"

Harding, indifferently: *"Nothing."* Then returning to his general theme: "There is nothing to make anyone comfortable any more. War is the art of spreading wretchedness and misery."

Gordon sits inattentive to Harding, looking at his sister.

Harding: "I remember when I was still a medical student, talking to a man named Cabal. About preventing war. I remember he said that if we did not end war, war would end us. Well, here we are!"

The sister moans and frets, rises and gropes about blindly. Wanders out. Gordon in great distress follows her.

Two wandering figures amidst ruins and desolation.

Flashes of their wanderings—among ruins, through a wrecked public garden, in a deserted railway station.

Sentinel who threatens with his rifle.

Gordon drags her away until another sanitary guard is encountered.

Gordon follows her until she drops. Then he sits by her side unwilling to believe her dead. He carries her to an improvised red cross mortuary. Attendants in hooded garments take her from him.

Interval of time indicated by bearers bringing in stretchers and Gordon re-emerges.

He prays: "God give me strength—help me God! Now I will live for one thing—to bring the world back to order. Somehow. I don't know how. I will work. . . . But save Mary—save my Mary. *That* I cannot endure."

Mary Harding appears.

"Oh, Mary, dear Mary!"

Mary holds out her arms to him and he weeps—like a child in her arms.

§22.

A stylograph sheet, very smudgy, stuck on a wall:

THE NEWS SHEET.
July 1970.
THE PESTILENCE QUITE OVER.
REVIVAL OF THE NATION'S LIFE
CATTLE RAIDING AGAIN.
RESUMPTION OF HOSTILITIES AGAINST THE HILL STATES.

No cases of Wandering Sickness have been notified in Everytown for six months. Clearly the scourge has passed. Everywhere there are signs of revival. Cultivation and grazing have been resumed almost to our front line at the foot of the hills. There however

§23.

A ruinous shed. Gordon struggling to get an old dynamo into order. Primitive and broken tools. He whistles.

Scene shifts to the ruined Market Square of Everytown. Familiar skyline. Ragged people. Marketing. A peasant with a horse-drawn motor car.

The scene presents a world of makeshift after the economic collapse of the pestilence and war.

Sound of an aeroplane which passes. Excitement of people, who are incredulous.

Mary Harding, who is now Mary Gordon, in a rough patched dress, is buying food. Gordon, in a very dirty, ill-cut sheepskin coat over breeches and puttees comes to help her carry home her stuff.

Gordon: "I have been trying to get that old dynamo at the Headquarters to work. But I can't get rubber-coated wire."

Mary: "You will think I am dreaming if I tell you something. But other people heard it. There was an aeroplane."

Gordon: "You're dreaming. There's been nothing in the air for five years. Gods, I'd like to see one of our birds in the sky again!"

Mary: "I am certain."

Gordon addresses the peasant with the horse-drawn car:

"Hullo, there, where did you get that car? What is it? It's a Ford-Morris-Austin, isn't it?"

The peasant: "It's a good pre-pestilence machine. Twenty years I've had it. Bought it secondhand in 1945."

Gordon: "Broken down?"

The peasant: "Not a bit of it. That engine could run to-day. I oil it and turn it over at times. But there's *no petrol left anywhere.*" (Confidentially). "Leastways what is left is hidden."

Gordon: "Ah, ah! You think you might want to go fast some day."

The peasant: "Don't you misunderstand me. I'm not saying I'm one of these petrol hoarders. No."

Gordon: "Did you hear anything of an airplane to-day?"

The peasant: "That's queer! I did hear something. . . . It couldn't have been an airplane. That's all dead and done for. . . . I said to my old missus here — — ."

Drum taps and a fife are heard. Everyone turns round. The Boss appears with his retinue followed by a company of soldiers. Everyone stiffens up.

The Boss can be a heavy, brutish-looking man of the condottiere type. He is in a rough costume between that of a boy scout, a Far West cowboy and a cossack. A rosette is his symbol and it is everywhere present; the last degradation of the English Tudor rose. He carries himself with a self-conscious swagger. He has roughly uniformed staff officers and guards with him (he never goes unattended). They all wear at least badges with the rosette symbol, and salute frequently. The soldiers have a rough uniform of sacking and carry rifles. The salute is made by standing up stiffly, hands by the side and nose in the air. No hand lifting. The producer should bear in mind that the Boss is not intended to be a caricature of a Fascist or Nazi leader. He is as much South American or Haytian or Gold Coast. He is something more ancient, more modern and more universal than any topical movements. There is a big flag with a rosette behind him.

Everyone stiffens up to attention, even Mary and Gordon do so mechanically.

The old peasant admires the troop. "That's the stuff to give the Hill men. They're the boys to end the war. If anything can."

Suddenly the fife and drums seem to lose breath and die away. Everyone becomes aware of a marvel. There is an aeroplane in the sky. It is a plane of the 1930–1940 type, but it roars cheerfully and circles over the town. The little armed party halts. All business stops.

Gordon: "This is too good to be true!"

Mary: "I heard something of this. They are flying again round the Mediterranean and across France."

Gordon: "It is almost as though civilisation was not dead. How good — to hear that old zoom again!"

The aeroplane shuts off and drops to make a landing. A move of the crowd as if to go and see it. The Boss begins to give directions, and three of his guards go off after the crowd. The Boss goes his way with the rest of his retinue. It is beneath his dignity to be astonished at anything.

§24.

The aeroplane in a desolate place.

Ragged figures running towards it, but afraid to go too near.

The aeroplane lands out of sight, and they line up against the sky looking at it.

They hesitate and begin to move off sideways.

A man appears in a modern (1975) flying kit, a shining black suit with a peculiar vizor that swings down upon his chest. He is John Cabal, now a man of seventy, but still hale and vigorous. He seems big and formidable in his strange vizor and black clothing.

This vizor of Cabal's is peculiar in structure. It is the lower part of a sort of huge (but light) helmet that encloses not only the head but the chest and shoulders. The lower forward part swings down to expose the face and throat, leaving a great semi-circular back, a kind of high vast collar or setting, behind the head.

Two guards come up at the double, but hesitate to approach this strange being closely.

§25.

A street opening into the square.

A little rabble of children and odd people follows Cabal. A rosette badged guard accompanies him. The guard is supposed to be in charge of a prisoner, but John Cabal is a headstrong man.

John Cabal: "I'll come to your Boss. All in good time. I've got lots to say to him. From the new World Transport Board. But first I want to talk to someone else and I've got to find him. There's a Doctor Harding here?"

Guard: "The Boss will be impatient."

John Cabal: "He must exercise self-control. Who would rule others must begin by ruling himself. My business begins with Doctor Harding."

§26.

The same laboratory as in §19, but still more impoverished. Meal in progress. No knives and forks. Potatoes in central dish. Cans. Harding is now fifty-five. He wears a shabby old steamer coat. He has aged somewhat, but is not nearly so lean and ill and frantic as in §19. Mary and Gordon, who are evidently man and wife, are telling Harding about the aeroplane.

Harding: "I did not know anything of the sort was still possible. This fool of a Boss of ours has what he calls his air force, but he has had no petrol for years. We have been so cut off."

A knocking.

"What is that?"

Mary with her hand to her heart: "Oh, not arrest!"

Gordon opens the door and John Cabal enters, followed by his guard.

John Cabal to the guard: "Go outside."

Guard salutes: "My duty is to remain with you and take you to the Boss."

John Cabal: "Not a bit of it. Wait outside until I am ready for this Boss of yours. Is that Doctor Harding? You don't remember me. I knew you as a medical student thirty-five years ago. You used to come to my house."

Harding (rising): "Of course! You're not so changed as all that; Mr. John Cabal."

John Cabal turning to the guard with a certain menace: "*Will* you go?"

Gordon stands ready (to help put out the guard if necessary).

The guard (saving his face): "I put you on your honour not to attempt escape."

Reassuring gesture from Cabal.

Guard retires and Gordon closes the door.

John Cabal removing his gas armour: "I was told you were here."

Cabal takes Harding by the shoulders and looks at him affectionately. "We used to make gadgets together. What has happened to you?"

Harding: "I'm a sort of mediaeval leech, a doctor without medicines or instruments. I do what I can in this broken down world. Good Heaven!—Do you remember, Sir, how I used to blow about the research I was going to do and the discoveries I was going to make? I can remember telling you some of my notions."

John Cabal: "Don't I. You will make your discoveries yet. But first I want advice. I am the commissioner from the Transport Union, the Air Traders. Never heard of us? You will. We've got together—we've scraped ourselves together. We are picking up what we can of the old air and sea lines of the world and restoring trade. Trade—which is civilization. We're the Hansa Merchants of a new world. We want to make this a district centre. Are there any mechanics left here—any scientific workers, any capable men? You—I know. I want a district commissioner and if possible a district council."

Harding: "There is your man." (Indicates Gordon.)

John Cabal scrutinises Gordon. "What are you?"

Gordon: "Ex air-mechanic, Sir. Here I am called the master engineer. A sort of handy man for any machinery we have left. Plumbing chiefly, now, and door handles."

Harding: "Pilot?"

Gordon: "Yes, Sir." Salutes mechanically in the old fashion. "Do you mean something is brewing—that this isn't just another brigand dictatorship?"

John Cabal: "That's the note I like to hear."

Gordon: "I've been looking for something to hitch on to—ever since the pestilence. What did you say—World Air Transport—strange words nowadays?"

§27.

The Boss at his Headquarters in his glory—at a vast desk in some large, partly ruined building—a city hall or a palace. Guards, attendants, Yes-men, about him. (N.B.—A broken down telephone. See §34).

At side-tables in respectful attitudes sit three or four lay councillors, who are also dressed in vague imitations of uniform. One of these is Simon Burton.

He is a wary man of the conservator accumulator type, the eternal conformist. He has a thin anxious face and he is watchful and quick.

Conspicuous among the entourage of the Boss is a woman, Roxana Black, obviously beautiful, in a picturesque costume with a long black robe and jewels. Several other women also barbarically adorned. One of these is a young woman and, by a glance and a gesture, a state of incipient rivalry between her and Roxana is indicated. Roxana watches proceedings—comes and stands close beside the Boss at his right hand. Whispers to him. She is proud and ostentatious of her role of mistress and inclined to be assertive of her general importance.

The atmosphere is electric. The Boss is impatient to see Cabal and Cabal does not come. Messengers sent and returning. Roxana excited and anxious to see Cabal.

Roxana: "But you can't go to him. He must come to you."

People talking in the street. Gestures to suggest effect: *"Where does he come from?"*

Crowd gathering outside Harding's house. "What does he come for?"

Sentry really becomes sentry to protect Cabal from disturbance.

Smaller crowd around aeroplane. A mother to her little boy: "Don't go near it, dear!"

§28.

Regrouping of the people in §26, to indicate they have talked for some time. It is twilight, and Mary Harding brings and lights a candle.

John Cabal: "War—breakdown—economic collapse—pestilence—disorder. Everywhere the old order of things is in complete decay. And struggling to keep alive. Everywhere these little semi-military dictators. Still robbing, still fighting—still carrying on their fragments of warfare. All over the world. In the name of patriotism. Before the war there were seventy sovereign states. Now seventy times seventy. Government broken to fragments. And so we who are all that is left of the old technical services, the old engineers and industrial machinists, are turning our hands to salvage it. We have the air-ways, what is left of them, we have the sea. We alone can pull the world together again."

Gordon, standing up in his excitement: "Oh! I have been waiting for this. Yours to command, Sir."

John Cabal: "No. No. No, not mine—no more bosses—don't let us begin that again. Civilisation's to command. The world state of air-men, sea-men, men of steel, men of knowledge, men of power."

Knocking at the door.

The guard appears in great distress, with others and a superior officer who have been sent after him: "God knows what will happen to me—if you do not come."

John Cabal rises.

§29.

The Headquarters of the Boss as before. Grouping similar.

Entry of Cabal followed respectfully by his guards. The Boss attempts a lordly pose but Cabal's bearing is easy and familiar.

Cabal: "Well, what do you want to talk about?"

The Boss: "I want some explanation from you. What are you doing here?"

Pause. There is a mute struggle between the two men to steal the situation so to speak. The Boss glances at the puzzled faces of his entourage and realises that he cannot carry matters with a high hand and that he may get the worst of a public encounter.

The Boss: "I think we must talk. I do not want to be hard with you...."

Leads the way to a small apartment.

There they converse with only Simon Burton hovering near.

The two men close up.

The Boss: "If we let your trading machines come into our territory, we do so under sufferance. You must pay dues to us. Considerable dues. You must alight where we indicate. Nowhere else. You must have no communication with our general population."

John Cabal, who listens with ironical calm: "We must have agents here."

The Boss: "An agent. One agent. Very well. And now furthermore— *We* have a flying force here."

John Cabal: "I'm told it doesn't fly."

The Boss: "For a very simple reason. No fuel supply. We are in hopes of capturing one, then you will see us in the air again. We have a highly skilled mechanic at our disposal— one Gordon."

John Cabal: "I want that man as my agent here."

The Boss: "That can be arranged. We can *lend* him to you. But we stand in need of mechanical aid and fuel for our air service. Our lads are gallant but unskilful. Frankly we need technical assistance. The war with the Hill men has gone on long enough. We want to end it."

John Cabal: "But the World Transport Board will help no one to make war."

The Boss: "*End* war! We want to make a victorious peace."

John Cabal: "H'm. (He thinks). You say you have no fuel?"

The Boss: "Unless we can borrow from you."

John Cabal: "We sell— we never lend."

The Boss: "After all, it is I who am giving *you* permission."

The two men face to face. Facial duel.

The expression on John Cabal's face hardly confirms the Boss's assertion.

The Boss tries to dominate and betrays that he is disconcerted.

Fade out.

§30.

Harding, Mary Harding and Gordon on a waste place with John Cabal, who is departing. "Good-bye, my valiant committee of three," says Cabal from the cockpit. "Do as I have said, and next time you shall have radio—all that is coming back again—and then there will be no more need to say good-bye."

§31.

But war is still afoot.

The Boss's people clattering off to attack the Hill men. Battle. "Victory!"

Glimpse of street in Everytown with flags. People asking questions. "We have captured the coal pits and the oil retorts and we have got oil at last."

Youngster in a state of patriotic exultation: "We'll bomb the Hill men to hell now!" He wears a rosette badge.

The Boss riding down the street; all his confidence restored.

§32.

The Headquarters of the Boss. Scene as in §27.

The Boss, Simon Burton, Roxana, courtiers, guards.

Gordon is under arrest, awaiting the attention of the Boss. Roxana finds Gordon has an interesting face. Her eyes come back to him. She cannot believe he is unaware of her. Possibly she is right.

The scene is not without a certain rude magnificence. So a barbarian chief with his captains and mistresses and ruffian courtiers might have sat amidst the ruins of an Imperial Roman city.

The Boss leaves his table, walks up and down and orates:

"Victory approaches. Our long struggle with the Hill men has come to its climax. Your sacrifices have not been in vain. Our victory at the old coal pits has brought a new supply of oil within reach. Once more we can take the air. We have some good bombs left—1940 bombs. We can renew the War in the Air. We have nearly forty airplanes. They can be adapted to use this new supply of fuel. Forty! We shall darken the sky over the heads of those obstinate enemies who have challenged our right to predominance. Nothing remains to be done but a conclusive bombing of the Hills. Then for a time we shall have a rich and rewarding peace, the peace of the strong man armed who keepeth his house.

"And now at this supreme crisis, you, Gordon, our master engineer, must needs refuse to adjust our old and trusted engines. You dare to tell me you must await orders from this World Transport Board, this conspiracy of foreigners and traitors before you do your duty."

Gordon: "The job is more difficult than you think. Half your machines here are hopelessly old. You haven't twenty sound ones – to be exact nineteen. You'll never get the others off the ground. The thing cannot be done as you imagine it. I want assistance from the Transport Board."

The Boss: "And you won't get help from your Transport Board. We've seen to that."

Gordon: "If you cut me off from the Transport Board, how can I do anything?"

The Boss: "This is a bluff. You know how things are with this World Transport Board of yours, and your confederate Harding knows. Yes – while you've been under arrest, he has been talking. He has been *made* to talk. Where is he?"

At a sign from the Boss, Harding is brought forward. He is rather dishevelled and handcuffed. He looks as if he had been manhandled.

The Boss: "Take off his handcuffs."

The Boss: "Well?"

Harding: "Well – what?"

The Boss: "The salute."

Harding: "*Damn* the salute."

Guard makes as if to strike Harding.

"No! No!" from Roxana.

The Boss takes his cue from her. "Never mind the salute now. We'll talk to him afterwards. You two have been dealing with what is practically a foreign power. We admit we conceded you a certain right to deal with this Transport Board, but it was on conditions. On definite conditions. We abate no atom of our sovereignty over you – we conceded you no release from your duty to the Combatant State. You, Gordon, to supply technical assstance to our air force. Your utmost. You, Harding, to help Gordon to deal with this fuel problem and to put your knowledge of poison gas at our disposal. Your utmost also. Never mind about your Transport Board – the Combatant State comes first."

Harding: "I tell you I will do nothing with poison gas. I am a doctor, not a poison dealer."

The Boss: "You've got the knowledge – if I have to wring it out of you."

Roxana intervenes and whispers.

The Boss: "Even if you have not the precise knowlege now, you have it at your finger ends. Don't pretend to be half-witted. The Combatant State is your father and your mother, your brother and your sister, your only protector, the totality of your interests. No discipline can be stern enough for the man who disdains that supreme obligation."

Harding: "Nonsense. We have our duty to civilisation; higher than any duty to flag or symbol or local state. You and your like are heading back to eternal barbarism."

Simon Burton: "But this is pure *treason*."

Harding: "In the name of civilisation, I protest against being dragged from my work here. Damn your silly war! I am working on the public health with the new material I have got from the Transport Board. Then suddenly I am handcuffed and hauled here. All my life has been interrupted and wasted and spoilt by war. I will not stand it any more."

Excitement of the retinue of the Boss.

Simon Burton shouts: "But this is Treason—Treason."

Guards rush upon Harding, seize him and twist his arms. He shouts with pain, astounded and dismayed.

Roxana protests: "No. No, not that."

Gordon starts forward as if to interfere and then stops short.

"Listen, my man, or it will be the worse for you."

Dr. Harding is sullenly silent. He is not used to pain.

The Boss: "We have need of your services."

Dr. Harding (hoarsely): "Well what do you *want?*"

The Boss: "You are conscripted. We enrol you as a scientific war worker. You are under my orders now and under no other orders in the world."

"Well?"

"Fuel and poison gas. Everyone knows you understand poison gas."

Dr. Harding: "I will have nothing to do with your air war. Not my business, I tell you, to help you to bomb the Hill people. I will not touch this work. Neither fuel nor gas."

The Boss: "You refuse?"

Dr. Harding: "Absolutely."

The Boss: "You are a most misguided and stiff-necked man, yet still I do not want to be forced to extremities. Nevertheless——."

He looks at one of the guards who carries a horse whip.

Simon Burton: "Sir, give him time for consideration—perhaps I might talk to him."

Roxana has been watching this scene. She intervenes now, whispering to the Boss with her eyes on Gordon. Gordon still ignores her, but she begins to feel he ignores her deliberately.

Gordon comes forward and salutes perfunctorily. There is latent insolence in his manner.

"Sir, may I have a word; I understand you want all those out-of-date crocks of yours, which you call your air force, to fly again—and to fly well."

The Boss: "Those are my orders."

Gordon: "I think that with Dr. Harding's help I could make several of them, a score of them, perhaps, fly reasonably well. The rest are hopeless."

Dr. Harding (astonished): "You are a traitor to civilisation. I won't touch it."

Gordon looks at him and then continues to address the Boss.

"If you will send Dr. Harding back to his laboratory and leave him free—and leave me free to talk to him, I promise you you will see all that is possible in your air force in the sky again—before the month is out."

Dr. Harding: "I will have nothing to do with it."

Gordon (to the Boss): "Leave that to me, Sir. I *must* have Harding to help about the fuel."

The Boss hesitates and then after a whisper or so with Roxana, gives a sign of assent.

He has an afterthought: "No sabotage?"

"You shall see better flying than you have seen for five years."

"If you play me false, make no mistake, the three of you suffer together. You—yes, and your wife, too—all hostages for each other. Hostages. Do you understand what that means?"

§33.

Harding's laboratory. Harding, his daughter and Gordon come in one after the other.

Harding turns and speaks angrily to Gordon: "So you agree to work and fly for these war makers? And you promise for me—*me* to help you. You do that to escape *discipline*. Since when did you become a coward, Gordon? Let us die like men. Think what will be the result of our surrender. Just when the World Transport Board has brought a gleam of hope to us. Have you no faith in that?"

Gordon: "I've thought out that."

Harding: "Well?"

Gordon: "This isn't the precise time for disobedience."

Harding: "You are going to put his machines right and put them up in the air for him?"

Gordon: "If you will help about the fuel."

Harding: "And bomb the people in the Hills?"

Gordon: "No. That won't follow."

Harding: "What do you mean?"

Gordon: "I prefer to begin disobeying the Boss—when I am well up in the air—and not before. Someone must tell the Transport Board they have got hold of this oil and that fighting is going on. There are no means of sending a message within three hundred miles. The only way—is to fly there. *Now* do you see?"

Mary: "He won't trust you. He'll send up a guard with you."

Gordon: "We won't meet trouble half-way. Perhaps he won't. What does concern me more is this; that you are hostages. I may have to be away three or four days. I don't know how soon the World Transport Board will be able to help us. . . . I shall be away—but you two will be here. . . ."

Hesitation.

Mary: "Yes—but you must go, my dear."

Harding: "I can stand it. We *have* to stand it. Go."

§34.

The Boss in his inner room with Simon Burton. (There is, by the bye, a broken down telephone in this room.)

Burton: "I suppose this World Transport Board *is* merely a trading company."

Boss: "Why do you keep harping on that? What else can it be? It is no sort of government as I understand governments."

Burton: "I suppose they haven't got bombs."

Boss: "Why should they have? If they had they would probably have been selling them to us before now. They are just traders."

Burton: "Ye-e-es. I wish we had news. If we had posts and telegraph as we used to do. Look at that old thing (telephone). It's just an antique. Nowadays, things happen and you don't know about them. I'd give something for a newspaper now. I'd give anything for a newspaper."

Boss: "What's worrying you?"

Burton: "This Transport Board. If it travels as far as *he* said it does, then it must be spreading all over the world—like a net."

Boss: "Well, what of it?"

Burton: "Suppose they say—suppose they take it into their heads to say "Stop" to our little war with the Hill men."

Boss hit for a moment: "*What!* Are we to be dictated to and told not to go to war by Air bus drivers? Of all people!"

§35.

The laboratory of Dr. Harding. Mary is alone. She is obviously in a state of great anxiety. She is clearing up the working bench, replacing light weights from the balance scales into their boxes, etc. She keeps looking out of the window.

She sees Simon Burton and Roxana approaching below. Tension.

Then they are in the room together.

Simon Burton: "We have wanted to come and see you."

Mary: "My father and my husband have gone to the new fuel tanks to see what can be done there."

Simon Burton: "Good news. Your father isn't as disloyal as he seemed. He was just in a passion."

Mary stands with her back to the bench defensively.

Roxana, ignoring Simon Burton and concentrating on Mary: "I have heard so much about you. I want so much to understand you. You see—you're so clever."

The two women are in marked contrast. Mary is dressed plainly and poorly without a trace of coquettishness. Her fair hair is cut short. Roxana is as smart and picturesque a creature as the barbaric resources of the age of disorder permit.

The two women are interested in and attracted by each other, but Simon Burton intervenes. He has something to say to Mary.

Simon Burton: "I do hope your father and your husband mean to stand by the Combatant State. We have this little war. .... Personally I'm all on your father's side. I'm all for peace and science and order. But we must end our little war first. You know—I hate all this brutality here—this compulsion."

Mary perplexed by this speech. She looks from him to Roxana and again scrutinizingly at him.

Simon Burton: "No, I'm a civilized man. It may be treason to say it. But the Boss—he's noble—creative—but his ways are rough. This whip business. This beating. (Confidentially.) I have intervened to save your father from beating. Already. I know—it is scandalous. But the Boss will brook no opposition. He—he beats women. He sticks at nothing. Rough!"

He affects discreet doubt. "I am saying too much."

Makes to go.

Roxana: "No, I want to talk to Mary."

§36.

Roxana and Mary talking together.

Roxana: "Why don't your father and your man help the Boss and work with him. Oh, I know—they are *pretending* to work with him now. To gain time. But why are they against him? What are they after, what are *you* after. I don't understand you."

Mary: "I suppose we think the Boss—*uncivilized*."

Roxana: "And where is civilization *now?*"

She thinks and perhaps repeats a phrase she has heard. "Has there ever been civilization? Mary, it's a dream."

Mary: "And what is not a dream?"

Roxana: *"This."*

Mary: "Squalor. War—incessant war and disorder."

Roxana: "War means victories. Disorder means adventures. Struggle means life. Do your men really *believe* in this civilization?"

Mary: "Even now—in civilization—in a wide world without war or cruelty."

Roxana: "And your Gordon looks so sane! Does *he* really believe stuff like that? Doesn't he adore *you?* Doesn't he want power and importance for your sake and his own?"

Mary: "I could not love him—if I thought him as small as that."

Roxana: "Small as that! Human as that! Mary, I *like* you. We are sisters. All this is madness. Look at things as they are. Why do your men struggle against the Boss and his gallant fighters? The Boss is glorious. He has restored the spirit of a dying nation. Oh, he *has!* I know. I believe it. That Gordon of yours could be a splendid fellow, too, lord of the air."

Mary (staring before her): "You think that war and struggle and chance happiness and general misery, all this squalid divided world about us, must go on for ever. Are you dreaming, or am I?"

Roxana: "*You.* You want an impossible world. You are asking too much from men and women. Particularly from women. What *do we* want? Knowledge, civilization, the good of mankind? Nonsense! Oh, nonsense! We want satisfaction—we want personal satisfaction. We want glory. Men and women, everyone, wants glory. No one can live without some sort of glory. I want the glory of being loved—the glory of being wanted—desired—splendidly desired—and the glory of feeling and looking splendid. Do men want anything different? My man too wants the glory of being loved—don't I know it? The glory of bossing things here—the glory of war and victory. This new world of yours will never come. This wonderful World of Reason. It won't be worth having if it does come. It will be dull and safe and—oh, dreary! No lovers—no warriors—no adventure."

Mary: "No adventure! No glory in helping make the world over—anew! It is *you* who are dreaming."

Roxana: "Helping men! Why should we work and toil for men? Let them work and toil for us? [*i.e.,!*—ed.]"

Mary: "But we can work *with* them!"

Roxana: "And what will *they* have to work for then?"

Mary: "Greater things."

Roxana: "There's no flavour in those greater things. I tell you, Mary—we are the salt of life. And if the salt has lost its savour wherewithal shall life be salted?"

Turns to the audience defiantly. She breaks through the film so to speak.

"Give me the love interest all the time—it's love that makes the world go round. Men and women are made for love making. All the rest—follows."

Is recalled to the story by the noise of an aeroplane outside . . .

Sound of an aeroplane in flight. "What was that? Who was that? Gordon?" They watch from the window.

Roxana: "He's *flying!* Look, that's looping the loop—just to show off— —!" The two women side by side at the window.

Roxana: "But where is he going?"

Fade out.

§37.

Scene from the air. Scenery so far as it is visible of a world largely in ruins. First the scenery. Then the aeroplane comes across it to blot it out.

Gordon pilots an old type machine first with anxiety and then with evident satisfaction at its performance. He listens to the engine. "Good!"

Behind him sits a rosette guard with a pistol.

It becomes evident that the aeroplane is not being flown according to instructions.

The guard protests. Gordon disregards him. The guard threatens. Still disregard. The guard points his pistol. Moment of mutual scrutiny. Gordon points downward. The guard insists menacingly. Gordon looks at the guard's undecided face, smiles, puts his thumb to his nose and spreads his fingers out. Then as the guard hesitates to shoot, Gordon loops the loop and then does the falling leaf trick. The guard drops the pistol and grips the sides. Gordon motions him to keep still and nothing further will happen.

The pistol is seen spinning down through the air and hitting the ground where it explodes.

Behind these things the scenery sways wildly and sweeps upside down, then as the pistol falls it rushes up until it comes to an abrupt stop as the pistol hits the ground and explodes. Effect of the scenery suddenly becoming still.

The aeroplane goes on in the distance—over the hills and far away.

Flash back to the two women at the window.

Roxana: "He's gone! He's left you."

§38.

Amidst the ruins of some great marine port or air port, the air mechanics are reconstituting their lives. This is the scene of the first Air Council. They have improvised an aerodrome among the ruins. There is no need for great hangars under the new conditions. Construction is going on. The new men here are working chiefly with helicopters of a novel type. The old familiar airplane is dying out.

Effect of helicopters and new flying machines coming from various directions to a central gathering.

§39.

The conference of the rebel savants and technicians. Gordon making his way into a great gathering in a hangar, in which a tribune has been erected.

The gathering is of mixed race and generally ill-dressed.

John Cabal, now a man of seventy, but upstanding and resolute, is addressing the crowd. His wife stands beside him and regards him loyally and proudly.

Cabal speaks:

"*Men who make* are tired of seeing their creations mis-used. Tired of having their work directed to base ends.

"We could give mankind universal health and long life—we have given poison gas.

"We could give universal plenty and we have given disorder.

"We have let the cheat, the bully, and the sneak be our masters. We have let ancient and outworn traditions, old hates and ape-like cunning, wreck the world.

"It has been *our* fault. We have not *insisted* that scientific methods could be applied to all human relations, to law and government—as well as material things. We have put new wine into old bottles and the bottles have burst and the wine has been wasted.

"But now we insist—

"Let our watchwords be:

"RESEARCH, INVENTION, WORLD PLANNING—AND SCIEN-TIFIC CONTROL.

"Freedom from the dead past.

"Freedom from the forestaller.

"Freedom from the cheat.

"Freedom from the gangster and terrorist.

"An end to demagogues? [i.e., !—ed.]

"An end to dictators!

"Let the Makers rule! Let us who know, take power!"

Acclamation. Not the excitement of men who hear a new idea, but the assent of men already decided in their minds.

§40.

Gordon making his way to the rostrum.

John Cabal is seen to ask what is it?

Gordon: "Everytown! Your native town."

John Cabal: "What of it?"

Gordon: "They have launched another idiotic war. Seized our offices. Taken hostages—Dr. Harding and my wife. We've got no radio there. No way of signalling. But it's urgent with us. Urgent!"

John Cabal goes back to the rostrum. He beats with a gaval [sic] to get a hearing. He holds up his hands. "We have to begin right away. There is a little war in the north west and there has been a battle. The Boss of Everytown has got some planes and is bombing the Hill men. One plane at least will have to go there now, whatever else we decide...."

§41.

The private apartment of the Boss. A large room in a once comfortable country house. Everything is large, lavish and squalid. The furniture is or looks like loot. Fabrics are threadbare and patching is rough. (See note about breakables in §21.) The Boss is in dishabille. His bed, recently slept in, is shown. He has been sleeping heavily and he listens almost stupidly to what Simon Burton tells him. A newly arrived messenger in oilskins stands at the back.

Simon Burton: "At last we have definite news."

The Boss: "Our intelligence department gets worse and worse. What is it?"

Simon Burton: "Bad news. Gordon didn't fall into the sea; that was a false report; he got away to the Western World Transport depot."

The Boss: "Well?"

Simon Burton: "He's coming back. In a new machine, a new sort of machine—and with gas bombs."

The Boss is waking up slowly. He gets up and walks a few paces. An attendant with food and coffee on a tray is disregarded.

The Boss: "Why didn't we leave their machines and chemicals alone? And hang the aviators and chemists."

The Boss: "I might have known. Why did I tamper with flying? Why didn't I see it before? Why didn't we see it before?"

Simon Burton: "We had to keep pace with the times."

The Boss: "We had to *stop* the pace of the times."

Simon Burton: "Well—we needed aeroplanes—against the Hill State. And somebody would have started in again with aeroplanes and gas and bombs if we hadn't."

The Boss: "Somebody would. Some fool would. Burton, I begin to see how things are. All this science and invention; its [sic] the enemy of everything that is natural in life. They will destroy nations, governments, loyalties; destroy all that men have valued and ruled their lives by, since history began. New machines, have they? New gas? I might have known. Didn't I tell you that you and I ought to have read more books, or forbidden them altogether?—stamped on all these new ideas, this knowledge, or made it our own. Either you conquer science or it conquers you."

Simon Burton: "You know the Hill States have succumbed already. Only too gladly. It saves them from us. We got that last night."

The Boss: "Dirty cowards. The sacred right of making war!"

Simon Burton (weighing the situation): "New machines—this new gas."

The Boss: "What do you know about the new gas?"

Simon Burton: "Nothing. I don't even know that it has been used anywhere."

The Boss: "Perhaps it's a bluff. I remember reading long ago that gas is over-rated. And their new machines—how many have they?"

Simon Burton: "Only two or three, it seems, in this part of the world, at any rate."

The Boss: "We have forty."

Simon Burton: "Eighteen that will fly."

The Boss: "And we have hostages. That's good. ... I'm glad now we haven't shot them already. I wonder if that fellow Harding. ... Of course! He can tell us what to do about the gas. If we have to wring his arms off and knock half his teeth down his throat to make him do it."

He is gathering courage again. He goes to his neglected coffee and gulps it down. "They have to come to earth sometime."

His confidence returns visibly. He eats and gesticulates with the food in his hand. He repeats, "They have to come to earth sometime."

The Boss: "What *is* this World Transport Board? A handful of men like ourselves. They're not—magic. They aren't invulnerable."

Simon Burton: "But—if all they say about this gas is true!"

Simon Burton's grimace.

§42.

Flash. The Boss is seen before the hangar exhorting a number of very young youngsters in flying kit. A strange miscellany of aeroplanes is seen—most of them with a touch of Heath Robinson about them.

(We want someone here who can make burlesque aeroplanes.)

The Boss: "To you is entrusted the defence of your race, your fatherland and the ancient order. To you I entrust these good old tried and tested machines. You are not mechanics—you are warriors. You have been saved from the corruption of excessive education. You have been taught not to think, but to do—and, if need be, die. I salute you. I your leader."

They salute and go off perhaps a little reluctantly, one by one. They are pitifully boyish. There seems to be some difficulty in starting some of the old machines. The drone of departing engines is heard as they go up. Several do not get off the ground, but remain hopping about and making unpleasant mechanical noises. One crashes in rising.

§43.

Intermittent noise of aeroplanes.

The Boss, leading a rather disorderly following of guards and officers through a muddy street of puddles amidst shattered and ruined buildings. "We fight to the last."

Roxana appears dramatically. She is dressed rather prettily in semi-military style and she salutes—gravely.

The Boss kisses her hand as gravely.

§44.

Flash to a great cavernous space under a ruined building, the space is arched over by a fallen girder and wreckage. It looks out over a foreground of rubble upon distant hills and the sky. (The familiar skyline of Everytown.) There is a sound of aeroplanes in the air. The air fight in this scene is not visible on the screen, except for one aeroplane that falls far away. The Boss and his entourage (but not Burton) stand partly covered and partly in the open.

Harding and his daughter are brought up by guards.

Harding is handcuffed.

The Boss: "We're expecting friend Gordon in a moment. But we have a question or so to ask you before he comes down."

Burton appears with men carrying masks. "We have found some masks."

Harding shakes his head.

The Boss: "What does he say?"

He goes towards Harding.

"What do you say?"

Harding: "*Those* masks won't help you."

The Boss: "Well, and they won't help *you*. How do you know they won't help me? Do you know about this gas?"

Roxana follows him.

Harding: "I know a little about it."

The Boss: "And you kept it from me?"

Harding: "I told you gas war wasn't my business."

The Boss: "You *filthy* traitor. You lie. Give me a mask, someone. Where are the masks?"

Simon Burton comes forward. "Here they are, for what they are worth."

The Boss takes one, but does not put it on. Other people start forward to secure gas masks.

The Boss: "Wait a moment. Wait a moment. My dear, you must have a mask."

Roxana: "I don't want a mask. I won't let that man find me dead in a mask. I don't believe he'll use gas."

Harding: "These gas masks are no use, I tell you."

The Boss: "You tell me that. Tell me something more. I mean to make you tell me more."

Simon Burton: "Look! the enemy." He points.

The whole assembly concentrates its attention on the fight in the air that now begins.

Simon Burton: "Gods, what a queer thing. With a queer noise. It's less like an aeroplane than a flying fort."

The Boss: "Only one. Our boys will have him down in five minutes."

Rattle of a machine gun. Whirr of planes and then an unfamiliar throbbing.

An officer cries involuntarily: "Oh, by God!" and half turns his face away. *Crash.*

The Boss: "Ah, but this one! Gallant lad. Up at him!"

Roxana: "Oh, poor boy. It's got him."

Loud report and a shrill screaming note. Far off an aeroplane is seen crashing and flaming. It flares up into a column of flame and then smoke.

Simon Burton: "They haven't a *chance*."

The Boss: "They're all coming down. That chap's making off. The young cur! Oh—a nose dive. Serve him right."

Roxana, struck by a sudden thought, turns to Mary.

Roxana: "But how can they use gas, if you are here?"

Simon Burton in dismay. "He's got us." The unfamiliar rhythm throbs up and dominates the scene. Everybody is looking up.

Simon Burton: "Can't we go out and wave flags—white flags?"

The Boss: "The white flag? *Never!*"

Roxana: "But *how* can they gas?"

The Boss suddenly becomes frantic (an explosion of nerves): "Seize that man. He wants to wave the white flag. Put him against the wall there."

Burton, astonished, is seized by guards.

The Boss: "I'm not done yet." To Harding: "Now, you old imposter, come out here. Bring him out. The girl too. Tie 'em. Tie 'em, I say. Yes, tie their hands. Tie them with anything. Out there in the open. Where they can be seen. I've a good mind to spread-eagle them. Hullo, up there. Don't you see? The fellow doesn't even look at us. His head's done up in a sort of balloon."

Simon Burton: "But *me*."

The Boss: "You—you and your white flag! Always I've suspected you."

Simon Burton: "But I want to gain time. You don't understand. I want to treat——." Insinuating expression.

The Boss: "Treat. You want to sell me. You think I'm done for. Time to sell out, eh? Take them into the open there. Put them against that bit of wall where they can be seen—all three of them. Get busy, I tell you. This isn't a parade. This is war."

The Boss, to Harding, who is smiling faintly: "What are you grinning at? Put them in a line over there. Get a firing party. Doesn't that fool up there understand? Here he comes again. Why doesn't he look down? Have you no way of signalling to him? Haven't you a code?"

The Boss, to the unseen aviator as he throbs loudly overhead: "I'll shoot 'em—if you don't come down. I'll shoot 'em, I swear."

A bomb drops and explodes with a soft heavy thud some way off.

Simon Burton: "By heaven! They're bombing their own hostages!"

The Boss becomes frantic: "Where's the firing party? Get on with the shooting."

Burton breaks with the guards who hold him and comes forward. "Haven't I always been loyal? Haven't I always been with you? What are you thinking of?"

The Boss: "*You!* As long as it suited you. But my eyes are open now."

He rushes out into the open and shouts up into the sky: "I tell you we have hostages. How dare you bomb women?"

Three deep thuds of ascendent loudness, and the droning throbbing comes very close. Drums in the music to the end of the scene.

The Boss, struck by an idea, rushes to Harding: "You know what to do. You've got a drug or something. Out with it!"

The Boss draws a pistol: "Out with, I say, out with it."

A bomb falls and explodes among the ruins quite close at hand. Fragments of masonry and a puff of dust fly across the scene.

This stuns the Boss for a moment. Then he remembers Harding: "Shoot *him*, anyhow."

Roxana dashes at the Boss and seizes his wrist just in time to save Harding. The pistol fires in the air and the Boss drops it. Harding puts his foot on it.

The Boss is so amazed by Roxana that he forgets to go on killing Harding. "What! *You* turned against me too. You as well as him."

Roxana: "Don't you see we are beaten? This gas *overcomes*, but it won't kill. Can't you see? Gordon has beaten you."

The Boss: "Absurd! Beaten! I'm not beaten."

Roxana to Mary: "We're beaten. It is I who was dreaming. Our world has worked itself out and your world begins. . . . Mary, I never did any harm to you. I saved your father."

She is afraid and clings to Mary. At the same time she looks up with a dim half disposition to catch Gordon's eye.

The first whiffs of the new gas are *seen* and felt. Everything now slows down, except for the Boss in the foreground who is the last to succumb. All the rest of the picture behind him is creeping down to immobility so to speak. Burton, leaning against the wall, covers his face with his hands. Harding (serene and confident) sits down on some wreckage. His daughter kneels beside him. Roxana close beside her, also sinks to her knees. But her eyes go up with a sort of perplexed curiosity.

The Boss comes up with his back to the auditorium. "Nobody shall say I showed the white flag. The old order dies fighting."

He makes a great effort against the creeping paralysis of the gas. "Shoot the devils as they stand, I say. Shoot them down. What are you all doing? Am I dreaming? Why don't you—*move?*"

Two men stagger and drop drowsily. The others droop.

The Boss: "I won't have it. I won't have it like this."

He wipes his hand across his face as if he can no longer see or think distinctly.

Close up of the Boss facing. He wipes his mouth and rubs his eyes. His face is suddenly distorted in a last violent effort to resist the gas. He bawls:

"Shoot, I say! Shoot. Shoot. We've never shot enough yet. We never shot enough. We spared them. Now they've *got* us. Our world or theirs. What did a few hundreds of them matter? We've been weak—*weak*. Kill them like vermin! Kill all of them! . . . Why should I be beaten like this? Weakness! Weakness! Weakness is fatal. . . . Shoot!"

He also falls.

Everyone becomes insensible.

Still figures. No contortion.

The droning throbbing rises to a climax and passes.

Receding explosions of bombs fainter and fainter.

Screen darkens down, irises out black and scene is restored slowly at daybreak in another part of the ruined town. Bodies lie about immobile.

§45.

Dawn.

Gordon in a new uniform of shining black material and a body helmet with a sort of under visor thrown back across his chest, is coming over the ruins.

Behind him come two men and two women similarly attired. They make tall, shining swift figures.

"They'll sleep for three or four days."

"Well, we've given them a whiff of civilization. The Gas of Peace. The last and best of gases."

"Nothing like putting the children to sleep when they are naughty."

Gordon leads the way. The rest are strangers to the town and follow him.

One or two rosette symbols are torn down as they are passed by the newcomers.

The group of insensible bodies under the great girder.

Gordon gathers up·Mary in his arms and looks at her. Kisses her: "My dear! It wasn't too late, my dear."

Women carry her off. Gordon shows great solicitude. "Take great care of her." He follows them some paces. Then he returns and speaks to the attendants who are carrying off Harding.

"Take care of them both."

"And as for *him*? (the Boss) tie him up in his infernal flag. Tie his hands and feet and oh!—*tie up his mouth.*"

He is about to turn away.

"And this man?" (referring to Burton).

Gordon stands over Simon Burton: "He's a difficult case. The sort of man who comes and goes. With you and against you. The commonest sort of man." He faces the audience and speaks to the man in the balcony. "Sometimes he's for freedom and sometimes he's for tyranny. He's never sure and always shifty. The utterly common man.

"When he comes too, will he serve? No. He will just hang on and seek some advantage for himself. He will tamper and muddle with our money if he can. Muddle with our politics if he can. Intrigue if he can. Scotched—not killed. Leave him to wake up to the new world in his own way and his own time. . . ."

He thinks of Mary and is about to follow her.

"There's still the Lady!"

Gordon with manifest reluctance turns back again.

The attendants have brought forward Roxana Black. She lies in a state of quite beautiful insensibility.

Gordon: "This is still more of a puzzle. Here's a pretty thing and a very pretty thing and what's to be done with this very pretty thing? . . . The eternal adventuress. A common pretty woman who doesn't work. A Lady! She has pluck. Charm. Brains enough for infinite mischief. And a sort of energy." The next few sentences are aimed at the Lady in the balcony seats: "She'll make her eyes at men to the end of her time. Now the bosses go the way of the money grubbers, I suppose it will be the turn of our engineers. Wherever power is, she will follow. Here they are both of them! Common souls. The common man who cannot be trusted with duty or machinery and the common woman who cannot be trusted with men! We can't always keep them under gas. We've got our work cut out for us still. Oh! Take her along."

Surveys the whole ruinous scene for a moment.

"And now for the World of the Airmen and a new start for mankind."

Flash outskirts of the town. Wondering people who have been outside the gas area coming in to town to see what has happened. They can be coming down the hillside against the familiar skyline.

Flash of these same people coming into the square. Sleeping figures being carried across.

"What has happened?"

The bunch of the New Airmen in their black costumes appear and walk across scene.

A man sleeping on a heap of rubbles in the foreground wakes up slowly and rubs his eyes. Yawns. Comic perplexity. He looks up in the air to see if the air fight is over. Sees these New Airmen in the distance.

He follows their movements.

He enquires (with the audience): "And *now*, what's going to happen?"

He struggles to his feet.

§46.
The Work Series.

A triumphant musical sequence.

Flash of a room, architecturally vast, unfurnished, with a great map of the world on a wall. A crowd of men (and some women) on the floor. On the platform, Cabal with a great pointer, and one or two other men.

Cabal: "This is where we concentrate. Here we can hold out if things go badly."

Flash of whirring planes rising from the conference. Droning and humming as they disperse. Effect of dispersal. Planes still make mechanical noises but N.B. the planes in the last part are to be absolutely silent.

Scenes of the Airmen's War.

Scenes of the suppression of rebels and robbers in the desert or wild mountain scenery, by flying machines of a new pattern. The robbers gallop and surrender as the shadows of the machines sweep over them.

A sequence of creative work and power.

Flashes to give a crescendo of strenuous creative activity to balance the first war crescendo.

In one Dr. Harding, his laboratory beautifully equipped again, is seen at work with his daughter. Gordon comes in to greet her. This is the last glimpse of that story.

Work in furnaces, upon embankments, in mines, upon great plantations. Men working in laboratories. This will have to be drawn from contemporary stuff, but that stuff must be *futurised* by putting unfamiliar flying machines in the air, projecting giant machines in the foreground, making great discs and curved forms swing and rotate enigmatically before the spectator. A lot of this may be contrived by blending small figures of workers with vast moving models of strange design.

Flashes of molten metal running.

Flash of some dark liquid dripping slowly while a man in a peculiar gas mask watches it.

Emphasise by banners, streamers and inscriptions:

RESEARCH
 INVENTION
  WORLD PLANNING and
   SCIENTIFIC CONTROL.

There is a progressive improvement in the clothing of the workers and the neatness and vigour of the machinery as this series goes through. New architectural forms appear presently, prevail for a few flashes and pass.

Compare the description of time-travelling in the TIME MACHINE.

§47.

A large space rather than a room partaking of the nature of a conservatory and large drawing room. There are neither pillars nor right-angle joins. The roof curves gently over the space. There are some beautiful plants in a sort of basin in which a fountain plays and beyond are other plants with a glimpse through a window of the city ways outside. At the far end the space is limited partly by this window which has no frame but is merely a piece of transparent soundproof wall and partly by an opaque barrier. An old gentleman, evidently very old, but in no way diseased or decrepit sits in an armchair close to a very pretty intelligent little girl (8 to 14) who lies prone on a couch and looks at a piece of apparatus on which pictures appear as she manipulates a few simple knobs. The old man wears a velvet cape with the exaggerated shoulders of the period (see later) and his hair though white is abundant. Some strange pet animal may repose on a rug or a capuchin monkey play with a ball. A doll (in an *exaggeration* of the costumes of the year 2054) sprawls in a corner.

General view and then come to the two people, the girl and the fine-featured old man.

The little girl: "I *love* history and I love history pictures. It's so exciting to see how the world has changed."

Old Man: "I've seen it change, my dear. When I was a little boy I saw John Cabal—I saw him with my own eyes. Yes—the great John Cabal. He was the great grandfather of Oswald Cabal the President of the Council."

The little girl: "Just as you are my great grandfather!"

She looks at her pictures. "What a funny place New York was—all sticking up and full of windows!"

(Picture displayed).

Old Man: "They built houses like that in the old days. It was the age of windows. They had no light inside their cities everywhere as we have. They just had the coming and going of the sunshine. So they had to stick the houses up into the light. Sometimes it was too hot. Sometimes it was too bright. Generally it was dark. They had no properly mixed and conditioned air. They opened and shut those windows to let in the wind and the wet and the cold. I don't know how to describe these windows to you but perhaps there are pictures...."

Two flashes of New York *en face* and from the air.

"Everybody lived half out of doors. Up staircases and elevators. They lived higher than the rooks. Windows, windows everywhere. Windows of soft glass. The age of windows. Lasted four centuries. Windows were always getting broken."

? Fantasy on the theme of windows. Casements, sash windows, cracked, dirty skylights. People trying to stop draughts. People working uncomfortably in a bad light, etc., etc.

"People never seemed to realise that we could light the interiors of our houses, night and day, with sunshine of our own, and better, so that there would be no need for windows and no need to poke our houses up ever so high into the air, and that it would be far more convenient for cities to nestle naturally into the hills. See what queer stuck-up shabby things their houses were!"

? Momentary flash of a row of early twentieth century villas.

Little Girl: "Weren't the people *tired* going up and down stairs?"

Old Man: "They were *all* tired and they had a disease called colds. Everybody had colds and coughed and sneezed and ran at the eyes."

Little Girl: "What's sneezing?"

Old Man: "*You* know. Atishoo!"

Little girl sits up very greatly delighted: "Atishoo. Everyone said Atishoo. That *must* have been funny."

Old Man: "Not so funny as you think."

Little Girl: "And you remember all that, great grandfather?"

Old Man: "I remember some of it. Colds we had and indigestion from the queer bad foods we ate. It was a poor life. Never really well."

Little Girl: "Did people laugh at it?"

Old Man: "They *had* a way of grinning at it. They called it humour. It was a pitiful grin at times. And then there was noise. Look at our mirror here—of the country outside."

The picture shows the old familiar skyline of hills, but now it is all graciously in order. It looks out over a sort of parapet (to give distance).

"Atishoo," says the little girl, amused.

Old Man: "There's our home Everytown and there's a million people perhaps living and busy within three miles of us. And it looks like what *they* would have called countryside."

"Garden?"

"Yes, garden. Garden is the word. Their countryside was just muddle and weeds. In the roadway there, there are scores of cars passing and we do not hear them. A hundred years ago it would have been all noise. But listen. (Apparatus.) How still the world is! And now look at Paris a hundred and twenty years ago. Listen to Paris."

Air view of Paris in 1934. Glimpse of congested streets with a great uproar of town noises—a drill at work, etc., etc.

Little Girl: "And that's the world John Cabal and his airmen tidied up. I'm glad *I* didn't live in it great grandfather."

Old Man: "That's only the best of it. I could hardly tell you of their wars, the pestilences. Oh—horrid."

Little Girl: "Horrid! I don't want to see or hear about it. The Wandering Sickness and all that. None of that will ever come again, great granddad? None of that will ever come again?"

Old Man: "Not if progress goes on."

Little Girl: "They keep on inventing new things now, don't they? And making life lovelier and lovelier?"

Old Man: "All this new music they are making—Yes." (Has his doubts). "Of course—*some* of it. I suppose I'm an old man, my dear, but it seems almost like going too far. This Space Gun of theirs that they keep on shooting."

Little Girl: "Great grandfather, what *is* this space gun? I don't understand it great grandfather."

Old Man: "It's a gun they fire by electricity—it's a lot of guns one inside the other—each one fires the next inside. *I* don't properly understand that. But the cylinder it fires out at last, goes so fast that it goes—swish—right away from the earth."

Little girl entranced: "What!—right out into the sky! To the stars."

Old Man: "They may get to the stars in time, but what they fire at now is the moon."

Little Girl: "You mean they shoot cylinders at the moon! Oh—*poor* old moon!"

Old Man: "Not exactly *at* it. No. They shoot it so that it spins round the other side of it and comes back—and there's a safe place in the Pacific Ocean where it drops. They get more and more accurate. They say they can tell within twenty miles where it will come back—and they keep the sea clear. You see?"

Little Girl: "But how splendid. And can people go in the cylinders? Can *I* go when I grow up? And see the other side of the moon!"

Old Man: "Oh! They haven't sent men and women yet. That's what all the trouble's about."

Little Girl: "What trouble?"

Old Man: "Oh, never mind."

Little Girl: "It wouldn't *hurt* to go?"

Old Man: "We don't know. Some people say yes—some people say no. They've sent mice round."

Little Girl: "Mice that have gone round the moon!"

Old Man: "They get broken up, poor little beasties! They don't know how to hold on, when the bumps come. That's why there's all this talk of sending—a man perhaps. He'd know how to hold on..."

Little Girl: "He'd have to be brave—wouldn't he! ... I wish *I* could fly round the moon."

§48.

A man's arm is seen resting and on it a gauntlet with gadgets. On this is a sort of identification disc with minute lettering which is brought up for the audience to read:—

Oswald Cabal

President of the Council

Recede to show the owner of the arm.

Oswald Cabal in his study.

He is a man of 38–40, very like the John Cabal of Scene I, but he is healthier, his hair is differently arranged. He wears a white tunic, which has a broad yoke with which various gadgets are connected. He has this gauntlet we have seen on his left arm and a small wristlet on his right—silk or metal shot or open-work trunk hose and light shoes. Modern fittings. The air is conditioned about him and the light perfect. It is a diffused light from the ceiling—no lamps. There are no windows and no hinged doors. There are cupboards like china cupboards with glass doors, and also two panels (which are sliding doors). Various small objects, the use of which is not evident nor explained. No pictures and very little bric-a-brac. If the pose of Oswald Cabal can recall the pose of John Cabal in §2 so much the better. Then all was dark and shadowy; now all is brightness and clearness, but there is the same suggestion of anxiety in the bearing of the grandson of John Cabal.

He touches a button on his arm and listens. A harsh voice speaks:

"What is all this Progress. What is the good of this Progress? Onward and onward. We demand a halt, we demand a rest. The object of life is happy living——."

He turns off the voice with a movement of impatience. "The same old complaints. One would think the object of life was everlasting repetition."

He muses and drums with his fingers. "Hm, what did he say?" He draws out a metal record from a piece of apparatus which is resting on the desk—a sort of small steel measuring tape rolled up—puts it through a small machine and the same words begin to repeat. "No, not that," he says, stops it and tries another part of the record, which says: "We will not have life sacrificed to experiment. Progress is not living, it should be only the preparation for living."

"Ugh," says Cabal and shuts it off again.

He swings round the movable blank frame, hesitates, touches a stud which buzzes and then says: "I want to see what is going on in the Great Hall of Drama in London."

There is a brief interval. The blank frame is brought up so as to nearly fill the screen. The audience just sees Oswald Cabal's profile and shoulders against it. At first the picture in the mirror is very faint and there is a remote drone like pebbles under breakers. Then this grows rapidly loud and plain as Cabal adjusts the focus. Every change in the focus of the picture is to be accompanied by some movement of Cabal as if adjusting it.

A vast hall is revealed—seats and a great screen. Effect of vast sweep of roof—like some such a mighty cavern as the Mas d'Azil in Provence. It is a hall in which sound pictures are usually shown, but at present no show is going on. Instead there is a meeting. A number of people sit in the seats. Many others stand. On the stage before the screen Theotocopulos is speaking. He is a tall, slender man, bearded, very fluent and full of gesture. His appearance suggests the artist. He looks like one of the figures in a picture by his ancestor El Greco. He has come to a rhetorical pause and the people before him are applauding. As the applause dies down he resumes:

"Let us be just to these people who rule over us. Let us not be ungrateful. They have tidied up the world. They have tidied it up marvellously. Order and magnificence is achieved, knowledge increases. Oh, God! how it increases!" (Laughter).

At this point Cabal vanishes. One sees a small hut in a blizzard on a high, snowy mountain with (obvious) meteorological apparatus, wind vane and so forth. The hut opens, we see a much wrapped-up observer sitting and listening to Theotocopulos on the televisor. The Great Hall again.

Theotocopulos proceeds: "And still the hard drive goes on. They find work for all of us. We thought this was to be the Age of Leisure. But is it? We must measure and compute, we must collect and sort, and count. We must sacrifice ourselves. We must live for—what is it?—the species. We must sacrifice ourselves—all day and every day to this incessant spreading of knowledge and order. We gain the whole world—and at what a price! Such a small price, such a tiny price. Just the silly happiness of the idle and the simple."

Observer: "Oh, *shut up!*" and switches off.

A number of people eat together at an elegant table. Above them is a frame in which Theotocopulos is speaking.

"And now we are to go to the moon. This great gun with which they are experimenting is to take human beings—human beings—and hurl them into empty space!"

A lazy man lies on a bed and listens to Theotocopulos.

"Think of it. Two young people are to be subjected to this horrible danger. Into vacancy—into death!"

The lazy man features agreement. He raises his eyebrows, compresses his lips, nods his head.

Return to Cabal listening and watching in his bureau.

"Shall we endure it?" says Theotocopulos.

Oswald Cabal puts the screen out of focus, and as he does so, the picture fogs to grey and the voice grows small, shrinks to a squeak and ends.

§49.

A faint musical sound. Cabal touches a stud on his gauntlet and listens.

A secretarial voice says: "Raymond Passworthy of General Fabrics—to talk to you."

"Who is Raymond Passworthy?"

"He is a textile director. His son knows your daughter. His son is the other one who has been chosen to go to the moon."

"Ah! the father of Maurice. What does he want to say?"

"He says he wants to talk to you face to face—urgently."

Oswald Cabal: "Can he come? . . . Good."

Raymond Passworthy on his way. Moving platforms, spiral ways vanishing into tunnels, exposed lifts. Drifts of people come and go. A vision of the city interior of the new age. General impression here of architecture and structure. Types of individual not shown. A little figure making its way to Oswald Cabal through these city effects is Raymond Passworthy.

Entry of Raymond Passworthy through a panel to Oswald Cabal in his apartment.

Passworthy is a compacter, sounder reproduction of Pipper Passworthy in Scene I. He wears a more ornate costume than Oswald Cabal and there is a touch of decoration on his shoes. If his entrance can, by some familiar gesture, recall the entrance of Passworthy in §2 so much the better. Hand on the mouth and pause, *e.g.*

Greetings.

Oswald Cabal is a trifle effusive and insincere in his manner: "So we are fathers of rebel children, eh? An old problem, Passworthy. What to do with sons and daughters? Fathers like you and I were asking that question in the Stone Age."

Passworthy: "They won't be asking it for many more generations if all the young people are to do what your daughter and my son want to do."

Oswald Cabal: "Humanity is tough stuff. If it wasn't for the desperate young people it wouldn't have gone far."

Passworthy: "But to attempt to get to the moon! It's—It's going *too* far."

Oswald Cabal looks at him thoughtfully. "Perhaps it is—going too far. But that is the way with young people."

Passworthy: "Everyone who attempts such an expedition must be killed."

Oswald Cabal: "They are not going *to* the moon; they are going round it."

Passworthy: "That's a quibble."

Oswald Cabal: "They will come back."

Passworthy: "If I could believe that!"

Oswald Cabal: "The best thing for us both is to believe it."

Passworthy walks about. "Why should *our* children be chosen for a thing like this?"

Oswald Cabal: "Science asks for the best."

Passworthy: "But my boy! Always such an impetuous little devil. All very well for you, Cabal. You are the great grandson of John Cabal, air dictator—experiment is in your blood. You—and your daughter! I'm—I'm more *normal*. I don't believe my boy would ever have thought of it. But the two of them go together."

Oswald Cabal: "They will come back together. This time there is to be no attempt to land on the moon."

Passworthy: "And when is this—this great experiment to be made? How long are we to have them before they go?"

Oswald Cabal (a little disingenuously): "I don't know."

Passworthy: "But when?"

Oswald Cabal: "When the space gun is ready again."

Passworthy: "You mean some time this year?"

Oswald Cabal: "I think so."

Passworthy: "In the old days it was different. Fathers had authority then. I should have said *No* and that would have settled it."

Oswald Cabal: "Fathers have said No since the Stone Age."

Passworthy: "Our families have always been pretty close together. You don't know that? Oh, yes. My great grandfather was a neighbour and friend of your grandfather before the Final Wars. Pipper Passworthy, he was called. Why, I've got letters of his describing a Christmas Party with a smudgy little snapshot of the Christmas Tree. Look! He took a snapshot to send to my grandfather who was a schoolboy in Wales." (Show reminder photograph of Scene §3). This enables him to show use of a sort of breast or hip pocket gadget or the gauntlet. "Queer how the generations mix; Eh! Here am I begging you to save our children from this modern madness."

Oswald Cabal regards him with a touch of kindly amusement. "But *would* it be saving our children."

Passworthy: "Yes—it would."

Oswald Cabal: "For what?"

Passworthy bursts out: "Children are born to be happy. Young people should take life lightly. There is something horrible in this immolation—it is nothing less than immolation—at eighteen and twenty-one!"

Oswald Cabal: "Do you think I have no feelings—feelings like yours? That I don't love my daughter. . . . I'm just snatching an hour to-day—just to see her and look at her—while I can. All the same, I shall let her go. When the time comes. She's away in the mountains at the water chutes—in training. I suppose your son is there. Come with me and see them. Face to face with them we may not feel just as we do here. Anyhow it will be well to be with them a bit. . . . It's fine outside. Will you come—do you mind coming out in the weather with me?"

Passworthy: "Mind? I'm an open-air man. This conditioned air may be better for us with its extra oxygen and so on, and the light here brighter and steadier, but give me the old sky and the wind on the heath and the snow and the rain, the quick changes and the nightfall. I don't *love* this human ant-hill in which we live. I'm conservative to the bone."

Oswald Cabal, standing ready: "We'll go and talk to the young people."

§50.

A group of four or five modellers at work upon clay figures which they are making. They listen to the television apparatus, in which Theotocopulos is heard perorating. The television has a characteristic frame so that it is immediately known for what it is. Perhaps only the lower part of that apparatus might appear here, showing Theotocopulos' legs and the front of the platform.

Theotocopulos is saying: "I have said all I have to say. Have these people the right to torment us by the spectacle of these human sacrifices? Have they the right to spoil the very peace of the starry heavens by their mad adventure?"

One modeller: "Hear, hear!"

Another dissenting: "No, No" (He stands up and turns the televisor off). "A man has a right to do what he likes with himself."

The First: "Never. That Space Gun ought to be destroyed. And *now*."

Another: "The thing ought to stop. Look!" (Holds up a model.)

All: "Good for Theotocopulos!"

Another: "But here!" Holds up an ugly caricature of Cabal.

They shake the figures at each other.

A group of young athletes in a bright light upon the edge of a shining swimming pool. Among them are Maurice Passworthy and Kate Cabal.

Above them is the now familiar frame of a television apparatus. One sees Theotocopulos bowing and turning away amidst a rush of applause which goes on as they talk.

Maurice: "This Theotocopulos is an old imbecile."

A Second Athlete: "The dear little children are not to take risks any more for ever. Just play with their little painties and sing their little songs."

A Third: "And find out nice new ways of making lovey-povey."

§51.

Oswald Cabal and Raymond Passworthy together walk along a path in what looks like a garden. At first very little is shown, but the path and the flowers beside it. These flowers are strange and beautiful.

Street scenes as Cabal and Passworthy pass along.

Galleries. Fountains. Moving platforms.

Here there is the best opportunity for showing social types. Men hurry by in working overalls. Others lounge or walk easily. Most of the women display much of the personal unconsciousness of the men, but the Eternal Feminine, in the form of a second Roxana (the same actress) in a consciously sex-appeal costume is still in the world. (This is the dress designer's best chance, so let it be taken.)

Passworthy: "Gallant lady."

Cabal looks back indifferently: "A pretty thing and a very pretty thing. But its [sic] strange to see her still flying her flags in a world that holds my daughter."

Passworthy: "Women change with the rest of the world."

Cabal: "Let's hope so. But look there! The butterflies are out to-day."

Another flaunting hussy passes.

The two men go through an archway into an establishment marked "OUTSIDE CLOTHING. 98B."

They are seen being measured by skilled tailors. At the end they are seen leaving the establishment by a portal opening on the exterior.

Their costumes are changed. The new clothing consists of tunics with leatherlike belts, trunk hose and cloaks with hoods. No hats. Shoulders very broad.

While they are being measured the small gadget on the gauntlet of Cabal's arm emits its note.

He answers: "Who is that?"

"Morden Mitani, very urgent."

"I am changing clothes at 98b. Can he come?"

"He is at the air station close by you. I will tell him – – ."

§52.

Cabal and Passworthy dressed for the open and about to leave the tailors.

Morden Mitani enters with an air of unusual urgency. Like Oswald Cabal he is a fit and capable looking man, clean shaven and fine featured. He wears similar clothing to Cabal's indoor clothes but of dark or black stuff.

Cabal leads him aside. The two talk closely.

Morden Mitani: "This trouble with Theotocopulos is more serious than we supposed. He ought not to have been allowed to talk on the television."

Oswald Cabal: "What can he do?"

Morden Mitani: "People are taking him seriously. They want to stop this firing of the Space Gun."

Oswald Cabal: "Why?"

Morden Mitani: "Theotocopulos has excited them. They object to sending human beings in the moon cylinder."

Oswald Cabal: "But if the human beings choose to go?"

Morden Mitani: "Still they object."

Oswald Cabal: "And if they object?"

Morden Mitani: "They may interfere with things. They may make—what did they use to call it—an insurrection."

"Against whom?"

"Against the Council."

Oswald Cabal: "I cannot imagine an insurrection. In the past insurrections were risings of downtrodden classes—and now we have no downtrodden classes. Everyone does a share in the work and everyone has a share in the abundance. Can mankind rise against itself? What is this Theotocopulos after?"

Morden Mitani: "What he calls the natural life of man. He talks of the loveliness and beauty of man's *little* life. Science he says is changing and destroying all that. He wants to call a halt to progress. He wants in particular to stop these extra terrestrial explorations with the Space Gun and the Moon Cylinder."

Oswald Cabal: "But how can he do that?"

Morden Mitani: "Suppose he gathers large crowds. We have no police, no troops, no weapons nowadays to keep crowds in order. We thought that was done with for ever. He has seized upon this experimental journey to the moon—these young people who are going— —."

Oswald Cabal: "Isn't one of them my daughter—my only daughter?"

Morden Mitani: "He says that shows your hardness of heart—shows what a monster science may make out of a man. He compares you to those Greek parents who sent their children to the Minotaur."

Oswald Cabal: "And if I sent other people's children—and saved my own!"

Morden Mitani: "You'd be in the wrong, anyhow."

Oswald Cabal: "But what can he do?"

Morden Mitani: "There is the Space Gun out on the seashore. It is hardly guarded at all. Suppose he incites a crowd! Nothing has been guarded in this planet for the past fifty years."

Oswald Cabal: "Then you'll have to organise a guard. After all you have your way-men and your inspection planes. And if there is—disturbance—isn't there still the Gas of Peace?"

Morden Mitani: "There *is* none. I want to call up the Council and get a sanction to make it. Meanwhile—(He smiles)—I have been having some made. Cabal, things are serious; I think it is a race against time—whether we can save that gun."

Oswald Cabal: "As bad as that!"

He rejoins Passworthy, moving gravely with a preoccupied air. He thinks and perhaps says: "Insurrection—against exploration—incredible!"

§53.

As Cabal and Passworthy go, Morden Mitani returns.

"One moment," he says. "I want you to see something."

He leads Cabal and Passworthy to a point where a high-flung bridge looks down on the city ways.

Far below a little straggle of people is gathering into a sort of procession. They are singing either the Marseillaise or music like it.

Morden Mitani: "Look at that. Listen to that!"

Passworthy: "But what's the trouble?"

Morden Mitani: "That's the outcome of Theotocopulos. That's—what do they call it?—a demonstration."

§54.

View outside the city in the year 2054. This has been glimpsed already in §47 in a mirror.

The scene, be it remembered, is a leap forward of ninety-five years from the age of disorder and one hundred and twenty from now and it must be sensationally better and *different* from any contemporary scene or the film will fall down.

The creative forces in mankind have triumphed and the face of the earth has changed.

There is serenity and beauty in the scenery of this last part. A novel vegetation of enlarged and modified forms blends with massive buildings built into the forms of the hills and mountains. Novel airships pass across the sky.

A very still scene of the world of 2054. Bright open air but not too bright. Real sky and cloud effects and a cloud shadow passing over the hills. Running water will also animate the effects. The interior scenes must be brighter than the exterior and more evenly lit.

N.B.—When an archway opens into the hill, the interior must be *brighter* than the world outside even in full daylight.

The general effect is of very beautiful, gentle hill country, agreeably wooded with a few groups of enigmatical buildings. *The same characteristic skyline of hill that we have seen since the beginning of the film reappears.* Men change, war changes to peace, but the hills are relatively eternal. It is the same place although every vestige of the old Everytown has vanished. There are great portals upon the hillside and minor doorways here and there. Through a great archway near at hand a varied traffic comes and goes and in the distance a few insect-like flying machines pass down to or rise from an unseen aerodrome. A few unfamiliar animals graze in the foreground (? Whipsnade or Tring). The vegetation of the outer scene is beautiful and healthy, but nothing like so rare and fine as the vegetation grown in conditioned air and soil and under special lighting within the city. The camera approaches the hillside until we see only the doorway by which Cabal and Passworthy come out of the city. They emerge.

Passworthy with an effort to be easy minded: "Here we are in the open air. Back to nature! Well, well—don't you feel the better for it?"

Cabal: "If I did I should make trouble for our ventilation department. I'll confess I like the varying breeze and the shadows of the clouds—for a change."

Passworthy: "There's some open air people playing at that old game of golf away there. It's a good game. I swing a club a bit myself. I don't suppose you do?"

Cabal: "I don't. Why do you?"

Passworthy: "It keeps one from thinking."

Oswald Cabal (expression).

Passworthy: "It couldn't keep me from thinking to-day anyhow. Oh, I can't keep my mind off it! These young people of ours! I want to see them. ... I'm out of sorts with this modern world and all this progress. I suppose our city is all very fine and vital, and this countryside trimmer and lovelier (if you like) than it was in the days of competition and scramble. I suppose there is hardly a bramble or a swamp or a thicket left in the world. Why can't we rest at this? Why must we go on—and go on more strenuous than ever?"

Oswald Cabal: "Stop thinking or toiling for ever more?"

Passworthy: "Take life as it comes."

Oswald Cabal: "Our whole world came very near to everlasting smash a hundred years ago—because it took life as it came."

§55.

Passworthy and Oswald Cabal still on their way to the Physical Exercise Centre. They go along a path of carven rocks amidst foaming rapids.

Then they are discovered waiting for their children in the Physical Exercise Centre. This is a half out-of-doors place, a sort of glazed loggia with immense windows of flexible unbreakable glass. Someone might lean a hand against this window—producing an optical distortion of the view if this can be contrived. There is a view of a series of chutes outside, down which water is pouring with great swiftness. Some are steeper and swifter than others and ever and again athletes (of either sex) flash by very swiftly. One or two spectators look out on these feats and Passworthy and Oswald Cabal do likewise.

Passworthy: "Here again every day some one is injured or killed! Why should anyone be killed?"

Oswald Cabal: "Everything is done to eliminate the clumsy ones before an accident occurs. But how are we to save the race from degeneration if this sort of thing does not go on?"

Passworthy: "My God! Look at that fellow!"

Rush to the window. A man flashes by evidently losing his balance.

Oswald Cabal: "He's all right."

Oswald Cabal: "Oh! Here they are!"

Turn.

§56.

The two young people appear in an archway – radiantly. They are exalted by some news they have to tell their parents.

They must be very fit and good-looking and not more than eighteen and one and twenty respectively. They must have good voices and Kate Cabal, the girl, must not have merely *pretty* features. She must be beautiful and not pretty-pretty. They are rather similarly dressed, she with a longer tunic and cross bands between her breasts. They have half hose and bare knees. They wear no gadgets. Theirs is a sort of gymnastic costume.

They wave their hands gaily in greeting. Everybody is trying to keep down any emotion.

Raymond Passworthy: "Well, you young people. How many killed to-day?"

Maurice Passworthy: "No one. One fellow slipped and broke his thigh – but he's being taken care of. He'll be well in a week. I just missed him as he fell. Or I might have come a cropper, too."

Raymond Passworthy: "Isn't life dangerous enough that you have to do these things?"

Maurice Passworthy: "My dear Father, it isn't nearly dangerous enough for a properly constituted animal. Since the world began life has lived by the skin of its teeth. It's used to it and it's built that way. And that's what's the matter with us now!"

Raymond Passworthy: "And to hell with Safety First!"

Maurice Passworthy: "To hell with Safety First! Live dangerously! That's the better motto."

Oswald Cabal: "Lunch first. Live dangerously if you like but not hungrily. Come into the city with us. And then we'll talk about all that."

Raymond Passworthy: "We'll talk about all that. Anyhow we've still plenty of time to talk."

A momentary pause.

This is to be a very intense moment. The two young people look at each other and then at their parents.

Maurice: "Not so very long now, father."

Another pause. The two older men realize that there is much in that sentence.

Kate seems about to speak but does not do so.

Raymond: "I suppose we have some *months* yet."

Cabal looks intently at his daughter.

Kate: *"There's just a few hours over one month.* Everything is ready now."

Maurice: "We could go now. The moon is coming into the right position even while we are talking. But they are waiting a month. To make sure."

Raymond: "You are going in four weeks! Four weeks! I forbid it!"

Cabal: "I thought — —"

Maurice Passworthy: "No, it is all arranged."

Raymond Passworthy: "Theotocopulos is right. This thing mustn't be. It is human sacrifice. Maurice my son!"

Cabal takes his arm. "Let us eat together and talk. Would you have your son go back on his word? There is still a month ahead of us. Let us talk it over calmly."

He speaks through his gauntlet. "Arrange for us to lunch at the Cupola. Tell Morden Mitani I shall be there in half an hour. Ask for the small Alcove over the city ways."

§57.

Insurrection Aflame.

The reception room of a dining place in the year 2054.

Enter Morden Mitani, excited and hurrying.

Morden Mitani: "Cabal! Cabal! It has happened sooner than I thought! Theotocopulos is out with a crowd of people — pleasure people, art people, producers, all sorts of followers. Not here — but he is going to the Space Gun. They are going to break it up. They say it is the symbol of science — and they want no more of that."

Oswald Cabal: "Have they any weapons?"

Morden Mitani: "Bars of metal. They can smash electric cables. They can do no end of mischief."

Oswald Cabal: "Are there no weapons on our side? Cannot your traffic control produce a police?"

Morden Mitani: "They have been warned. They are coming. And there is that old gas — the gas that makes people insensible. The Gas of Peace. I have been preparing it for days. I felt this coming. But this is so sudden. We must hold these people back — at any cost — for a time. Until our planes can come."

Raymond Passworthy: "Look!"

He points to the streets far below. A great crowd of people are seen marching. He opens a sound-proof window and the new revolutionary air (or the Marseillaise?) is heard.

Enter a technical assistant. Like Morden Mitani, he is darkly clad. He speaks but is inaudible. Cabal makes gesture to the window which Morden Mitani closes.

Technical Assistant: "It is a mob. It is a riot. It is barbarism come back. How can I get back to the gun in time?"

Cabal: "Who are you?"

Technical Assistant shows a sort of identification disc on his gauntlet. *William Jeans, Astronomical Staff – Space Gun.*

Morden Mitani, surveying crowd: "They will take two hours or more to march there. *Then* they will hestitate."

Technical Assistant: "Meanwhile we can fly. Oh, that gun must not be broken up! The pity of it! – if they smash the Space Gun! When the trial experiments had been made! When everything was ready!"

Maurice, echoing – with an idea growing in his head – "When everything was ready!"

Raymond also thinking the situation out: "And if they smash up this infernal gun – then honour is satisfied and you need not go!"

Maurice: "Oh, Father! *Father!*"

Cabal: *"They* won't smash the gun."

Maurice to Technical Assistant: "Tell me something. Suppose the gun was touched off and it was fired now. Would the cylinder reach the moon?"

The Technical Assistant looks at his watch. "No. It would miss and fly into space. But – It is now four. If the gun is fired at about seven to-night. Between seven and eight."

Kate: "And it *could* be?"

Technical Assistant: *"Yes."*

Maurice and Kate: "Then! – we go now."

Raymond: "I protest! . . . Oh! I don't know what to say. Don't go. Don't *go!"*

Cabal: "Let them go."

Morden Mitani: "We could have a plane ready for you in half an hour. I can send directions. . . . It can be done."

Cabal: "It *must* be done."

Morden Mitani: "You can have your meal here – all the same. It will give you something to do. We can come for you. We can hold them off – long enough for that anyhow. . . ."

§58.

The four sit at table in an alcove (lit from above) after the main part of the lunch has been eaten. The table is on a sort of glazed-in balcony looking down on the city ways. Far below are streets and people moving about. The table has no cloth, but there is fruit (unfamiliar) and fine and dark wine. No smoking. The glass and everything is very simple. Everything is pellucid and clean. There are no waiters or servants. The four help themselves and each other, but anything that is done with is put on a glassy band at the back and carried away. Behind this band in the recess on the alcove are flowers. This scene ought to be as beautiful a picture as possible.

Raymond Passworthy: "Isn't life good enough for you here? Here you are in a safe and lovely world. Young lovers. Just beginning love. And you want to go into that outer horror! Into the cold and darkness, the deadly cold silence of outer space. Let some old man go in that accursed moon sphere! Let some one go who is sick of life."

Kate Cabal: "They want fit young people. Alert and quick. And we are fit young people. We can observe, we can come back and tell."

Maurice Passworthy: "That's why we are in training."

Raymond Passworthy: "Cabal! I want to ask you one plain question. Why do you let your daughter, your only daughter, dream of going on this mad moon journey?"

Oswald Cabal answers slowly with his eyes on his daughter. "Because I love her. Because I want her to live to the best effect. Dragging out life to the last possible second isn't living to the best effect. The nearer the bone, the sweeter the meat. The best of life, Passworthy, lies nearest to the edge of death."

He suddenly takes his daughter's hand which has been stretched out towards him.

"And besides—how can *we* ask others to do what we dare not do ourselves?"

Raymond Passworthy: "I am a broken man. I do not know where honour lies."

Oswald Cabal, to his daughter: "My dear, I love you—and I have no doubt."

Maurice Passworthy: "A century ago, no man who was worth his salt hesitated to give his life in war. When I read about these fellows in the trenches."

Oswald Cabal: "No. Only a few men *gave their lives* in war. Those men were caught by some tragic and noble necessity. What the rest did was to *risk* their lives.

"And that is all you two have to do. You two have to do your utmost to come back safe and sound. . . .

"And you are not the only ones who are taking risks to-day. Have we not men exploring the depths of the sea, training and making friends with dangerous animals and with dangers in every shape and form, playing with gigantic physical forces, balancing on the rims of lakes of molten metal— —."

Raymond Passworthy: "But all that is to make this world safe for Man— safe for happiness."

Oswald Cabal: "No. The world will never be safe for man—and there is no happiness in safety. You haven't got things right, Passworthy. Our fathers and our fathers' fathers cleaned up the old order of things because it killed *children*, because it killed people unprepared for death, because it tormented people in vain, because it outraged human pride and dignity, because it was an ugly spectacle of waste. But *that* was only the beginning. There is nothing wrong in suffering if you suffer for a purpose. Our Revolution has not abolished danger or death. It has made danger and death worth while."

§59.

Cabal, Passworthy, Maurice Passworthy and Kate Cabal, wrapped in cloaks, and climbing into an aeroplane of modern design. Here the aeroplane designer gets his chance.

Effect of purposeful hurried departure.

§60.

The works about the Space Gun and the Moon Cylinder. The gun is a vast mortar-like shell-within-shell gun. The Moon Cylinder is a metallic cylinder 30×10 feet in diameter, poised above the gun. It looks very small in comparison with the concentric shell of the Space Gun. These great bulks are seen indistinctly through an intricate fine scaffolding. The general effect is one of *monstrous* structures upheld by a delicate lattice. Great cables surround the Space Gun. The human figures are entirely dwarfed when the whole scene is shown. Later they are brought into importance by closer shots.

Through the midst of this vast structural mass swirls a torrent of turbine water. Great turbines spin silently in the background. This rush of water must be introduced to establish the gigantic scale of the thing and correct any suggestion that we are dealing (as we are) with a model. It may add to this effect if the scene is laid near the sea and sunlit breakers swirl among the outer piers of the scaffolding.

The whole body of the works can be situated in a sort of chine among high cliffs. Huge water pipes deliver the water to the turbines from above, and the main bulk of the gun emplacement must be separated by a space from the cliff and minor scaffolding against it, amidst which the would-be attackers appear.

Young athletes (men and women), mechanical workers, aviators and suchlike people are seen rallying upon the framework about the gun and cylinder. Then closer shots show Cabal, Passworthy and the two young people mounting through the scaffolding to a great platform of metal close below the cylinder, that furnishes a sort of rostrum for the ensuing speech. Morden Mitani, already in control, greets them. Other defenders cheer. Cries of "Cabal, Cabal!"

The insurrectionary song already heard in the city ways again becomes audible.

N.B. – The attackers are not "proletarians." They are the social equals of the defenders and wear quite similar clothes. But being rather on the artistic side their clothing is rather more vivid and varied. They appear first as stragglers, far below, or amidst the cliff scaffolding. Then over a cliff brow appear banners and then the roughly formed procession of men and women unarmed or armed only with metal bars, following Theotocopulos.

Theotocopulos comes out to a position on the cliff edge so as to confront, across a sort of gulf, Oswald Cabal and his group, standing on their quasi-rostrum close up to the cylinder.

These men are going to shout at one another across a big space. Someone may appear behind Cabal and fix something suggestive of an amplifier. This is merely to meet the critical objection that may be felt in the audience that normal human voices would be lost in the big space of the works about the Space Gun. It has no other importance.

Theotocopulos: "There is the man who would offer up his daughter to the Devil of Science!"

Oswald Cabal: "What do you want?"

Theotocopulos: "We want to save these young people from your experiments. We want to put an end to this inhuman foolery. We want to make the world safe for men. We mean to destroy that gun."

Oswald Cabal: "And how will you do that?"

Theotocopulos: "We have electricians with us. We shall find out what to do."

Oswald Cabal: "We have a right to do what we like with our own lives."

Theotocopulos: "*No.*"

Oswald Cabal: "We do not grudge you your artistic life. You have safety, plenty—all you need."

Theotocopulos: "Except freedom."

Oswald Cabal: "No one compels you."

Theotocopulos: "We want to live the common ancient life of man."

Oswald Cabal: "No one prevents you."

Theotocopulos: "How can we do that when your science and inventions are perpetually changing life for us—when you are everlastingly rebuilding and contriving strange things about us? When you make what we think great, seem small. When you make what we think strong, seem feeble. We don't want this expedition. We don't want mankind to go out to the moon and the planets. We shall hate you more if you succeed than if you fail. Is there never to be rest in this world?"

Passworthy breaks out. He stands up beside Cabal and shouts partly at him and partly at the people below: "Yes, I, too, ask you, is there never to be rest? Never? This is my son. And he has rebelled against me. What he does, he does against the instincts of my heart. Cabal, I implore you. Is there never to be calm and happiness for mankind?"

Oswald Cabal: "Listen. Listen to me, Theotocopulos. Listen to me, Passworthy. If I wished to give way to you, I *could* not. It is not us who war against the order of things, but you. Either you go forward or you go back."

Theotocopulos: "We will destroy the gun."

Cabal: "Before you can destroy the gun, the gun will be fired. It is ready now. Beware."

§61.

Crisis.

Theotocopulos seen close up gesticulating to his following. Men armed with bars scrambling down by the lattice work.

Then in contrast, the little orderly group about Cabal and the two young people, who are climbing up towards the cylinder. Return to the people pouring down the lattice frameworks opposite the Space Gun.

Cabal calling across to Theotocopulos: "Beware of the concussion. That framework is not safe."

"This framework is not safe."

People are seen hesitating on the lattice and then scrambling down and running away.

§62.

Interior of the moon cylinder. It is padded. There are lockers with padded doors and grips for the two space travellers to hold by. The lower end of the cylinder is open and Maurice and Kate clamber in. They grasp their grips. Leather straps are bound across them tightly. They are bound in at last so that only faces show and hands. But it is shown that they can release themselves. They are posed as if crucified.

"Hold tight."

"Do you want to go back?"

She shakes her head smiling.

"All's well. Close and lower away."

The assistants disappear from the opening and it is closed.

§63.

The great chine. The cylinder is being lowered into the gun.

Commotion of people clearing out of the way. At a distance, they pause to look back. Then a re-arrangement of all the people to show passage of time. It has grown darker and the clouds in the sky have moved. Stillness.

The gun fires.

Whirlwind. Collapse of a subsidiary fabric of girders.

Theotocopulos and his staff are seen buffeted and torn by the wild rush of air.

Cloaks, sun hats, papers, banners, light gadgets, straws, dead leaves, everything, flying wild.

§64.

Cabal and Passworthy very still on a great enclosed platform above the city in starlight, not peeping through a telescope or tube of any sort, but watching a disc.

Cabal and Passworthy interested in the telescope disc. "There! There they go! That faint gleam of light."

Passworthy: "I feel—what we have done is—*monstrous.*"

Cabal: "What *they* have done is magnificent."

Passworthy: "Will they return?"

Cabal: "Yes. And go again. And again—until the landing can be made and the moon is conquered. This is only a beginning."

Passworthy: "And if they don't return—my son and your daughter? What of that, Cabal?"

Cabal, with a catch in his voice, but resolute: "Then presently—others will go."

Passworthy: "My God! Is there never to be peace for mankind? No rest?"

Cabal: "Rest enough for the individual man. Too much of it and too soon—and we call it death. But for *Man*, no rest and no ending. He must go on—conquest beyond conquest. This little planet and its winds and ways, and all the laws of matter that restrain him. Then the planets about him, and at last out across immensity to the stars. And when he has conquered all the deeps of space and all the mysteries of time—still he will be beginning."

Passworthy: "But we are such *little* creatures. Poor humanity. So fragile—so weak."

Cabal: "Little animals, eh?"

Passworthy: "Little animals."

Cabal: "If we are no more than animals—we must live and suffer and pass and matter no more—than all the other animals do or have done. It is that—or this? All the universe—or nothingness."

His hand goes out across the stars. "Which will it be, Passworthy?"

The two men fade out against the starry background, then across that starry background, the opening question reappears:

WHITHER MANKIND?

Music.

THE END.

(Here follow appendices, I. and II.)

§[65].

APPENDICES

I. ODD NOTES.

Items for the detail and forms of the latter scenes. Anno 2054.

Immense architectural spans.

No wood, no wooden objects or patterns.

An immense use of artificial substances of the bakelite type.

No bolts or screwed together parts or joins in apparatus or machinery. No beams or obvious stays.

All glass is unbreakable. If something of glass can be dropped and not break, good. If someone can lean against a glass pane which *gives* elastically without breaking – good.

If a cat or dog appears it must be of the rarest breed.

A research for unfamiliar objects must be made.

Odd mechanical forms must be seen going along roadways, through arches, amidst hills, or in the distance. All cars streamlined.

Elephants or lamas or yaks or suchlike unfamiliar animals may be glimpsed incidentally in the background.

A Capuchin monkey or any such pretty pet, gay lizards or big (very big) chameleons might stray through some branches. Or gazelles pass in an endless troupe behind the scene.

Large and strange plants and trees especially *within* the city. No hedges in the open air scenes. No farm houses. No telegraph poles, pylons or other familiar lines or tracks. No pollarded or other trimmed trees.

§[66].
NOTES FOR CASTING.

(Please make your suggestions).

Three *clever* little boys aged between six and ten will be needed for the first part and several other pretty children.

John Cabal is a man of 35 with a sensitive, intelligent face and a fine voice, reasonably well built, and a quiet, restrained, good actor. He is the Maker, and the main figure throughout. He is the Father in the first part, the English aviator in the second part and (as a ripe man of 70) the leader of the revolt in the third part.

Oswald Cabal, the principal speaker in the fourth part is his grandson. He is presented by the same actor as John Cabal. He is a man of 38–45, but he is fitter and more plainly *healthy* than his grandfather.

Pipper Passworthy, 40–50, the optimist in the first part, is stoutish, with a fat voice and a fat laugh, a back-slapping, cheerful fellow. "Kind as they make them."

Raymond Passworthy, 40–48, in the fourth part, is his grandson. He is a rather finer version of the same character. Less demonstrative in his gestures. He should be the same actor as Pipper.

Maurice Passworthy, the son of Raymond, is a very good-looking youngster of 19–23, tall and well grown.

Edward Harding, a medical student in the first part, a middle-aged doctor in the third part, a distinguished old man in the final flash.

Richard Gordon, the air mechanic in the third part. Intelligent revolutionary type about 37.

Simon Burton, in the third part, a lean, wary-faced watchful man. The sort of man who always attaches himself to the established thing and strives to support it.

Theotocopulos (as described).

Morden Mitani (as described).

The second aviator in the second part may have a foreign accent.

The Bully, the Boss, in the third part. Might be a Laughton part, or he could be a heavy, solemn lout of the blackshirt type.

Mrs. Cabal, a good looking woman.

Kate Cabal, 18–20, the daughter of Oswald Cabal, is a handsome, fine-grown girl.

Mary Harding, later Mary Gordon, the daughter in the third part. Blonde, intellectual and dignified. Capable of strong feeling, but dignified and restrained. She is 18 in the pestilence scene and 28 in the scenes with the Boss.

Janet Gordon, the sister of Richard Gordon. Slender and pitiful.

Roxana Black, handsome and expressive, vigorously and picturesquely costumed.

The little girl of 2054.

Her great grandfather.

A beauty chorus of particularly good-looking, well-built young men and women as passers-by, etc., for the 2054 scenes.
No one in the 2054 scenes is to seem more than middle-aged.
Cadaverous people for the sick in the Pestilence Series and everyone in that phase of the story to be lean and pale.
The name of the Boss need not be given.
The christian name of the Mrs. Cabal need not be given.
No other characters are named.

THINGS TO COME

The Release Script
of the London Films Production

Reel 1

FADE IN:
1. TRADE MARK 23ft. 10frs.
   Big Ben   CHIMES OF BIG BEN
                               A   Music
                    LONDON FILM PRODUCTION
            FADE IN: FADE OUT:
2. 122 ft. 1fr.   H.G. Wells
                                                     DISSOLVE:
3.   "THINGS TO COME"
                                                     DISSOLVE:
4.   Produced by
                       ALEXANDER KORDA
                                                     DISSOLVE:
5.   Directed by
                  WILLIAM CAMERON MENZIES
                                                     DISSOLVE:
6.   Settings designed
                             by
                        VINCENT KORDA
                                                     DISSOLVE:
7.   Photography
                             by
                      GEORGES PERINAL
                                                     DISSOLVE:
8.   Special Effects
                          Directed by

NED MANN
DISSOLVE:
9.   Music Specially Composed by
ARTHUR BLISS
Musical Director
MUIR MATHIESON
Recorded on Western Electric Noiseless System
DISSOLVE:
10.   Costumes Designed by
JOHN ARMSTRONG, RENE HUBERT,
& THE MARCHIONESS OF QUEENSBERRY
Production Manager
DAVID B. CUNYNGHAME
DISSOLVE:

11. Recording Director . . . .   A.W. WATKINS
    Assistant Art Director . . . .   FRANK WELLS
    Aeronautical Advisor . . . .   NIGEL TANGYE
    Supervising Editor . . . .   WILLIAM HORNBECK
DISSOLVE:
12. Film Editors . . . .   CHARLES CRICHTON
                                                      & FRANCIS LYON

    Special Effects photographed by . .   EDWARD COHEN A.S.C.
    Assistant Special Effects . . . .   LAWRENCE BUTLER
    Assistant Director . . . .   GEOFFREY BOOTHBY
    Camera Operator . . . .   ROBERT KRASKER
DISSOLVE:
13.   *THE CAST*
    RAYMOND MASSEY . . . .   JOHN CABAL
                                                      OSWALD CABAL
    EDWARD CHAPMAN . . . .   PIPPA PASSWORTHY
                                                      RAYMOND PASSWORTHY
    RALPH RICHARDSON . . . .   THE BOSS
    MARGUERETTA SCOTT . . . . . .   ROXANA
                                                      ROWENA
    CEDRIC HARDWICKE . . . .   THEOTOCOPULOS
    MAURICE BRADELL . . . .   DR. HARDING
    SOPHIE STEWART . . . .   MRS. CABAL
    DERRICK de MARNEY . . . .   RICHARD GORDON
    ANN TODD . . . .   MARY GORDON
    PEARL ARGYLE . . . .   CATHERINE CABAL
    KENNETH VILLIERS . . . .   MAURICE PASSWORTHY
    IVAN BRANDT . . . .   MORDEN MITANI
    ANNE McLAREN . . . .   THE CHILD
    PATRICIA HILLIARD . . . .   JANET GORDON
    CHARLES CARSON . . . .   GREAT GRANDFATHER
DISSOLVE:
14.   DISTRIBUTED
by
UNITED ARTISTS

FADE OUT:

FADE IN:
15. VERY LONG SHOT 29ft. 11frs.
Of Everytown over which Titles
appear.

1940
CHRISTMAS
EVERYTOWN

DISSOLVE:
16. LONG SHOT   MIXED WITH MUSIC IS THE
The town.   NOISE OF NEWSBOYS YELL-
ING AND GENERAL TRAFFIC
AND STREET NOISE.
DISSOLVE:

17. MEDIUM SHOT
Small boy standing by a toy-shop
window in which stands a Christmas tree and a fort.
18. CLOSE UP 4ft. 8frs.
The boy's face alight with pleasure.
19. CLOSE SHOT 5ft.
The fort he is looking at.
20. CLOSE UP 3ft.
The boy's face.
21. CLOSE UP 5ft. 6frs.   VENDOR:
A hollyvendor, yelling.   Holly all berry, holly all berry.

22. MEDIUM SHOT 8ft. 4frs.
The vendor still yelling—people
pass. A bus draws up, on which is
a war poster.
23. CLOSE SHOT 7ft. 2frs.
The feet of shoppers as they walk
over the pavement on which
Christmas greetings have been
written by a pavement artist.
24. MEDIUM SHOT 5ft. 1fr.
The pavement artist at work.
25. MEDIUM SHOT 11ft. 8frs.
A group of carol singers pass along
in front of posters announcing the
rumour of war.
26. CLOSE SHOT 10ft. 7frs.
The group pass and leave the war
posters visible.
27. LONG SHOT 5ft. 7frs.
The city square, alive with Christmas traffic.
28. LONG SHOT 5ft. 7frs.

Man wheels a fruit barrow down a
cockney street.
29. LONG SHOT 6ft. 11frs.
    Outside a cinema, people hurrying
    past, and traffic driving across the
    street.
30. LONG SHOT 2ft. 7frs.
    Car with man and girl stops.
    There is a Christmas tree in the
    back of the car.
31. CLOSE SHOT 3ft. 7frs.
    The man and girl in the car. A
    bus with a war poster on the side,
    is beside them.
32. MEDIUM SHOT 6ft. 7frs.
    A woman laden with Christmas
    parcels scrambles on to the bus,
    on the side of which is a war
    poster.
33. LONG SHOT 9ft. 15frs.
    Outside entrance to pit of theatre,
    people hurry by. A man carrying
    a war poster walks up to the
    CAMERA.
34. LONG SHOT 6ft. 2frs.
    Square.

                                        POULTERER:
                                          Christmas ain't Christmas with-
                                          out a turkey.
35. MEDIUM SHOT 7ft. 2frs.   WOMAN:
                                          That's quite right, Mr. Denison.
36. MEDIUM SHOT 2ft. 9frs.
    Two women leaning out of their
    windows, a large war poster be-   1ST WOMAN:
    tween them.   What you got for Christmas
                                            dinner?

37. CLOSE SHOT 5ft. 13frs.
    Children in front of large war   2ND WOMAN:
    poster on the wall.   Half a pig's head and a couple of
                                            trotters.
38. CLOSE SHOT 4ft. 9frs.
    Poster — WAR SCARE   1ST WOMAN:
                                            Oh Blimey!
39. LONG SHOT 4ft. 6frs.
    Crowd coming out of theatre.
40. CLOSE SHOT 5ft.
    The crowd.
41. CLOSE SHOT 4ft. 6frs.

Poster—WAR SCARE
42. CLOSE SHOT 6ft. 12frs.
Poster—WAR SCARE
A man is carrying it, and he
comes closer, and closer up to
CAMERA.
43. CLOSE SHOT 3ft. 1fr.
Christmas turkeys sign over poul-
terer's shop.
44. CLOSE SHOT 3ft. 1fr.
A Father Christmas doll on the
pavement as it is held by a street
vendor.
45. CLOSE SHOT 2ft.
Poster—WAR STORM
46. CLOSE SHOT 1ft. 15frs.
The woman by a poster blowing
paper streamers.
47. CLOSE UP 1ft. 15frs.
Poster—WAR STORM
48. CLOSE UP 1ft. 10frs.
Poster—WARNING TO EUROPE
49. CLOSE UP 1ft. 11frs.
Another poster—1000 FIGHTERS
50. CLOSE UP 1ft. 9frs.
Poster—ALARMING SPEECH
51. CLOSE SHOT 1ft.
Poster—WAR SCARE
52. CLOSE UP 0ft. 13frs.
Poster—EUROPE IS ARMING
53. CLOSE UP 1ft. 1fr.
Poster—WARNING TO EUROPE
54. CLOSE SHOT 0ft. 9frs.
Along pavement showing several
war posters.
55. CLOSE UP 0ft. 9frs.
Poster—WAR SCARE
56. CLOSE SHOT 0ft. 9frs.
Along pavement showing war
poster.
57. LONG SHOT 0ft. 8frs.
The vendor with the Father
Christmas doll, in front of a large
war poster.
58. CLOSE UP 38ft. 1fr.
WAR poster.   MUSIC & STREET NOISES
                                         FADE OUT:
                                         DISSOLVE:

59. Start on CLOSE UP paper held in

Cabal's hands, with headline of
war scare. TRUCK BACK to
show Cabal seated in his study;
Harding enters.

CABAL:
　Hullo, young Harding. You're
　early.
HARDING:
　Yes, I'd finished up. It was too
　late to start anything fresh.
　What's all this fuss about in the
　papers tonight, Mr. Cabal?
CABAL:
　Wars and rumours of wars.
HARDING:
　Crying wolf?
CABAL:
　Some day the wolf will come.

60. CLOSE SHOT 3ft. 2frs.
　　Cabal over Harding's shoulder.

CABAL:
　Those fools are capable of. . . .
　anything.

61. CLOSE SHOT 5ft. 13frs.
　　Harding over Cabal's shoulder.

HARDING:
　In that case what happens to
　medical research?
CABAL:
　It has to stop.

62. LONG SHOT 20ft. 14frs.
　　The two in the room.

HARDING:
　That'll mess me up.
CABAL:
　Mess you up! Mess everything
　up. My God! If war gets loose
　again. . .

Passworthy enters and commences
to sing.

PASSWORTHY:
　Happy Christmas everyone.
　While shepherds watch their
　flocks by night, all seated on the
　ground. . . . What's the matter
　with you fellows?. . .

63. CLOSE SHOT 32ft. 2frs.
　　All three, favour Passworthy, they
　　show him the paper. PAN across
　　to hold him and Harding, when
　　he talks to him, and then over to
　　hold all three again.

　　. . . .Oh that. This little upset
　　across the water doesn't mean
　　anything. Threatened men live

long, and threatened wars never occur. Another speech by him? I tell you there's nothing in it. It's just to buck up people about the air estimates. Now why meet wars half way? Why not look on the bright side of things? You're all right. Your business is going up. . . .

64. CLOSE SHOT 13ft. 11frs.
All three, favour Cabal.

. . . . You've got a jolly wife, a pretty home. . .
CABAL:
All's right with the world, eh? All's right with the world?
PASSWORTHY:
Certainly.
CABAL:
Passworthy, you should have been called Pippa Passworthy
. . . . .

65. CLOSE SHOT 9ft. 15frs.
All three, favour Passworthy.

PASSWORTHY:
Oh, and Cabal. You've been smoking too much. You're not . . . you're not eupeptic. Oh — come on. It's Christmas.

66. CLOSE SHOT 45ft. 6frs.
All three. Favour Cabal. They all start to sing.

PASSWORTHY & CABAL:
Noel, Noel, Noel, Noel, Born is the King of Israel. . . .
DISSOLVE:
MUSIC STARTS

67. MEDIUM SHOT
Children playing. TRUCK BACK to show whole room, a party at Cabal's house, the parents and the grandfather playing with the children's toys with them.

GRANDFATHER:
Nice toys they have now-a-days. Nice toys. The toys we had were simpler. Ever so much simpler. Noah's arks and wooden soldiers. . .

68. CLOSE SHOT 12ft. 12frs.
Grandfather.

. . . Nothing complex like these. You know — I wonder sometimes if perhaps all these new toys aren't a bit too much for them.

69. CLOSE SHOT 3ft. 12frs.
Mrs. Cabal.

MRS. CABAL:
It teaches them to use their
hands.

70. LONG SHOT 6ft. 13frs.
Whole room.

GRANDFATHER:
Well, I suppose their grandchildren will see even more wonderful things...

71. CLOSE UP 10ft. 6frs.
Grandfather.

...Progress...Progress...I'd like
to see the wonders they'll see.

72. CLOSE UP 11ft. 11frs.
Cabal.

CABAL:
Don't be too sure of progress.
PASSWORTHY:
Oh listen to the incurable pessi-
mist.
GRANDFATHER:
What's to stop progress nowa-
days?
CABAL:
War.

73. CLOSE SHOT 8ft. 14frs.
Passworthy and son.

PASSWORTHY:
Firstly there isn't going to be a
war, and secondly war doesn't
stop progress. It stimulates progress.

74. CLOSE UP 6ft. 14frs.
Cabal.

CABAL:
Yes. War can be a highly stimu-
lating thing. But you can overdo
a stimulant.

75. LONG SHOT 9ft. 3frs.
Room.

PASSWORTHY:
Oh well, after all, aren't we ex-
aggerating the horrors of war.
Don't we rather overdo that
song.

76. CLOSE SHOT 11ft. 12frs.
Passworthy and son.

...After all, you know, the last
war wasn't as bad as people
make out. We didn't worry.
Something—something great
seemed to have got hold of us.

77. CLOSE UP 8ft. 14frs.
Cabal.

CABAL:
Something greater still may get

78. CLOSE SHOT 2ft. 14frs.
    Passworthy and son.

79. CLOSE UP 4ft. 1fr.
    Cabal.

80. CLOSE UP 33ft.
    Mrs. Cabal.

81. CHRISTMAS TREE LIGHTED
    UP.

82. CHRISTMAS TREE WITH
    LIGHTS EXTINGUISHED.

83. LONG SHOT
    Exterior house.
84. MEDIUM CLOSE SHOT 30ft.
    4frs.
    All four, they come out.

85. LONG SHOT 9ft. 13frs.
    Group—searchlights in sky.

86. MEDIUM SHOT 2ft. 12frs.
    All four.
87. LONG SHOT 2ft. 8frs.
    Searchlights in sky.
88. MEDIUM SHOT 14ft. 14frs.

hold of us next time. If we don't
end war, war will end us.

PASSWORTHY:
    Well...what can you do?

CABAL:
    Yes.

What can we do?
                    DISSOLVE:

                    DISSOLVE:

                    DISSOLVE:
MIXED WITH MUSIC IS THE
NOISE OF CHRISTMAS BELLS

PASSWORTHY:
    Peace on earth, goodwill towards
    men. Real old fashioned Christ-
    mas this year.
GUNSHOT
    Fresh and a little snow, with a
    nip in the air, eh?
MRS. CABAL:
    What was that? It sounded like a
    gun.
PASSWORTHY:
    No, no guns here. Merry Christ-
    mas Cabal. Here's to another
    good year for all of us. Another
    year of recovery, eh?

MRS. CABAL:
    What are searchlights doing
    now?
PASSWORTHY:
    Yes....

    ....Well, it must be anti-

    ...aircraft manoeuvres.

All four.

CABAL:
> Manoeuvres at Christmas? No.

GUN SHOT

HARDING:
> Listen, guns again.

89. LONG SHOT 8ft. 13frs.
All four, Cabal runs in.

90. MEDIUM SHOT 26ft. 5frs.
The three outside the house.

TELEPHONE RINGS IN
HOUSE.

CABAL (off):
> Yes, Cabal speaking. At the hill-
> town aerodrome at three. I'll be
> there.

He joins them outside.

> Mobilisation.

MRS. CABAL:
> Oh God!

PASSWORTHY:
> Perhaps it's only precautionary
> mobilisation.

CABAL:
> Let's hear the radio.

91. LONG SHOT 13ft. 9frs.
In house, Cabal runs in and turns
on radio, they all come in and
listen.

MUSIC STOPS AS ANNOUN-
CER STARTS

RADIO ANNOUNCER:
> The unknown aircraft passed
> over Seabeach and dropped
> bombs within a few hundred
> yards of the waterworks. They
> then turned southward
> again. . . .

92. CLOSE UP 13ft. 13frs.
Harding and Mrs. Cabal. TRUCK
IN to Big Head C.U. of Harding.

> . . . .By this time they had been
> picked up by the searchlights, of
> the Battleship Dinosaur, and be-
> fore they could mount out of
> range she had opened upon
> them with her antiaircraft guns.
> Unfortunately without re-
> sult. . . .

93. LONG SHOT 12ft. 15frs.
All four. Cabal stands.

HARDING:
> . . . .Of course everyone has said
> this time they'll start without
> any declaration of war.

MRS. CABAL:

Oh, listen!

RADIO ANNOUNCER:
We do not yet know the nationality of these aircraft, though of course there can be little doubt of their place of origin....

Big Head CLOSE UP 6 ft. 3frs.
Of Mrs. Cabal.

....But before all things it is necessary for the country to keep calm.

94. CLOSE UP 5ft. 15frs.
Passworthy.

....No doubt the losses suffered by the fleet are serious.

PASSWORTHY:
What's that? Losses of the fleet?

95. LONG SHOT 5ft. 7frs.
All four.

MRS. CABAL:
Listen—listen.

RADIO ANNOUNCER:
And it is imperative that the whole nation should at once stand to arms...

96. CLOSE UP 9ft. 1fr.
Cabal.

...Orders for a general mobilisation have been issued and the precautionary civilian organisation against gas...

97. CLOSE UP 2ft. 15frs.
Mrs. Cabal.

...will at once be put into operation.

98. CLOSE UP 2ft. 15frs.
Cabal.

...Ah—instructions have come to hand...

99. CLOSE UP 2ft. 14frs.
Passworthy.

...We shall cut off for five minutes...

100. CLOSE UP 2ft. 12frs.
Harding.

...and then read you the general instructions...

101. MEDIUM SHOT 76ft.
All four.

...Please call in all your friends. Call in everyone you can.

CABAL:
You've got your stimulant Passworthy. Something great has got you. War has come.

DISSOLVE:

102. MEDIUM SHOT
Passworthy and Harding.

TRUCK BACK as they walk forward.

PASSWORTHY:
My God, if they've attacked without a declaration of war... then it's vengeance. No quarter ...vengeance. Punishment, condign punishment...or else the end of civilization altogether. But it's just possible there's some mistake, you know. I cling to that. If not, then it's war to the knife. No it's...it's not a war. It's extermination of dangerous vermin. A vermin hunt without pause or pity. Well, goodnight.

End of Reel 1

Reel 2

103. MEDIUM SHOT 10ft. 4frs.   MUSIC
    Crowd looking at poster, on which is the NATIONAL DEFENSE ACT.
104. CLOSE SHOT 10ft. 13frs.
    Bus passes on which is a STAND TO ARMS poster.
105. LONG SHOT 11ft. 3frs.
    City Square.
106. MEDIUM SHOT 8ft. 2frs.
    Newsboy with poster, GENERAL MOBILISATION. He is standing by entrance to Underground—a couple kiss goodbye.
107. LONG SHOT 10ft. 2frs.
    Street. People crowd around a truck.
108. LONG SHOT 8ft. 14frs.
    Square. Motor cycle squad ride through.
109. LONG SHOT 5ft. 3frs.
    Another angle showing statue and the Town Hall. Lorry drives through with soldiers in it.
110. LONG SHOT 3ft. 6frs.
    Closer than above—guns in front of Town Hall.
111. CLOSE SHOT 7ft. 1fr.

A gun passes Sanderson's.
112. LONG SHOT 9ft. 14frs.
Street by Sanderson's. Motor cycle squad drives through.
113. LONG SHOT 3ft. 3frs.
By Town Hall.
114. LONG SHOT 8ft. 5frs.
Motor cycle squad.
115. LONG SHOT 4ft. 8frs.
Announcer's car comes into
Square.
116. LONG SHOT 9ft. 11frs.
Announcer's car comes in and
draws up. The announcer in
CLOSE SHOT.

MUSIC STOPS

ANNOUNCER:
Please keep still and listen. War
has broken out suddenly...

117. LONG SHOT 6ft. 5frs.
Square.

...There may be an air raid but
it is not likely to be a very serious one...

118. CLOSE SHOT 2ft. 10frs.
Announcer.

...You must be prepared for
it...

119. LONG SHOT 2ft. 12frs.
Town Hall.

...The danger will not be
great...

120. VERY LONG SHOT 2ft. 3frs.
Square.

...As soon as the danger is
over...

121. LONG SHOT 2ft. 14frs.
Shooting down on a group of
people in a cockney street.

...bugles will sound all clear...

122. LONG SHOT 2ft. 12frs.
Square.

...The streets will be dangerous...

123. LONG SHOT 2ft. 4frs.
Group of people outside Sanderson's listening to announcer.

...Do not assemble in
crowds...

124. LONG SHOT 2ft. 11frs.
The announcer's truck with a
crowd around it.

...Keep indoors. Go home. Go
home...

125. CLOSE UP 1ft. 15frs.
Girl's face.

...Those who are far from
home...

126. CLOSE UP 1ft. 11frs.
Man's face.

...can take refuge in the

under...

127. MEDIUM SHOT 1ft. 8frs.
     Group of men's faces.   ...ground railways...
128. CLOSE UP 1ft. 7frs.
     Another girl's face—crowd press-
     ing behind her.   ...Go home...
129. CLOSE UP 1ft. 3frs.
     Men's faces, as they press for-
     ward past the CAMERA.   ...Go home...
130. CLOSE UP 11frs.
     Girl's face.   ...Go...
131. CLOSE UP 1ft. 1fr.
     Man's face.   ...home...
132. LONG SHOT 4ft. 3frs.
     Crowd round announcer's truck.   ...Get out of the square, get
                                              out of the streets...
133. LONG SHOT 2ft. 8frs.
     Street, statue in foreground.   ...Go home and keep home...
134. CLOSE SHOT 1ft. 9frs.
     Announcer.   ...Put out your lights...
135. CLOSE SHOT 4ft. 1fr.
     Man and woman look out of
     window, they drop the curtain.   ...Close the windows, put a
                                              wet sheet or a wet...
136. CLOSE SHOT 4ft. 8frs.
     Woman looking out of window.
     She puts out the light.   ...blanket over doors and win-
                                              dows...Keep indoors...
137. LONG SHOT 2ft. 8frs.
     Square.   ...Keep indoors...
138. LONG SHOT 2ft. 2frs.
     Lorry in cockney street.   ...Get out of the streets...
139. LONG SHOT 2ft. 1fr.
     Town Hall in square.   ...Go home and keep home...
140. LONG SHOT 1ft. 14frs.
     Cockney street.   ...Keep indoors...
141. LONG SHOT 2ft. 8frs.
     People run past Sanderson's.   ...Go home...
142. MEDIUM SHOT 2ft. 2frs.
     Ambulance passes Sanderson's.   ...Go home...
143. MEDIUM SHOT 8ft. 6frs.
     Crowd in front of Town Hall.   ...Do not assemble in
                                              crowds...
                                                        DISSOLVE:

144. MEDIUM SHOT
     Two children in bed.
145. LONG SHOT 3ft. 11frs.
     Cabal and Mrs. Cabal standing
     beside the two sleeping children.

146. CLOSE SHOT 62ft. 10frs.
    Cabal and Mrs. Cabal.

MRS. CABAL:
  My dear, my dear, are you sorry
  we had these children?
CABAL:
  No, life must carry on. Why
  should we surrender life to the
  brutes and the fools?
MRS. CABAL:
  I loved you. I wanted to serve
  you and make life happy for
  you, but think of the things that
  may happen to them. Were we
  selfish?
CABAL:
  You weren't afraid to bear
  them—*we* were children yesterday. We are anxious, but we're
  not afraid—really...

147. MEDIUM LONG SHOT 18ft.
    7frs.
    The two by the bed.

  ...Courage my dear. And may
  that little heart have courage.

148. LONG SHOT
    People in fog outside. They pass
    CAMERA.
149. LONG SHOT 13ft. 5frs.
    Outside Cabal's house. He comes
    out with his case and goes off.
150. LONG SHOT 6ft. 15frs.
    Gate to Passworthy's garden.
    Passworthy and son come out.

151. MEDIUM SHOT 24ft. 11frs.
    The two.

HORRIE:
  Are you an officer, daddy?

PASSWORTHY:
  Well you've got to do your bit
  you know sonny, you've got to
  do your bit.
HORRIE:
  I'm an officer too, daddy.
PASSWORTHY:
  That's the spirit. Carry on, sir,
  carry on. Goodbye son. There.
  Now then. Quick march.

They salute. Passworthy picks up
his son and kisses him. He puts
Horrie down, and picking up his
suitcase starts to beat it as if it
were a drum and marches off,

Horrie marching behind him.

152. LONG SHOT 33ft. 10frs.
The two marching. Passworthy
goes and leaves Horrie marching
up and down with his drum.

Huge shadowgraph phantoms
marching behind Horrie.

Back to Horrie marching up and
down.

153. CLOSE SHOT
An army truck passes in the
square.

154. LONG SHOT 3ft.
Square.

155. LONG SHOT 3ft. 2frs.
Silhouette man, crowd behind
him, shooting from inside a
truck.

156. CLOSE SHOT 4ft. 11frs.
TRUCK passes GAS MASKS on
the side of the truck, crowd runs
after it.

157. LONG SHOT 2ft. 6frs.
Underground subway. People
crowd down.

158. MEDIUM SHOT 2ft. 12frs.
Crowd from above, going down
underground.

159. LONG SHOT 4ft. 4frs.
Gun passes Sanderson's.

160. LONG SHOT 2ft. 7frs.
Man on gun.

MUSIC STARTS

DISSOLVE:

DISSOLVE:

DISSOLVE:

The announcer's voice is heard
over a general noise of panic
and an ever increasing drone of
approaching aeroplanes.
VOICE:
An air raid is approaching
Everytown...

...An air raid is approaching
Everytown...

...Gas masks are being distributed...

...See that they fit tightly behind the ears...

...Get to cover...Get under
cover at once...

...The enemy are not in any
great force...

...and our anti-aircraft gunners
will speedily dispose of them...

THE VOICE OF THE AN-
NOUNCER IS DROWNED BY
THE PLANES & OTHER

NOISES.

161. LONG SHOT 2ft. 10frs.
Square.
162. LONG SHOT 2ft. 6frs.
From above. Announcer's truck.
Crowd around it.
163. LONG SHOT 1ft. 10frs.
Street. People running about in
panic in front of Sanderson's.
164. VERY LONG SHOT 2ft. 1fr.
Square.
165. LONG SHOT 2ft. 7frs.
People in front of Town Hall.
166. LONG SHOT 1ft. 12frs.
Group in street in front of
Sanderson's.
167. LONG SHOT 1ft. 14frs.
People pass gun.
168. LONG SHOT 1ft. 11frs.
People move along in front of
Town Hall.
169. VERY LONG SHOT 1ft. 14frs.
Square.
170. CLOSE SHOT 3ft. 14frs.
Poster – WAR THE TRUTH,
people pass by it.
171. MEDIUM SHOT 2ft. 15frs.
People pass across CAMERA
down cockney street.
172. LONG SHOT 2ft. 12frs.
Crowd round a gun.
173. CLOSE SHOT 4ft. 1fr.
Pavement. "Christmas" written
on it. People pass.
174. MEDIUM SHOT 4ft. 1fr.
Man trying to hold people from
going past a CLOSED notice.
They push him aside and scramble past.
175. LONG SHOT 3ft. 1fr.
Corner of square, GAS MASKS
truck passes.
176. MEDIUM SHOT 3ft. 11frs.
People scramble over cars which
are piled up in a block.
177. LONG SHOT 3ft. 7frs.
A gun.
178. LONG SHOT 4ft. 4frs.
A darkened alley-way.

179. MEDIUM SHOT 3ft. 5frs.
Crowd pushing down the
Underground subway.
180. MEDIUM SHOT 2ft. 14frs.
Shooting down from above to
the crowd going down the
Underground subway.
181. LONG SHOT 3ft. 6frs.
Gun in position, crowd standing
round.
182. MEDIUM SHOT 3ft. 11frs.
Fire engine down street past
Sanderson's.
183. MEDIUM SHOT 2ft. 15frs.
Soldiers on a gun as it turns
round.
184. MEDIUM SHOT 2ft. 6frs.
People climbing over cars.
185. LONG SHOT 1ft. 9frs.
 Soldiers on a gun.
186. CLOSE SHOT 1ft. 4frs.
From inside the gas mask truck.
A man hands out masks.
187. MEDIUM SHOT 1ft. 6frs.
People scramble over cars.
188. LONG SHOT 1ft. 8frs.
People run past Sanderson's.
189. LONG SHOT 15frs.
In front of the Town Hall, an
ambulance pulls up.
190. CLOSE SHOT 1ft. 9frs.
Pavement. Scurrying feet.
191. LONG SHOT 1ft. 7frs.
A gun in front of Town Hall.
192. MEDIUM SHOT 1ft.
Gun against Town Hall.
193. LONG SHOT ?frs.
Gun.
194. LONG SHOT 12frs.
Another gun.
195. CLOSE SHOT 10frs.
Lower part of gun.
196. LONG SHOT 9frs.
Gun and soldiers.
197. MEDIUM SHOT 7frs.
Lower part of gun.
198. MEDIUM SHOT 1ft.   MUSIC STOPS
Top of gun as it fires.
199. CLOSE UP 15frs.

Man's face.
200. MEDIUM SHOT 13frs.
Gun fires.
201. LONG SHOT 1ft. 4frs.
Gun in front of Town Hall—it
fires.
202. MEDIUM SHOT 14frs.
Gun fires.
203. CLOSE SHOT 1ft. 7frs.
Soldiers round gun.
204. MEDIUM SHOT 2ft. 4frs.
Gun fires.
205. VERY LONG SHOT 3ft. 12frs.
Darkened square.
206. LONG SHOT 3ft. 3frs.
Gun in front of Town Hall—it
fires.
207. MEDIUM SHOT 1ft. 4frs.
Gun firing.
208. LONG SHOT 1ft. 1fr.
Gun firing.
209. MEDIUM SHOT 13frs.
Gun firing.
210. LONG SHOT 13frs.
Gun firing.
211. LONG SHOT 10frs.
Another gun firing.
212. LONG SHOT 12frs.
Another gun fires.
213. LONG SHOT 9frs.
Another gun fires.
214. MEDIUM SHOT 9frs.
Gun fires.
215. LONG SHOT 9ft. 2frs.
Cinema explosion—wreckage
falls.
216. LONG SHOT 1ft. 2frs.
Gun firing.
217. LONG SHOT 1ft. 11frs.
Another gun firing.
218. LONG SHOT 5ft. 15frs.
Cockney street—explosion—
chimney falls.
219. LONG SHOT 1ft. 14frs.
A street—a fire engine rushes
through in CLOSE SHOT.
220. LONG SHOT 8ft. 5frs.
Cockney street, another
explosion.

221. LONG SHOT 15frs.
     Gun in front of Town
     Hall—firing.
222. LONG SHOT 15frs.
     Gun from above, firing.
223. LONG SHOT 1ft.
     Gun in front of Town Hall.
224. LONG SHOT 5 ft. 2frs.
     Sanderson's blows up.
225. MEDIUM SHOT 5ft. 2frs.
     People reaching up for gas masks.
226. LONG SHOT 2ft. 7frs.
     Low set up—lorry passes.
227. LONG SHOT 1ft. 14frs.
     Gun in front of Town Hall.
228. MEDIUM SHOT 3ft. 1fr.
     Shooting through wreckage—
     people rush past.
229. MEDIUM SHOT 3ft. 9frs.
     People getting gas masks—
     explosion they all fall.
230. LONG SHOT 13frs.
     Bus—explosion.
231. CLOSE SHOT 2ft. 5frs.
     Man—head lolling out of car
     window.
232. LONG SHOT 1ft. 13frs.
     Street—fire engine passes.
233. MEDIUM SHOT 2ft. 12frs.
     Wrecked car on its
     side—explosion.
234. LONG SHOT 2ft. 11frs.
     Crowd of people running along
     pavement—man shakes his fist in
     the air—explosion.
235. EXPLOSION 4frs.
236. LONG SHOT 16ft. 14frs.
     PAN over as people try to scram-
     ble over wreckage.
237. LONG SHOT 5ft. 6frs.
     Wrecked square.
238. CLOSE SHOT 7ft. 9frs.
     Man—head lolling out of car—
     girl leaning on bonnet—
     explosion—she is blown up.
239. LONG SHOT 3ft. 10frs.
     Men in gas masks try to pick up
     wounded.
240. MEDIUM CLOSE SHOT 2ft.

12frs.
People on top of bus.
241. MEDIUM SHOT 3ft. 8frs.
Men with gas masks on carry
stretchers.
242. LONG SHOT 3ft. 12frs.
Wreckage.
243. LONG SHOT 4ft.
Men among wreckage.
244. MEDIUM SHOT 3ft. 4frs.
Over pile of corpses.
245. LONG SHOT 5ft. 13frs.
Wrecked cockney street—
wounded try to get up.
246. LONG SHOT 4ft. 5frs.
Shooting over corpses.
247. LONG SHOT 5ft. 11frs.
Wrecked cinema.
248. MEDIUM SHOT 3ft. 9frs.
Wreckage.
249. LONG SHOT 39ft. 6frs.
Outside Passworthy house. PAN
DOWN over wreckage to Horrie
who lies dead in the midst.

DISSOLVE:

250. LONG SHOT
Wrecked buildings.

DISSOLVE:

251. LONG SHOT
Burning square.

DISSOLVE:

252. LONG SHOT
Another smouldering ruin.

DISSOLVE:

253. LONG SHOT
Another smouldering house.

FADE OUT:

FADE IN:
254. 17ft. 2frs.
A dissolve and mixes sequence.
Over a shot of lines of huge
shadows of marching soldiers is
superimposed a shot of tanks on
their way to war, then back to
the lines of marching soldiers.
Mix to lines of battleships.
255. 15ft. 12frs.
Shooting through part of one
ship to other ships, over this is

mixed shot of tanks coming
down hill, mix with tanks moving over a pond.
256. 4ft. 9frs.
Tanks advancing over waste
land.
257. 8ft. 7frs.
A shot of a tank mixes with
shots of tanks moving over a
pond—explosions.
258. 3ft. 6frs.
A shot of a tank mixes with
shots of tanks moving.
259. 14ft. 2frs.
A lot of tanks on their way—
many explosions—mix with a
shot of a tank crushing down a
building.

FADE OUT:

FADE IN:
260. LONG SHOT 30ft. 2frs.
Cliffs of Dover.

DISSOLVE:

261. LONG SHOT
Of the sky full of travelling
planes.
262. LONG SHOT 27ft. 13frs.
The planes fly over the Dover
cliffs.
263. LONG SHOT 4ft. 7frs.
Shooting down to the edge of
the cliff from a plane, showing
the sea below.
264. LONG SHOT 7ft. 9frs.
Swarms of planes in the sky.
265. LONG SHOT 4ft. 3frs.
Shooting down again to the
coast as we fly over it.
266. LONG SHOT 7ft. 13frs.
Airplanes in the sky.
267. LONG SHOT 38ft.
Shooting over the roofs of the
houses of a village, the swarm of
airplanes flies over.

DISSOLVE:

268. LONG SHOT
The air filled with planes.

DISSOLVE:

269. Another angle the planes fly over.

End of Reel 2

Reel 3

270. LONG SHOT 22ft. 5frs.
Sky full of hundreds of planes.

DISSOLVE:

271. CLOSE SHOT
Enemy airman looking back.

272. CLOSE SHOT 13ft. 3frs.
Cabal, shooting from behind.

273. LONG SHOT 18ft. 3frs.
Enemy plane, shooting through
Cabal's plane.

274. CLOSE SHOT 3ft. 9frs.
Cabal looks over the side of his
plane.

275. CLOSE SHOT 3ft. 1fr.
Enemy airman, looking back.

276. CLOSE SHOT 3ft. 14frs.
Cabal shooting from behind.

277. CLOSE SHOT 1ft. 6frs.
Enemy airman.

278. LONG SHOT 2ft. 3frs.
Cabal's plane, swooping to attack
enemy plane.

279. CLOSE SHOT 1ft. 7frs.
Enemy airman looking back.

280. MEDIUM SHOT 1ft. 5frs.
Cabal's plane, coming towards
camera.

281. CLOSE SHOT 3ft. 2frs.
Enemy airman. Cabal's plane
behind him. Cabal swoops and
hits enemy with his machine
gun.

282. LONG SHOT 4ft.
Cabal's plane.

283. CLOSE SHOT 11ft. 9frs.
Enemy airman; he is badly
wounded and his plane is in a
tail spin, falling to earth, he
makes an effort to right it.

284. LONG SHOT 8ft.
Enemy plane falling to earth.

285. LONG SHOT 5ft. 5frs.
The plane falls into picture and
crashes on ground.

286. LONG SHOT 19ft. 2frs.

Cabal's plane coming down.

DISSOLVE:

287. LONG SHOT
     The wrecked plane, Cabal's plane
     lands behind it.
288. MEDIUM SHOT 8ft. 13frs.
     Cabal goes out of plane.
289. MEDIUM LONG SHOT 5ft.
     8frs.
     Wrecked plane, with Cabal's
     plane in background, the
     wounded airman starts to
     clamber out.
290. MEDIUM SHOT 6ft. 12frs.
     Wrecked plane. Cabal comes and
     helps his enemy out of the
     wreckage.
291. LONG SHOT 7ft. 8frs.
     The wreckage with Cabal's plane
     in background.
292. LONG SHOT 13ft. 5frs.
     Cabal helps his enemy to the
     grass near his own plane and
     takes off his helmet.

293. MEDIUM SHOT 15ft. 2frs.
     The two.

CABAL:
  Bad shape, eh?

  Why has it come to this? God,
  why do we have to murder each
  other!
ENEMY:
  Go my friend! That is my gas,
  and it's a bad gas.

294. LONG SHOT 3ft. 1fr.
     The field, gas is seen to be
     approaching.
295. CLOSE SHOT 20ft. 13frs.
     Cabal and enemy—Cabal puts
     his enemy's gas mask on then
     starts to put on his own.

ENEMY:
  Funny if I'm killed by my own
  poison.
CABAL:
  Quick get this on.

296. LONG SHOT 4ft. 10frs.
     Small girl running across the
     field, trying to escape from the
     gas.
297. LONG SHOT 4ft. 2frs.
     She runs up to Cabal and enemy

airman, Cabal starts to take off
his gas mask to give it to her.

298. MEDIUM SHOT 26ft. 11frs.
Cabal, the enemy airman and
the little girl, the wounded man
insists on the child having his gas
mask and Cabal retaining his
own.

CABAL:
Here. Get this on quickly.

ENEMY:
Give it to her. I've given plenty
to others, why should I not
have some myself? Give it to
her, I'm done.
CABAL:
Breathe through your mouth.

299. LONG SHOT 20ft. 6frs.
All three. Cabal and the child
with their gas masks on start to
go to his airplane, Cabal turns
back and throws a revolver to
the wounded man.

300. MEDIUM CLOSE SHOT 45ft.
13frs.
The enemy airman, the gas enve-
lopes him, he coughs very badly.

ENEMY:
I dropped the gas on her. Maybe
I've killed her father and
mother, maybe I've killed her
whole family, and then I go and
give up my mask to save her.
That's funny. That's...a joke.

301. LONG SHOT 7ft. 15frs.
The child and Cabal get into his
plane.

REVOLVER SHOT HEARD
OFF.

302. LONG SHOT 17ft. 4frs.
The burning wreckage of the
enemy plane, Cabal's plane takes
off in the background.

FADE IN:
303. LONG SHOT 72ft. 11frs.
Waste strip of land, tanks come
over a hill top—firing.

FADE OUT:

MUSIC

304. Tanks move across the screen, in
the background huge figures of a
date 1945 come up.

DISSOLVE:

DISSOLVE:

305. LONG SHOT
     In the foreground some men lie
     against barbed wire, the date
     1955 shows behind.

                                                    DISSOLVE:

306. LONG SHOT
     Some very ragged looking
     soldiers with old fashioned
     weapons run up over a wall.

                                                    DISSOLVE:

307. LONG SHOT
     Some more of the ragged men
     run towards the CAMERA with
     their old weapons.

                                                    DISSOLVE:

308. CLOSE SHOT
     Two dishevelled-looking men
     with rifles.

                                                    DISSOLVE:

309. LONG SHOT
     Some ragged soldiers pulling a
     cart, the date 1960 is seen in
     background.

                                                    DISSOLVE:

310. MEDIUM SHOT
     A dead man hanging over some
     barbed wire.

                                                    DISSOLVE:

311. TO the same wire—rags only are
     left in place of the dead man.

                                                    FADE OUT:

                FADE IN:
312. LONG SHOT 60ft. 12frs.
     Waste land—some old papers are
     seen blowing about, one is
     caught on the branch of a tree.

                                                    DISSOLVE:

313. INSERT the paper, the
     CAMERA moves up so that we
     can read it:
                    NATIONAL BULLETIN
                 The end is in sight. Victory is coming.
                 The enemy is near breaking point and
                 defeated on land and sea have neverthe-
                 less retained a few aeroplanes which are
                 difficult to locate and destroy. These
                 they are using to spread the WANDER-
                 ING SICKNESS, a new fever of mind
                 and body. Avoid sites where bombs

have fallen. Do not drink stagnant
water.

FADE OUT:

FADE IN:
314. A VERY LONG SHOT 10ft.
14frs.
Of Everytown, showing the
familiar hill, over this is a title:
EVERYTOWN 1966
315. VERY LONG SHOT 30ft. 12frs.
The square in Everytown, a few
stragglers are walking about.

DISSOLVE:

316. LONG SHOT
Some people lying on some steps.
A ragged-looking man comes
down with a basket of bread and
gives some to a woman and her
child.

DISSOLVE:

317. LONG SHOT
Outside a sewer, a weary-looking
man taps a woman on the
shoulder and they move off.

DISSOLVE:

318. LONG SHOT
Inside sewer, a man comes
down the steps, a woman and
child are by the stove in the
foreground.

FADE OUT:

FADE IN:
319. LONG SHOT 26ft. 7frs.   MUSIC STOPS
Woman pulling a plough by
hand. Over this a title fades in:
IN THE WAKE OF WAR AND SOCIAL
BREAKDOWN A STRANGE AND TER-
RIBLE PESTILENCE, THE WANDERING
SICKNESS, SPREAD UNCHECKED
THROUGHOUT THE WORLD.

FADE OUT:

FADE IN:
320. CLOSE UP 29ft. 3frs.   MUSIC
Man's hand as it holds on to a
post outside a ruined building
marked "Hospital." The man
pulls himself up by his hand and
comes into the picture.
321. LONG SHOT 7ft. 14frs.

He comes out and starts to
wander across the square, eyes
staring wildly.

322. LONG SHOT 5ft. 3frs.
The ruined square, a man in the
foreground sees the sick wanderer
and calls out a warning.

MAN:
Look...He's carrying the infection.

323. EXT. LONG SHOT 10ft.
The square, the sick man
wandering, people fleeing from
him.

DISSOLVE:

324. INSERT:
Dr. Harding, chalked roughly on
a door.

325. LONG SHOT 4ft. 10frs.
Harding and Mary in their
laboratory.

HARDING:
Iodine, please...

326. CLOSE SHOT 8ft. 13frs.
Mary takes a bottle from a shelf.

...Mary, iodine.

327. CLOSE SHOT 8ft. 2frs.
Harding looking through a
microscope. Mary joins him.

MARY:
There's no more, father. That is
the last drop.

328. MEDIUM LONG SHOT 24ft.
2frs.
The two. They go to the window
and are there in LONG SHOT.

HARDING:
No more iodine. God—what is
the use of trying to save this
mad world from its punishment.
MARY:
Oh father, if only you could get
some sleep.
HARDING:
How can I sleep? See how they
wander out to die?

329. LONG SHOT 5ft. 1fr.
Outside, shooting through an
arch, the wanderer passes.

WANDERING MOTIVE
STARTS IN MUSIC

330. LONG SHOT 5ft. 4frs.
He comes through an arch, people run away from him.

331. MEDIUM LONG SHOT 2ft.

12frs.
Man and woman see him and
run away.
332. VERY LONG SHOT 3ft.
Square, the man wandering
round.
333. LONG SHOT 1ft. 15frs.
Steps to ruined buildings, people
run away at his approach.
334. MEDIUM SHOT 2ft. 12frs.
Two women see him and run.
335. CLOSE SHOT 4ft. 8frs.
Shooting up at the sky,
wanderer's head appears, he
comes nearer and nearer to
CAMERA.
336. MEDIUM SHOT 6ft. 7frs.
The Boss by a ruined building
calls a man to him.

337. CLOSE SHOT 9ft. 1fr.

338. VERY LONG SHOT 2ft. 2frs.
The square.
339. LONG SHOT 5ft. 12frs.
Man running to get a rifle. He
comes back with one.
340. CLOSE SHOT 3ft. 6frs.
Man and another behind him.
He takes aim.
341. LONG SHOT 6ft. 1fr.
Wanderer in square, arms up, he
is shot.

342. CLOSE SHOT 8ft. 12frs.
Mary and Harding looking out of
the window.

343. MEDIUM SHOT 3ft. 6frs.
Entrance to room. Gordon
enters.
344. MEDIUM SHOT 21ft. 2frs.
Harding and Mary; Gordon joins
them. PAN.

BOSS:
Why don't you shoot them...
...It's their lives or ours. Let's
get guards and make a cordon.

MUSIC STOPS.
SHOT
MUSIC STARTS AGAIN

HARDING:
That's how they dealt with pestilence in the Dark Ages.

MARY:
Richard.
GORDON:
My sister.
HARDING:

Gordon, how do you know?

GORDON:

Her heart beats fast, and she feels faint. And she won't answer. What can I do for her?

345. CLOSE SHOT 11ft. 8frs.
Mary and Gordon.

...I thought something might be known.

MARY:

Oh, Janet. And you, you poor dear Richard.

GORDON:

I might be infected.

346. MEDIUM SHOT 10ft. 5frs.
The two, they leave.

DISSOLVE:

347. MEDIUM SHOT
Janet in bed.

348. LONG SHOT 22ft. 3frs.
The room. Janet in bed, Harding, Mary and Gordon standing by.

GORDON:

Is there nothing to make her comfortable?

HARDING:

Nothing. There's nothing will make anyone comfortable any more.

349. MEDIUM SHOT 6ft. 11frs.
Harding goes out.

350. LONG SHOT 13ft. 5frs.
Guard on wall overlooking square. He holds a rifle.

DISSOLVE:

351. LONG SHOT
Janet in bed.

352. CLOSE UP 5ft.
Janet. She tosses about and starts to get up.

353. LONG SHOT 17ft. 15frs.
She gets out of bed and starts out of the room.

354. MEDIUM SHOT 9ft. 6frs.
She passes the CAMERA and wanders out.

WANDERING MOTIVE
STARTS IN MUSIC

355. LONG SHOT 3ft. 2frs.
Guard on wall.

356. MEDIUM SHOT 10ft. 2frs.
Man and some women run away

as Janet comes out from her
ruined house and starts to
wander across the square.

357. LONG SHOT 9ft. 14frs.
Janet's empty room. Gordon
comes in and finds her gone. He
dashes out after her.

358. MEDIUM SHOT 2ft. 10frs.
The guard with his rifle.

359. LONG SHOT 4ft. 9frs.
Janet wandering across the
square.

360. MEDIUM SHOT 1ft. 13frs.
Guard taking aim.

361. LONG SHOT 6ft. 8frs.
The square. Gordon looks round
for Janet.

362. CLOSE UP 2ft. 14frs.
Gordon. He looks up and sees
the guard.

GORDON:
No—Don't shoot.

363. MEDIUM SHOT 6ft. 1fr.
Guard. Boss joins him, he takes
the rifle from him and aims at
Janet.

BOSS:
Shoot, I tell you—shoot.

364. LONG SHOT 4ft. 12frs.
Janet staggers across the square,
she falls.

MUSIC STOPS.
SHOT

End of Reel 3

Reel 4

365. MEDIUM SHOT 10ft. 13frs.
Guard and Boss.

BOSS:
That's the way to do it. Shoot
'em.

FADE OUT:

FADE IN:
366. TITLE 35ft. 14frs.

1967
NO MAN HAS EVER RECKONED
THE RAVAGES OF THE WANDER-
ING SICKNESS. LIKE THE BLACK
DEATH IN THE MIDDLE AGES IT
KILLED MORE THAN HALF THE
HUMAN RACE. NO ONE WHO

CAUGHT IT SURVIVED. ONLY
GRADUALLY DID MEN REALIZE
THAT THE EPIDEMIC WAS OVER
AND THAT SOCIAL VITALITY WAS
RETURNING.
1970
FADE OUT:

FADE IN:

367. EXT. LONG SHOT 6ft. 15frs.
The built-up square, the living
accommodations consist in many
cases of converted buses or badly
repaired buildings.

368. LONG SHOT 4ft.
The square.

BELL RINGS

369. MEDIUM SHOT 13ft.
A group round the bell ringer,
he is reading out a proclamation
which is fixed upon a board.

BELL RINGER:
May Day 1970. The pestilence
has ceased...

370. MEDIUM SHOT 4ft. 5frs.
A potter working on a wheel, his
assistant beside him.

...Thanks to the determined
action of our Chief...

371. LONG SHOT 3ft. 6frs.
People walking across the square.

...in shooting all wanderers...

372. LONG SHOT 3ft. 8frs.
Some children run into a broken
down building past a standing
horse.

...there have been no cases for
two months...

373. MEDIUM SHOT 4ft. 14frs.
A man milking a cow.

...The pestilence has been conquered...

374. MEDIUM SHOT 4ft. 13frs.
A Cobbler at work.

...The Chief is preparing to resume hostilities...

375. MEDIUM SHOT 4ft. 3frs.
Man weaving.

...against the hill people with
the utmost vigour...

376. MEDIUM SHOT 5ft. 5frs.
A butcher chopping some meat
by a converted bus.

...Soon we shall have victory
and peace.

377. MEDIUM SHOT 4ft. 15frs.
Mary walks across the square
with a basket and buys some
vegetables.

...All is well. God save the

Chief...

...God save our land.

378. MEDIUM SHOT 4ft. 9frs.
Group round the bell ringer.

379. LONG SHOT 5ft. 11frs.
A wrecked aerodrome. Gordon
and two mechanics.

380. CLOSE UP 34ft. 3frs.
Gordon. He throws down a piece
of broken wire disgustedly.

GORDON:
Have we any more insulated
wire?

ASST:
We've got no rubbered wire at
all, sir.

GORDON:
Any rubber tape?

ASST:
There's not a scrap left in the
place. We used the last on the
other motor.

GORDON:
Oh what's the use? There's no
petrol anyway. I don't believe
there's three gallons of petrol left
in this accursed ruin of a town.
What's the good of setting me at
a job like this. Nothing'll ever
fly again. Flying's over. Civilization's dead.

381. LONG SHOT 17ft. 15frs.
A part of the square. A woman
is bathing a baby in a tub, Mary
crosses the square and a Rolls
Royce, drawn by a horse, pulls
up beside her.

382. MEDIUM SHOT 6ft. 7frs.
Gordon as he comes from the
airport by a wrecked bus and
looks around for Mary. He walks
up to C.S.

383. MEDIUM SHOT 14ft. 3frs.
Of Rolls, the peasant driver is
out of the car and standing back
to CAMERA. Mary in on the
farther side of the car. Gordon
joins her.

MARY:
Hullo.

GORDON:
It's a Rolls, isn't it?

384. CLOSE SHOT 3ft. 9frs.
Mary and Gordon.

385. CLOSE SHOT 19ft. 9frs.
Peasant, shooting between Mary
and Gordon.

386. MEDIUM SHOT 17ft. 10frs.
The three, shooting towards
Mary and Gordon.

He gets in the car and starts to
make the horses draw the car
out.

387. LONG SHOT 5ft. 9frs.
The peasant drives out in his car
pulled by the horse.

388. MEDIUM SHOT 14ft.
Mary and Gordon.

389. CLOSE SHOT 7ft. 13frs.
The two.

PEASANT:
Yes, it's a good pre-pestilence
machine. I oil it and turn it over
at times.

GORDON:
D'you think it'll go fast some
day, still?

PEASANT:
Oh, I'm not one of your petrol
hoarders. But all the same
that engine turns over still.
Why, I remember when I was a
lad—when it was new—we
thought nothing of going a hundred miles in it...

...a whole hundred miles. Less
than three hours I've done it in.
But that sort of thing's all gone
now. Gone forever.

GORDON:
Afraid so.

MARY:
Richard.
GORDON:
What is it?
MARY:
You won't think me mad?
GORDON:
Why darling?
MARY:
I thought I heard an aeroplane
this morning...at dawn. I
thought it was a dream but...

GORDON:
Nonsense. I tell you flying's finished. We shall never get into
the air again. Never.

390. LONG SHOT 9ft. 13frs.
The Chief on horseback, followed by his men ride across.
They are seen in silhouette
through an arch.
391. MEDIUM SHOT 4ft. 2frs.
A man milking a cow. A soldier
comes into the picture, kicks
him.

392. MEDIUM SHOT 2ft. 10frs.
A butcher.
393. MEDIUM SHOT 2ft. 6frs.
A small girl runs up to two men
weaving, and peering through
the strings calls out to them.

394. MEDIUM SHOT 2ft. 3frs.
Man with a chair.
395. MEDIUM SHOT 2ft. 2frs.
Men drinking. They raise up
their mugs.

396. EXT. LONG SHOT 4ft.
The square. People hurry across
to greet the Boss.
397. LONG SHOT 3ft. 11frs.
They run to meet him.
398. LONG SHOT 5ft. 14frs.
Another angle, they run to greet
him.
399. LONG SHOT 4ft. 3frs.
By some chairs and a statue,
they run forward to see him pass.
400. MEDIUM SHOT 4ft. 13frs.
The Boss's procession comes
towards the CAMERA. A
horseman, drummers behind
them. People wave as they pass.
401. EXT. LONG SHOT 4ft. 9frs.
The square, as the procession
comes closer, the Boss leading.
402. LONG SHOT 4ft. 7frs.
He rides through files of cheering
people.
403. LONG SHOT 8ft. 14frs.
Corner of the square, crowds
cheer the Boss.

MUSIC STARTS

SOLDIER:
Hi, come on, the Boss...

...Look, the Boss.

GIRL:
The Boss is coming.

MEN:
Here's to the Boss.
CHEERS FROM THE CROWD

404. MEDIUM SHOT 2ft. 6frs.
The Boss riding past.

405. LONG SHOT 4ft. 2frs.
People clear away from foreground and show Mary and Gordon standing together, the Boss
rides up to them.

MUSIC FADES OUT AS PRO-
CESSION MOVES OFF

BOSS:
Anything to report, Gordon?
GORDON:
Nothing very hopeful, Chief.

406. MEDIUM SHOT 61ft. 7frs.
The three.

BOSS:
I must have these aeroplanes—
somehow.
GORDON:
I'll do what I can, but you can't
fly without petrol.
BOSS:
I'll get petrol for you, trust me.
You look after the machines. I
know you haven't got the stuff—
but you can get round that. For
example transfer parts. Use bits
of one to mend another. Give
me only ten machines in working order. Give me only five. I
don't want them all, and we'll
end this war of ours forever. I'll
see you get your reward...

Boss gets off his horse.

...This your wife, Gordon? You
keep her well hidden. Salutation
lady. You must use your influence with our Master Mechanic. The combatant state
wants his service.
MARY:
I'm sure my husband does his
best for you.
BOSS:
That's hardly enough, lady. The
combatant state demands miracles.

407. CLOSE SHOT 10ft. 4frs.
Favour Mary, shooting over Gordon and the Boss. The Boss puts
his hand under Mary's chin.

MARY:
Not everyone can work miracles
as you do Chief.
BOSS:

Oh, I'm sure you could work
miracles if you tried, lady.

ROXANA (off):
Rudolf!

408. MEDIUM SHOT 10ft. 4frs.
The group. Roxana comes up to
them followed by Wadsky. She
comes right up to the Boss, Mary
and Gordon.

WADSKY:
Lady, lady, I showed it to you
but you said you didn't want
it . . .

BOSS:
If Wadsky's been up to his tricks
again, he'll have to answer for
them.

409. CLOSE UP 3ft. 1fr.
Roxana, Wadsky behind her.

ROXANA:
But he's been keeping things
back from me again.

410. MEDIUM SHOT 9ft. 4frs.
Boss, Gordon, Mary and
Roxana.

BOSS:
Not only Wadsky keeps things
back. What do you think of our
Master Mechanic here—that
won't give me planes to end this
war of ours with the hill men.

411. CLOSE UP 5ft. 13frs.
Roxana.

ROXANA:
Well, can't you make him? I
thought you could make everybody do everything.

412. MEDIUM SHOT 34ft. 8frs.
The four.

GORDON:
Some things you can't do
Madam. You can't fly without
petrol. You can't mend machines without tools or material.
We've gone back too far. Flying's
become a lost skill in Everytown.

ROXANA:
Are you really as stupid as that?

GORDON:
I'm as helpless as that.

ROXANA:
And now, Chief, what are you
going to do about it?

SOUND OF DISTANT PLANE
BOSS:
  He's going to let me have those
  machines and I'm going to let
  him have coal-stuff to make oil.
GORDON:
  It's a lost skill, it's a dream of
  the . . .

413. LONG SHOT 6ft. 3frs.
  A black plane in the sky.
414. CLOSE SHOT 3ft. 7frs.
  Mary and Gordon as they look
  up. TRUCK to C.U. of Gordon   GORDON:
  as he sees a plane.   There it is . . .

415. CLOSE UP 1ft. 11frs.   . . . you were right . . .
  Boss as he sees it.
416. CLOSE UP 2ft. 2frs.
  Roxana, Wadsky behind her, as
  they look up and see the ap-
  proaching plane.   . . . a plane once more!
417. LONG SHOT 8ft. 8frs.
  The black plane in the sky.
418. LONG SHOT 3ft. 10frs.
  The men drinking see the plane
  as they look up.   MAN:
                                         Look there he is.
419. MEDIUM SHOT 1ft. 5frs.
  People by statue look up.
420. CLOSE UP 1ft. 15frs.
  The Boss looking up.
421. LONG SHOT 3ft. 11frs.
  The plane in the sky.
422. LONG SHOT 4ft. 13frs.
  The Boss, Gordon, Mary and
  Roxana in front of crowd.   GORDON:
                                       He's shutting off. He's coming
                                       down.
                                     BOSS:
                                       What's the meaning of . . .
423. MEDIUM SHOT 21ft. 1fr.
  Some steps. Boss runs up them.   . . . this? They've got aeroplanes
                                       before us? And you told me we
                                       couldn't fly any more. While
                                       we've been fumbling they've
                                       been active. Here some of you.
                                       You and you. Find out who this
                                       is and what it means. There's
                                       only one man in it. Hold him.

424. CLOSE SHOT 16ft. 8frs.
Gordon, Mary and Roxana in
foreground, Boss behind them on
steps.

GORDON:
    Somewhere they can still make
    new machines. I didn't dream it
    was still possible.
ROXANA:
    Yes, but who is this man? How
    does he dare to come here?
BOSS:
    Fetch him to the Town Hall.
    Guard his machine and bring
    him to me there.

Boss comes down.

425. LONG SHOT 5ft.
Plane shooting through ruined
pillars as plane lands.
426. LONG SHOT 2ft. 4frs.
All moving off to see the plane.
427. CLOSE SHOT 4ft. 2frs.
Mary and Gordon.

GORDON:
    Come along, Mary. I must see
    that machine.

428. LONG SHOT 13ft. 5frs.
Shooting through ruined pillars.
Plane taxis forward and comes to
a standstill.
429. LONG SHOT 4ft.
Crowd by ruined pillars come
forward towards CAMERA.
430. LONG SHOT 4ft. 4frs.
Black plane from the side. Airman starts to get out.
431. LONG SHOT 6ft. 5frs.
From the front an airman in
black gas mask who is now seen
to be Cabal, stands up.
432. LONG SHOT 2ft. 14frs.
(closer than above). Crowd approaching CAMERA.
433. LONG SHOT 5ft. 11frs.
Cabal walks away from
CAMERA towards crowd.
434. LONG SHOT 7ft. 7frs.
Crowd led by a guard ap-
proaches CAMERA.
435. MEDIUM SHOT 7ft.
Favouring Cabal as Cabal
reaches the guard.

CABAL:

Who's in control of this part of
the country.
GUARD:
The Chief. What we call the
Boss.

436. CLOSE SHOT 2ft. 15frs.
Cabal and guard, favouring
Cabal.

CABAL:
Good, I want to see him.

437. CLOSE SHOT 2ft. 11frs.
The two. Favour guard.

GUARD:
He sent me to arrest you.

438. CLOSE SHOT 5ft. 12frs.
The two. Favour Cabal.

CABAL:
You can't do that. But I'll come
and see him.

439. CLOSE SHOT 6ft. 7frs.
The two. Favour guard.

GUARD:
Well you're under arrest.
Whether you'll admit it or not.
The country's in a state...

440. CLOSE SHOT 3ft. 12frs.
The two. Favour Cabal.

...of war.
CABAL:
Well, come along...

441. LONG SHOT 27ft. 3frs.
The two. Favour the guard. The
crowd behind them. He turns
and Cabal walks off through the
crowd.

...I know the way.
DISSOLVE:

442. LONG SHOT
The ruined square, the crowd led
by Cabal comes to the top of a
bank. Cabal stands, the crowd
around him.

CABAL:
I remember this place well—I
used to live over there. For
years. Ever heard of a man
named Passworthy?
MURMURING.. No.

443. MEDIUM SHOT 3ft. 5frs.
Cabal, guard and woman.

CABAL:
Harding?
MURMURING. Yes.

444. LONG SHOT 8ft. 7frs.
As before, they all move out.

MAN:
Look! Here he comes now.

445. LONG SHOT 16ft. 3frs.

Children run across. Cabal joins
Harding, who approaches
through the crowd.

CABAL:
So you're Harding?
HARDING:
I seem to remember something
about you.
CABAL:
You were a young man.

446. LONG SHOT 49ft. 1fr.
Shooting from above, the group.

HARDING:
You're John Cabal. I remember
you. I used to visit your house
here endless years ago, before
the wars. And you're still flying!
Your hair is grey, but you look
young enough.
CABAL:
How are things here? Who's in
control in this place?
HARDING:
Oh. We have a Chief, a war
lord.
CABAL:
The usual thing. I want to look
up your war lord. Where can we
go and talk?
HARDING:
I should think my laboratory
the best thing—it's just over
here.

They all move off.

CABAL:
Right!

447. LONG SHOT 7ft. 8frs.
Outside Harding's laboratory, as
the group comes up.
448. MEDIUM SHOT 18ft. 5frs.
Mary followed by Cabal and
Harding, the guard comes up.

GUARD:
Here you can't go in there.
You're under arrest. You've got
to go with me to the Chief.
CABAL:
All in good time. I must see this
gentleman first.
GUARD:
Well you've got to go with me.
Orders are orders. The Boss
first.

449. LONG SHOT 21ft. 13frs.
Inside the laboratory, they all
enter. The guard is pushed outside, and Gordon shuts the door.

PAN over to hold the group,
Harding, Mary, Gordon and
Cabal in the room.

CABAL:
Stay outside...

...So you came back here after
the war?
HARDING:
Yes, became a sort of medieval
leech. A doctor without any
medicines or instruments.

450. CLOSE SHOT 7ft. 6frs.
Cabal and Harding.

CABAL:
But tell me—how are things
here? Are there any mechanics
left? Any good technical workers?

451. LONG SHOT 9ft. 6frs.
All four.

HARDING:
The very man!
CABAL:
What are you?
GORDON:
Ex-air-mechanic sir. Jack of all
trades now.

452. CLOSE SHOT 10ft. 1fr.
Cabal, Gordon and Harding.

The last engineer in Every-
town.
CABAL:
Pilot?
GORDON:
Yes, sir. But not very skillful,
I'm afraid. I'm not a very good
mechanic.

453. LONG SHOT 24ft. 10frs.
Guard comes in.

GUARD:
My orders are...
CABAL:
Never mind your orders. Shut
that door.

He is pushed out again. Mary
starts to put food before Cabal
who sits at the table.

Now tell me, what about this
Boss of yours. What sort of a
man's got hold of this part of
the world?

End of Reel 4

Reel 5

454. LONG SHOT 15ft. 4frs.
Roxana by the window of Boss's
Head Quarters. Boss is sitting at
his table, Burton waiting behind
him. Roxana walks over to Boss.

BOSS:
Where is this man? Why isn't he
brought here?

BURTON:
Well, he's gone off with Dr.
Harding.

455. MEDIUM SHOT 13ft. 11frs.
Boss, Burton and Roxana. Boss
rises.

BOSS:
He has to be brought here. I
must deal with him.

ROXANA:
Here, you can't go to him. He
must come to you.

Boss sits down again.

BOSS:
Well, send another man for him.
Send three men. He's got to be
brought here.

456. MEDIUM SHOT 33ft. 4frs.
Cabal, Harding, Mary and Gordon in Harding's laboratory.
Cabal is walking about as he
talks, the others are seated.

CABAL:
So that's the sort of man your
Boss is. Not an unusual type.
Everywhere we find these little
semi-military upstarts, robbing
and fighting. That's what endless
warfare had led to — brigandage.
What else could happen? But
we, who are all that are left of
the old engineers and mechanics
have pledged ourselves to salvage the world. We have the air-
ways, all that's left of them. We
have the seas, and we have ideas
in common...

457. CLOSE UP 14ft. 1fr.
Cabal.

...the Brotherhood of efficiency, the free masonry of
Science. We're the last trustees
of civilization when everything
else has failed.

458. MEDIUM SHOT 34ft. 13frs.
The four.

GORDON:
I've been waiting for this. I'm
yours to command.
CABAL:
Not mine. Not mine. No more
bosses. Civilization's to command.

The doors are thrown open and
two other messengers from the
Boss with the original guard
come in.

GUARD:
Tell him he'll have to come. If
he won't come on foot, well,
we'll have to carry him.
GUARD:
I don't know what'll happen to
me, sir, if you don't come.

Cabal goes out followed by the
three guards.

FADE OUT:

FADE IN:
459. LONG SHOT 10ft. 5frs.
The doors of the Boss's Headquarters are opened to show
Cabal in doorway in foreground,
back to CAMERA and the Boss
and group at the table in the
background. The Boss stands.

CABAL:
Well, what do you want to see
me about?

460. MEDIUM SHOT 3ft. 13frs.
Boss and Burton at table. Burton
walks out of picture.

BOSS:
Who are you? Do you know this
country's at war?

461. LONG SHOT 3ft. 13frs.
Cabal goes towards Boss. Cabal
back to CAMERA.

CABAL:
At war!

462. CLOSE UP 2ft. 14frs.
Cabal coming towards
CAMERA.

...Still at it, eh?

463. MEDIUM SHOT 11ft. 4frs.
Cabal, Boss, Roxana and
Burton.

...We must clean that up.
BOSS:
What do you mean? We must
clean that up? War's war. Who

are you I say?

CABAL:
The Law...

...Law and Sanity.

464. CLOSE UP 2ft. 6frs.
Cabal.

465. CLOSE SHOT 2ft. 14frs.
Boss and Roxana.

BOSS:
I'm the law here.

CABAL:
I said law and sanity.

467. MEDIUM SHOT 10ft. 15frs.
Cabal, Boss, Roxana and
Burton.

BOSS:
Where do you come from? Who
are you?

CABAL:
Wings over the World.

BOSS:
Well, you know, you can't come
into a country like this in this
fashion.

468. MEDIUM SHOT 6ft. 13frs.
Reverse shot of the four. Cabal
sits.

CABAL:
I'm here. Do you mind if I sit
down?

469. MEDIUM SHOT 30ft. 2frs.
The four, favouring the Boss.

BOSS:
And now for the fourth time,
who are you?

CABAL:
I tell you "Wings over the
World."

BOSS:
That's nothing. What government are you under?

CABAL:
Commonsense. I belong to
World Communications. We
just run ourselves.

BOSS:
Eh? You'll run into trouble if
you try and land here in war
time. What's the game?

CABAL:
Order and trade...

470. MEDIUM SHOT 5ft. 0frs.
Boss, Roxana and Cabal. Favour
Boss. He rises.

BOSS:

Trade, eh? Can you do anything
in munitions?

471. CLOSE UP 1ft. 11frs.
     Cabal.

CABAL:
Not our line of business.

472. CLOSE UP 9ft. 6frs.
     Boss.

BOSS:
Fuel—spare parts? We've got
planes—we've got planes—I've
got boys who've trained a bit on
the ground. We've got no fuel. It
hampers us. We might do a
deal.

473. CLOSE UP 3ft. 6frs.
     Roxana.

CABAL:
We might.
BOSS:
I know where I can get some
fuel...

474. MEDIUM SHOT 6ft. 11frs.
     Boss, Cabal and Roxana.

...I've got my plans later. But if
you can manage a temporary ac-
commodation—we'd do business.

475. CLOSE UP 3ft. 9frs.
     Cabal.

CABAL:
World Communications helps
no one to make war.

476. CLOSE SHOT 2ft. 11frs.
     Boss and Roxana.

BOSS:
End war. End war.

477. CLOSE UP 9ft. 15frs.
     Cabal.

...I want to make victorious
peace.
CABAL:
I seem to have heard that phrase
before. When I was a young
man...

478. CLOSE SHOT 14ft. 12frs.
     Boss and Roxana.

...but it made no end of war.
BOSS:
Now look here Mr. Aviator.
Let's see how we stand. Come
down to actuality. The way you
swagger you don't seem to
realise you're under arrest...

479. CLOSE UP 8ft. 6frs.
     Cabal.

...You and your machine.
CABAL:
You'll find other planes looking

480. CLOSE UP 1ft. 15frs.
     Boss.

481. MEDIUM SHOT 15ft. 6frs.
     Cabal, Boss and Roxana.

482. CLOSE UP 4ft. 3frs.
     Cabal.

483. CLOSE SHOT 14ft. 8frs.
     Boss and Roxana.

484. MEDIUM SHOT 24ft. 15frs.
     Boss, Roxana and Cabal from
     the front of the room.

     Boss walks away and Roxana
     comes over to Cabal.

485. CLOSE UP 13ft. 3frs.
     Cabal gets up and walks round
     table.

486. MEDIUM SHOT 5ft. 4frs.
     Boss, Cabal and Roxana.

for me if I happen to be delayed.

BOSS:
We'll deal with them later...

...Now you can start a trading
agency here if you like. I've no
objection. The first thing we
shall want is to get our planes in
the air again.
CABAL:
Quite a laudable ambition...

...But our new order has an
objection to private aeroplanes.

ROXANA:
The impudence!
BOSS:
I'm not talking about private
aeroplanes. Our aeroplanes are
public aeroplanes. This is...an
independent sovereign state—at
war...

...I know nothing about any
new order. I'm the chief here,
and I'm not taking any orders—
old or new from you.
CABAL:
I suppose I've walked into trouble.
BOSS:
Yes—you can take that as right.

ROXANA:
Where do you come from?

CABAL:
I flew from our headquarters at
Basra this morning...We have
some hundreds of new type
planes, and we're building more
—fast. The factories are working
again.

...We're gradually restoring

487. CLOSE SHOT 9ft. 9frs.
     Cabal and Boss, favour Boss.

order and trade in the whole
Mediterranean area...

...We're scouting this region
now to see how things are.
BOSS:
You've found out. This is an independent sovereign state.

488. MEDIUM SHOT 11ft. 14frs.
     The three, favour Cabal.

CABAL:
Yes, we must talk about that.
BOSS:
We won't discuss it.
CABAL:
We don't approve of indepen-
dent sovereign states.
BOSS:
You don't approve!

489. CLOSE UP 1ft. 15frs.
     Cabal.

CABAL:
We mean to stop them.

490. CLOSE UP 1ft. 8frs.
     Boss.

BOSS:
That's war.

491. CLOSE UP 1ft. 13frs.
     Cabal.

CABAL:
If you will.

492. MEDIUM SHOT 20ft. 7frs.
     The three. Burton comes up to
     Boss, TRUCK BACK to hold
     group in LONG SHOT.

BOSS:
All right—I think we know how
we stand. Burton, take this
man. If he gives you any trouble, club him. Do you hear that,
Mr. Wings over your Wits?

493. CLOSE UP 9ft. 14frs.
     Cabal.

CABAL:
My friends know my where-
abouts—if I don't come back,
they'll send a force to find me.

494. CLOSE UP 6ft. 13frs.
     Boss, shooting over Cabal's
     shoulder.

BOSS:
Perhaps they won't find you.
CABAL:
They'll find you.
BOSS:
They'll find me ready...

495. MEDIUM SHOT 5ft. 14frs.
Cabal, Boss, Roxana and
Burton.

Boss walks over to his bedroom.
496. LONG SHOT 12ft. 5frs.
Boss enters his bedroom and lies
down on the bed.
497. MEDIUM SHOT 5ft. 11frs.
Roxana enters the room and
walks up to M.S. as she stands at
the foot of the bed, looking at
Boss.

498. LONG SHOT 14ft. 13frs.
Boss and Roxana.

499. MEDIUM SHOT 3ft. 10frs.
Roxana.

500. MEDIUM SHOT 9ft. 5frs.
Boss.

501. MEDIUM SHOT 4ft. 11frs.
Roxana.

502. LONG SHOT 11ft. 0frs.
The two.

Boss gets up and goes over to get
himself a drink.

...Take him to the detention
room downstairs.

ROXANA:
Now was that wise?

BOSS:
Wise?
ROXANA:
Yes, wise to quarrel with him at
once?
BOSS:
Quarrel with him! Confound
him—he began to quarrel with
me. We must clean that up!
Clean that up!...

BOSS:
...My war!
ROXANA:
But there's things behind him.

BOSS:
Things behind him. Some sort
of aerial bus driver. Standing up
to me...

...like an equal.
ROXANA:
So you lost your temper, and
you bullied him.

BOSS:
I don't bully. I just handled the
man.
ROXANA:
No. You bully. And you bully
too soon.

BOSS:

503. CLOSE UP 12ft. 13frs.
Boss, Roxana joins him, as they
walk back to M.S.

Ah, I don't seem able to please
you today.

ROXANA:
Well, if you must go from one
tactless thing to another. Weak-
ening your authority, sacrificing
dignity.
BOSS:
Here, what's the matter with
you?
ROXANA:
Oh, I saw...

504. CLOSE SHOT 6ft. 12frs.
The two.

...There's your head mechanic
—the essential man for the job,
and you can't keep your eyes off
his wife...

505. MEDIUM SHOT 33ft. 8frs.
The two, they walk up to
CLOSE SHOT.

...Don't I know you? But never
mind that, I'm accustomed to
overlooking that sort of thing.
What I'm asking you now,
whether you bully or not—was it
wise to take this man in this
way?
BOSS:
How else could I have treated
him?
ROXANA:

They sit on the bed in C.S.

He's the first real aviator that
has come this way for years.
Think of what that means, my
dear. You want aeroplanes don't
you? You want your aeroplanes
put in order?...

506. LONG SHOT 4ft. 7frs.
The two sitting on the bed. Roxana rises.

...A really clever man could
have had some of those machines up long ago...

507. CLOSE SHOT 18ft. 0frs.
The two, the Boss rises also.

....I'm sure of it.
BOSS:
So along comes this stranger
who is going to clean me up,
and you expect me to hand my

planes over to him, lock, stock
and barrel.

ROXANA:

Why talk nonsense, you could
have persuaded him—under
supervision.

BOSS:

Supervision!...

508. MEDIUM SHOT 13ft. 3frs.
The two.

...The sort of oafs I've got here
to supervise him. He'd be too
much for them.

ROXANA:

Oh well of course, if he's going
to be too much for you, why
don't you hang him and hide his
machine before the others are
after you.

509. CLOSE SHOT 5ft. 14frs.
Roxana.

BOSS:

I don't agree with you. I don't
agree with you. Now this
stranger...

510. LONG SHOT 13ft. 14frs.
The two, the Boss crosses the
room and sits in a chair.

...hasn't taken me by surprise. I
knew he was coming. Yes, I
knew he was coming. I felt...

511. CLOSE SHOT 5ft. 4frs.
Boss.

...this conspiracy of air bus
drivers brewing somewhere in
the world...

512. LONG SHOT 6ft. 9frs.
The two.

...I felt they were getting ahead
with their aeroplanes down
there somewhere. Very well....

513. CLOSE UP 5ft. 9frs.
Boss.

...Now's our chance. We've got
this fellow bottled up. They
won't even begin to miss him...

514. CLOSE UP 3ft. 11frs.
Roxana.

...for days...

515. CLOSE UP 16ft. 2frs.
Boss.

...I've got everything fixed now
for an attack straight away on
the Floss Valley to the old coal
and shale pits—where there's oil
too—Then...up we buzz.

DISSOLVE:

516. LONG SHOT   MUSIC OF ATTACK STARTS
     Hillside—men rush forward to
     attack.
517. LONG SHOT 4ft. 9frs.
     Mine. Boss's men rush forward to
     attack.
518. LONG SHOT 2ft. 11frs.
     Closer than above as men attack.
519. MEDIUM SHOT 2ft. 14frs.
     Boss with two of his men looking
     over a wall—he gives a signal.
520. CLOSE SHOT 1ft. 7frs.
     Shooting behind a man working
     a machine gun towards the mine.
521. CLOSE SHOT 1ft. 7frs.
     Man comes up to a corner of a
     wall and throws a bomb.
522. CLOSE SHOT 2ft. 8frs.
     Two men in foreground—backs
     to CAMERA—shooting.
523. CLOSE SHOT 2ft. 13frs.
     Man working a machine gun.
524. MEDIUM SHOT 2ft. 8frs.
     Men come over a wall.
525. MEDIUM SHOT 1ft. 4frs.
     Men running away from
     CAMERA.
526. MEDIUM SHOT 4ft. 1fr.
     Men fighting with bayonets pass
     the CAMERA.
527. MEDIUM SHOT 2ft. 5frs.
     Men come through a hole in the
     wall.
528. MEDIUM SHOT 2ft. 3frs.
     Boss in foreground—back to
     CAMERA—the mine in
     background.
529. LONG SHOT 2ft. 2frs.
     Horsemen gallop past a wall of
     the mine.
530. MEDIUM SHOT 2ft. 14frs.
     The fight—shooting through a
     girder.
531. MEDIUM SHOT 1ft. 8frs.
     Horsemen ride past.
532. LONG SHOT 2ft. 15frs.
     Man climbs up a girder with the
     Boss's flag.
533. MEDIUM SHOT 2ft. 8frs.

Horses gallop past a girder.

534. LONG SHOT 2ft. 4frs.
The enemy flag falling from the
top of the girder—a man with a
bayonet passes in the foreground.

535. MEDIUM SHOT 3ft. 1fr.
Boss and one of his men—Boss
points up to where his flag now
flies.

536. LONG SHOT 15ft. 7frs.
The man fixing the Boss's flag in
position on the top of the girder.

MUSIC CHANGES TO THE
TRIUMPHAL RETURN
MARCH
DISSOLVE:

537. LONG SHOT
Crowds cheering outside the
Town Hall as the Boss rides up
among them.

538. LONG SHOT 5ft. 7frs.
Another angle—the Boss is more
clearly seen with Roxana.

539. MEDIUM SHOT 5ft. 12frs.
Boss and Roxana dismount.

540. MEDIUM CLOSE SHOT 2ft.
6frs.
Crowd of cheering women.

541. LONG SHOT 82ft. 3frs.
Boss, Roxana and some of their
followers going to the Town
Hall, the crowd still cheering.

DISSOLVE:
THE MUSIC OF THE MARCH
UNDERLIES ALL THIS SCENE

542. LONG SHOT
Towards the stairway down to
the hall of the Boss's Headquarters. The Boss marches into
the room.

BOSS:
Victory approaches. Your sacrifices have not been in vain. Our
old struggle with the hill men
has come to its climax. Our new
victory at the old coal pits has
brought a great supply of oil
within our reach...Once more
we may hope to take the air and
look our invaders in the face.
We've forty aeroplanes, as large
a force I venture to say, as any
in the world. This new oil can

He walks up to a chair and
strikes a pose, flinging his cloak
over the back of the chair.

PAN with him as he walks across to Gordon and Burton who are standing by a pillar in front of a fire. They are all held in L.S.

be adapted to our needs. That's quite a simple business. Nothing remains but the conclusive bombing of the hills. Then for a time we can hope for a rich rewarding peace. The peace of the strong man, armed, who keepeth his house. And now at this supreme crisis you, Gordon, our Master Mechanic, refuse your help...

Turns round to Gordon.

543. MEDIUM SHOT 36ft. 3frs.
Boss, Gordon and Burton.

...Where are my planes?
GORDON:
The job's more difficult than you think. Half your machines are hopelessly old. You haven't twenty sound ones, to be exact, nineteen. You'll never get the others off the ground. The thing can't be done as you imagined it. I want assistance.
BOSS:
What assistance?
GORDON:
Your prisoner.
BOSS:
What, you want that chap in black—that Wings over the World? You want him released?
GORDON:
He knows his business. I don't enough. Make him my technical advisor.

544. CLOSE SHOT 35ft. 8frs.
Boss and Gordon.

BOSS:
I don't trust you technical chaps.
GORDON:
Then you won't get an aeroplane up.
BOSS:
I want those planes.

Gordon shrugs his shoulder.

...Well, if you get him?
GORDON:
Then I want Dr. Harding out too.
BOSS:

They're old associates.

GORDON:

I can't help that. If anybody in
Everytown can adapt that crude
oil for our aeroplanes it's Harding. If not it can't be done.

BOSS:

Well, we've had a bit of an argument with Harding lately.

GORDON:

He's the only man who can do
this work for you.

545. MEDIUM SHOT 5ft. 5frs.
Boss, Gordon and Burton. Burton leaves to fetch Harding.

BOSS:

Get him.

546. LONG SHOT 6ft. 10frs.
Towards the door. Burton leaves
and Roxana enters.

MUSIC FADES OUT

End of Reel 5

Reel 6

547. MEDIUM SHOT 63ft. 9frs.
Boss in foreground with his back
to the CAMERA, Roxana and
others standing in background.
Burton comes in and stands with
Harding near Roxana.

BOSS:

Undo his hands. Well?

HARDING:

Well, what?

BOSS:

The salute.

HARDING:

Damn the salute.

Burton and others start to molest
Harding.

ROXANA:

No, no, no, no.

BOSS:

Never mind the salute now.
We'll talk about that later. Now
look here, let's see how we
stand. You, Gordon, are to undertake the reconstruction of

Gordon steps into picture.

our air force. The prisoner
Cabal is to be placed at your
disposal. Everywhere he goes he
is to be under guard and obser-

vation. No relaxing on that. Neither you nor he are to go within a hundred yards of his aeroplane. Mind that. Now you, Harding, are to assist Gordon with his fuel problem and place your knowledge of poison gas at our disposal.

HARDING:

I'll have nothing to do with poison gas.

BOSS:

You've got the knowledge if I have to wring it out of you.

548. CLOSE SHOT 4ft. 15frs.
Boss over Harding's shoulder.

BOSS:

The State's your mother—your father...

549. LONG SHOT 23ft. 14frs.
The whole group.

...the totality of your interests. No discipline can be too severe for the man that denies that by word or deed.

HARDING:

Nonsense. We have a duty to civilization. You and your sort are driving us straight back to eternal barbarism.

BURTON:

But this is pure treason.

Boss walks away out of picture.

550. LONG SHOT 61ft. 11frs.
The whole group—longer than above. The Boss is standing with his back to CAMERA in the foreground.

HARDING:

I protest being dragged away from my work. Confound your silly war and your war material and all the rest of it. All my life has been interrupted and wasted and spoilt by war. I'll not stand it any longer.

BURTON:

But this is treason—treason.

ROXANA:

No, no, no, no. Stop that.

BOSS:

We've need of your service.

HARDING:

They start to molest Harding.

Boss walks up to the group again.

Well, what do you want?

BOSS:
You're conscripted. You're under my orders now and under no other orders in the world.

551. CLOSE SHOT 9ft. 6frs.
Reverse of above, the Boss walks up to the group.

552. MEDIUM SHOT 51ft. 9frs.
The group, Boss, Roxana, Harding and Burton—favour Boss, Roxana behind him.

I'm master here. I'm the State. I need fuel and gas.

HARDING:
Neither fuel nor gas.
BOSS:
You refuse?
HARDING:
Absolutely.
BOSS:
I don't want to be forced to extremities.
GORDON:

Gordon comes into shot.

May I have a word? I understand you want all of those out-of-date crocks of yours, which you call your air force—to fly again—and fly well?
BOSS:
They shall.
GORDON:
With the help of that man— Cabal—you have in the cells and Doctor Harding here—you may even have a dozen of your planes in the air again.
HARDING:
You—you're a traitor to civilization. I won't touch it.
GORDON:
If you give me Cabal...

553. MEDIUM SHOT 39ft. 1fr.
The group—favour Gordon.

...and if you leave me free to talk with Harding, I promise you you'll see your air force—a third of it at any rate—in the sky again.
BOSS:
You talk as if you're driving a

bargain with me.
GORDON:
I'm sorry, Chief. It's not I who
makes these conditions. It is the
nature of things. You cannot
have technical services, you cannot have scientific help without
treating the men who give it to
you properly.
ROXANA:
That's what I said all along.
You're bullying too hard, my
dear, and there's a limit to bullying...

554. CLOSE SHOT 7ft. 11frs.
The group. Favour Boss and
Roxana.

...Why! you can't make a dog
hunt by beating it.
BOSS:
I want those planes.
MUSIC

555. LONG SHOT 27ft. 6frs.
The torchlight procession outside
the Town Hall.

556. LONG SHOT
The whole banqueting room,
showing the blonde sitting at the
left hand of the Boss, a Captain
on the Boss's right, and Roxana
next to him. Other people at the
table. All are feasting. The Captain rises.

DISSOLVE:

CAPTAIN:
Chief and Commanders! A
health. Our War Leader. Our
Peace Maker, Rudolf the Victor-
ious.
CRIES OF "RUDOLF" –
"SPEECH"

557. MEDIUM SHOT 17ft. 13frs.
The group round the Boss at the
table, the Boss rises.

BOSS:
My Captains, my Commanders,
I greet you. Could anything in
life be better than this moment?
You've faced difficulties and
dangers...

558. LONG SHOT 16ft. 14frs.
The whole room.

...But now at this bright moment of victory we relax, to

559. CLOSE SHOT 8ft. 14frs.
Roxana, she does not share the
Boss's enthusiasm.

560. CLOSE SHOT 11ft. 14frs.
Boss and the blonde, as he gives
her an amorous pat on the head.

561. MEDIUM SHOT 15ft. 8frs.
The group round the Boss.

562. CLOSE UP 7ft. 1fr.
Roxana.

563. MEDIUM SHOT 24ft. 10frs.
The group, Roxana rises and
goes, the Boss hardly noticing
her departure.

564. LONG SHOT
Cabal sitting in his cell. Shooting
towards the door, Cabal rises as
he sees Roxana coming through
the door.

565. MEDIUM SHOT 8ft. 2frs.
Roxana as she comes down the
steps.

566. LONG SHOT 4ft. 2frs.
The two, Cabal back to
CAMERA in the foreground,
Roxana facing him in the
background.

gather strength for the supreme
effort that'll make this land forever ours...

...A Man's land we're making,
a land for strength and for courage...

...None but the brave deserve
the land, none but the brave
deserve the fair....
LAUGHTER

...Our dear old world! Our
dear old land! There are some
among us that dare to run down
our land. It isn't this—it isn't
that. It isn't...

...what it used to be. We
haven't got chemists. Well, who
wants chemists?...

...They don't print books any
more. Who wants books to
muddle their thoughts and their
ideas? We can't travel any more.
Well, isn't our land good enough
for us?
DISSOLVE:
MUSIC FADES OUT

ROXANA:
I want to look at you.

CABAL:

I am at your service, Madame.

567. CLOSE SHOT 17ft. 14frs.
Roxana. PAN with her as she
goes over to Cabal, hold the two
in LONG SHOT.

ROXANA:
You're the most interesting thing
that has happened in Everytown
for years.
CABAL:
You honour me.
ROXANA:
You come from outside. I'd be-
gun to forget there was anything
outside...

568. LONG SHOT 15ft. 9frs.
The two, Cabal back to
CAMERA. Roxana comes up to
him, she sits. Cabal sits on edge
of table.

...I want to hear about it.
CABAL:
May I offer you my only chair?
ROXANA:
You know, I'm not a stupid wo-
man.
CABAL:
I am sure.
ROXANA:
This life here—is limited...

569. LONG SHOT 3ft. 7frs.
Reverse of above, favour Cabal.

...War—always going on and
never ending...

570. CLOSE SHOT 36ft. 6frs.
The two, from the side.

...Flags, marching. Oh I adore
the Chief. I've always adored
him since he took control in the
Pestilence Days when everyone
else lost heart. He rules...He's
firm. Everyone—every woman
finds him strong and attractive.
I can't complain. I have everything that is to be had here.
And yet...This is a small limited world we live in...

571. CLOSE SHOT 23ft. 7frs.
The two, favour Roxana.

...You bring in the breath of
something greater. When I saw
you swooping down out of the
air. When I saw you marching
in to the Town Hall—I felt this

man lives in a greater world.
And you spoke of the Mediterranean and the East—of your
camps and factories.

572. CLOSE SHOT 6ft. 13frs.
The two, favour Cabal.

ROXANA:
I've read about the Mediterran-
ean and Egypt and Greece—and
India.

573. CLOSE SHOT 17ft. 13frs.
The two, favour Roxana.

...Oh—I can read—a lot of
those old books. I'm not like
most of the younger people here.
I learnt a lot before education
stopped and the schools closed
down. I want to see that
world...

574. CLOSE SHOT 37ft. 7frs.
The two, from the side.

...Skies, snowy mountains, blue
seas. Sunshine. Palms.
CABAL:
If I had my way—you could fly
to all that in a couple of hours.
ROXANA:
If you were free—and if I was
free...I don't suppose any man
has understood any woman
since the beginning of things.
You don't understand our imag-
inations. How wild our imagina-
tions can be. I wish I were a
man...

575. MEDIUM SHOT 4ft. 4frs.
The two. She rises and walks
away to L.S.
576. CLOSE UP 5ft. 4frs.
Roxana.

...Oh—if I were a man...

...What are your people trying
to do to us?

577. CLOSE UP 2ft. 3frs.
Cabal.
578. CLOSE UP 5ft. 10frs.
Roxana.

579. CLOSE UP 4ft. 7frs.
Cabal.

...What are you going to do to
this Boss of mine?

580. CLOSE UP 6ft. 6frs.
Roxana.

CABAL:
The immediate question seems
what does he mean to do to me?

ROXANA:

581. MEDIUM SHOT 14ft. 11frs.
The two.

Cabal rises and goes over to the window.

582. CLOSE SHOT 21ft. 8frs.
The two, shooting from outside the window through the bars to the two of them.

583. LONG SHOT 14ft. 10frs.
The two.

584. MEDIUM SHOT 48ft. 8frs.
The two.

Something violent and foolish—unless I prevent it.

CABAL:
That's how I see things.
ROXANA:
And if he kills you...

CABAL:
We shall come here and clean things up.
ROXANA:
But if you're killed—how can you say we?

CABAL:
We go on. That's how things are. We are taking hold of things. In Science and Government—in the long run—no man is indispensable. The human things go on. We—forever.

ROXANA:
I see—and this war-like State of ours here?
CABAL:
It has to vanish, like the Tyrannosaurus and the saber-toothed tiger.

ROXANA:
Why can't I—help you? I know this place. I'm a sort of Queen here. Am I nothing to you at all?
CABAL:
Do you think you could get me to my plane? They haven't put it out of action, have they?
ROXANA:
No, he wants to use it and he doesn't know how to. There it stands with six guards night and day. Even I couldn't get at that just now.
CABAL:

What are you proposing to me?

ROXANA:

Nothing. I came to see you. I wanted to look at you. I'm interested in you.

CABAL:

Well?

585. CLOSE SHOT 26ft. 11frs.
The two, from the side.

ROXANA:

And now I find you more interesting than ever. A woman loves to help, she loves to give. I could help you so much now... and if I help?

CABAL:

We wouldn't forget.

ROXANA:

We wouldn't forget. Who cares about we? Would you forget it?

CABAL:

Why should I in particular?

586. MEDIUM SHOT 24ft. 3frs.
The two.

ROXANA:

Are you a stupid man, or are you insulting me? I tell you I find you the most interesting man in the world—a great eagle out of the air. And you stare at me with that ugly face of yours and pretend not to understand. Ugly you are and grey. It doesn't matter. Oh why should we go on fencing?...

587. CLOSE SHOT 18ft. 15frs.
The two.

...Don't you understand? Don't you see? I'm yours if you want me. I'm for you. Now—now will you let me help you?

They look round as they hear the noise of a door opening.

588. LONG SHOT 25ft. 7frs.
Shooting towards the door of cellar. Boss enters and comes down. Roxana and Cabal step into foreground. Their backs to the CAMERA.

BOSS:

Ah. So here you are.

ROXANA:

I said I should talk to him and I

have.
BOSS:
I told you to leave that fellow alone.
ROXANA:
Yes, and sat up there drinking and swaggering and looking as proud as you could. Rudolf the Victorious. And here I am trying to find out what this black invader means.

Cabal walks out of picture.

589. CLOSE SHOT 17ft. 8frs.
Roxana and Boss, favouring Boss.

Do you think I wanted to come and talk to him, this cold grey man? While you're swaggering here, there are more planes away there at Basra getting ready.
BOSS:
Basra?
ROXANA:
His headquarters. Have you never heard of Basra?

Boss walks down to her.

590. MEDIUM SHOT 22ft. 14frs.
Boss and Roxana.

BOSS:
These are matters for us to talk about.
CABAL:
This lady has been putting me through a severe cross examination. But the gist of it is—that away there in Basra new aeroplanes are rising night and day like hornets round a hornets' nest.

Cabal comes into picture.

591. CLOSE SHOT 23ft. 5frs.
Boss and Cabal. Shooting from the side.

What happens to me is a small affair. They'll finish you. The new world of united airmen will finish you. Listen! You can almost hear them coming now.
BOSS:
Not a bit of it.

592. LONG SHOT 34ft. 5frs.
All three, favouring Boss and Roxana.

ROXANA:
What he says is the truth.

BOSS:
What he says is bluff.
ROXANA:
Make peace with the airmen and let him go.
BOSS:
That means surrender of our sovereign independence.
ROXANA:
But more machines will be coming and more and more.
BOSS:
Yes. And he's here—hostage for their good behavior. Come, madam, enough of this little diplomatic mission of yours.

Roxana runs up the steps, turns at the door and calls down to the Boss.

ROXANA:
You've got the subtlety of a— bullfrog.
BOSS:
Yes, I don't know what she's been saying to you. I don't much care. There's no making peace between you and me. It's your world or mine. And it's going to be mine and for all your threats of swarms of hornets and so on...

She leaves, the Boss laughs.

...you're a hostage. Remember that...

594. CLOSE UP 3ft. 1fr.

595. MEDIUM SHOT 24ft. 12frs.
The two. Boss puts candle out.

...And don't be too sure you'll win. So just sit there and think that over, Mr. Wings over the World.
FADE OUT:

End of Reel 6

Reel 7

FADE IN:
596. LONG SHOT 12ft. 7frs.
Cabal and Gordon working on a plane, a guard stands by them.

CABAL:
Now get round to the other side and look at these engine bearer

braces—quickly . . .

597. CLOSE SHOT 9ft. 7frs.
Shooting from behind Cabal's
head to Gordon on the other
side of the plane.

(whispering):
. . . If I could get to my plane
there's a wireless there.
GORDON:
Hopeless, they won't even trust
me.
CABAL:
We shall have to make a job of
this.

598. LONG SHOT 6ft. 10frs.
Guard walks up to listen to what
they are saying.
599. CLOSE SHOT 10ft. 6frs.
Cabal, shooting from behind
Gordon's back.

GORDON:
I can manage to get your reserve
petrol. They'll let me have that
for this plane.
CABAL:
Good.
GORDON:
It won't be easy to make a get-
away . . .

600. MEDIUM SHOT 7ft. 10frs.
Behind Cabal showing guard,
listening.

CABAL (aloud):
These oil pump connections
aren't very good. But we'll have
to risk it.

601. CLOSE SHOT 7ft. 9frs.
Shooting from behind Gordon's
back to Cabal on other side of
plane.

GORDON (whispering):
I think we'll manage it all right
now that Harding knows his
part of the job.
CABAL:
Good.
                    FADE OUT:

FADE IN:
602. LONG SHOT 7ft. 1fr.
Roxana and Mary in Harding's
laboratory.

ROXANA:
It's not only that I want to protect you from the insults of the

603. CLOSE UP 7ft. 3frs.
Roxana.

604. LONG SHOT 19ft. 11frs.
The two—Roxana crosses over to
Mary.

605. CLOSE UP 6ft. 9frs.
Roxana.

606. CLOSE UP 4ft. 8frs.
Mary.

607. MEDIUM SHOT 15ft. 10frs.
& The two.
608.

609. CLOSE SHOT 17ft. 15frs.
The two.

610. CLOSE UP 8ft. 10frs.
The two.

Chief—I know him...

...But I want to talk to you
about this man Cabal and this
airmen's world they talk
about...

...What is this new world that's
coming? Is it a new world really?
Or only the old world dressed
up in a new way? Do you understand him? Is he flesh and
blood?
MARY:
He's a great man.

ROXANA:
If this new world of yours—all
airships and order and science
comes about...

...what will happen to us wo-
men?
MARY:
We'll work like the men.

ROXANA:
Men—when I think of lean grim
Cabal—I believe this world of
yours must come. And then I
think—it can't come—it can't.
It'll seem to come and it won't
come...

MARY:
Do you really believe that war
and struggle, mere chance
gleams of happiness, and general
misery, do you think that this
will last forever?
ROXANA:
You want an impossible world.
You're asking too much from
men and women...

...What do we want, we women? Knowledge, civilization,
the good of mankind?...

611. MEDIUM SHOT 29ft. 11frs.
     The two.

     . . . Nonsense—Nonsense—We
     want satisfaction. We want
     glory. The glory of being loved—
     the glory of being wanted—de-
     sired—splendidly desired—and
     Mary goes out of picture. Roxana
     sits.
     the glory of feeling and looking
     splendid. Do you want anything
     different? Of course you don't.
     But you haven't learnt to look
     things in the face yet.

612. CLOSE UP 6ft. 10frs.
     Mary.

     . . . This brave new world of
     yours will never come. This
     wonderful world of reason . . .

613. CLOSE SHOT 35ft. 15frs.
     Roxana goes up to Mary.

     . . . and it wouldn't be worth
     having if it does come. It would
     be dull and safe and—oh,
     dreary. No lovers—no warriors—
     no danger—no adventure.
     MARY:
     No adventure. No glory in help-
     ing, to make the world over
     anew. It's you who are dream-
     ing.
     ROXANA:
     Helping men. Why should we
     work and toil for them? Let
     them work and toil for us.
     MARY:
     Yes—but we could work with
     them.
     ROXANA:
     And what would they have to
     work and toil for then?

614. MEDIUM SHOT 7ft. 7frs.
     The two. TRUCK back as Rox-
     ana crosses.

     MARY:
     Greater things.
     ROXANA:
     There's no flavour in these
     greater things. No flavour, no
     flavour at all . . .

615. CLOSE UP 11ft. 8frs.
     Roxana.

     . . . These airmen—they will con-
     quer the world. Then we shall
     conquer them. Lean and stern
     and sober though they are.

616. MEDIUM SHOT 21ft. 13frs.
The two.

MARY:
If I thought that was all we
could work for...
ROXANA:
This is all we can work for.
Have you learnt nothing from
marriage with Gordon?
PLANE NOISE HEARD OFF

They cross over to the window
and look out. PAN over with
them as they cross.

617. LONG SHOT 11ft. 15frs.
Gordon's plane flying.

ROXANA:
Look! It's your Gordon...

...he's flying at last.
FADE OUT:

FADE IN:
618. VERY LONG SHOT 12ft. 8frs.
At Basra showing one of the
huge Basra bombers, and a lot of
men going to and fro.
619. LONG SHOT 6ft. 7frs.
The plane, the men by it.
620. LONG SHOT 9ft. 6frs.
Closer than above, a young airman is going up the steps to the
plane, he turns and looks off.

621. CLOSE SHOT 3ft.
The young airman.
622. LONG SHOT 4ft. 9frs.
The group round the foot of the
steps to the plane. A chief
engineer comes out of the plane
and stands on the steps. Gordon,
and the guard who accompanied
him, are brought to the foot of
the steps.
623. LONG SHOT 13ft. 11frs.
Shooting from behind the chief
engineer to Gordon and the
group below.

AIRMAN:
Look, an aeroplane out of the
Ark boys.

It's pre-war.

ENGINEER:
Where do you come from?
AIRMAN:
He comes from the North, sir.
From Everytown. He says Cabal
is a prisoner there.
GORDON:

624. CLOSE SHOT 2ft. 1fr.
     The chief engineer.

625. CLOSE SHOT 4ft. 8frs.
     Gordon.

626. CLOSE SHOT 2ft. 3frs.
     Chief engineer.

627. CLOSE SHOT 5ft. 5frs.
     Young airman.

628. LONG SHOT 34ft. 1fr.
     Shooting towards the chief on
     the steps, the group in the
     foreground.

629. MEDIUM SHOT
     Burton comes to the Boss, who is
     lying on his bed asleep, and
     wakes him up.

630. LONG SHOT 7ft. 9frs.
     The room—a man enters with

They've got him, sir. And he's
in danger. I had great difficulty
in getting here.

ENGINEER:
You say Cabal's in danger?

GORDON:
Very great danger. The Boss of
Everytown is a violent tough.

ENGINEER:
Job for our new squadron.

AIMAN:
Well, now we've got a chance to
try the new Gas of Peace on
somebody.

GORDON:
There's no time to lose, sir. May
I report to Headquarters?
ENGINEER:
Yes. Take him to the Council.
                          DISSOLVE:

BURTON:
At last we have definite news.
BOSS:
What is it?
BURTON:
Gordon didn't fall into the sea.
He got away. A fishing boat saw
him making for the French
coast. Perhaps he reached his
pals.
BOSS:
Well?
BURTON:
Well—he'll be coming back. He'll
be bringing the others with him.
BOSS:
Curse these...

the Boss's coffee on a tray.

631. CLOSE UP 42ft. 3frs.
Boss.

Boss crosses to Burton, hold the
two in CLOSE SHOT.

632. LONG SHOT 47ft. 12frs.
Boss walks across room. Burton
follows.

World Communications.
Curse all airmen and...

...gas men and machine men.
Why didn't we leave their machines and their sciences alone?
I might have known. Why did I
tamper with flying?

BURTON:
Well—we needed aeroplanes—
against the Hill State. Somebody
else would have started in again
with aeroplanes and gas and
bombs if we didn't. These people
would have come interfering
anyhow.
BOSS:
Why was all this science ever allowed? Why was it ever let begin? Science! It's an enemy of
everything that's natural in life.
I dreamt of those fellows last
night. Great ugly black inhuman
chaps.

Half like machines...Bomb-
ing and bombing.
BURTON:
Yes—I guess they'll come bombing all right.
BOSS:
Then we'll fight 'em. Since Gordon got away I've had these air
boys up to see me. They've got
guts, they'll do something still
...We'll fight 'em. We'll fight
'em. We've got hostages...I'm
glad I didn't shoot them anyway. There's that chap Harding.
Of course...He can tell us what
to do against this gas. If I have
to pull his arm off and knock
his teeth down his throat. Get
him—get him...
BURTON:
Go and get Dr. Harding.

The man goes.

633. CLOSE UP 30ft. 8frs.
     Boss walks up to window and
     starts to eat his breakfast—
     Burton stands in background.

BOSS:
     They have to come to earth
     sometime. What is this World
     Communications? A handful of
     men like ourselves. They're not
     magic.
                    DISSOLVE:

634. LONG SHOT
     Airmen at Basra as they go into
     one of the big planes. They have
     parachutes on their backs.
635. MEDIUM SHOT 3ft. 12frs.
     Of the steps up to the plane, as
     we see the feet of the men going
     up.
636. CLOSE SHOT 4ft.
     Some men putting boxes of gas
     bombs on to a rail and sending
     them into the plane.
637. CLOSE SHOT 2ft. 7frs.
     Shooting up the steps as more
     men go inside.
638. MEDIUM SHOT 1ft. 14frs.
     Men packing gas bombs.
640. MEDIUM SHOT 2ft. 8frs.
     Some men take the rail away.
641. MEDIUM SHOT 11ft. 4frs.
     Of the steps into the plane as the
     last few go up, then the door
     closes.

642. LONG SHOT
     The Boss's planes lined up in a
     field against some ruined pillars.
     The airmen are lined up by their
     machines. The Boss and Roxana
     are in the foreground, their backs
     to the CAMERA, the Boss on a
     raised platform—Roxana standing
     below.

                    DISSOLVE:

643. CLOSE SHOT 12ft. 11frs.
     Boss and Roxana.

BOSS:
     To you I entrust these good,
     tried, tested machines...

     ...You are not mechanics—you
     are warriors. You have been
     trained not to think, but to

do. . .

644. LONG SHOT 4ft. 4frs.
Shooting from behind the Boss
to the planes.

. . .maybe to die. . .

645. CLOSE SHOT 7ft. 13frs.
Boss and Roxana. He lifts up
both arms.

. . .I salute you—I your Chief.

646. LONG SHOT 10ft. 13frs.
Shooting from behind the Boss.
They all salute.

FADE IN:

647. LONG SHOT 9ft. 14frs.
The square—the people ner-
vously expecting an attack.

648. LONG SHOT 10ft. 7frs.
The Boss standing by the steps of
the Town Hall. Roxana is there
among a crowd of others.

649. MED. LONG SHOT 10ft. 14frs.
Shooting to the steps, Boss goes
up the steps to Harding, who is
standing with Mary in the
doorway.

FADE OUT:

BOSS:
What do you know about these
World Communications people?
Have they got gas? What sort of
gas?

650. MEDIUM SHOT 22ft. 11frs.
Boss, Harding, Roxana and
Mary.

HARDING:
I know nothing about gas.
BOSS:
Tell us about these masks,
anyway.

Harding examines the masks that
are passed to him.

HARDING:
Well, they're rotten. They're no
good at all.
BOSS:
What sort of gas have they got?
HARDING:
I tell you gas isn't my business.
BOSS:
Well they can't gas us when
you're here anyway.
BASRA PLANE NOISE IS
HEARD
BURTON:

651. LONG SHOT 3ft. 9frs.
The whole group, shooting from
the bottom of the steps.

652. LONG SHOT 11ft. 12frs.
Basra plane coming out of a
cloud past the CAMERA R to L.

653. LONG SHOT 9ft. 12frs.
Several Basra planes pass the
CAMERA.

654. LONG SHOT 7ft. 7frs.
A single plane flies past the
CAMERA.

655. MEDIUM LONG SHOT 2ft. 1fr.
The group in the square below,
Harding, Mary, Boss, Roxana
and Burton. They look up at the
approaching planes.

656. CLOSE UP 2ft. 8frs.
The Boss reacting.

657. MEDIUM LONG SHOT 2ft.
7frs.
A group of women look up.

658. LONG SHOT 2ft. 9frs.
A group of people run out and
look up at the oncoming planes.

659. LONG SHOT 10ft. 0frs.
A Basra plane flies towards the
CAMERA.

660. MEDIUM LONG SHOT 3ft.
2frs.
Shooting behind an airman in
the control room, towards a set
of dials.

661. LONG SHOT 4ft. 8frs.
Inside one of the Basra machines
as Gordon and another airman
go to the rail, backs to
CAMERA, and look out.

662. MEDIUM SHOT 6ft. 5frs.
The two from behind.

The other man leaves.

663. LONG SHOT 11ft. 8frs.
The Boss's planes run along the
ground past the CAMERA, trying to take off. Some of them fly

Here they are...

...Listen. They're coming already.

GORDON:
We're here. Tell them to stand
by.

up a little way, the engines back-
firing badly.
664. LONG SHOT 13ft. 5frs.
Shooting through the ruined
pillars to the planes, still back-
firing badly, as some of them
mount into the air.
665. LONG SHOT 4ft. 7frs.
Several bombers fly past.
666. LONG SHOT 11ft. 7frs.
In the square. The Boss in the
foreground, looking up at the
planes. Burton and Roxana stand
behind him and many other
people.

BOSS:
Clumsy great things—our boys'll
have 'em down in no time—
they're too clumsy!

667. LONG SHOT 13ft. 15frs.
A Basra plane flies towards the
CAMERA.
668. LONG SHOT 3ft. 10frs.
Inside one of the Basra planes—
some of the Boss's planes are seen
through the window.
669. LONG SHOT 3ft. 9frs.
Some Basra bombers fly past the
CAMERA.
670. LONG SHOT 4ft. 12frs.
One of the Boss's planes dives.
671. LONG SHOT 2ft. 1fr.
Some Basra bombers flying past
the CAMERA.
672. LONG SHOT 3ft. 13frs.
Inside one of the Basra planes.
Some of the airmen watch the
fight through the window—one
of the Boss's planes falls towards
the earth.
673. LONG SHOT 3ft. 10frs.
Several of the Boss's planes
swooping in the air.
674. LONG SHOT 6ft. 2frs.
The square. The Boss with Burton and Roxana behind him are
in front of the crowd.

BOSS:
What! Only six of us up—where
are the rest of our fellows? Go
on—up at him!

675. LONG SHOT 2ft. 13frs.
     Several Basra planes fly past
     CAMERA.
676. LONG SHOT 1ft. 14frs.
     A Boss's plane falling.
677. LONG SHOT 0ft. 15frs.
     A Boss's plane falling.
678. LONG SHOT 10ft. 0frs.
     A Basra plane flies past the
     CAMERA.
679. LONG SHOT 4ft. 12frs.
     Inside a Basra plane—airmen
     watch a Boss's plane fall in
     flames.
680. LONG SHOT 30ft. 5frs.
     The square. The Boss with Bur-
     ton and Roxana behind him are
     in front of the crowd.

ROXANA:
  Poor boy—it's got him.
BOSS:
  They're both coming down.
  Cowards.
ROXANA:
  But they can't use gas when we
  have hostages.
BOSS:
  The hostages! I'm not done yet.
  Go on, fetch them. Bring them
  out here. Out in the open tie
  'em up where they can be
  seen...

Harding and Mary are brought
forward and tied to posts.

...Where's the other fellow?
He's the Prize Hostage. He's
the best of the lot. They'll know
him. Fetch him.

681. LONG SHOT 3ft. 5frs.
     People running away from a
     cloud of gas.
682. CLOSE UP 4ft. 4frs.
     Burton, the Boss behind him.

BURTON:
  Look! Is that gas?

683. CLOSE SHOT 4ft. 1fr.
     A man in the control room in a
     Basra bomber. Shooting from the
     side, he drops a bomb.
684. LONG SHOT 4ft. 10frs.
     A crowd of Basra bombers pass.
685. LONG SHOT 4ft. 1fr.

A gas bomb is dropped in the square, people start to be overcome by gas.

686. CLOSE SHOT 8ft. 4frs.
Boss and Harding, the Boss brings his pistol out.

BOSS:
Anyway you won't get out of this.

You!

Roxana comes up to restrain him.

ROXANA:
Don't you see—we're beaten.

687. LONG SHOT 5ft. 2frs.
Part of the square, a railing in the foreground. People succumbing to the gas.

688. LONG SHOT 6ft. 14frs.
The Boss in the middle of the square, people are staggering around him.

BOSS:
Shoot them. What are you all doing? Why don't you move?

689. MEDIUM LONG SHOT 5ft. 7frs.
Roxana and Mary, Harding is tied to a post in the foreground, the Boss is standing in the background.

ROXANA:
I never did you any harm—I saved your father and I saved you...

690. CLOSE SHOT 7ft. 14frs.
Roxana and Mary, the gas starts to blow past them.

...Couldn't you call up to your man there to stop this?

691. LONG SHOT 7ft. 0frs.
The Boss in the square, the people around him all falling down under the effect of the gas.

692. CLOSE SHOT 11ft. 6frs.
The Boss, he fights against the gas, he pulls out his pistol and starts to shoot, not aiming but shooting wildly in the air.

BOSS:
I won't have it like this.

...What's happening? Everything's swimming. Shoot.

693. LONG SHOT 8ft. 12frs.
The Boss, now the only one who has not fallen down under the

effects of the gas, climbs up the steps.

Shoot! We never shot enough yet. We haven't...

694. CLOSE SHOT 46ft. 9frs.
The Boss, he falls down. He rises and still shooting his pistol grabs hold of the bell which hangs beside the National Bulletin Board. The Boss falls out of picture. PAN over the Board and stay on the words at the end of the Bulletin: "LONG LIVE THE CHIEF."

...shot enough. We've spared them and now they've got us. Our world or theirs. Why should I be beaten like this? Shoot! Shoot! Shoot! Shoot!
BELL RINGS

End of Reel 7

Reel 8

695. LONG SHOT 12ft. 11frs.
Shooting towards the steps of the Town Hall. All the people, now including the Boss, are lying prostrate on the ground.

696. LONG SHOT
A Basra bomber flies past the CAMERA, parachutes falling out of it.

DISSOLVE:
MUSIC STARTS

697. LONG SHOT 3ft. 10frs.
Some of the airmen jumping from a Basra plane with their parachutes, showing another plane in the background.

698. MEDIUM LONG SHOT 2ft. 11frs.
The interior of a bomber—some of the airmen looking out, another plane can be seen through the window.

699. LONG SHOT 11ft. 14frs.
A Basra plane flies towards the CAMERA.

700. LONG SHOT 7ft. 15frs.
The air filled with parachutes.

701. LONG SHOT 3ft. 9frs.

Some more airmen jumping out
of a plane with their parachutes.

702. LONG SHOT 3ft. 8frs.
A Basra plane flies towards the
CAMERA.

703. LONG SHOT 5ft. 8frs.
The air filled with parachutes.

704. LONG SHOT 21ft. 11frs.
A group of Basra bombers flies
past the CAMERA.

DISSOLVE:

705. LONG SHOT
A line of the new world airmen
seen in silhouette, as we shoot at
them through an arch, they walk
on their way to Everytown.

DISSOLVE:

706. VERY LONG SHOT
The Basra airmen walk through
the square, among the prostrate
bodies.

707. LONG SHOT 22ft. 14frs.
Shooting towards the Town Hall
steps, Gordon and some of the
Basra airmen come up to where
Mary and Roxana are lying.

GORDON:
There they are. Mary! No, no
she's not hurt. She's asleep, like
the others.

708. MEDIUM LONG SHOT 3ft.
13frs.
Shooting towards the door of the
Town Hall, two Basra airmen
run out, followed by Cabal, who
carries his gas mask.

AIRMAN:
Cabal's safe!

709. LONG SHOT 2ft. 13frs.
Gordon in the foreground. Cabal
and the others on the steps.

GORDON:
Cabal!

710. MEDIUM LONG SHOT 29ft.
13frs.
The three on the steps.

CABAL:
Well done, Gordon. Well, they
laughed at me for sticking to my
gas mask—but thanks to that
I'm here—and everyone else is
sleeping. I wonder if they'll ever
use gas masks again?

PAN over with Cabal as he goes
to the young man who kneels
beside the body of the Boss.
Hold the three in L.S.

AIRMAN (off):
Sire?

CABAL:
What is it?
AIRMAN:
This man's not sleeping. He's
dead.

711. MEDIUM SHOT 32ft. 7frs.
Cabal.

CABAL:
Dead and his world dead with
him, and a new world beginning. Poor old Boss. He and his
flags and his follies. And now
for the rule of the airmen, and a
new life for mankind.
                    DISSOLVE:

712. LONG SHOT
Cabal comes up to Roxana who
is lying asleep.

CABAL:
Roxana.

713. MEDIUM LONG SHOT 28ft.
14frs.
The two, he kneels beside her.

The eternal adventuress!
You've pluck and charm, and
brains for infinite mischief.
Where power is you'll follow.
You'll play your eyes at men till
the end of your time. Now that
the Bosses have gone the way of
the money grubbers I suppose it
will be our turn.

714. LONG SHOT 3ft. 6frs.
The two as Cabal stands up.
715. CLOSE SHOT 9ft. 3frs.
Cabal.

A new world, with the old
stuff. Our job is only beginning.

716. LONG SHOT 7ft. 1fr.
The Basra airmen walk through
the square, as the people on all
sides start to awaken.
717. MEDIUM LONG SHOT 5ft.
7frs.
Some people lying by an old bus
wake up, and start to rise.
718. LONG SHOT 7ft. 9frs.
The airmen walk among the

waking people and collect the
rifles and weapons from the men,
and pile them in the centre of
the square.
719. VERY LONG SHOT 12ft. 10frs.
The square, as the airmen walk
among the people.

720. LONG SHOT
Cabal is addressing the Council
at Basra.

DISSOLVE:

CABAL:
Our job is only beginning.

721. CLOSE SHOT 40ft. 15frs.
Cabal standing.

For now we have to put the
world in order. It will be a long
and complicated struggle.

722. LONG SHOT 11ft. 1fr.
Revealing that Cabal is addressing a meeting of men assembled
round a table in a room at Basra.
He sits down.

But we have the unity of a
common order and a common
knowledge. This is how I con-
ceive our plan of operations.

723. MEDIUM SHOT 19ft. 3frs.
Cabal and the group round him
at the table.

First a roundup of brigands.
The last dismal vestige of ancient predatory soldiering. The
last would-be conquerors. Then
settle, organize, advance. This
zone, then that.

724. CLOSE SHOT 11ft. 0frs.
Cabal.

MUSIC ENDS
And at last, wings over the
whole world and the new world
begins.
FADE OUT:

FADE IN:
725. LONG SHOT 95ft. 11frs.
Everytown in ruins, showing the
hill in the background. PAN
OVER to where some immense
digging machines are in operation making a hole in the
ground.

MIXED WITH MUSIC OVER
THIS SHOT COMES CABAL'S
VOICE

CABAL'S VOICE:
Do you realise the immense task
we shall undertake, when we set
ourselves to an active and aggressive peace, when we direct

our energies to tear out the
wealth of this planet, and exploit all these giant possibilities
of science that have been squandered hitherto upon war and
senseless competition. We shall
excavate the eternal hills. We
shall make such use of the treasures of sky and sea and earth as
men have never dreamt of hitherto. I would that I could see
our children's children in this
world we shall win for them.
But in them and through them
we shall live again.
DISSOLVE:
MUSIC CONTINUES

726. LONG SHOT
A digger comes toward the
CAMERA.

727. LONG SHOT
Some men raising some planks.

DISSOLVE:

728. LONG SHOT
A digger moving across past the
CAMERA.

DISSOLVE:

729. LONG SHOT
The head of a digger.
730. LONG SHOT 5ft. 14frs.
A digger at work.
731. CLOSE SHOT 7ft. 7frs.
Head of a digger, showing the
huge jaws.
732. LONG SHOT 4ft. 14frs.
Showing the workman's platform
below the digger.
733. LONG SHOT 4ft. 11frs.
Closer than above, showing men
climbing off the platform.
734. CLOSE SHOT 2ft. 2frs.
The head of a digger, the jaws
close, and a flame spurts out.
735. LONG SHOT 9ft. 14frs.
The head of another digger at
work. Explosion.

DISSOLVE:

736. LONG SHOT
Some men in protective helmets

standing by some massive coils.
737. MEDIUM SHOT 4ft. 7frs.
The two men.
738. LONG SHOT 4ft. 1fr.
The two by the coils.
739. CLOSE SHOT 2ft. 4frs.
The jaws of a digger firing.
740. LONG SHOT 7ft. 6frs.
A digger at work, rocks crumble
down.
741. LONG SHOT 6ft. 1fr.
Shooting up the length of a
digger — explosions.
742. LONG SHOT 3ft. 15frs.
Digger — side view — explosions.
743. LONG SHOT 12ft. 7frs.
Many diggers at
work — explosions.
744. LONG SHOT 3ft. 4frs.
A digger comes towards the
CAMERA.
745. LONG SHOT 2ft. 7frs.
The head of a digger passes the
CAMERA.
746. LONG SHOT 44ft. 10frs.
Many diggers at work — many
explosions.

DISSOLVE:

747. LONG SHOT
Men by some vast tapping
machines.

DISSOLVE:

748. LONG SHOT
Some machinery, a crane lowers
a plank.

DISSOLVE:

749. LONG SHOT
Some men move about on
trolleys.

DISSOLVE:

750. MEDIUM SHOT
Some leaves turn over.

DISSOLVE:

751. LONG SHOT
Some light squares falling.

DISSOLVE:

752. LONG SHOT
Shooting down on light patterned circle.

DISSOLVE:

753. LONG SHOT
     TRUCK along past some rolling
     machines.

754. LONG SHOT
     Shooting from inside a moving
     truck, a man in foreground, a
     crane seen through the window.

DISSOLVE:

755. LONG SHOT 116ft. 4frs.
     An enormous factory—a man on
     a trolley rises in the foreground.

DISSOLVE:

756. LONG SHOT
     Shooting from ground level, a
     man on a trolley comes along the
     floor of the factory.

DISSOLVE:

757. LONG SHOT
     A man on ascending trolley.

DISSOLVE:

758. LONG SHOT
     Man on a trolley—on ground of
     factory, gets off and climbs some
     steps.

DISSOLVE:

759. LONG SHOT
     Rolling machinery.

DISSOLVE:

760. LONG SHOT
     Factory, spiral in foreground.

DISSOLVE:

761. MEDIUM SHOT
     The spiral.

DISSOLVE:

762. MEDIUM SHOT
     Man on trolley below turning
     machines.

DISSOLVE:

763. LONG SHOT
     Factory, showing spiral up to
     roof.

DISSOLVE:

764. CLOSE SHOT
     Spinning tubes.

DISSOLVE:

765. CLOSER SHOT
     Than above, the spinning tubes.

DISSOLVE:

766. LONG SHOT
Rollers going up, a man on a
moving trolley in foreground.

767. Folding leaves.

DISSOLVE:

768. Spinning cube in a circle.

DISSOLVE:

769. Lighted numbers on a board.

DISSOLVE:

770. CLOSE SHOT
A diver in a black helmet walking away from CAMERA, he
turns and looks up.

DISSOLVE:

771. LONG SHOT
Enormous tanks that he sees.

DISSOLVE:

772. LONG SHOT
Men walking up steps to these
tanks.

DISSOLVE:

773. LONG SHOT
Shooting down factory, man in
foreground controlling moving
machinery.

774. LONG SHOT 5ft. 14frs.
Shooting down factory, from a
high angle.

775. LONG SHOT 50ft. 13frs.
Shooting down to man on trolley
travelling along the factory.

776. Glass globe behind rails.

DISSOLVE:

777. CLOSE SHOT
Man behind corrugated glass.

DISSOLVE:

778. CLOSE SHOT
Light jet.

DISSOLVE:

779. CLOSE SHOT
Man behind corrugated glass, he
gives a signal and walks off.

DISSOLVE:

780. Lava pouring over some bars.

DISSOLVE:

781. Funnel hissing out steam.

782. LONG SHOT

Man climbs up steps on
machinery beside this funnel.
783. VERY LONG SHOT 5ft. 3frs.
Huge wall making machines.
784. CLOSE SHOT 3ft. 5frs.
Hissing funnel.
785. LONG SHOT 5ft. 3frs.
The funnel pouring stuff down
into the wall moulders.
786. CLOSE SHOT 4ft.
The funnel.
787. VERY LONG SHOT 12ft. 9frs.
Wall moulders.
788. LONG SHOT 7ft. 1fr.
Shooting end on to moulders,
the sides slide back disclosing a
finished wall.
789. VERY LONG SHOT 6ft. 1fr.
The moulder with the sides back,
now no steam coming from funnel, the wall starts to move out.
790. LONG SHOT 5ft. 8frs.
The wall coming towards the
CAMERA.
791. LONG SHOT 30ft. 2frs.
Shooting sideways to the wall as
it moves out and comes to an
exit from the factory.

DISSOLVE:

792. LONG SHOT
Reverse of above, shooting
through the opening back to the
factory, the wall now having
come out, the exit closes.

DISSOLVE:

793. LONG SHOT
Several walls moving along — man
directing operations of a huge
machine to put the walls in place
on buildings. The walls move out
of picture.
794. LONG SHOT 5ft. 6frs.
Closer than above of the wall
fixing machine in operation.
795. LONG SHOT 5ft. 13frs.
The men directing the wall fixing
machine.
796. CLOSE SHOT 4ft. 7frs.
The sucker at the end of the arm

of this machine, it lifts a wall up
and carries it near its position.

797. LONG SHOT 5ft. 11frs.
The wall being put nearer still
into its position.

[798]

DISSOLVE:

799. VERY LONG SHOT
Everytown, again showing the
hill, now the ruins have been
cleared away and trees grow in
their place. PAN round and
down to the hole seen at the
beginning of the sequence. Now
as we PAN down the hole we see
the new Everytown, a city of
white smooth walls built
underground. Over the white
comes a title:

MUSIC ENDS

CROWD IS HEARD MURMUR-
ING

2036
EVERYTOWN

DISSOLVE:

800. LONG SHOT
Closer than above, PAN down
to show more of the city, a moving bridge across between several
buildings. PAN down past this to
a crowd of people in the City
Ways.

DISSOLVE:

801. VERY LONG SHOT
PAN down on large statue to
show Theotocopulos at work on
the statue.

THEOTOCOPULOS:
Is it any better world than it
used to be? I rebel against this
Progress.

802. LONG SHOT 15ft. 8frs.
Theotocopulos by statue. Assistant walks up steps to join him
on platform.

What has this Progress—this
World Civilization done for us?
Machines and marvels. They've
built these great cities of theirs.
Yes. They've prolonged life.
Yes.

803. MEDIUM SHOT 16ft. 12frs.
Theotocopulos by statue.

They've conquered nature,
they say, and made a great

white world. Is it any jollier
than the world used to be? In
the good old days when life was
short and hot and merry, and
the devil took the hindermost . . .

804. LONG SHOT 8ft. 10frs.
     The two.

ASSISTANT:
  All the same, what can we do
  about it?
THEOTOCOPULOS:
  Rebel. And rebel now. Now.
  Now's the time.
ASSISTANT:
  Why now in particular?

805. MEDIUM CLOSE SHOT 9ft.
     15frs.
     Theotocopulos.

THEOTOCOPULOS:
  Why—Because of this Space
  Gun business. Because of this
  project to shoot human beings
  at the stars.

806. LONG SHOT 10ft. 15frs.
     Theotocopulos and Assistant.

THEOTOCOPULOS:
  People don't like it. Shooting
  humans away into hard frozen
  darkness. They're murmuring.
ASSISTANT:
  They've murmured before. And
  nothing came of it.

End of Reel 8

Reel 9

807. MEDIUM CLOSE SHOT 20ft.
     11frs.
     Theotocopulos. He walks up
     towards CAMERA.

THEOTOCOPULOS:
  Because they had no leader. But
  now. Suppose someone cried
  "Halt. Stop this Progress."

808. LONG SHOT 13ft. 11frs.
     The two.

Suppose I shouted to the
world, "Make an end to this
Progress." I could talk. Talk.
Radio is everywhere. This modern world is full of voices.

809. CLOSE SHOT 20ft. 1fr.

Theotocopulos. The Assistant
enters shot.

I'm a Master Craftsman. I
have the right to talk.
ASSISTANT:
Yes. But will they listen to you?
THEOTOCOPULOS:
They'll listen. Trust them. If I
shout. Arise. Awake...

810. VERY LONG SHOT 13ft. 3frs.
Large statue, Theotocopulos and
Assistant as tiny figures below.

Stop this Progress before it
is too late.
DISSOLVE:

811. LONG SHOT
Of the City Ways, crowds of
people are there, some of them
come up the steps.
812. LONG SHOT 16ft. 3frs.
Another angle of the City Ways.
PAN up and past some balconies
to one particular balcony, a little
girl runs out and looks over the
railing.
813. LONG SHOT 4ft. 5frs.
Closer than above, shooting up
to the child looking down.
814. LONG SHOT 4ft. 14frs.
Shooting down from above the
child to the square below, the
child runs in.
815. LONG SHOT 6ft. 9frs.
Inside the room, shooting
through a television screen, to an
old man on the other side of it,
the child runs to him.

CHILD:
I like these history lessons.

816. MEDIUM SHOT 46ft. 12frs.
The two, shooting from their
side of the screen, as they look at
it. On the screen are pictures of
New York and other cities, these
pictures change as the dialogue
goes on.

What a funny place New
York was, all sticking up and
full of windows.
OLD MAN:
They built houses like that in
the old days.
CHILD:

Why?

OLD MAN:

They'd no light inside their cities as we have. So they had to stick them up into the daylight, what there was of it. They'd no properly mixed and conditioned air. Everybody lived half out of doors. They had windows of brittle glass. The Age of Windows lasted four centuries.

The pictures on the screen change to a succession of shots of windows. The old man goes out of the picture.

817. LONG SHOT 12ft. 5frs.
Reverse of the above showing the old man in the foreground. He sits on a glass chair, and the child is seen sitting by the television screen in the background.

They never seemed to realise that we could light the interiors of our houses with sunshine of our own, so there was no need to stick them up ever so high in the air.

818. MEDIUM SHOT 6ft. 3frs.
The child.

CHILD:

Weren't people tired of going up and down those stairs?

819. LONG SHOT 8ft. 14frs.
The old man.

OLD MAN:

They were all tired. And they had a disease—colds. Everybody had colds.

820. MEDIUM SHOT 4ft. 10frs.
The child.

...And they coughed and sneezed and ran at the eyes.

821. LONG SHOT 5ft. 7frs.
The two, the grandfather in the foreground, the child and the screen in the background. She rises and crosses over to him.

CHILD:

Sneezed! What's sneezed?

OLD MAN:

Oh, you...

822. CLOSE UP 47ft. 1fr.
Old man, shooting over child's shoulder.

...know. Atishoo.

CHILD:

Atishoo. Everybody said atishoo. That must have been funny.

OLD MAN:
Not so funny as you think.
CHILD:
And you remember all that,
great grandfather?
OLD MAN:
Well, I remember some of it.
Colds we had and indigestion
too—from the queer bad foods
we ate. Oh it was a poor life.
Never really well.
CHILD:
Did people laugh at it?
OLD MAN:
Well, they had a way of grin-
ning at it. They used to call it
humour. We had to have a lot
of humour.

I've lived through some horrid times, my dear. Oh, horrid.

CHILD:
Horrid. I don't want to hear
about that.

823. CLOSE SHOT 10ft. 15frs.
The two.

The child starts to walk over the
room again.

824. LONG SHOT 9ft. 5frs.
Shooting through the television
screen, on which are now no pictures, as the child crosses the
room and sits beside the screen.

The wars, the Wandering
Sickness, and all those dreadful
years.

825. MEDIUM SHOT 5ft. 6frs.
The child sitting.

...None of that will come
again, great grandfather? Ever?

826. LONG SHOT 30ft.

OLD MAN:
Well not if progress goes on.
CHILD:
They keep on inventing new
things now don't they, and making life lovelier and lovelier.
OLD MAN:
Lovelier—yes—and bolder. I suppose I'm an old man my dear,
but some of it seems like going
too far. This Space Gu ₁ of
theirs that they keep on shooting.

827. MEDIUM SHOT 5ft. 5frs.

The child.

828. LONG SHOT 16ft. 5frs.
Shooting through the television
screen. The old man crosses over
to the child and sits beside it.

829. CLOSE SHOT 5ft. 9frs.
The two.

830. LONG SHOT 18ft. 13frs.
The two, shooting through the
televisor.

831. CLOSE SHOT 22ft. 9frs.
The two, favour the old man.

832. CLOSE UP 3ft. 8frs.
Child.

833. CLOSE UP 7ft.
Old man.

CHILD:
What is this Space Gun, great
grandfather?

OLD MAN:
Well it's a gun they discharge by
electricity—it's a lot of guns inside one another, and each one
discharges the gun next inside. I
don't properly understand it.

But the cylinder it shoots out
at last—goes swish—right away
from the earth.

CHILD:
What! Right out into the sky?
To the stars?
OLD MAN:
Well I suppose they'll get to the
stars in time, but just now they
only shoot at the moon.
CHILD:
Do you mean they shoot cylin-
ders at the moon?

OLD MAN:
Well, not exactly at it. They
shoot the cylinder so that it
travels round the other side of
the moon and comes back into
the Pacific where it drops.
There's a safe place there.
They're getting more and more
accurate. They can tell within
twenty miles where it's going to
drop, then they keep the sea
clear for it, you see.

CHILD:
And can people go in the cylinders?

OLD MAN:
Well they haven't sent men and
women yet—that's what Theoto-

834. CLOSE SHOT 10ft. 15frs.
The two, favour the old man.

copulos is making all the trouble about.

CHILD:
It wouldn't hurt to go to the moon?

OLD MAN:
Well, we don't know. Some people say yes—some say no. They've sent mice round the moon.

835. CLOSE UP 14ft. 5frs.
Old man.

And they get all broken up, poor little beasties. They don't know how to hold on when the bumps come. That's why there's this talk of sending a man per-haps. He'd know how to hold on...

836. CLOSE UP 8ft.
Child.

CHILD:
He'd have to be brave, wouldn't he?...I wish I could fly round the moon.

837. MEDIUM SHOT 44ft.
The two. Old man rises.

OLD MAN:
Well that in time. Won't you come back to your history pic-tures again?

CHILD:
I'm glad I didn't live in the old world. I know that John Cabal and his airmen tidied it all up. Did you see John Cabal, great grand-dad?

OLD MAN:
Well, you can see him in your pictures.

CHILD:
Did you see him when he lived, you really saw him?

He sits again.

OLD MAN:
Yes. I saw the great John Cabal with my own eyes when I was a little boy. He was a lean brown old man with hair as white as mine.

838. MEDIUM SHOT 14ft. 13frs.
The two. Another angle, to show

the television screen. The old
man turns a button and a picture
of John Cabal appears on the
screen.

He was the great grandfather
of Oswald Cabal, the President
of our Council.
CHILD:
Just as you are my great grandfather?
                    DISSOLVE:

839. CLOSE SHOT
     Cabal sitting at his desk.
840. LONG SHOT 15ft. 5frs.
     Shooting towards Cabal, show-
     ing him in a large room, the fur-
     niture all made of glass.

CABAL:
I take it the Space Gun's passed
all its preliminary trials and
there's nothing left now but to
choose the two who are to go.

An Engineer comes up to his
desk from the right of the
picture.

1ST ENGINEER:
That's going to be the trouble.
2ND ENGINEER (off):
Thousands of young people have
been applying.

841. LONG SHOT 5ft. 15frs.
     Another angle, showing the sec-
     ond engineer seated in the
     foreground, Cabal and the other
     engineer in the background.

Young men and women. I
never dreamt the moon was so
attractive.

842. LONG SHOT 29ft. 2frs.
     Shooting towards the desk,
     Cabal and engineer.

1ST ENGINEER:
Practically the gun is perfect
now. There are risks, but reasonable risks. And the position
of the moon in the next three
or four months gives us the best
conditions for getting there. It's
only the choice of the two now
that matters.
CABAL:
Well?
1ST ENGINEER:
There are going to be difficulties.

Cabal rises.

843. VERY LONG SHOT 8ft. 7frs.
As Cabal starts to cross to 2nd
engineer — showing the landscape
out of the window behind them.

844. LONG SHOT 9ft. 2frs.

845. LONG SHOT 8ft. 5frs.
Reverse of above, showing the
three in the foreground and the
landscape behind them.

846. LONG SHOT 22ft. 12frs.
The three, shooting from outside
the window.

Cabal starts to cross the room.

847. LONG SHOT 2ft. 1fr.
Cabal crossing room, he looks at
a small televisor on his wrist.
848. CLOSE UP 10ft. 6frs.
Cabal and instrument on his
wrist, as he raises his hand and
looks at it.

That man Theotocopulos is talk-
ing on the radio about it.
CABAL:
He's a fantastic fellow.

2ND ENGINEER:
Yes, but he's making trouble. It's
not going to be easy to choose
these young people.
CABAL:
With all these thousands offering themselves?
1ST ENGINEER:
We've looked into thousands of
cases. We've rejected everyone of
imperfect...

...health, or anyone who's had
friends who objected. And the
fact is we want you to talk to
two people.

There's Raymond Passworthy of
General Fabrics. You know him?
CABAL:
Yes, I know him.
1ST ENGINEER:
We want you to see the son,
Maurice Passworthy.
CABAL:
Why?
1ST ENGINEER:
He asks to go.
2ND ENGINEER:
We think you ought to see him.
He's waiting here.

CABAL:
Is Maurice Passworthy there?

SECRETARY (off):
He's on his way.
CABAL:
Good.

849. LONG SHOT 20ft. 6frs.
A plane starting to land. PAN
down with it as it flies lower and
down by an arch and lands in
the City Ways, a crowd of people
round it.

DISSOLVE:

850. LONG SHOT
Cabal and the two engineers in
his room. The door opens and
Maurice comes in, the two
engineers leave.

CABAL:
You want to talk to me?
MAURICE:
Forgive me, sir. I came straight
to you.
CABAL:
You're asking a...

851. LONG SHOT 53ft. 10frs.
The two, they stand behind a
desk.

...favour.
MAURICE:
A very big favour. I want to be
one of the first two human beings to go round the moon.
CABAL:
It means danger. Great hardship
anyhow. You realise there's an
even chance of never coming
back alive, a still greater chance
of coming back a cripple.
MAURICE:
Give me credit for not minding
that, sir.

Cabal walks away from the
CAMERA and then turns
round.

CABAL:
Yes, a lot of you young people
don't mind that. But why
should I give you a favour?
MAURICE:
Well, I'm the son of a friend of
yours, and people seem to feel—
you oughtn't to send someone
you don't know, sir.

Maurice joins him.

CABAL:
Go on...
MAURICE:
We've talked about this over
and over again.
CABAL:
We?

852. CLOSE SHOT 28ft. 10frs.
Of the two. Favour Cabal.

MAURICE:
You, both of us. It's her idea
even more than it's mine.
CABAL:
Her idea? Who is she?
MAURICE:
Someone much closer to you
than I am, sir.
CABAL:
Go on.
MAURICE:
It's Catherine your daughter.
She says you can't possibly send
anybody's child but your own.

853. LONG SHOT 36ft.
The two. Cabal comes forward
again.

CABAL:
I might have known.
MAURICE:
You see sir...
CABAL:
Yes...I see. Funny I never
thought of her as anything but a
little girl. Quite out of all this.
MAURICE:
She's eighteen...

854. LONG SHOT 22ft. 1fr.
A room outside the television
chamber. Theotocopulos and
some of his followers arrive.

THEOTOCOPULOS:
Today I am going to put it to
the world—plainly. Is this thing
to go on, or are we sane and
normal human beings to put an
end to it—and an end to all
such follies forever.

Theotocopulos goes inside the
television chamber.
855. LONG SHOT 17ft. 6frs.
Inside the chamber.
Theotocopulos raises his hand

and the lights go on.

856. LONG SHOT 12ft. 13frs.
In the square, the television
screen is lowered.

857. LONG SHOT 23ft. 6frs.
Closer than above, the image of
Theotocopulos appears on the
screen in LONG SHOT and
Theotocopulos starts his speech.

THEOTOCOPULOS:
What is this Progress? What is
the good of all this Progress? Onward and onward. We demand a
halt, we demand a rest. The object of life is happy living.

858. LONG SHOT 10ft. 13frs.
Theotocopulos in the B.B.C.
showing both Theotocopulos
himself and his image on the
small televisor beside the television operator.

We will not have human life
sacrificed to experiment...Pro-
gress is not living, it should only
be the preparation for living.

859. CLOSE SHOT 6ft.
Cabal, from the front.

Let us be fair to these people
who rule over us.

860. CLOSE SHOT 7ft. 5frs.
Shooting over Cabal's shoulder
to his television screen on his
desk.

Let me not be ungrateful. They
have tidied up the world. They
have tidied it up marvellously.

861. MEDIUM SHOT 10ft. 1fr.
Three men looking at their
televisor, which is a round one.

Order and magnificence is
achieved, knowledge increases.
Oh God, how it increases.

862. LONG SHOT 17ft. 3frs.
In the B.B.C. showing
Theotocopulos and his image on
the small screen.

Still the hard drive goes on.
They have found work for all of
us. We thought this was to be
the Age of Leisure. But is it?
We must measure and compute.
We must collect and sort and...

863. CLOSE SHOT 9ft. 3frs.
The small televisor in the B.B.C.

...count. We must sacrifice ourselves. We must live for—what is

it? — the species.

864. LONG SHOT 17ft. 7frs.
Theotocopulos in the B.B.C.

Greater sacrifices and still greater. Until at last they lead us back to the supreme sacrifice — the sacrifice of human life.

865. CLOSE SHOT 24ft. 0frs.
Cabal, front view.

They stage the old Greek tragedy again, and father offers up his daughter to his evil gods.

Over Theotocopulos's voice
Cabal speaks:
And that voice is sounding to the whole world. We might suppress it. No. They'll have to hear him and make what they can of him.

But have they really left us? No. The old slaveries have taken new names and fresh masks.

866. LONG SHOT 16ft. 14frs.
In the square, showing the L.S. of Theotocopulos on the screen.

What does this Space Gun portend? Make no mistake about it. The slaveries they put upon themselves today they will impose tomorrow upon the whole world.

867. CLOSE SHOT 11ft. 13frs.
A boy and a girl by their televisor.

Is man never to rest, never to be free? A time will come...

868. LONG SHOT 14ft. 2frs.
A boy and girl by a televisor, crowds are moving about in the background. L.S. of Theotocopulos on the televisor.

...when you in your turn will be forced away to take your chance upon strange planets and in dreary abominable places beyond the stars.

End of Reel 9

Reel 10

869a. CLOSE SHOT 6ft. 8frs.
Cabal front view, he is no longer looking at his televisor.

THEOTOCOPULOS:
An end to Progress. Make an end to this Progress...

869b. LONG SHOT 23ft. 6frs.
The crowd in the City Ways, still

looking at the televisor, on which is a L.S. of Theotocopulos.

The image fades off the screen.

870. CLOSE UP 7ft. 2frs.
Cabal, front view.

871. LONG SHOT 12ft. 13frs.
The City Ways, now no image on the television screen. Some of the crowd start to leave the City Ways.

872. LONG SHOT
Cabal and Passworthy come up the stairs to the ante-room.

873. MEDIUM SHOT 24ft. 5frs.
The two. They are walking along the balcony.

874. LONG SHOT 3ft. 13frs.
They move out of shot.

875. LONG SHOT 13ft. 6frs.
The two. They continue walking.

...now. Let this be the last day of the Scientific Age. Make the Space Gun the symbol of all that drives us...and destroy it now.

CROWD CHEER

CABAL:
I wonder what they will make of him.

DISSOLVE:

PASSWORTHY:
It's all very well for you, Cabal. You're the great grandson of John Cabal...

...the air dictator. The man who changed the whole course of the world. You've got experiment in your blood—you and your daughter. But I'm—I'm more normal. I don't believe my boy would have thought of it, the two of them must have got together.

CABAL:
They'll come back together. This time there's no attempt to land on the moon.

PASSWORTHY:
And when...when is this great experiment to be made? How much longer have we got before they go?

CABAL:
When the Space Gun is ready.

PASSWORTHY:
Some time this year you mean?

876. MEDIUM SHOT 16ft. 3frs.
The two as they walk.

877. LONG SHOT 9ft. 13frs.
The two walking.

878. CLOSE SHOT 22ft. 3frs.
The two.

879. LONG SHOT 10ft. 14frs.
The two, shooting towards the
stairs—the boy and girl join them.

880. MEDIUM SHOT 31ft. 2frs.
The group of four.

CABAL:
Soon.

PASSWORTHY:
Then is there no way of saving
our children from this madness?
CABAL:
But would it be saving our
children?
PASSWORTHY:
Children are born to be happy.

PASSWORTHY:
Young people ought to take life
lightly. There's something horrible about this immolation of
eighteen and twenty-one.

CABAL:
Do you think I haven't the same
feelings as you? Do you think I
don't love my daughter? I'm
snatching an hour today—just to
see her, just to look at her while
I can. All the same I shall let
her go...when the time comes.

PASSWORTHY:
Well, here they are.
CATHERINE:
Father, we're to go?
CABAL:
Yes—you're to go.
CATHERINE:
It's announced?
CABAL:
Two hours ago.

PASSWORTHY:
Already.
CABAL:
Why not?
PASSWORTHY:
But—my son.
CABAL:
He's of age. He's volunteered.
PASSWORTHY:
Yes, but I want to talk it over

first. I must talk it over. Why
have you announced this so
soon? There is still time to talk
it over, isn't there?
MAURICE:
Not so very long now, father.
PASSWORTHY:
We've got several months yet,
surely.
CATHERINE:
It's just one month and three
days. Everything's ready.
MAURICE:
And the moon's coming into the
right position even while we're
talking now.

881. CLOSE SHOT 3ft. 3frs.
Cabal and Catherine.

They're leaving it a month
longer to make sure.

882. CLOSE SHOT 7ft.
Passworthy and Maurice. Favour
Passworthy.

PASSWORTHY:
You mean you're going in four
weeks. Four weeks! I forbid it.

883. MEDIUM SHOT 2ft. 2frs.
The four. Passworthy crosses.

This man Theotocopulos is
right.

884. CLOSE SHOT 2ft. 5frs.
Cabal and Catherine.

This thing must not be.

885. MEDIUM SHOT 2ft. 3frs.
The four.

It's human sacrifice.

886. LONG SHOT 4ft. 6frs.
City Ways, the bridge angle, the
screen is no longer there, the
people start rushing out of the
City Ways up the steps.
887. LONG SHOT 4ft. 12frs.
Shooting down over a balcony to
the rushing crowd below.
888. LONG SHOT 5ft. 13frs.
The City Ways, as more people
run up the steps.
889. LONG SHOT 4ft. 9frs.
Theotocopulos outside the
B.B.C., some of his followers
standing by him. A man comes
running to him.

MAN:
Your speech has struck fire.

890. CLOSE SHOT 40ft. 7frs.

The group.

...All the people are excited and angry. Some are already going out of the city towards the Space Gun. Nothing is wanted now but leading.

THEOTOCOPULOS:
We must go right on with this. To the Space Gun. And so—we end an age.

He rises.

He goes out followed by his supporters.

DISSOLVE:

891. LONG SHOT
Cabal, Maurice and Catherine and Passworthy in the ante-room. Maurice and Catherine seated and Cabal standing behind them, Passworthy seated in the foreground.

PASSWORTHY:
Young people just beginning life. And you want to go into that outer Horror. Why don't you send somebody who's sick of life?

892. MEDIUM SHOT 9ft. 8frs.
Two-shot, Catherine and Maurice.

CATHERINE:
They want fit young people, alert and quick. And we're fit young people. We can observe and come back and tell.

893. LONG SHOT 4ft. 5frs.
The four.

PASSWORTHY:
Cabal. I just want to ask you one plain question.

894. LONG SHOT 5ft. 8frs.
Passworthy.

Why did you let your daughter dream of going on this mad moon journey?

895. MEDIUM SHOT 23ft.
Three-shot. Cabal, Maurice and Catherine.

CABAL:
Because I love her and I want her to live to the best effect. Dragging out life to the last possible second is not living to the best effect. The nearer the bone, the sweeter the meat. The best of life, Passworthy, lies nearest to

896. LONG SHOT 10ft. 15frs.
Passworthy alone.

897. MEDIUM SHOT 7ft. 5frs.
Cabal, Maurice and Catherine.

898. LONG SHOT 10ft. 15frs.
All four.

899. MEDIUM SHOT 36ft. 4frs.
Cabal, Maurice and Catherine.

900. LONG SHOT 4ft. 9frs.
Passworthy alone.

901. CLOSE SHOT 4ft. 12frs.
Cabal, Maurice and Catherine.

902. LONG SHOT 7ft. 1fr.
Passworthy alone.

903. CLOSE SHOT 8ft. 6frs.
Cabal.

904. LONG SHOT 11ft. 5frs.
All four.

the edge of death.

PASSWORTHY:
I'm—I'm a broken man. I don't know where honour lies.

CABAL:
My dear, I love you—and I have no doubt.

MAURICE:
A century ago, no man worth his salt hesitated to give his life in war. When I think of those fellows in the trenches...

CABAL:
No. Very few men gave their lives in war, and those few were caught up in a tragic and noble necessity. What the rest did was to risk their lives—and that's all you two have to do. You must do your utmost to come back safe and sound. And you're not the only people who are risking their lives daily. Haven't we men exploring the depths of the sea, training and making friends with danger in every shape and form...

...playing with gigantic physical forces...

...balancing on the rims of lakes of molten metal...

PASSWORTHY:
Yes, but that's to make the world safe for men—safe for happiness.

CABAL:
No, the world will never be safe for man—and there's no happiness in safety.

You've got things wrong,

905. CLOSE SHOT 6ft. 12frs.
Cabal.

Passworthy. Our fathers and our fathers' fathers cleaned up the old order of things because it killed children.

It killed those who were unprepared for death, because it tormented people in vain...

906. CLOSE SHOT 3ft. 3frs.
Maurice and Catherine.

...because it outraged human pride and dignity...

907. CLOSE SHOT 8ft. 1fr.
Cabal.

...because it was an ugly spectacle of waste. But that was only a beginning.

908. LONG SHOT 4ft.
Passworthy.

There's nothing wrong in suffering...

909. CLOSE SHOT 13ft. 13frs.
Cabal.

...if you suffer for a purpose. Our revolution didn't abolish danger and death, it simply made danger and death worthwhile.

910. LONG SHOT 2ft. 11frs.
The four, in the room, they look up.

MITANI (off):
Cabal!

911. TWO-SHOT 4ft. 6frs.
Favour Mitani. Shooting towards door over Cabal's shoulder. Mitani enters and comes to Cabal.

Cabal. The gun's in urgent danger.
It's a race against time now to save it.

912. LONG SHOT 2ft. 10frs.

913. CLOSE SHOT 5ft. 8frs.
Mitani and Cabal. Favour Cabal.

Theotocopulos is out with a crowd of people already. He's going to the Space Gun now. They're going to break it up. They say it's the symbol of your tyranny.

914. CLOSE SHOT 9ft. 1fr.

CABAL:
Have they weapons?
MITANI:
Bars of metal. They can smash delicate apparatus.

915. TWO-SHOT 6ft. 9frs.

Favour Cabal.

916. LONG SHOT 6ft. 11frs.
    All five.

917. TWO-SHOT 6ft. 5frs.
    Cabal and Mitani. Favour Cabal.

918. LONG SHOT 88ft. 7frs.
    They cross the room.

919. LONG SHOT 5ft. 5frs.
    Shooting up to their balcony as
    they all come out and look down.
920. LONG SHOT 4ft. 3frs.
    Balcony. They look down.
921. VERY LONG SHOT 3ft. 9frs.
    The crowd surging in the City
    Ways below.
922. VERY LONG SHOT 7ft. 11frs.
    Another angle, shooting down
    on to top of an obelisk standing
    in the centre of the square.
923. LONG SHOT 4ft. 1fr.
    Shooting up to the group on the
    balcony.
924. LONG SHOT 26ft. 13frs.
    All five. A man comes hurrying
    in.

They can do endless mischief.
CABAL:
    But you have the Traffic Con-
    trol. Can't thay produce the po-
    lice?

MITANI:
    Very few. We've nothing but the
    Gas of Peace. And it isn't ready.
    It'll take hours yet.

We must hold this crowd
back—at any cost—for a time.
Until the Gas of Peace is ready.
CROWD NOISES

PASSWORTHY:
    Listen.

Look.

JEANS:
    Cabal! They're rioting. It's bar-
    barism come back.
CABAL:
    Who are you?
JEANS:
    William Jeans, astronomical de-
    partment, Space Gun.
MITANI:
    Well, we've stopped the airways,
    they'll have to go afoot and
    they'll take an hour or more to
    get there, even those who've al-
    ready started.

925. THREE-SHOT 5ft. 12frs.
Passworthy, Catherine and
Mitani.

926. LONG SHOT 33ft.
All the group.

JEANS:
That gun mustn't be broken up
after all the final experiments
have been made. When everything was ready.
MAURICE:
When everything was ready?

PASSWORTHY:
If they smash up that infernal
gun then honour is satisfied and
you needn't go.

CABAL:
They won't smash the gun.
MAURICE:
Suppose the gun was fired now.
Would the cylinder reach the
moon?
JEANS:
It would miss and fly into outer
space. But it's five now, if the
gun were fired before seven...
CATHERINE:
And it could be...?
JEANS:
Yes.
CATHERINE:
Then...
MAURICE:
We go now.
PASSWORTHY:
No, no, no. Oh, I don't know
what to say, but don't go. Don't
go.
MAURICE:
Oh, but father, we must go now
or we may never go, and then
for the rest of our lives we'll feel
we've shirked and lived in vain.
We must go now.

927. LONG SHOT 10ft. 1fr.
Shooting up to the balcony
where the group are standing
from the City Ways, PAN across
past other balconies.

End of Reel 10

Reel 11

928. LONG SHOT 7ft. 3frs.
The City Ways. Crowds are
there, surrounding a plane.
929. MEDIUM SHOT 9ft. 15frs.
Men open the door of the plane.
Cabal, Passworthy, Maurice and
Catherine come up.
930. MEDIUM SHOT 8ft. 3frs.
Another angle from above of the
plane. Cabal, Passworthy,
Maurice and Catherine get in.
931. MEDIUM SHOT 5ft. 5frs.
Inside the plane. Cabal sits at
the wheel in the foreground.
932. LONG SHOT 6ft. 9frs.
The City. The plane rising.
933. LONG SHOT 2ft. 15frs.
Reverse angle, the plane rising.
934. LONG SHOT 6ft. 4frs.
The plane in the sky.
935. LONG SHOT 8ft.
Crowds rush up the steps from
the City Ways to go to the gun.
936. LONG SHOT 6ft. 6frs.
Plane flying.
937. LONG SHOT 24ft. 15frs.
We fly through the clouds, and
see the plane circling round the
Moon Gun.
938. LONG SHOT 13ft. 8frs.
Shooting down on top of gun as
the plane flies round.
939. LONG SHOT 23ft. 7frs.
Plane flies past gun, PAN with it
as it goes behind gun.
940. LONG SHOT 4ft.
As the plane descends vertically
by a girder by the gun.
941. MEDIUM SHOT 4ft. 2frs.
Showing the four inside the
plane, the girder in the
background, as they fly down.
942. MEDIUM SHOT 4ft. 8frs.
The girder as they see it, while
they descend.
943. MEDIUM SHOT 4ft. 9frs.
Showing the four inside the

plane as they descend.
944. LONG SHOT 9ft. 7frs.
The plane reaches the ground.
945. LONG SHOT 11ft. 2frs.
Another angle, the plane taxiing
along. PAN up to show some of
the base of the gun's framework.
946. LONG SHOT 6ft. 14frs.
Mitani comes out to greet plane.
947. LONG SHOT 7ft. 4frs.
Closer than above. They get out
of the plane as Mitani comes up.
948. LONG SHOT 3ft. 9frs.
Low angle shooting up to the
gun.
949. LONG SHOT 4ft. 6frs.
The group by the plane.

MITANI:
Quickly, this way!

950. They start off towards the interior of the gun.
951. EXT. LONG SHOT 12ft. 10frs.

ELECTRIC HUM STARTS

The gun, as the arm of the girder
loaded with the shell swings
over. There is a tree in the
foreground of the picture.
952. LONG SHOT 16ft. 11frs.
Cabal, Passworthy, Maurice and
Catherine follow Mitani down a
passage, they come to a lift.

MITANI:
If you go up to the platform,
we'll guard this below.
CABAL:
Right.

The four get in the lift and go
up.
953. MEDIUM LONG SHOT 6ft.
2frs.
PAN up with the lift as it rises
beside the girder.
954. LONG SHOT 4ft. 3frs.
The gun as the arm swings further over.
955. LONG SHOT 7ft. 5frs.
Passworthy and Cabal standing
on the platform. Lift comes up.
956. LONG SHOT 8ft. 1fr.
Maurice and Catherine coming
out of the lift.
957. LONG SHOT 3ft. ?frs.

All four on the platform.
958. LONG SHOT 15ft. 13frs.
The shell is lowered to the platform. PAN down with the shell.
959. LONG SHOT 15ft. 6frs.
All four standing on the platform
as the shell comes into the picture and comes to rest beside the
platform.
960. LONG SHOT 6ft. 12frs.
Closer than above. The four as
they go to the door of the shell.
961. LONG SHOT 5ft. 14frs.
Closer still. The door is opened.
962. LONG SHOT 12ft.
Still closer. The two children say
goodbye to their parents and
then hurry inside the shell.
963. LONG SHOT 16ft. 13frs.
From the top of the shell,
shooting down into it. Maurice
and Catherine are helped into
position by two engineers.

ENGINEER:
Contract all your muscles when
the concussion comes. In five
minutes you'll be able to get
loose and move about.

964. LONG SHOT 7ft. 13frs.
From outside as the door starts
to close. Cabal and Passworthy
are standing there, the engineers
come out.
965. CLOSE UP 3ft. 6frs.
Passworthy reacting to the closing of the door.
966. CLOSE SHOT 2ft. 9frs.
From Passworthy's angle, as the
door closes still further.
967. LONG SHOT 7ft. 12frs.
Shooting from top of shell, showing the door closing.
968. LONG SHOT 5ft. 1fr.
In control room. Two men come
up to some instruments.
969. VERY LONG SHOT 11ft. 14frs.
As the shell rises, showing Cabal
and Passworthy looking up at it.
970. EXT. LONG SHOT 6ft. 6frs.   CROWD NOISES
The shell rises—shooting through

a girder in the foreground.
971. EXT. LONG SHOT 6ft.
The cliff. Theotocopulos arrives
with a crowd following him.
972. LONG SHOT 3ft. 12frs.
Theotocopulos and his followers
on the cliff.

THEOTOCOPULOS:
There's the man...

973. LONG SHOT 6ft. 5frs.
Cabal and Passworthy on the
bridge.

...There is the man who would
offer up his daughter to the
Devil of Science.

974. LONG SHOT 3ft. 2frs.
Closer than above of Cabal and
Passworthy.

CABAL:
What do you want here?

975. LONG SHOT 4ft. 8frs.
Theotocopulos.

THEOTOCOPULOS:
We want to save these young
people from your experiments...

976. VERY LONG SHOT 5ft. 5frs.
The crowd on the cliff top.

...we want to put an end to
this inhuman foolery.

977. CLOSE SHOT 4ft.
Theotocopulos.
978. LONG SHOT 5ft. 13frs.
The shell rising.

...we mean to destroy that gun.

CABAL:
We have a right to do what we
like with our lives—with our sort
of lives...

979. LONG SHOT 7ft. 4frs.
Cabal and Passworthy on the
bridge.

...We don't grudge you your
artistic life. You have safety,
plenty, all you want.

980. VERY LONG SHOT 6ft. 2frs.
The crowd on the cliff.

THEOTOCOPULOS:
We want to make the world safe
for men.
CABAL:
No one prevents you.

981. LONG SHOT 6ft. 12frs.
The shell rises.

THEOTOCOPULOS:
How can we do that when your
science and inventions are perpetually changing life for us...

982. CLOSE SHOT 9ft. 15frs.
Some machinery inside the gun.

...when you're everlastingly

983. LONG SHOT 5ft. 2frs.
The crowd on the cliff.

984. CLOSE SHOT 3ft. 11frs.
Theotocopulos.

985. LONG SHOT 8ft. 8frs.
Shooting through a girder in the
foreground.

986. CLOSE SHOT 8ft. 6frs.
Theotocopulos.

987. VERY LONG SHOT 4ft. 7frs.
The crowd on the cliff top start
off towards the gun.
988. LONG SHOT 5ft.
Cabal and Passworthy.

989. LONG SHOT 5ft. 7frs.
A platform slides back on rail
away from the base of the gun.
990. VERY LONG SHOT 5ft. 1fr.
The cliff top.
991. LONG SHOT 5ft. 15frs.
Shooting up as the shell is
lowered into the gun.
992. VERY LONG SHOT 4ft. 9frs.
The cliff.
993. LONG SHOT 2ft. 15frs.
Cabal and Passworthy leave the
bridge.
994. LONG SHOT ?ft. 14frs.
The shell is going into the gun.
995. CLOSE SHOT 6ft. 7frs.
Shooting from above, the shell is
lowered into the mouth of the
gun.
996. LONG SHOT 5ft. 1fr.
Shooting down to Maurice and
Catherine inside the shell.
997. CLOSE SHOT 5ft. 3frs.

contriving strange things. When
you make what we think great
seem small...

...When you make what we
think strong seem feeble.

We don't want you in the
same world with us...

...We don't want this expedition. We don't want mankind to
go out to the moon and to the
planets.

We shall hate you more if
you succeed than if you fail. Destroy the gun!

CABAL:
Before you can even reach the
base of the gun, it will be fired...

...Beware of the concussion!

...Beware of the concussion!

MUSIC OF ATTACK STARTS

Mitani sitting by an instruction
board.

MITANI:
  Stand by control room.

998. LONG SHOT 4ft. 12frs.
   Shooting down to the two men
   in the control room—the lights
   go out.
999. LONG SHOT 3ft. 12frs.
   Some people run past Cabal's
   plane at the foot of the gun to
   the interior.
1000. LONG SHOT 3ft. 14frs.
   Another angle as more people
   rush past to attack.
1001. LONG SHOT 3ft. 2frs.
   Shooting down into the darkened
   control room.
1002. CLOSE SHOT 6ft. 3frs.
   The pincers which originally held
   the shell coming back out of the
   mouth of the gun.
1003. VERY LONG SHOT 5ft. 15frs.
   People running round the base of
   the gun.
1004. CLOSE SHOT 3ft. 15frs.
   Mitani.

MITANI:
  Clear all outside observers.

1005. LONG SHOT 3ft. 1fr.
   From below—shooting up to gun.
1006. LONG SHOT 5ft. 11frs.
   Cabal and Passworthy running
   across a bridge to the interior of
   the gun.
1007. VERY LONG SHOT 4ft. 15frs.
   A few men climbing a girder up
   the side of the gun.
1008. VERY LONG SHOT 13ft. 9frs.
   PAN past the gun to show
   swarms of people running round
   the base of the gun.
1009. LONG SHOT 2ft. 14frs.
   People run past the plane to the
   gun.
1010. VERY LONG SHOT 4ft. 0frs.
   People running round the base of
   the gun.
1011. LONG SHOT 2ft. 12frs.
   People run down a passage in the
   interior of the gun.

1012. VERY LONG SHOT 3ft. 13frs.
Shooting through some girders to
some people swarming round the
base of the gun.
1013. VERY LONG SHOT 4ft. 14frs.
Another angle of the mob.
1014. VERY LONG SHOT 3ft. 7frs.
The arm of the gun, with the
pincers now not holding the
shell, swings back away from the
mouth of the gun.
1015. CLOSE SHOT 3ft. 3frs.
Mitani.

MITANI:
Stand by to fire.

1016. VERY LONG SHOT 2ft. 10frs.
More people climbing a girder.
1017. EXT. LONG SHOT 3ft. 2frs.
Crowds running to base of gun,
shooting through a girder.
1018. LONG SHOT 2ft. 10frs.
Shooting down on people running round the girders of the gun.
1019. LONG SHOT 2ft. 3frs.
Shooting from above to the
engineers in control room.
1020. MEDIUM SHOT 2ft. 11frs.
Some dials in the control room.
1021. LONG SHOT 1ft. 14frs.
Some people running along a
passage in the interior of the gun.
1022. LONG SHOT 1ft. 13frs.
People dash over a bridge.
1023. LONG SHOT 2ft. 4frs.
People rush past the plane at the
foot of the gun.
1024. LONG SHOT 1ft. 13frs.
Control room from above.
1025. CLOSE SHOT 1ft. 10frs.
A hand on a lever.
1026. LONG SHOT 1ft. 9frs.
The interior of the shell, Maurice
and Catherine, shooting from
above.
1027. CLOSE SHOT 1ft. 8frs.
A portion of a dial.
1028. CLOSE SHOT 1ft. 7frs.
Hand pulls the lever.
1029. LONG SHOT 3ft. 12frs.
Shooting up to the gun, as it

comes slowly down before
shooting the shell out.

1030. CLOSE SHOT 3ft. 15frs.
Some machinery of the gun moving down.

1031. CLOSE SHOT 4ft. 7frs.
The top of the gun as it goes
down.

1032. LONG SHOT 2ft. 15frs.
Low set up again, shooting up to
the gun as it goes back again.

ROAR OF GUN MIXED WITH
MUSICAL MACHINERY
NOISE

1033. CLOSE SHOT 29ft. 2frs.
The clouds curl back to make
way for shell.

DISSOLVE:

1034. CLOSE SHOT
Another section of rolling clouds.

DISSOLVE:

1035. CLOSE SHOT
Another section of rolling clouds.

DISSOLVE:

1036. CLOSE SHOT
Another section of rolling clouds.

DISSOLVE:

1037. CLOSE SHOT
Another section of rolling clouds.

DISSOLVE:

1038. CLOSE SHOT
Another section of rolling clouds.

DISSOLVE:

1039. LONG SHOT
Starry sky.

DISSOLVE:

1040. VERY LONG SHOT
Cabal and Passworthy walk up to
large reflector of telescope (backs
to CAMERA).

1041. VERY LONG SHOT 8ft. 4frs.
Cabal and Passworthy shooting
from the front, through some
astronomical instruments.

1042. MEDIUM SHOT 36ft. 11frs.
The two men from front.

CABAL:
There. There they go. That
faint gleam of light.
PASSWORTHY:
I feel that what we've done is
monstrous.
CABAL:

What they've done is magnificent.

PASSWORTHY:

Will they come back?

CABAL:

Yes, and go again and again, until the landing is made and the moon is conquered. This is only a beginning.

PASSWORTHY:

And if they don't come back? My son and your daughter? What of that, Cabal?

CABAL:

Then presently others will go.

1043. CLOSE UP 8ft. 0frs.
Passworthy.

PASSWORTHY:

Oh God, is there never to be any age of happiness? Is there never to be any rest?

1044. CLOSE UP 16ft. 9frs.
Cabal.

CABAL:

Rest enough for the individual man. Too much and too soon, and we call it death. But for Man no rest and no ending. He must go on. Conquest beyond conquest.

1045. VERY LONG SHOT 22ft. 5frs.
The two from the front, shooting through the instruments.

First this little planet with its winds and waves. And all the laws of mind and matter that restrain him. Then the planets about him. And at last out across immensity to the stars.

1046. CLOSE UP 13ft. 3frs.
Cabal.

And when he has conquered all the deeps of space and all the mysteries of time—still he will be beginning.

1047. CLOSE SHOT 13ft. 15frs.
The two men from the back.

PASSWORTHY:

But we're such little creatures. Poor humanity, so fragile, so weak—little animals.

1048. CLOSE UP 25ft. 1fr.
Cabal.

CABAL:

Little animals, eh? And if we're

no more than animals we must snatch each little scrap of happiness and live and suffer and pass, mattering no more than all the other animals do or have done.

1049. CLOSE SHOT 84ft. 1fr.
The two from the back. Their heads against the starry sky.
TRACK IN to C.U. of Cabal.

Cabal's head fades out leaving a L.S. of the starry sky.

It is this or that. All the universe or nothingness.

Which shall it be, Passworthy? Which shall it be? Which shall it be?
MUSICAL CHORUS:
WHICH SHALL IT BE?

FADE OUT.

End of Reel 11

Editorial note: Numbered feet and frames in the above camera shots are faithfully transcribed from a hectographed copy of this in-house record. Its manifest errors here and there were made by the studio typist in cutting stencils from some original document, now lost. No corrections have been supplied even when it seems clear the typist frequently slipped in striking "0" for "9."

INDEX TO PAGES xv–116